Evening by Evening

To Dana
with Love from
Jeanne xxx

Evening by Evening

365-DAY DEVOTIONAL

CHARLES SPURGEON

WHITAKER
HOUSE

Publisher's note:
In this new edition from Whitaker House, we have lightly edited the
unabridged original text for the modern reader. Words, expressions,
and sentence structure have been updated for clarity and readability,
while retaining the entirety of Spurgeon's original writings.

All Scripture quotations are taken from the King James Version
of the Holy Bible.

EVENING BY EVENING

ISBN-13: 978-0-88368-646-1
Printed in the United States of America
© 2001 by Whitaker House

Whitaker House
1030 Hunt Valley Circle
New Kensington, PA 15068
www.whitakerhouse.com

Library of Congress Cataloging-in-Publication Data

Spurgeon, C. H. (Charles Haddon), 1834–1892.
Evening by evening / Charles Spurgeon.
    p. cm.
ISBN 0-88368-646-5 (pbk.)
1. Devotional calendars—Baptists. I. Title.
BV4811 .S665 2001
242'.2—dc21

                                        2001004214

5 6 7 8 9 10 11 12 13 **ᴡ** 22 21 20 19 18 17 16

Preface

When the noise and turmoil of the day are over, it is sweet to commune with God. The cool and calm of evening agree most delightfully with prayer and praise. The hours of the declining sun are like quiet alleys in the garden of time wherein man may find his Maker waiting to commune with him, even as of old the Lord God walked with Adam in Paradise in the cool of the day.

It is fitting that we should set apart a peaceful season before the day has quite ended, a season of thanksgiving for abounding grace, of repentance for multiplied follies, of self-examination for insinuating evils. To leap from day to day like a mad hunter beating the bushes is an omen of being delivered over to destruction. But the solemn pause, the deliberate consideration—these are means of grace and signs of an indwelling life. The ocean tide stays awhile at ebb before it resolves to flood again; the moon sometimes lingers at its fullest size. There are distinct hedges in nature set between the seasons—even the strike of the bell is a little warning that men should not remove landmarks; instead, they should frequently examine the boundaries in their lives and keep up with due interval and solemnity the remembrance of the passing of days and months and years. Each evening it would be well to traverse the boundaries of the day and take note of all that it has brought and all that it has seen.

The drops of the night come from the same Fount as the dew of the morning. He who met Abraham at the break of day communed with Isaac in the field at evening. He who opens the doors of the day with the hand of mercy draws the curtains of the night around His people. By His shining presence, He makes the *"outgoings of the morning and evening to rejoice"* (Ps. 65:8). A promise at dawn and a sure word at sunset crown the brow of day with light and sandal its feet with love. To breakfast with Jesus and to dine with Him also is to enjoy the days of heaven on earth.

It is dangerous to fall asleep before the head is leaned on Jesus' bosom. When divine love puts its finger on weary eyelids, it is brave sleeping; but so that the Lord's beloved may have such sleep given to him, it is necessary that he should make a near approach to the throne and unburden his soul before the great Preserver of men. To enter into the blaze of Jehovah's presence by way of the atoning blood is the sure method of refining ourselves of earthly dross and renewing the soul after exhausting service.

The reading of the Word and prayer are as gates of precious stones to admit us into the presence of the august Majesty. He is most blessed who most frequently swings those gates on their sapphire hinges. When the stars are revealed and all the hosts of heaven walk in golden glory, then surely that is the time when the solemn temple is lit up and the worshipper is invited to enter. If one hour can be endowed with a sacredness above the others, it must be the hour when the Lord looses the cords of Orion and leads forth the Bear and its cubs. (See Job 38:31–32.) Then voices from worlds afar call us to contemplation and adoration, and the stillness of the lower world prepares an oratory for the devout soul. He surely never prays at all who does not end the day as all men wish to end their lives—in prayer.

In many households the gathering of the family for evening prayer is easier than the morning opportunity, and in all the tents of our Israel, the evening sacrifice should be solemnly remembered. Before we take refuge underneath the wings of the Eternal, let us entreat Him to deliver us from the terror by night and give us safe dwelling in His secret place. It is blessed work to set the night watchmen in their posts by supplication, and then to commit ourselves without fear to the embraces of divine love.

Having had the seal of our Master's blessing set upon our former volume, entitled *Morning by Morning*, we have felt encouraged to give our best attention to the present series of brief meditations, and I send them forth with importunate prayer for a blessing to rest on every reader. May the Father's smile be their benediction. I have striven to keep out of the common track; hence, I have used unusual texts and have brought forward neglected subjects. The vice of many religious works is their dullness—from this I have tried to be free: my friends must judge how successful I have been. I have drawn much of my subject matter out of my own experience, and I have always felt assured that a truth that has been sanctified to our own good will not be without an anointing for others. If I may lead one heart upward that otherwise would have drooped, or sow in a single mind a holy purpose that otherwise never would have been conceived, I will be grateful. May the Lord send us such results in thousands of instances, and His will be all the praise. The longer I live, the more deeply I am conscious that the Holy Spirit alone can make truth profitable to the heart; therefore, in earnest prayer, I commit this volume and its companion to His care.

—*C. H. Spurgeon*

We will be glad and rejoice in thee.
—Song of Solomon 1:4

e will be glad and rejoice in thee." We will not open the gates of the year to the dolorous notes of the trombone, but to the sweet strains of the harp of joy and the grand sounds of the cymbals of gladness. *"O come, let us sing unto the LORD: let us make a joyful noise to the rock of our salvation"* (Ps. 95:1). We, the called and faithful and chosen, will drive away our griefs and set up our banners of confidence in the name of God. Let others lament over their troubles; we who have the sweetening tree to cast into Marah's bitter pool (see Exodus 15:23) will magnify the Lord with joy. Eternal Spirit, our precious Comforter, we, who are the temples in which You dwell, will never cease from adoring and blessing the name of Jesus. *"We will"*—we are resolved about it. Jesus must have the crown of our hearts' delight. We will not dishonor our Bridegroom by mourning in His presence. We are ordained to be the minstrels of the skies; let us rehearse our everlasting anthem before we sing it in the halls of the New Jerusalem. *"We will be glad and rejoice."* These words have one sense: double joy, blessing upon blessing. Does there need to be any limit to our rejoicing in the Lord? Do not men of grace find their Lord to be precious even now? What better fragrance do they have in heaven itself? *"We will be glad and rejoice in thee."* That last word is the meat in the dish, the kernel of the nut, the soul of the text. What blessings are laid up in Jesus! What rivers of infinite bliss have their source, yes, and every drop of their fullness, in Him! Since, O sweet Lord Jesus, You are the present portion of Your people, favor us this year with such a sense of Your preciousness that, from its first to its last day, we may be glad and rejoice in You. Let January open with joy in the Lord, and December close with gladness in Jesus.

Let the people renew their strength.
—Isaiah 41:1

ll things on earth need to be renewed. No created thing continues by itself. *"Thou renewest the face of the earth"* (Ps. 104:30) was the psalmist's utterance. Even the trees, which do not wear themselves out with care or shorten their lives with labor, must drink of the rain of heaven and draw from the hidden treasures of the soil. The cedars of Lebanon, which God has planted, live only because, day by day, they are full of sap freshly drawn from the earth. Neither can man's life be sustained without renewal from God. As it is necessary to prevent the wasting away of the body by frequent meals, so we must restore the hungry soul by listening to the preached Word or by feeding on the Book of God or the soul-fattening table of the ordinances. How depressed are our graces when means are neglected! What poor starvelings some saints are who live without the diligent use of the Word of God and secret prayer! If our piety can live without God, it is not of divine creating; it is but a dream. For if God had begotten it, it would wait on Him as the flowers wait on the dew. Without constant restoration, we are not ready for the perpetual assaults of hell or the stern afflictions of heaven or even the conflicts within. When the whirlwind is loosed, woe to the tree that has not sucked up fresh sap and grasped the rock with many intertwined roots. When tempests arise, woe to the mariners who have not strengthened their masts, cast their anchors, or sought a haven. If we allow the good to grow weaker, the evil will surely gather strength and struggle desperately for mastery over us; and so, perhaps, a painful desolation and a lamentable disgrace may follow. Let us draw near to the footstool of divine mercy in humble entreaty. Then we will realize the fulfillment of the promise, *"They that wait upon the LORD shall renew their strength"* (Isa. 40:31).

*The voice of one crying in the wilderness, Prepare ye the way of the
Lord, make his paths straight.*
—Luke 3:4

he voice crying in the wilderness demanded a way for
the Lord to be prepared, a way prepared in the wilderness. I would be attentive to the Master's proclamation and give Him a road into my heart, built, by gracious operations, through the desert of my nature. The four
directives in Isaiah 40, from which today's text comes (v. 3),
must have my serious attention: *"Every valley shall be exalted"* (v. 4). Low and groveling thoughts of God must be
given up, doubting and despairing must be removed, and
self-seeking and carnal delights must be forsaken. Across
these deep valleys, a glorious causeway of grace must be
raised. *"Every mountain and hill shall be made low"* (v. 4).
Proud creature-sufficiency and boastful self-righteousness
must be leveled to make a highway for the King of Kings.
Divine fellowship is never granted to haughty, high-minded
sinners. The Lord shows respect to the lowly and visits the
contrite in heart, but the arrogant are an abomination to
Him. My soul, beseech the Holy Spirit to set you right in
this respect. *"The crooked shall be made straight"* (v. 4). The
wavering heart must have a straight path of decision for
God and holiness marked out for it. Double-minded men
are strangers to the God of truth. My soul, take heed that
you are honest and true in all things, as in the sight of the
heart-searching God. *"The rough places* [shall be made]
plain" (v. 4). Stumbling blocks of sin must be removed, and
thorns and briers of rebellion must be uprooted. So great a
Visitor must not find miry ways and stony places when He
comes to honor His favored ones with His company. Oh,
that this evening the Lord would find in my heart a highway made ready by His grace, so that He may make a tri-
umphal progression through the utmost boundaries of my
soul, from the beginning of this year even to the end of it.

And Joseph knew his brethren, but they knew not him.
—Genesis 42:8

his morning our prayer went forth for growth in grace and in the knowledge of our Lord Jesus; it may be well tonight to consider a related topic, namely, our heavenly Joseph's knowledge of us. This knowledge was most blessedly perfect long before we had the slightest knowledge of Him. *"Thine eyes did see my substance, yet being unperfect; and in thy book all my members were written,…when as yet there was none of them"* (Ps. 139:16). Before we existed in the world, we existed in His heart. When we were enemies to Him, He knew us, with our misery, our foolishness, and our wickedness. When we wept bitterly in despairing repentance and viewed Him as only a judge and a ruler, He viewed us as His well-beloved brethren, and His heart yearned toward us. He never mistook His chosen, but always beheld them as objects of His infinite affection. *"The Lord knoweth them that are his"* (2 Tim. 2:19) is as true of the prodigals who are feeding swine as of the children who sit at the table. But, alas, we did not know our Royal Brother, and out of this ignorance grew a host of sins. We withheld our hearts from Him and allowed Him no entrance to our love. We mistrusted Him and gave no credit to His words. We rebelled against Him and paid Him no loving homage. The *"Sun of righteousness"* (Mal. 4:2) shone forth, and we could not see Him. Heaven came down to earth, and earth perceived it not. Let God be praised, for those days are over for us; yet even now we know but little of Jesus compared with what He knows of us. We have but begun to study Him, but He knows us completely. It is a blessed circumstance that the ignorance is not on His side, for then it would be a hopeless case for us. He will not say to us, *"I never knew you"* (Matt. 7:23). He will confess our names in the day of His appearing; meanwhile, He will manifest Himself to us as He does not to the world.

And God saw the light.
—Genesis 1:4

his morning we noticed the goodness of the light, and the Lord's dividing it from the darkness. We now note the special eye that the Lord had for the light: *"God saw the light."* He looked at it with satisfaction, gazed on it with pleasure, and saw that it *"was good"* (Gen. 1:4). If the Lord has given you light, dear reader, He looks on that light with special interest, not only because it is dear to Him as His own handiwork, but also because it is like Himself, for *"God is light"* (1 John 1:5). It is pleasant to the believer to know that God's eye is thus tenderly observant of that work of grace that He has begun in him. He never loses sight of the treasure that He has placed in our earthen vessels. Sometimes we cannot see the light, but God always sees the light, and that is much better than our seeing it. Better for the judge to see my innocence than for me to think I see it. It is very comfortable for me to know that I am one of God's people; but whether I know it or not, if the Lord knows it, I am still safe. This is the foundation: *"The Lord knoweth them that are his"* (2 Tim. 2:19). You may be sighing and groaning because of inbred sin and mourning over your darkness, yet the Lord sees light in your heart, for He has put it there. All the cloudiness and gloom of your soul cannot conceal your light from His gracious eye. You may have sunk low in despondency and even despair, but if your soul has any longing toward Christ, and if you are seeking to rest in His finished work, God sees the light. He not only sees it, but also preserves it in you. *"I the LORD do keep it"* (Isa. 27:3). This is a precious thought to those who, after anxious watching and guarding of themselves, feel their own powerlessness to keep themselves. The light thus preserved by God's grace He will one day develop into the splendor of noonday and the fullness of glory. The light within is the dawn of the eternal day.

Now the hand of the LORD was upon me in the evening.
—Ezekiel 33:22

In the way of judgment, this may be the case, and, if so, it is mine to consider the reason for such a visitation and to bear the rod and Him who has appointed it. I am not the only one who is chastened in the night season; let me cheerfully submit to the affliction and carefully endeavor to be profited by it. But the hand of the Lord may also be felt in another manner—strengthening the soul and lifting the spirit up toward eternal things. Oh, that I may in this sense feel the Lord dealing with me! A sense of the divine presence and indwelling bears the soul toward heaven as on the wings of eagles. At such times we are full to the brim with spiritual joy, and we forget the cares and sorrows of earth. The invisible is near, and the visible loses its power over us. The servant-body waits at the foot of the hill, and the master-spirit worships on the summit in the presence of the Lord. Oh, that a hallowed season of divine communion may be granted to me this evening! The Lord knows that I need it very greatly. My graces languish, my corruptions rage, my faith is weak, and my devotion is cold; all these are reasons why His healing hand should be laid upon me. His hand can cool the heat of my burning brow and stop the tumult of my palpitating heart. The glorious right hand that molded the world can create my mind anew. The unwearied hand that bears up the earth's huge pillars can sustain my spirit. The loving hand that encloses all the saints can cherish me. And the mighty hand that breaks the enemy in pieces can subdue my sins. Why should I not feel that hand touching me this evening? Come, my soul. Address your God with the potent plea that Jesus' hands were pierced for your redemption, and you will surely feel that same hand on you that once touched Daniel and drew him to his knees so that he might see visions of God.

My sister, my spouse.
—Song of Solomon 4:12

bserve the sweet titles with which the heavenly Solomon addresses His bride, the church, with intense affection: "'*My sister*'—one near to Me by ties of nature, partaker of the same sympathies. '*My spouse*'—nearest and dearest, united to Me by the tenderest bonds of love; My sweet companion, part of My own self. '*My sister*' by My incarnation, which makes Me bone of your bone and flesh of your flesh. '*My spouse*' by heavenly betrothal, in which I have attached you to Myself in righteousness. '*My sister*,' whom I knew of old, and over whom I watched from her earliest infancy. '*My spouse*,' taken from among the daughters, embraced by arms of love, and betrothed to Me forever." See how true it is that our royal Kinsman is not ashamed of us, for He dwells with manifest delight on this twofold relationship. We have the word *"my"* twice in our text, as if Christ dwelt with rapture on His possession of His church. His *"delights were with the sons of men"* (Prov. 8:31), because those sons of men were His own chosen ones. He, the Shepherd, sought the sheep, because they were His sheep. He has gone about *"to seek and to save that which was lost"* (Luke 19:10), because what was lost was His long before it was lost to itself or lost to Him. The church is the exclusive portion of her Lord; no one else may claim a partnership or pretend to share her love. Jesus, Your church delights to have it so! Let every believing soul drink solace out of these wells. Soul, Christ is near to you in ties of relationship. Christ is dear to you in bonds of marriage union, and you are dear to Him! Behold, He grasps both of your hands with both of His own, saying, *"My sister, my spouse."* Note the two sacred anchors by which your Lord secures such a double hold of you that He neither can nor will ever let you go. O beloved, do not be slow to return the hallowed flame of His love.

Thy love is better than wine.
—Song of Solomon 1:2

Nothing gives the believer as much joy as fellowship with Christ. He has enjoyment, as others have, in the common mercies of life. He can be glad both in God's gifts and God's works; but in all of these separately, yes, and in all of them added together, he does not find such substantial delight as in the matchless person of his Lord Jesus. The believer has wine that no vineyard on earth ever yielded; he has bread that all the cornfields of Egypt could never bring forth. Where can such sweetness be found as we have tasted in communion with our Beloved? In our judgment, the joys of earth are little better than husks for swine compared with Jesus, the heavenly Manna. We would rather have one mouthful of Christ's love and a sip of His fellowship than a whole world full of carnal delights. What is the chaff compared with the wheat? What is the sparkling artificial gem compared with the true diamond? What is a dream compared with the glorious reality? What is earth's greatest enjoyment compared with our Lord Jesus in His most despised estate? If you know anything of the inner life, you will confess that our highest, purest, and most enduring joys must be the fruit of the Tree of Life, which is in the midst of the Paradise of God. No spring yields such sweet water as that well of God that was dug with the soldier's spear. (See John 19:34.) All earthly bliss is *"of the earth, earthy"* (1 Cor. 15:47), but the comforts of Christ's presence are like Himself, heavenly. We can review our communion with Jesus and find no regrets of emptiness therein; no dregs are in this wine, no dead flies in this ointment. The joy of the Lord is solid and enduring. Vanity has not looked on it, but discretion and prudence testify that it abides the test of years and is, in time and eternity, worthy to be called the only true delight. For nourishment, consolation, exhilaration, and refreshment, no wine can rival the love of Jesus. Let us drink to the full this evening.

Serve the LORD with gladness.
—Psalm 100:2

elight in divine service is a token of acceptance. Those who serve God with a sad countenance, because they do what is unpleasant to them, are not serving Him at all; they bring the form of homage, but the life is absent. Our God requires no slaves to grace His throne. He is the Lord of the empire of love, and He would have His servants dressed in the uniform of joy. The angels of God serve Him with songs, not with groans. A murmur or a sigh would be mutiny in their ranks. Obedience that is not voluntary is disobedience, for the Lord looks at the heart, and if He sees that we serve Him from force, and not because we love Him, He will reject our offering. Service coupled with cheerfulness is heart-service and, therefore, true. Take away joyful willingness from the Christian, and you have removed the test of his sincerity. If a man is driven to battle, he is no patriot; but he who marches into the fray with flashing eye and beaming face, singing, "It is sweet to die for one's country," proves himself to be sincere in his patriotism. Cheerfulness is the support of our strength; in the joy of the Lord we are strong. It acts as the remover of difficulties. It is to our service what oil is to the wheels of a railroad car. Without oil the axle soon grows hot, and accidents occur; if there is not a holy cheerfulness to oil our wheels, our spirits will be clogged with weariness. The man who is cheerful in his service to God proves that obedience is his element; he can sing,

> Make me to walk in Your commands,
> 'Tis a delightful road.

Reader, let me put this question to you: Do you *"serve the LORD with gladness"*? Let us show the people of the world, who think our religion is slavery, that to us it is a delight and a joy! Let our gladness proclaim that we serve a good Master.

In my flesh shall I see God.
—Job 19:26

Note the subject of Job's devout anticipation: "I will see God." He does not say, "I will see the saints"— though, doubtless, that will be untold happiness— but "I will see God." It is not, "I will see the pearly gates; I will behold the walls of jasper; I will gaze upon the crowns of gold," but "I will see God." This is the sum and substance of heaven; this is the joyful hope of all believers. By faith, it is their delight to see Him now in the ordinances. They love to behold Him in communion and in prayer; but there in heaven they will have open and unclouded vision, and seeing *"him as he is"* (1 John 3:2), they will be made completely like Him. Likeness to God—what more can we wish for? A sight of God—what can we desire that is better? Some read the passage, *"In my flesh shall I see God,"* and find there an allusion to Christ as the *"Word...made flesh"* (John 14:1) and that glorious beholding of Him that will be the splendor of the latter days. Whether this is so or not, it is certain that Christ will be the object of our eternal vision; we will never wish for any joy beyond that of seeing Him. Do not think that this will be a narrow sphere for the mind to dwell in. It is but one source of delight, yet that source is infinite. All His attributes will be subjects for contemplation, and as He is infinite in each aspect, there is no fear of exhausting them. His works, His gifts, His love for us, and His glory in all His purposes and in all His actions—these will make a theme that will be ever new. The patriarch looked forward to this sight of God as a personal enjoyment. *"Whom...mine eyes shall behold, and not another"* (Job 19:27). Consider the reality of heaven's bliss; think what heaven will be to you. *"Thine eyes shall see the king in his beauty"* (Isa. 33:17). All earthly brightness fades and darkens as we gaze on it, but here is a brightness that can never dim, a glory that can never fade: I will see God.

I have prayed for thee, that thy faith fail not.
—Luke 22:32

ow encouraging is the thought of the Redeemer's never-ceasing intercession for us. When we pray, He pleads for us; and when we are not praying, He is advocating our cause, and by His supplications shielding us from unseen dangers. Notice the word of comfort addressed to Peter: *"Simon, Simon, behold, Satan hath desired to have you, that he may sift you as wheat: but…"* (Luke 22:31–32). But what? "But go and pray for yourself"? That would be good advice, but that is not what is written. Neither did our Lord say, "But I will keep you watchful, and so you will be preserved." That, too, would be a great blessing. But no, He said, *"I have prayed for thee, that thy faith fail not."* We know little of what we owe to our Savior's prayers. When we reach the hilltops of heaven and look back on all the ways in which the Lord our God has led us, how we will praise Him who, before the eternal throne, undid the mischief that Satan was doing on earth! How we will thank Him because He never withheld His peace, but day and night He pointed to the wounds on His hands and carried our names on His breastplate! Even before Satan had begun to tempt, Jesus had forestalled him and entered a plea in heaven. Mercy outruns malice. Note that He did not say, "Satan hath sifted you; therefore, I will pray," but He said, *"Satan hath desired to have you."* He checked Satan even in his very desire and nipped it in the bud. He did not say, "But I have desired to pray for you." No, He said, *"'I have prayed for thee.'* I have done it already. I have gone to court and entered a counterplea even before an accusation is made." O Jesus, what a comfort it is that You have pleaded our cause against our unseen enemies, disarmed their mines, and unmasked their ambushes. This is a matter for joy, gratitude, hope, and confidence.

I have yet to speak on God's behalf.
—Job 36:2

We should not court publicity for our virtue or fame for our zeal; but, at the same time, it is a sin to be always seeking to hide that which God has bestowed on us for the good of others. A Christian is not to be a village in a valley, but a *"city that is set on an hill"* (Matt. 5:14). He or she is not to be a candle *"under a bushel"* (v. 15), but a candle in a candlestick, giving light to all. Retirement may be lovely in its season, and to hide oneself is no doubt modest, but the hiding of Christ in us can never be justified, and the keeping back of truth that is precious to ourselves is a sin against others and an offense against God. If you are of a nervous temperament and a retiring disposition, take care that you do not indulge this trembling propensity too much, lest you should be useless to the church. Seek, in the name of Him who was not ashamed of you, to do what you can to tell others what Christ has told you. If you cannot speak with trumpet tongue, use the still small voice. If the pulpit cannot be your tribune, if the press may not carry on its wings your words, yet say with Peter and John, *"Silver and gold have I none; but such as I have give I thee"* (Acts 3:6). Talk to the Samaritan woman by Sychar's well, if you cannot preach a sermon on the mountain. Utter the praises of Jesus in a small group, if not among the whole congregation; in the field, if not at a busy intersection; in the midst of your own household, if you cannot speak of Him in the midst of the great family of humankind. From the hidden springs within, let sweetly flowing rivulets of testimony flow forth, giving drink to every passerby. Do not hide your talent. Trade with it, and you will bring in good interest to your Lord and Master. To speak for God will be refreshing to ourselves, cheering to saints, useful to sinners, and honoring to the Savior. Lord, unloose all your children's tongues.

The iron did swim.
—2 Kings 6:6

he ax head seemed hopelessly lost. Since it was borrowed, the honor of the prophetic band was likely to be imperiled, and thus the name of their God would be compromised. Contrary to all expectation, the ax head was made to mount from the depth of the stream and to swim, for things impossible with men are possible with God. Just a few years ago, I knew of a Christian who was called to undertake a work far exceeding his strength. It appeared so difficult as to involve absurdity in the mere idea of attempting it. Yet he was called to do it, and his faith rose with the occasion. God honored his faith, unlooked-for aid was sent, and *"the iron did swim."* Another of the Lord's family was in grievous financial straits. He would have been able to meet all claims, and much more, if he could have realized a certain portion of his estate, but he was overtaken by a sudden financial constraint. In vain he sought for the help of friends, but faith led him to the unfailing Helper; remarkably, the trouble was averted, his footsteps were enlarged, and *"the iron did swim."* A third had a sorrowful case of depravity to deal with. He had taught, reproved, warned, invited, and interceded, but all in vain. At first, the carnal spirit of Old Adam was too strong for this reformer's prayerful influence; the stubborn spirit of the sinner would not relent. Then came an agony of prayer, and before long, a blessed answer was sent from heaven. The hard heart was broken; *"the iron did swim."* Beloved reader, what is your desperate circumstance? What heavy matter do you have in hand this evening? Bring it forth. The God of the prophets lives and lives to help His saints. He will not allow you to lack any good thing. Believe in the Lord of Hosts! Pleading the name of Jesus, approach Him, and the iron will swim; you, too, will see the hand of God working marvels for His people. *"According to your faith be it unto you"* (Matt. 9:29), and yet again the iron will swim.

Beginning to sink, [Peter] cried, saying, Lord, save me.
—Matthew 14:30

Sinking times are praying times with the Lord's servants. Peter neglected prayer when starting on his daring journey; but when he began to sink, his danger made him a suppliant, and his cry, though late, was not too late. In our hours of bodily pain and mental anguish, we find ourselves as naturally driven to prayer as a shipwreck is driven upon the shore by the waves. The fox hurries to its hole for protection; the bird flies to the wood for shelter; even so the tried believer hastens to the mercy seat for safety. Heaven's great harbor of refuge is "All-prayer"; thousands of weather-beaten vessels have found a haven there, and the moment a storm comes on, it is wise for us to make for it with all sail. Short prayers are long enough. There were only three words in the petition that Peter gasped out, but they were sufficient for his purpose. Not length but strength is desirable. A sense of need is a mighty teacher of brevity. If our prayers had less of the tail feathers of pride and more wing, they would be all the better. Verbiage is to devotion as chaff is to wheat. Precious things lie in small spaces, and all that is real prayer in many a long address might have been uttered in a petition as short as that of Peter's. Our extremities are the Lord's opportunities. Immediately, a keen sense of danger forces an anxious cry from us that the ear of Jesus hears, and with Him, ear and heart go together, and the hand does not long linger. At the last moment we appeal to our Master, but His swift hand makes up for our delays by instant, effective action. Are we nearly engulfed by the boisterous waters of affliction? Let us then lift up our souls to our Savior, and we may rest assured that He will not allow us to perish. When we can do nothing, Jesus can do all things; let us enlist His powerful aid on our side, and all will be well.

But I give myself unto prayer.
—Psalm 109:4

Lying tongues were busy against the reputation of David, but he did not defend himself; he moved the case into a higher court and pleaded before the great King Himself. Prayer is the safest method of replying to words of hatred. The psalmist did not pray in a coldhearted manner; he gave himself to the exercise—threw his whole soul and heart into it—straining every sinew and muscle, as Jacob did when wrestling with the angel. In this way, and only in this way, will any of us speed to the throne of grace. As a shadow has no power because there is no substance in it, even so the supplication in which a man's proper self is not thoroughly present in agonizing earnestness and vehement desire is utterly ineffective, for it lacks that which would give it force. "Fervent prayer," said an old churchman, "like a cannon planted at the gates of heaven, makes them fly open." The common fault with most of us is our readiness to yield to distractions. Our thoughts go roving here and there, and we make little progress toward our desired end. Like mercury, our minds will not hold together, but they roll off this way and that. How great an evil this is! It injures us, and what is worse, it insults our God. What would we think of a petitioner, if, while having an audience with a prince, he played with a feather or tried to catch a fly? Continuance and perseverance are intended in the expression of our text. David did not cry once and then relapse into silence; his holy clamor continued until it brought down the blessing. Prayer must not be our accidental work, but our daily business, our habit, and vocation. As artists give themselves to their models and poets to their classical pursuits, so we must addict ourselves to prayer. We must be immersed in prayer as in our element, and so *"pray without ceasing"* (1 Thess. 5:17). Lord, teach us to pray so that we may be more and more prevalent in supplication.

Messiah [shall] be cut off, but not for himself.
—Daniel 9:26

Blessed be His name, there was no cause of death in Him. Neither original nor actual sin had defiled Him; therefore, death had no claim on Him. No man could have taken His life from Him justly, for He had done no man wrong. No man could have even struck Him down by force unless He had been pleased to yield Himself to die. But one sins and another suffers. Justice was offended by us, but it found its satisfaction in Him. Rivers of tears, mountains of offerings, seas of the blood of bullocks, and hills of frankincense could not have accomplished the removal of sin. But Jesus was cut off for us, and the cause of wrath was cut off at once, for sin was put away forever. Herein is wisdom, whereby substitution, the sure and speedy way of atonement, was devised! Herein is condescension, which brought Messiah, the Prince, to wear a crown of thorns and to die on the cross! Herein is love, which led the Redeemer to lay down His life for His enemies! It is not enough, however, to admire the spectacle of the innocent bleeding for the guilty; we must make sure of our interest in it. The special purpose of the Messiah's death was the salvation of His church. Have we a part and a lot among those for whom He gave His life as a ransom? Did the Lord Jesus stand as our Representative? Are we healed by His stripes? It would be a terrible thing indeed if we would come short of a portion in His sacrifice; it would be better for us if we had never been born. Solemn as the question is, it is a joyful circumstance that it is one that may be answered clearly and without mistake. To all who believe on Him, the Lord Jesus is a present Savior, and upon them all the blood of reconciliation has been sprinkled. Let all who trust in the merit of Messiah's death be joyful at every remembrance of Him, and let their holy gratitude lead them to the fullest consecration to His cause.

*And it came to pass in an eveningtide, that David arose from off his
bed, and walked upon the roof of the king's house.*
—2 Samuel 11:2

A t that hour of night, David saw Bathsheba. We are
never out of the reach of temptation. Both at home
and abroad, we are liable to meet with allurements
to evil; the morning opens with peril, and the shades of
evening find us still in jeopardy. They are well kept whom
God keeps, but woe to those who go forth into the world,
or even dare to walk unarmed around their own house.
Those who think they are secure are more exposed to danger than any others. The armor-bearer of sin is self-
confidence. David should have been engaged in fighting the
Lord's battles; instead, he tarried at Jerusalem and gave
himself up to luxurious repose, for he arose from his bed in
the evening. Idleness and luxury are the devil's jackals, and
they find him abundant prey. In stagnant waters noxious
creatures swarm, and neglected soil soon yields a dense
tangle of weeds and briars. Oh, for the constraining love of
Jesus to keep us active and useful! When I see the king of
Israel sluggishly leaving his couch at the close of the day
and falling at once into temptation, let me take warning and
set holy watchfulness to guard my door. Is it possible that
the king had mounted his housetop for retirement and devotion? If so, what a caution is given to us to consider no
place, however secret, a sanctuary from sin! Because our
hearts are so like a tinderbox and sparks are so plentiful, we
need to use all diligence in all places to prevent a blaze. Satan can climb housetops and enter prayer closets. Even if
we could shut out that foul fiend, our own corruptions are
enough to work our ruin unless grace prevents it. Reader,
beware of evening temptations. Do not be secure. The sun
is down, but sin is up. We need a watchman for the night as
well as a guardian for the day. O blessed Spirit, keep us
from all evil this night. Amen.

*He expounded unto them in all the scriptures
the things concerning himself.*
—Luke 24:27

he two disciples on the road to Emmaus had a most profitable journey. Their companion and teacher was the best of tutors, their interpreter one of a thousand, *"in whom are hid all the treasures of wisdom and knowledge"* (Col. 2:3). The Lord Jesus condescended to become a preacher of the Gospel, and He was not ashamed to exercise His calling before an audience of two persons; neither does He now refuse to become the teacher of even one. Let us court the company of so excellent an Instructor, for until He is *"made unto us wisdom"* (1 Cor. 1:30), we will never be *"wise unto salvation"* (2 Tim. 3:15). This unrivalled Tutor used as His textbook the Best of Books. Although able to reveal fresh truth, He preferred to expound the old. He knew by His omniscience what was the most instructive way of teaching, and by turning immediately to Moses and the prophets, He showed us that the surest road to wisdom is not speculating, reasoning, or reading human books, but meditating on the Word of God. The readiest way to be spiritually rich in heavenly knowledge is to dig in this mine of diamonds, to gather pearls from this heavenly sea. When Jesus Himself sought to enrich others, He dug in the quarry of Holy Scripture. The favored pair were led to consider the best of subjects, for Jesus *"expounded...the things concerning himself."* Here the diamond cut the diamond, and what could be more admirable? The Master of the house unlocked His own doors, conducted the guests to His table, and placed His own delicacies on it. He who hid the treasure in the field guided the searchers to it Himself. Our Lord would naturally discourse upon the sweetest of topics, and He could find none sweeter than His own person and work. With an eye to these truths, we should always search the Word. Oh, for grace to study the Bible with Jesus as both our Teacher and our Lesson!

*Then opened he their understanding, that they might
understand the scriptures.*
—Luke 24:45

Jesus, whom we viewed last evening as opening Scripture, we see here opening the understanding of the two on the road to Emmaus. In the first work of opening the Scriptures, Jesus has many fellow laborers, but in the second, opening a person's understanding, He stands alone. Many can bring the Scriptures to the mind, but the Lord alone can prepare the mind to receive the Scriptures. Our Lord Jesus differs from all other teachers. They reach the ear, but He instructs the heart; they deal with the outward letter, but He imparts an inward taste for the truth, by which we perceive its savor and spirit. The most uneducated men become mature scholars in the school of grace when the Lord Jesus by His Holy Spirit unfolds the mysteries of the kingdom to them and grants the divine anointing by which they are enabled to behold the invisible. We are blessed if we have had our understanding cleared and strengthened by the Master! How many men of profound learning are ignorant of eternal things! They know the killing letter of revelation, but its killing spirit they cannot discern. They have a veil over their hearts that the eyes of carnal reason cannot penetrate. Such was our case a little time ago. We who now see were once utterly blind. Truth was to us as beauty in the dark, a thing unnoticed and neglected. Had it not been for the love of Jesus, we would have remained to this moment in utter ignorance, for without His gracious opening of our understanding, we could no more have attained spiritual knowledge than an infant can climb the pyramids or an ostrich can fly up to the stars. Jesus' college is the only one in which God's truth can really be learned; other schools may teach us what is to be believed, but Christ's alone can show us how to believe it. Let us sit at the feet of Jesus and, by earnest prayer, call in His blessed aid, so that our dull wits may grow brighter and our feeble understanding may receive heavenly things.

Turn away mine eyes from beholding vanity;
and quicken thou me in thy way.
—Psalm 119:37

here are various kinds of vanity. The cap and bells of the fool, the mirth of the world, the dance, the lyre, and the cup of the indulgent—all these things men know to be vanities. They display their proper name and title prominently. Far more treacherous are those equally conceited things, *"the cares of this world, and the deceitfulness of riches"* (Mark 4:19). A person may follow vanity as much in his business as an actor seeks it in the theater. If he is spending his life in amassing wealth, he passes his days in a vain show. Unless we follow Christ and make God the great purpose of our lives, we differ only in appearance from the most frivolous. It is clear that there is much need of the first prayer of our text, *"Turn away mine eyes from beholding vanity."* In the second prayer, *"Quicken thou me in thy way,"* the psalmist confessed that he was dull, heavy, lethargic, all but dead. Perhaps, dear reader, you feel the same. We are so sluggish that the best motives cannot quicken us, apart from the Lord Himself. What! Will not hell quicken me? Will I think of sinners perishing, and yet not be awakened? Will not heaven quicken me? Can I think of the reward that awaits the righteous and yet be cold? Will not death quicken me? Can I think of dying and standing before my God yet be slothful in my Master's service? Will not Christ's love constrain me? Can I think of His dear wounds, can I sit at the foot of His cross and not be stirred with fervency and zeal? It seems so! No mere consideration can quicken us to zeal, but God Himself must do it; hence, the cry, *"Quicken **thou** me"* (emphasis added). The psalmist breathed out his whole soul in vehement pleadings; his body and his soul united in prayer. *"Turn away mine eyes,"* says the body. *"Quicken thou me,"* cries the soul. This is an appropriate prayer for every day. O Lord, hear it in my case this night.

*He was sore athirst, and called on the LORD, and said, Thou hast
given this great deliverance into the hand of thy servant:
and now shall I die for thirst?*
—Judges 15:18

amson was thirsty and ready to die. The difficulty was
totally different from any that the hero had met before. Merely to get thirst assuaged is not nearly as
great a matter as to be delivered from a thousand Philistines! But when the thirst was upon him, Samson felt that
this little present difficulty was more weighty than the
great past difficulty out of which he had been so wonder-
fully delivered. It is very common for God's people, after
they have enjoyed a great deliverance, to find a little trouble too much for them. Samson slew a thousand Philistines
and piled them up in heaps—then he fainted for a little water! Jacob wrestled with God at Peniel and overcame Omnipotence itself, and then went limping on his hip! It is
strange that there must be a shrinking of the sinew whenever we win the day. It is as if the Lord must teach us our
littleness, our nothingness, in order to keep us within
bounds. Samson boasted very loudly when he said, *"I
[have] slain a thousand men"* (Judg. 15:16). His boastful
throat soon grew hoarse with thirst, and he resorted to
prayer. God has many ways of humbling His people. Dear
child of God, if after receiving great mercy you are laid
very low, your case is not an unusual one. When David had
mounted the throne of Israel, he said, *"I am this day weak,
though anointed king"* (2 Sam. 3:39). You must expect to feel
weakest when you are enjoying your greatest triumph. If
God has won for you great deliverances in the past, your
present difficulty is only like Samson's thirst, and the Lord
will not let you faint or allow your enemies to triumph over
you. The road of sorrow is the road to heaven, but there are
wells of refreshing water all along the route. So, tried ones,
cheer your hearts with Samson's words, and rest assured
that God will deliver you before long.

Doth Job fear God for nought?
—Job 1:9

This was the wicked question of Satan concerning Job, that upright man of old. Sadly, there are many people today about whom it might be asked with legitimacy, for they love God after a fashion because He prospers them. But if things were to go badly for them, they would give up all their boasted faith in God. If they can clearly see that since the time of their supposed conversion they have enjoyed prosperity, then they will love God in their poor carnal way; but if they endure adversity, they rebel against the Lord. Their love is the love of the table, not of the Host; a love of the cupboard, not of the Master of the house. As for the true Christian, he expects to have his reward in the next life and to endure hardness in this life. The promise of the old covenant is adversity. Remember Christ's words, *"Every branch in me that beareth not fruit he taketh away: and every branch that beareth fruit..."* (John 15:2). What happens to a branch that does bear fruit? *"He purgeth it, that it may bring forth more fruit"* (v. 2). If you bring forth fruit, you will have to endure affliction. "Alas" you say, "that is a terrible prospect!" But this affliction works out such precious results that the Christian who is the subject of it must learn to rejoice in tribulations, because as his tribulations abound, so his consolations abound by Christ Jesus. Rest assured, if you are a child of God, you will be no stranger to the rod. Sooner or later, every bar of gold must pass through the fire. Do not fear, but rather rejoice that fruitful times are in store for you, for in them you will be weaned from earth and made ready for heaven. You will be delivered from clinging to the present and caused to long for those eternal things that are so soon to be revealed to you. When you feel that you would gladly serve God without the promise of any benefits in this life, you will then rejoice in the infinite reward of the future.

We will remember thy love more than wine.
—Song of Solomon 1:4

esus will not let His people forget His love. If all the love they have enjoyed should be forgotten, He will visit them with fresh love. "Do you forget My Cross?" He asks. "I will cause you to remember it, for at My Table I will manifest Myself anew to you. Do you forget what I did for you in the council chamber of eternity? I will remind you of it, for you will need a counselor and will find Me ready at your call." Mothers do not let their children forget them. If a boy has gone to Australia and does not write home, his mother writes, "Has John forgotten his mother?" Then a sweet letter comes back, which proves that the gentle reminder was not in vain. So is it with Jesus. He says to us, "Remember Me," and our response is, *"We will remember thy love.'* We will remember Your love and its matchless history. It is as ancient as *'the glory which* [You] *had with* [the Father] *before the world was'* (John 17:5). O Jesus, we remember Your eternal love when You became our Surety and espoused us as Your betrothed. We remember the love that suggested the sacrifice of Yourself, the love that, until the fullness of time, mused over that sacrifice. We long for the hour of which in the volume of the Book it was written of You, *'Lo, I come'* (Heb. 10:7). We remember Your love, O Jesus, as it was manifested to us in Your holy life, from the manger of Bethlehem to the Garden of Gethsemane. We track You from the cradle to the grave—for every word and deed of Yours was love—and we rejoice in Your love, which death did not exhaust, Your love that shone resplendent in Your resurrection. We remember that burning fire of love that will never let You hold Your peace until Your chosen ones are all safely housed, until Zion is glorified, and Jerusalem is settled on her everlasting foundations of light and love in heaven."

Martha was cumbered about much serving.
—Luke 10:40

Martha's fault was not that she served, for the condition of a servant well becomes every Christian. "I serve" should be the motto of all the princes of the royal family of heaven. Nor was it her fault that she had *"much serving."* We cannot do too much. Let us do all that we possibly can. Let head and heart and hands be engaged in the Master's service. It was no fault of hers that she was busy preparing a feast for the Master. Happy Martha, to have an opportunity of entertaining so blessed a Guest, and happy, too, to have the spirit to throw her whole soul so heartily into the engagement. Her fault was that she grew *"cumbered about much serving,"* so that she forgot Him and only remembered the service. She allowed service to override communion, and so she presented one duty stained with the blood of another. We ought to be Martha and Mary in one: we should do much service and have much communion at the same time. For this we need great grace. It is easier to serve than to commune. Joshua never grew weary in fighting with the Amalekites; but Moses, on the top of the mountain in prayer, needed two helpers to sustain his hands. The more spiritual the exercise, the sooner we tire in it. The choicest fruits are the hardest to grow; the most heavenly graces are the most difficult to cultivate. Beloved, while we do not neglect external things, which are good enough in themselves, we also ought to see to it that we enjoy living, personal fellowship with Jesus. See to it that sitting at the Savior's feet is not neglected, even though it may be under the seeming purpose of doing Him service. The first thing for our soul's health, the first thing for His glory, and the first thing for our own usefulness is to keep ourselves in perpetual communion with the Lord Jesus and to see that the vital spirituality of our religion is maintained over and above everything else in the world.

Do we then make void the law through faith?
God forbid: yea, we establish the law.
—Romans 3:31

hen the believer is adopted into the Lord's family, his relationship to Old Adam and the law ceases at once; but then he is under a new rule and a new covenant. Believer, you are God's child. It is your first duty to obey your heavenly Father. You have nothing to do with a servile spirit: you are not a slave but a child. And now, inasmuch as you are a beloved child, you are bound to obey your Father's faintest wish, the least intimation of His will. Does He bid you to fulfill a sacred ordinance? It is at your peril that you neglect it, for you will be disobeying your Father. Does He command you to seek the image of Jesus? Is it not your joy to do so? Does Jesus tell you, *"Be ye therefore perfect, even as your Father which is in heaven is perfect"* (Matt. 5:48)? Then not because the law commands, but because your Savior directs, you will labor to be perfect in holiness. Does He bid His saints to love one another? Do it, not because the law says, *"Love thy neighbour"* (Lev. 19:18), but because Jesus says, *"If ye love me, keep my commandments"* (John 14:15). This is the commandment that He has given to you, *"That ye love one another"* (John 13:34). Are you told to give to the poor? Do it, not because charity is a burden that you dare not shirk, but because Jesus teaches, *"Give to every man that asketh of thee"* (Luke 6:30). Does the Word say, "Love God with all your heart"? (See Deuteronomy 6:5.) Look at the commandment and reply, "Ah, commandment, Christ has fulfilled you already. I have no need, therefore, to fulfill you for my salvation, but I rejoice to yield obedience to you because God is my Father now, and He has a claim on me that I would not dispute." May the Holy Spirit make your heart obedient to the constraining power of Christ's love, so that your prayer may be, *"Make me to go in the path of thy commandments; for therein do I delight"* (Ps. 119:35). Grace is the mother and nurse of holiness, and not the apologist of sin.

All they that heard it wondered at those things.
—Luke 2:18

e must not cease to wonder at the great marvels of our God. It would be very difficult to draw a line between holy wonder and real worship, for when the soul is overwhelmed with the majesty of God's glory, though it may not express itself in song or even utter its voice with bowed head in humble prayer, yet it silently adores. Our incarnate God is to be worshipped as "the Wonderful." That God should consider His fallen creature, man, and, instead of sweeping him away with the *"besom [broom] of destruction"* (Isa. 14:23), should Himself undertake to be man's Redeemer and to pay his ransom price, is, indeed, marvelous! But to each believer redemption is most marvelous as he views it in relation to himself. It is a miracle of grace, indeed, that Jesus would forsake the thrones and royalties above to suffer a shameful death below *for you.* Let your soul lose itself in wonder, for wonder is, in this way, a very practical emotion. Holy wonder will lead you to grateful worship and heartfelt thanksgiving. It will cause within you godly watchfulness. You will be afraid to sin against such a love as this. Feeling the presence of the mighty God in the gift of His dear Son, you will *"put off thy shoes from off thy feet, for the place whereon thou standest is holy ground"* (Exod. 3:5). You will be moved at the same time to glorious hope. If Jesus has done such marvelous things on your behalf, you will feel that heaven itself is not too great for your expectation. Who can be astonished at anything, when he has once been astonished at the manger and the Cross? What is left that is wonderful after one has seen the Savior? Dear reader, it may be that, from the quietness and solitude of your life, you are scarcely able to imitate the shepherds of Bethlehem, who told what they had seen and heard, but you can, at least, fill up the circle of the worshippers before the throne by wondering at what God has done.

But Mary kept all these things,
and pondered them in her heart.
—Luke 2:19

his blessed woman exercised three powers of her being: her *memory*—she *"kept all these things"*; her *affec-*
tions—she *"kept...them in her heart"*; and her *intellect*—
she *"pondered them."* Memory, affection, and understanding
were all exercised about the things that she had heard. Beloved, remember what you have heard of your Lord Jesus
and what He has done for you. Make your heart the golden
pot of manna to preserve the memorial of the heavenly
Bread on which you have fed in days gone by. Let your
memory treasure up everything about Christ that you have
either felt, known, or believed, and then let your fond affections hold Him fast forevermore. Love the person of your
Lord! Bring forth the alabaster box of your heart, even
though it may be broken, and let all the precious ointment
of your affection come streaming on His pierced feet. Let
your intellect be exercised concerning the Lord Jesus.
Meditate on what you read. Do not stop at the surface; dive
into the depths. Do not be like the swallow that touches the
brook with its wing, but be like the fish that penetrates the
lowest wave. Abide with your Lord. Do not let Him be to
you as a wayfaring man, who tarries for a night; but constrain Him, saying, *"Abide with us: for...the day is far spent"*
(Luke 24:29). Hold Him, and do not let Him go. The word
ponder means "to weigh." Make ready the balances of judgment. Oh, but where are the scales that can weigh the Lord
Christ? He *"weighed the mountains in scales"* (v. 12)—in what
scales shall we weigh *Him? "He taketh up the isles as a very*
little thing" (Isa. 40:15)—who will take *Him* up? Even so, if
your understanding cannot comprehend, let your affections
do so. If your spirit cannot encompass the Lord Jesus in the
grasp of understanding, let it embrace Him in the arms of
affection.

And the shepherds returned, glorifying and praising God for all the things that they had heard and seen, as it was told unto them.
—Luke 2:20

hat was the subject of the shepherds' praise? They praised God for what they had *"heard,"* for the *"good tidings of great joy"* (Luke 2:10) that a Savior had been born unto them. Let us imitate them. Let us also raise a song of thanksgiving that we have heard of Jesus and His salvation. Moreover, they praised God for what they had *"seen."* That is the sweetest music—what we have experienced, what we have felt within, what we have made our own: *"The things which* [we] *have made touching the king"* (Ps. 45:1). It is not enough to hear about Jesus; mere hearing may tune the harp, but the fingers of living faith must create the music. If you have seen Jesus with the God-giving sight of faith, allow no cobwebs to linger among the harpstrings. Awake your psaltery and harp and loudly praise His sovereign grace. One point for which they praised God was the agreement between what they had heard and what they had seen. Observe the last part of the sentence: *"As it was told unto them."* Have you not found the Gospel to be in yourself just what the Bible said it would be? Jesus said He would give you rest—have you not enjoyed the sweetest peace in Him? He said you would have joy, comfort, and life through believing in Him—have you not received all these? Are His ways not *"ways of pleasantness"* (Prov. 3:17) and His paths not paths of peace (v. 17)? Surely, you can say with the queen of Sheba, *"The half was not told me"* (1 Kings 10:7). I have found Christ sweeter than His servants ever said He was. I looked on His likeness as they painted it, but it was a crude portrait compared with Himself; for the King in His beauty outshines all imaginable loveliness. Surely, what we have seen not only keeps pace with, but far exceeds what we have heard. Let us, then, glorify and praise God for a Savior so precious and so satisfying.

The dove came in to him in the evening.
—Genesis 8:11

Blessed be the Lord for another day of mercy, even though I am now weary from its labor. I lift my song of gratitude to the Preserver of men. The dove found no rest outside the ark so it returned to it, and my soul has learned more than ever, this day, that there is no satisfaction to be found in earthly things—God alone can give rest to my spirit. As to my business, my possessions, my family, my accomplishments, these are all well enough in their way, but they cannot fulfill the desires of my immortal nature. *"Return unto thy rest, O my soul; for the LORD hath dealt bountifully with thee"* (Ps. 116:7). It was at the still hour, when the gates of the day were closing, that with weary wing the dove came back to its master. O Lord, enable me this evening thus to return to Jesus. The dove could not endure to spend a night hovering over the restless waste; neither can I bear to be even for another hour away from Jesus, the Rest of my heart, the Home of my spirit. The bird did not merely alight on the roof of the ark; it *"came in to him."* Even so would my longing spirit look into the secrets of the Lord, pierce to the interior of truth, enter into that which is *"within the veil"* (Heb. 6:19), and reach to my Beloved. To Jesus I must come. Short of the nearest and dearest communion with Him, my panting spirit cannot stand firm. Blessed Lord Jesus, be with me, reveal Yourself, and abide with me all night, so that, when I awake, I may still be with You. I note that the dove brought in its mouth an olive branch that it had plucked off, a memorial of the past day and a prophecy of the future. Have I no pleasing record to bring home, no pledge and earnest of lovingkindness yet to come? Yes, my Lord, I present You my grateful acknowledgments for tender mercies that have been *"new every morning"* (Lam. 3:23) and fresh every evening. Now, I pray You, put forth Your hand and take Your dove in to Yourself.

In whom also we have obtained an inheritance.
—Ephesians 1:11

When Jesus gave Himself for us, He gave us all the rights and privileges that are in Him. Although, as eternal God, He has essential rights to which no creature may venture to claim, as Jesus, the Mediator, the federal Head of the covenant of grace, He now has no heritage apart from us. All the glorious consequences of His obedience unto death are the joint riches of all who are in Him and on whose behalf He accomplished the divine will. Note that He entered into glory, but not for Himself alone, for it is written, *"Whither the forerunner is **for us** entered"* (Heb. 6:20, emphasis added). Does He stand in the presence of God? He appears *"in the presence of God **for us**"* (Heb. 9:24, emphasis added). Consider this, believer: you have no right to heaven in yourself; your right lies in Christ. If you are pardoned, it is through His blood. If you are justified, it is through His righteousness. If you are sanctified, it is because you are in Jesus, *"who of God is made unto [you] ...sanctification"* (1 Cor. 1:30). If you will be kept from falling, it will be because you are preserved in Christ Jesus; and if you are perfected at the last, it will be because you are *"complete in him"* (Col. 2:10). Thus Jesus is magnified, for all is in Him and by Him. The inheritance is made certain to us, for it is obtained in Him, and each blessing is sweeter—even heaven itself the brighter—because it is Jesus our Beloved *"in whom also we have obtained"* all. Where is the person who can estimate our divine portion? Weigh the riches of Christ and His treasure; then try to count the treasures that belong to the saints. Reach the bottom of Christ's sea of joy; then hope to understand the bliss *"which God hath prepared for them that love him"* (1 Cor. 2:9). Hurdle the boundaries of Christ's possessions; then dream of a limit to the fair inheritance of the elect. *"All things are yours;...ye are Christ's; and Christ is God's"* (1 Cor. 3:21, 23).

Then Ahimaaz ran by the way of the plain, and overran Cushi.
—2 Samuel 18:23

Running is not everything. The path that we select is also significant. A swift foot over hill and down dale will not keep pace with a slower traveler who is on level ground. How is it with my spiritual journey? Am I laboring up the hill of my own works and down into the ravines of my own humiliations and resolutions, or do I run by the unobstructed way of "believe and live"? (See John 20:31.) How blessed it is to wait on the Lord by faith! The soul runs without weariness and walks without fainting when it operates in faith. Christ Jesus is the way of life, and He is a plain way, a pleasant way, a way suitable for the tottering feet and feeble knees of trembling sinners. Am I on His path, or am I hunting after another track, such as one that false religions or philosophy may promise me? I read of *"the way of holiness"* in which *"the wayfaring men, though fools, shall not err"* (Isa. 35:8). Have I been delivered from proud reason and been brought as a little child to rest in Jesus' love and blood? If so, by God's grace I will outrun the strongest runner who chooses any other path. This truth I may remember to my profit in my daily cares and needs. It will be my wisest course to go at once to my God and not to wander in a roundabout manner to this friend and that. He knows my needs and can relieve them. To whom should I go but to Himself by the direct appeal of prayer and the plain argument of the promise? "Straightforward makes the best runner." I will not confer with the servants but hasten to their master. In reading this passage, it strikes me that if men vie with each other over common matters, and one outruns the other, I ought to be in solemn earnestness to run in such a way that I may obtain the prize. Lord, help me to *"gird up the loins of* [my] *mind"* (1 Pet. 1:13). May *"I press toward the mark for the prize of the high calling of God in Christ Jesus"* (Phil. 3:14).

Thy love to me was wonderful.
—2 Samuel 1:26

ome, dear readers, and let each one of us speak for himself of the wonderful love, not of Jonathan, but of Jesus. We will not relate what we have been told, but the things that we have tasted and handled of the love of Christ. Your love for me, O Jesus, was wonderful when I was a stranger wandering far from You, fulfilling the desires of the flesh and of the mind. Your love restrained me from committing the *"sin unto death"* (Rom. 6:16) and withheld me from self-destruction. Your love held back the ax when Justice said, "Cut it down! Why trouble the ground with it?" Your love drew me into the wilderness, stripped me there, and made me feel the guilt of my sin and the burden of my iniquity. Your love spoke gently to me when I was very dismayed: *"Come unto me...and I will give you rest"* (Matt. 11:28). Oh, how matchless was Your love when, in a moment, You washed my sins away and made my polluted soul, which was crimson with the blood of my birth and black with the grime of my transgressions, to be white as the driven snow and pure as the finest wool. How You showed me Your love when You whispered in my ears, "I am yours and you are Mine." Your words were so kind when You said, *"The Father himself loveth you"* (John 16:27). And sweet the moments, surpassing sweet, when You declared to me *"the love of the Spirit"* (Rom. 15:30). My soul will never forget those times of fellowship where You have unveiled Yourself to me. Did Moses have his cleft in the rock, where he saw the train, the back, of his God? We, too, have had our clefts in the rock where we have seen the full splendor of the Godhead in the person of Christ. Did David remember the tracks of the wild goat, the land of Jordan, and the heights of Hermon? We, too, can remember places that are dear to our memories, equal to these in blessedness. Precious Lord Jesus, give us a fresh portion of Your wondrous love with which to begin the month. Amen.

And these are ancient things.
—1 Chronicles 4:22

hese things are not as ancient as those precious things that delight our souls. Let us for a moment recall them, recounting them as misers delight in calculating the worth of their gold. The sovereign choice of the Father, by which He elected us to eternal life, before *"the earth was"* (Prov. 8:23), is a matter of vast antiquity, since no date can be conceived for it in the mind of man. We were *"chosen...in him before the foundation of the world"* (Eph. 1:4). Everlasting love went with the choice, for it was not a mere act of divine will by which we were set apart, but divine affection was also involved. The Father loved us in and from the beginning. Here is a theme for daily contemplation. The eternal purpose to redeem us from our foreseen ruin, to cleanse and sanctify us, and, at last, to glorify us was of infinite antiquity; it runs side by side with immutable love and absolute sovereignty. The covenant is always described as being everlasting, and Jesus, the second party in it, was actively involved from the start. He struck hands in sacred suretyship long before the first of the stars began to shine, and it was in Him that the elect were ordained to eternal life. Thus in the divine purpose a most blessed covenant union was established between the Son of God and His elect people, which will remain as the foundation of their safety when time will be no more. Is it not well to be conversant with these ancient things? Is it not shameful that they should be so much neglected and even rejected by the majority of believers? If they knew more of their own sin, would they not be more ready to adore His amazing grace? Let us both admire and adore Him tonight, as we sing,

> A monument of grace,
> A sinner saved by blood!
> The streams of love I trace
> Up to the Fountain, God;
> And in His sacred bosom see
> Eternal thoughts of love to me.

*Tell me…where thou feedest, where thou
makest thy flock to rest at noon.*
—Song of Solomon 1:7

hese words express the desire of the believer to follow
Christ and his longing for present communion with
Him. Where do You feed Your flock? In Your house? I
will go, if I may find You there. In private prayer? Then I
will pray without ceasing. In the Word? Then I will read it
diligently. In Your commandments? Then I will walk in
them with all my heart. Tell me where You feed, for wherever You stand as the Shepherd, there will I lie down as a
sheep; for none but You can supply my need. I cannot be
satisfied to be apart from You. My soul hungers and thirsts
for the refreshment of Your presence. "Where do You make
Your flock to rest at noon?" For whether it is at dawn or at
noon, my only rest must be where You are and Your beloved
flock. My soul's rest must be a grace-given rest, and it can be
found only in You. Where is the shadow of that rock? Why
should I not repose underneath it? *"Why should I be as one
that turneth aside by the flocks of thy companions?"* (Song 1:7).
You have companions—why should I not be one? Satan tells
me that I am unworthy, but I always was unworthy. Yet You
have long loved me; therefore, my unworthiness cannot be a
barrier to my having fellowship with You now. It is true I
am weak in faith and prone to fall, but my very feebleness is
the reason why I should always be where You feed Your
flock, so that I may be strengthened and preserved in safety
beside the still waters. Why should I turn away from You?
There is no reason why I should, but there are a thousand
reasons why I should not, for Jesus beckons me to come. If
He withdrew Himself a little, it was only to make me prize
His presence more. Now that I am grieved and distressed at
being away from Him, He will lead me once again to that
sheltered nook where the lambs of His fold are shielded from
the burning sun.

Your refuge from the avenger of blood.
—Joshua 20:3

t is said that in the land of Canaan, cities of refuge were set up so that any man might reach one of them within half a day at the most. Likewise, the word of our salvation is near to us. Jesus is a present Savior, and the distance to Him is short. It requires only a simple renunciation of our own merit and a laying hold of Jesus to be our all in all. With regard to the roads leading to the cities of refuge, we are told that they were carefully preserved. Every river was bridged and every obstruction removed, so that the man who fled might find an easy passage to safety. Once a year the elders went along the roads and saw to their order, so that nothing might impede the flight of anyone or cause him, through delay, to be overtaken and slain. How graciously do the promises of the Gospel remove stumbling blocks from our paths! Wherever there were hidden roads or turns, there were signs placed, with this inscription on them: "To the city of refuge!" This is a picture of the road to Christ Jesus. It is no roundabout road of the law. It does not involve obeying endless rules; it is a straight road: "Believe and live." (See John 20:31.) It is a road so hard that no self-righteous man can ever tread it, but so easy that every sinner, who knows himself to be a sinner, may by it find his way to heaven. No sooner did the manslayer reach the outskirts of the city than he was safe. It was not necessary for him to pass far within the walls, for the suburbs themselves were sufficient protection. Learn that if you touch just the hem of Christ's garment, you will be made whole; if you will only lay hold on him with *faith as a grain of mustard seed"* (Matt. 17:20), you will be safe.

> A little genuine grace ensures
> The death of all our sins.

Do not waste any time. Do not loiter by the way, for *"the avenger of blood"* is swift of foot; it may be that he is at your heels on this quiet, evening hour.

At that time Jesus answered.
—Matthew 11:25

his is an unusual way in which to begin a verse—*"At that time Jesus answered."* If you look at the context, you will notice that no one had asked Him a question and that He was not in conversation with any human being. Yet it is written, *"Jesus answered and said, I thank thee, O Father"* (Matt. 11:25). When a man answers, he answers a person who has been speaking to him. Who, then, had spoken to Christ? His Father. Yet there is no record of it. This should teach us that Jesus had constant fellowship with His Father; God spoke to His heart so often, so continually, that it was not a circumstance uncommon enough to be recorded. It was the habit and life of Jesus to talk with God. Even as Jesus was, in this world, so are we; let us, therefore, learn the lesson that this simple statement concerning Him teaches us. May we likewise have silent fellowship with the Father, so that often we may answer Him. Though the world does not know to whom we speak, may we be responsive to that secret voice unheard by any other ear, which our own ears, opened by the Spirit of God, recognize with joy. God has spoken to us; let us speak to God—either to set our seal that God is true and faithful to His promise, to confess the sin of which the Spirit of God has convicted us, to acknowledge the mercy that God's providence has given, or to express assent to the great truths that God the Holy Spirit has opened to our understanding. What a privilege is intimate communion with the Father of our spirits! It is a secret hidden from the world, a joy with which even the dearest friend cannot share. If we would hear the whispers of God's love, our ears must be purged and ready to listen to His voice. This very evening may our hearts be in such a state so that, when God speaks to us, we, like Jesus, may be prepared at once to answer Him.

Pray one for another.
—James 5:16

s an encouragement to offer intercessory prayer cheerfully, remember that such prayer is the sweetest God ever hears, for the prayer of Christ is of this same character. In all the incense that our Great High Priest now puts into the golden censer, there is not a single grain for Himself. His intercession must be the most acceptable of all supplications—and the more our prayer is like Christ's, the sweeter it will be. Thus while petitions for ourselves will be accepted, our pleadings for others, having in them more of the fruits of the Spirit—more love, more faith, more brotherly kindness—will be, through the precious merits of Jesus, the sweetest offering that we can present to God, the very fat of our sacrifice. Remember, also, that intercessory prayer is exceedingly prevalent. What wonders it has brought about! The Word of God teems with its marvelous deeds. Believer, you have a mighty engine in your hand; use it well, and use it constantly. Use it with faith, and you will surely be a benefactor to your brethren. When you have the King's ear, speak to Him for the suffering members of His body. When you are favored to draw very near to His throne, and the King says to you, *"Whatsoever ye shall ask the Father in my name, he will give it you"* (John 16:23), let your petitions be, not for yourself alone, but for the many who need His aid. If you have grace at all and you are not an intercessor, that grace must be as small as a grain of mustard seed. You have just enough grace to float your soul clear from the quicksand, but you have no deep floods of grace. Otherwise, you would carry in your joyous boat a weighty cargo of the needs of others, and you would bring back from your Lord rich blessings, which without you they might not have obtained.

> Oh, let my hands forget their skill,
> My tongue be silent, cold, and still,
> This bounding heart forget to beat,
> If I forget the mercy seat!

And they heard a great voice from heaven
saying unto them, Come up hither.
—Revelation 11:12

Without considering these words in their prophetic connection, let us regard them as the invitation of our great Forerunner to His sanctified people. In due time, every believer will hear *"a great voice from heaven,"* saying, *"Come up hither."* To the saints, this should be the subject of joyful anticipation. Instead of dreading the time when we will leave this world to go to the Father, we should be panting for the hour of our emancipation. Our song should be,

> My heart is with Him on His throne,
> And ill can brook delay;
> Each moment listening for the voice,
> "Rise up and come away."

We are not called down to the grave, but up to the skies. Our heaven-born spirits should long for their native air, yet the celestial summons should be the object of patient waiting. Our God knows best when to bid us, *"Come up hither."* We must not wish to hasten the period of our departure. I know that strong love will make us cry,

> O Lord of Hosts, the waves divide,
> And land us all in heaven.

But patience must have her perfect work. God ordains with accurate wisdom the most fitting time for the redeemed to abide below. Surely, if there could be regrets in heaven, the saints might mourn that they did not live longer here to do more good. Oh, for more sheaves for my Lord's garner— more jewels for His crown! But how, unless there is more work? It is true that living so briefly, our sins are fewer; but oh, when we are fully serving God and He is giving us precious seed to scatter and to reap a hundredfold, we would even say it is well for us to remain where we are. Whether our Master says "go" or "stay," let us be equally well pleased as long as He continues to bless us with His presence.

He shall save his people from their sins.
—Matthew 1:21

any persons, when asked what they mean by salvation, will reply, "Being saved from hell and taken to heaven." This is one result of salvation, but it is not one tenth of what is contained in that blessing. It is true that our Lord Jesus Christ redeems all His people from the wrath to come. He saves them from the fearful condemnation that their sins have brought upon them, but His triumph is far more complete than this. He saves His people *"from their sins."* Oh, sweet deliverance from our worst foes! Where Christ works a saving work, He casts Satan from his throne and will not let him be master any longer. No man is a true Christian if sin reigns in his mortal body. Sin will be in us; it will never be utterly expelled until the spirit enters glory, but it will never have dominion. There will be a striving for dominion—a lusting against the new law and the new spirit that God has implanted—but sin will never get the upper hand so as to be absolute monarch of our natures. Christ will be the Master of the heart, and sin must be mortified. The Lion of the tribe of Judah will prevail, and the dragon will be cast out. Believer, is sin subdued in you? If your life is unholy, your heart is unchanged; and if your heart is unchanged, you are an unsaved person. If the Savior has not sanctified you, renewed you, given you a hatred of sin and a love of holiness, He has done nothing in you of a saving character. Grace that does not make a man better than others is a worthless counterfeit. Christ saves His people, not *in* their sins, but *from* them. Without *"holiness,…no man shall see the Lord"* (Heb. 12:14). *"Let every one that nameth the name of Christ depart from iniquity"* (2 Tim. 2:19). If we are not saved from sin, how will we hope to be counted among His people? Lord, save me now from all evil and enable me to honor my Savior.

Lead us not into temptation;
but deliver us from evil [or, the evil one].
—Luke 11:4

What we are taught to seek or shun in prayer, we should equally pursue or avoid in action. Therefore, we should avoid temptation earnestly, seeking to walk guardedly in the path of obedience, so that we may never tempt the devil to tempt us. We are not to enter the thicket in search of the lion. Dearly might we pay for such presumption. A lion may cross our paths or leap on us from the thicket, but we have nothing to do with hunting it. He who meets with a lion, even though he wins the day, will find it a stern struggle. Let the Christian pray that he may be spared from the encounter. Our Savior, who experienced what temptation meant, thus earnestly admonished His disciples: *"Pray that ye enter not into temptation"* (Luke 22:40). But no matter what we do, we will be tempted; hence the prayer *"deliver us from evil."* God had one Son without sin; but He has no son without temptation. The natural *"man is born unto trouble, as the sparks fly upward,"* (Job 5:7), and the Christian man is born to temptation just as certainly. We must always be on watch against Satan, because, like a thief, he gives no warning of his approach. Believers who have had experience in the ways of Satan know that there are certain seasons when he will most probably make an attack, just as at certain seasons bleak winds may be expected. Thus the Christian is put on a double guard by fear of danger, and the danger is averted by preparing to meet it. Prevention is better than cure: it is better to be so well armed that the devil will not attack you than to endure the perils of the fight, even though you come off a conqueror. Pray this evening first that you may not be tempted, and next that if temptation is permitted, you may be delivered from the evil one.

I have blotted out, as a thick cloud, thy transgressions, and, as a
cloud, thy sins: return unto me; for I have redeemed thee.
—Isaiah 44:22

arefully observe the instructive comparison made here: our sins are like a cloud. As clouds are of many shapes and shades, so are our transgressions. As clouds obscure the light of the sun and darken the landscape below, so do our sins hide from us the light of Jehovah's face and cause us to sit in the shadow of death. They are earthborn things and rise from the miry places of our nature. When so collected that their measure is full, they threaten us with storm and tempest. Sadly, unlike clouds, our sins do not yield any beneficial showers; rather, they threaten to deluge us with a fiery flood of destruction. O black clouds of sin, how can it be fair weather with our souls while you remain? Let our joyful eyes dwell on the notable act of divine mercy—blotting out. God Himself appears on the scene, and in divine graciousness, instead of manifesting His anger, He reveals His grace. At once and forever, He effectively removes the mischief, not by blowing away the cloud, but by blotting it out from existence once and for all. No sin remains against the justified man; the great transaction of the Cross has eternally removed his transgressions from him. On Calvary's summit the great deed, by which the sin of all the chosen was forever put away, was completely and effectively performed. Practically, let us obey the gracious command, *"Return unto me."* Why should pardoned sinners live at a distance from their God? If we have been forgiven of all our sins, let no fear keep us from the boldest access to our Lord. Let us regret any backslidings, but let us not persevere in them. To the greatest possible nearness of communion with the Lord, let us, in the power of the Holy Spirit, strive mightily to return. O Lord, this night restore us!

Thou hast left thy first love.
—Revelation 2:4

We will always remember that best and brightest of hours when we first saw the Lord. We lost our burdens, received His promises, rejoiced in full salvation, and went on our way in peace. It was springtime in the soul. The winter was past. The mutterings of Sinai's thunders were hushed, and the flashings of its lightning were no more perceived. God and man were reconciled; the law threatened no vengeance, and justice demanded no punishment. Then the flowers appeared in our hearts. Hope, love, peace, and patience sprang from the sod. The hyacinth of repentance, the snowdrop of pure holiness, the crocus of golden faith, the daffodil of early love—all arrayed the garden of the soul. The *"time of the singing of birds"* (Song 2:12) came, and we rejoiced with thanksgiving. We magnified the holy name of our forgiving God, and our resolve was, "Lord, I am Yours, wholly Yours. All I am and all I have, I would devote to You. You have bought me with Your blood; let me spend myself and be spent in Your service. In life and in death, let me be consecrated to You." How have we kept this resolve? Our first love burned with a holy flame of devotion to Jesus; is it the same now? Might not Jesus well say to us, *"I have somewhat against thee, because thou hast left thy first love"* (Rev. 2:4)? Alas, we have done but little for our Master's glory! Our winter has lasted all too long. We are as cold as ice when we should feel a summer's glow and bloom with sacred flowers. We give God pennies when He deserves dollars. No, He deserves our hearts' blood to be invested in the service of His church and of His truth. Will we continue to do so? Lord, after You have so richly blessed us, will we be ungrateful and become indifferent to Your good cause and work? Quicken us so that we may return to our first love and do our first works! Sun of Righteousness, send us a refreshing spring.

He shall give you another Comforter,
that he may abide with you for ever.
—John 14:16

Our great Father revealed Himself to believers of old before the coming of His Son. He was known to Abraham, Isaac, and Jacob as God Almighty. Then Jesus came, and the ever-blessed Son in His own proper person was the delight of His people's eyes. At the time of the Redeemer's ascension, the Holy Spirit became the Head of the present dispensation, and His power was gloriously manifested in and after Pentecost. He remains at this hour the present Immanuel—God with us, dwelling in and with His people, quickening, guiding, and ruling in their midst. Is His presence recognized as it ought to be? We cannot control His working. He is most sovereign in all His operations, but are we sufficiently anxious to obtain His help or sufficiently watchful lest we provoke Him to withdraw His aid? Without Him we can do nothing, but by His almighty energy, the most extraordinary results can be produced. Everything depends on His manifesting or concealing His power. Do we always look up to Him both for our inner lives and our outward service with the respectful dependence that is fitting? Do we not too often run before His call and act independently of His aid? Let us humble ourselves this evening for past failures, and now entreat the heavenly dew to rest upon us, the sacred oil to anoint us, and the celestial flame to burn within us. The Holy Spirit is no temporary gift; He abides with the saints. We have but to seek Him aright, and He will be found by us. He is jealous, but He is compassionate. If He leaves in anger, He returns in mercy. Gracious and tender, He does not weary of us, but He waits to be merciful still.

> Sin has been hammering my soul
> Unto a hardness, void of love.
> Let grace work, too, and o'er my soul
> Drop from above.

There is therefore now no condemnation.
—Romans 8:1

ome, my soul, think of this: By believing in Jesus, you are actually and effectively cleared from guilt. You are released from your prison. No longer chained like a slave, you are delivered from the bondage of the law. You are freed from sin and can walk as a freeman. Your Savior's blood has obtained your full pardon. Now, you have the right to approach your Father's throne. No flames of vengeance and no fiery swords are there to scare you. Justice cannot smite the innocent. Your disabilities are taken away. You were once unable to see your Father's face; you can see it now. You could not speak with Him, but now you have access with boldness. Once the fear of hell was upon you. But you have no fear of it now, for how can there be punishment for the guiltless? He who believes is not condemned and cannot be punished. And more than all, the privileges you might have enjoyed, if you had never sinned, are yours now that you are justified. All the blessings that you would have had if you had kept the law, and more, are yours, because Christ has kept it for you. All the love and the acceptance that perfect obedience could have obtained from God belong to you, because Christ was perfectly obedient on your behalf. He has imputed all His merits to your account so that you might be exceedingly rich through Him, who for your sake became exceedingly poor. Oh, how great the debt of love and gratitude you owe to your Savior!

> A debtor to mercy alone,
> Of covenant mercy I sing;
> Nor fear with Your righteousness on,
> My person and offerings to bring:
> The terrors of law and of God,
> With me can have nothing to do;
> My Savior's obedience and blood
> Hide all my transgressions from view.

She was healed immediately.
—Luke 8:47

ne of the most touching and teaching of the Savior's miracles is before us tonight. The woman was very ignorant. She imagined that virtue came out of Christ by a law of necessity, without His knowledge or direct will. Moreover, she was a stranger to the generosity of Jesus' character, or she would not have gone behind Him to steal the cure that He was so ready to give. Misery should always place itself right in the face of mercy. Had she known the love of Jesus' heart, she would have said, "I have but to put myself where He can see me. Then His omniscience will reveal my situation to Him, and His love will work my cure immediately." We admire her faith, but we marvel at her ignorance. After she had obtained the cure, she rejoiced with trembling. She was glad that the divine virtue had worked a miracle in her, but she feared lest Christ might retract the blessing and cancel the grant of His grace. Little did she comprehend the fullness of His love! We do not have as clear a view of Him as we could wish. We do not know the heights and depths of His love, but we know with certainty that He is too good to withdraw from a trembling soul the gift that it has been able to obtain. But here is the marvel of it: little as her knowledge was, her faith, because it was real faith, saved her, and saved her at once. There was no tedious delay—faith's miracle was instantaneous. If we have faith as a grain of mustard seed, salvation is our present and eternal possession. If, in the list of the Lord's children, we are written as the weakest of the family, yet, being heirs through faith, no power, human or devilish, can eject us from salvation. Even if we do not dare to lean our heads on His bosom as John did, yet we can venture into the crowd behind Him and touch the hem of His garment, and we will be made whole. Courage, timid one! Your faith has saved you. Go in peace. *"Being justified by faith, we have peace with God"* (Rom. 5:1).

Whereby they have made thee glad.
—Psalm 45:8

Who are the ones who are privileged to make the Savior glad? His church—His people. But is it possible? He makes us glad, but how can we make Him glad? By our love. We think our love is so cold and so faint; indeed, we must sorrowfully confess it to be, but it is very sweet to Christ. Hear His own eulogy of that love in the golden Song of Solomon: *"How fair is thy love, my sister, my spouse! how much better is thy love than wine!"* (Song 4:10). See, loving heart, how He delights in you. When you lean your head on His bosom, you not only receive, but also give Him joy. When you gaze with love on His all-glorious face, you not only obtain comfort, but also impart delight. Our praise, too, gives Him joy—not the song of the lips alone, but the melody of the heart's deep gratitude. Our gifts, too, are very pleasant to Him. He loves to see us lay our time, our talents, and our substance upon the altar, not for the value of what we give, but for the sake of the motive from which the gift springs. To Him, the lowly offerings of His saints are more acceptable than the thousands of offerings of gold and silver. Holiness is like frankincense and myrrh to Him. Forgive your enemy, and you make Christ glad. Distribute of your substance to the poor, and He rejoices. Be the means of saving souls, and you give Him the opportunity to see the fruit of His soul's labors. Proclaim His Gospel, and you are a sweet aroma to Him. Go among the ignorant and lift up the Cross, and you have given Him honor. It is in your power even now to break the alabaster box and pour the precious oil of joy upon His head, as did the woman of old, whose memorial is told to this day wherever the Gospel is preached. Will you be backward then? Will you not perfume your beloved Lord with the myrrh, aloes, and cinnamon of your heart's praise? Yes, ivory palaces, you will hear the songs of the saints!

Thy good spirit.
—Nehemiah 9:20

ommon, too common, is the sin of forgetting the Holy Spirit. This is folly and ingratitude. He deserves our best, for He is good, supremely good. As God, He is good essentially. He shares in the threefold ascription of *"Holy, holy, holy"* (Isa. 6:3; Rev. 4:8), which ascends to the triune Jehovah. He is purity, truth, and grace. He is good benevolently, tenderly bearing with our waywardness and striving with our rebellious wills. He quickens us from our death in sin, and then He trains us for the skies as a loving nurse fosters her child. How generous, forgiving, and tender is this patient Spirit of God! He is good operatively. All His works are good in the most eminent degree. He suggests good thoughts, prompts good actions, reveals good truths, applies good promises, assists in good attainments, and leads to good results. There is no spiritual good in all the world of which He is not the author and sustainer; heaven itself will owe the perfect character of its redeemed inhabitants to His work. He is good officially. Whether as Comforter, Instructor, Guide, Sanctifier, Quickener, or Intercessor, He fulfills His office well, and each work is laden with the highest good to the church of God. Those who yield to His influences become good, those who obey His impulses do good, and those who live under His power receive good. Let us then act toward so good a person according to the dictates of gratitude. Let us revere and adore Him, *"who is over all, God blessed for ever"* (Rom. 9:5). Let us recognize His power and admit our need of Him by waiting on Him in all our holy enterprises. Let us hourly seek His aid and never grieve Him. And let us praise Him whenever any opportunity to do so arises. The church will never prosper until more reverently it believes in the Holy Spirit. He is so good and kind that it is sad indeed that He should be grieved by slights and neglect.

Whereas the LORD was there.
—Ezekiel 35:10

E dom's princes saw the whole country left desolate, and they counted upon its easy conquest. But there was one great difficulty in their way that was quite unknown to them: *"The LORD was there."* In His presence lay the special security of the chosen land. Whatever may be the schemes and devices of the enemies of God's people, there is still the same effective barrier to thwart their plans. The saints belong to God, and He is in the midst of them. He will protect His own. What comfort this assurance provides for us in our troubles and spiritual conflicts! We are constantly opposed yet perpetually preserved! How often Satan shoots his arrows against our faith, but our faith defies the power of hell's fiery darts. They are not only turned aside, but they are quenched upon its shield, for *"the LORD is there."* Our good works are the subjects of Satan's attacks. A saint never yet had a virtue or a grace that was not the target for hellish bullets. Whether it was a bright and sparkling hope, a warm and fervent love, an all-enduring patience, or a zeal flaming like coals of fire, the old enemy of everything that is good has tried to destroy it. The only reason why anything virtuous or lovely survives in us is this: *"The LORD is there."* If the Lord is with us through life, we do not need to fear for our dying confidence; for when we come to die, we will find that *"the LORD is there."* Where the billows are the most tempestuous and the water is the coldest, we will feel the bottom and know that it is secure. When time is passing away, our feet will stand upon the Rock of Ages. Beloved, from the first of a Christian's life to the last, the only reason why he does not perish is that *"the LORD is there."* When the God of everlasting love changes or leaves His elect to perish, then may the church of God be destroyed; but not until then, because it is written, JEHOVAH SHAMMAH, *"The LORD is there."*

Father, I have sinned.
—Luke 15:18

It is quite certain that those whom Christ has washed in His precious blood do not need to make a confession of sin as culprits or criminals before God the Judge. Christ has forever taken away all their sins in a legal sense, so that they no longer stand where they can be condemned, but they are once and for all *"accepted in the beloved"* (Eph. 1:6). But having become children, and offending as children, should they not every day go before their heavenly Father and confess their sin and acknowledge their iniquity in that character? Nature teaches that it is the duty of erring children to make a confession to their earthly father, and the grace of God in the heart teaches us that we, as Christians, owe the same duty to our heavenly Father. We daily offend and should not rest without daily pardon. Suppose that my trespasses against my Father are not at once taken to Him to be washed away by the cleansing power of the Lord Jesus; what will be the consequence? If I have not sought forgiveness and been cleansed from these offenses against my Father, I will feel at a distance from Him. I will doubt His love for me. I will tremble in His presence, and I will be afraid to pray to Him. I will become like the Prodigal, who, although he was his father's child, was still far away from his father. But if, with a child's sorrow at offending so gracious and loving a Parent, I go to Him and tell Him all, and I do not rest until I realize that I am forgiven, then I will feel a holy love toward my Father. I will go through my Christian life not only as saved, but also as one enjoying present peace in God through Jesus Christ my Lord. There is a wide distinction between confessing sin as a culprit and confessing sin as a child. The Father's heart is the place for penitent confessions. We have been cleansed once and for all, but, as children of God, our feet still need to be washed from the defilement of our daily walk.

[Andrew] first findeth his own brother Simon.
—John 1:41

This case is an excellent example of what happens when spiritual life is vital. As soon as a man has found Christ, he begins to find others. I will not believe that you have tasted of the honey of the Gospel if you can eat it all yourself. True grace puts an end to all spiritual monopoly. Andrew first found his own brother Simon and then others. Relationship has a very strong demand upon our initial individual efforts. Andrew did well to begin with Simon. I do not doubt that there are some Christians giving away tracts at other people's houses who would do well to give away a tract at their own. Likewise, I wonder whether there are not some who are engaged in works of ministry abroad who are neglecting their special sphere of usefulness at home. You may or may not be called to evangelize people in a particular locality, but certainly you are called to see after your own household, your own relatives, and your acquaintances. Let your religion begin at home. Many tradesmen export their best commodities—the Christian should not. All his conversation everywhere should carry the best aroma; but let him pay special care to put forth the sweetest fruit of spiritual life and testimony among his own family. When Andrew went to find his brother, he could not have imagined how eminent Simon would become. Simon Peter was worth ten Andrews as far as we can gather from sacred history, yet Andrew was instrumental in bringing him to Jesus. You may be very deficient in talent yourself, yet you may be the means of drawing to Christ one who will become prominent in grace and service. Dear friend, little do you know the possibilities that are in you. You may merely speak a word to a child, and in that child there may be slumbering a noble heart that will stir the Christian church in years to come. Andrew had only two talents, but he found Peter. Go and do likewise.

*Then was Jesus led up of the Spirit into the wilderness
to be tempted of the devil.*
—Matthew 4:1

A holy character does not avert temptation: Jesus was tempted. When Satan tempts us, his sparks fall upon kindling. In Christ's case, however, it was like striking sparks on water. Yet the enemy continued his evil work. Now, if the devil goes on striking when there is no result, how much more will he do it when he knows what flammable stuff our hearts are made of. Though you become greatly sanctified by the Holy Spirit, expect that the great dog of hell will still bark at you. In the company of men, we expect to be tempted; but even seclusion will not guard us from the same trial. Jesus Christ was led away from human society into the wilderness and was tempted by the devil. Solitude has its charms and its benefits and may be useful in checking the lust of the eye and the pride of life, but the devil will follow us into the most lovely retreats. Do not suppose that it is only the worldly-minded who have dreadful thoughts and blasphemous temptations, for even spiritually-minded persons endure the same. We may suffer the darkest temptation in the holiest place. The utmost consecration of spirit will not insure you against satanic temptation. Christ was consecrated through and through. It was His meat and drink to do the will of Him who sent Him, yet He was tempted! Your heart may glow with an angelic flame of love for Jesus, yet the devil will try to bring you down to Laodicean lukewarmness. If you tell me when God permits a Christian to lay aside his armor, I will tell you when Satan gives up temptation. Like the old knights in wartime, we must sleep with helmet and breastplate buckled on, for the arch-deceiver will seize our first unguarded hour to make us his prey. May the Lord keep us watchful in all seasons and give us a final escape from the jaw of the lion and the paw of the bear.

Understandest thou what thou readest?
—Acts 8:30

If we sought to have a more intelligent understanding of the Word of God, we would be better teachers of others and less likely to be carried about by *"every wind of doctrine"* (Eph. 4:14). Only the Holy Spirit, the Author of the Scriptures, can enlighten us properly to understand them; therefore, we should constantly pray for His teaching and His guidance into all truth. When the prophet Daniel needed to interpret Nebuchadnezzar's dream, what did he do? He earnestly prayed that God would open up the vision. The apostle John, in his vision at Patmos, saw a book sealed with seven seals that no one was found worthy to open or even to look upon. The book was later opened by the Lion of the tribe of Judah, who had prevailed to open it; but it is written first, *"I wept much"* (Rev. 5:4). The tears of John were his liquid prayers. As far as he was concerned, they were the sacred keys by which the folded book was opened. If, for your own benefit and the benefit of others, you desire to be *"filled with the knowledge of [God's] will in all wisdom and spiritual understanding"* (Col. 1:9), remember that prayer is your best means of study. Like Daniel, you will understand the dream and its interpretation when you have sought God. Like John, you will see the seven seals of precious truth loosed after you have wept much. Stones are not broken except by an earnest use of the hammer. The one who desires to break the stones must go down on his knees. Use the hammer of diligence, and let the knee of prayer be exercised. There is not a stony doctrine in revelation that is useful for you to understand that will not fly into pieces under the exercise of prayer and faith. You may force your way through anything with the leverage of prayer. Thoughts and arguments are like the steel wedges that give a hold upon truth; but prayer is the lever that forces open the iron chest of sacred mystery so that we may obtain the treasure hidden within.

The LORD is slow to anger, and great in power.
—Nahum 1:3

ehovah *"is slow to anger."* When mercy comes into the world, it drives winged steeds; the axles of its chariot wheels are red-hot with speed. But when wrath goes forth, it toils on with sluggish footsteps, for God takes no pleasure in the sinner's death. God's rod of mercy is always in His outstretched hands. His sword of justice is in its sheath, held down by the pierced hand of love that bled for the sins of men. *"The LORD is slow to anger"* because He is great in power. He is truly great in power who has power over himself. When God's power restrains Himself, then it is power indeed: the power that binds omnipotence surpasses omnipotence. A man who has a strong mind can bear to be insulted for a long time, and he resents the wrong only when a sense of right demands his action. The weak mind is irritated by little things, but the strong mind bears irritation like a rock that does not move, even though a thousand breakers dash upon it and cast their pitiful malice in spray upon its summit. God sees His enemies, yet He does not rouse Himself to action, but holds in His anger. If He were less divine than He is, long before this, He would have sent forth the whole of His thunders and emptied the magazines of heaven. Long before this, He would have blasted the earth with the wondrous fires of its lower regions, and man would have been utterly destroyed. But the greatness of His power brings us mercy. Dear reader, what is your state of mind this evening? Can you by humble faith look to Jesus and say, "My Substitute, You are my rock and my trust"? Then, beloved, do not be afraid of God's power. If by faith you have fled to Christ for refuge, the power of God no longer needs to terrify you any more than the shield and sword of the warrior terrifies those whom he loves. Instead, rejoice that He who is *"great in power"* is your Father and Friend.

Take up the cross, and follow me.
—Mark 10:21

You are not to construct your own cross, although unbelief is a master carpenter at cross-making. Neither are you permitted to choose your own cross, although self-will would gladly be lord and master. But your cross is prepared and appointed for you by divine love, and you are to accept it cheerfully. You are to take up the cross as your chosen badge and burden, not stand around complaining about it. This night Jesus invites you to submit your shoulder to His easy yoke. Do not kick at it in petulance, trample on it in pride, fall under it in despair, or run away from it in fear. Take it up like a true follower of Jesus. Jesus was a cross-bearer; He leads the way in the path of sorrow. Surely you could not desire a better guide! And if He carried a cross, what nobler burden would you desire? The *Via Crucis* is the way of safety; do not fear to tread its thorny paths. Beloved, the cross is not made of feathers or lined with velvet. It is heavy and galling to disobedient shoulders, but it is not an iron cross, though your fears have painted it with iron colors. It is a wooden cross, and a man can carry it, for the Man of Sorrows first bore the load. Take up your cross, and by the power of the Spirit of God, you will soon be so in love with it that, like Moses, you would not exchange *"the reproach of Christ* [for all] *the treasures in Egypt"* (Heb. 11:26). Remember that Jesus carried it, and it will smell sweetly; remember that soon it will be followed by the crown, and the thought of the coming weight of glory will greatly lighten the present heaviness of trouble. May the Lord help you to bow your spirit in submission to the divine will before you fall asleep this night so that waking with tomorrow's sun, you may go forth to the day's cross with the holy and submissive spirit that becomes a follower of the Crucified One.

*O LORD of hosts, how long wilt thou not have mercy
on Jerusalem?…And the LORD answered the angel…
with good words and comfortable words.*
—Zechariah 1:12–13

What a sweet answer to an anxious inquiry! This
night let us rejoice in it. O Zion, there are good
things in store for you. Your time of travail will
soon be over. Your children will be brought forth, and your
captivity will end. Patiently bear the rod for a season, and
in the darkness still trust in God, for His love burns toward
you. God loves the church with a love too deep for human
imagination. He loves her with all His infinite heart; therefore, let her sons be of good courage. She cannot be far from
prosperity to whom God speaks *"good words and comfortable
words."* The prophet goes on to tell us what these comfortable words are: *"I am jealous for Jerusalem and for Zion with a
great jealousy"* (Zech. 1:14). The Lord loves His church so
much that He cannot bear that she would go astray to others; when she has done so, He cannot bear that she would
suffer too much or too heavily. He will not have His enemies afflict her. He is displeased with them because they
increase her misery. When God seems to have left His
church, His heart is still warm toward her. History shows
us that whenever God uses a rod to chasten His servants,
He always breaks it afterward, as if He loathed the rod that
gave His children pain. *"Like as a father pitieth his children, so
the LORD pitieth them that fear him"* (Ps. 103:13). God has not
forgotten us because He chastens us; His correction is no
evidence of a lack of love. If this is true of His church col-
lectively, it is also true of each individual member. You may
fear that the Lord has passed you by, but that is not so. He
who counts the stars and calls them by their names is in no
danger of forgetting His own children. He knows your
situation as thoroughly as if you were the only creature He
ever made or the only saint He ever loved. Approach Him,
and be at peace.

But Jonah rose up to flee unto Tarshish from the presence of the
LORD, and went down to Joppa.
—Jonah 1:3

Instead of going to Nineveh to preach the Word as God commanded him, Jonah disliked the work and went to Joppa to escape from it. There are occasions when God's servants shrink from duty. But what is the consequence? What did Jonah lose by his conduct? He lost the presence and comfortable enjoyment of God's love. When we serve our Lord Jesus as believers should, our God is with us. Though we have the whole world against us, if we have God with us, what does it matter? But the moment we turn back and seek our own desires, we are at sea without a pilot. Then may we bitterly lament and groan, "O my God, where have You gone? How could I have been so foolish as to shun Your service and thus lose all the brightness of Your face? This price is too high. Let me return to my allegiance so that I may rejoice in Your presence." Jonah also lost all peace of mind. Sin soon destroys a believer's comfort. Sin is like the poisonous mulberry tree, from whose leaves distill deadly drops that destroy the life of joy and peace. Jonah lost everything on which he might have drawn comfort in any other situation. He could not plead the promise of divine protection, for he was not in God's will. He could not say, "Lord, I met with these difficulties in the course of my duty; therefore, help me through them." He was reaping his own deeds; he was filled with his own ways. Christian, do not act like Jonah, unless you wish to have all the waves and the billows rolling over your head. In the long run, you will find that it is far harder to shun the work and will of God than to yield yourself to it immediately. Jonah lost his time, for he had to go to Tarshish after all. It is hard to contend with God. Let us yield ourselves to Him right now.

Behold, if the leprosy have covered all his flesh,
he shall pronounce him clean that hath the plague.
—Leviticus 13:13

lthough this regulation appears to be strange, there was wisdom in it. The outward manifestation of the disease proved that the leper's constitution was sound. It may be well for us to see the symbolic meaning of so unusual a rule. We, too, are lepers and may apply the law of the leper to ourselves. When a man sees himself to be altogether lost and ruined, covered with the defilement of sin, and in no part free from pollution; when he disclaims all righteousness of his own and pleads guilty before the Lord, then he is clean through the blood of Jesus and the grace of God. Hidden, unfelt, unconfessed iniquity is the true leprosy; but when sin is seen and felt, it has received its death-blow, and the Lord looks with eyes of mercy on the afflicted soul. Nothing is more deadly than self-righteousness or more hopeful than repentance. We must confess that we are sinful, for no confession short of this will be the whole truth. If the Holy Spirit is at work in us, convicting us of sin, there will be no difficulty about making such an acknowledgment—it will spring spontaneously from our lips. What comfort the text gives to truly awakened sinners: the very circumstance that so grievously discouraged them is here turned into a sign of a hopeful condition! Stripping comes before clothing; digging out the foundation is the first thing in building—and a thorough sense of sin is one of the earliest works of grace. Poor, leprous sinner, take heart from the text, and come as you are to Jesus.

> For let our debts be what they may,
> However great or small,
> As soon as we have nought to pay,
> Our Lord forgives us all.
> 'Tis perfect poverty alone
> That sets the soul at large:
> While we can call one mite our own,
> We have no full discharge.

Whose goings forth have been from of old, from everlasting.
—Micah 5:2

The Lord Jesus represented His people before the throne long before they appeared on the stage of time. It was *"from everlasting"* that He signed the covenant with His Father that He would pay blood for blood, suffering for suffering, agony for agony, and death for death on behalf of His people. It was *"from everlasting"* that He gave Himself up without murmuring a word. From the crown of His head to the soles of His feet, He sweat great drops of blood. He was spat upon, pierced, mocked, torn asunder, and crushed beneath the pains of death. His offering Himself as our Surety was *"from everlasting."* Pause, my soul, and wonder! You have been loved by Jesus *"from everlasting."* Not only when you were born into the world did Christ love you, but His *"delights were with the sons of men"* (Prov. 8:31) before there were any sons of men! He thought of them often; from everlasting to everlasting He had set His affection upon them. Has He planned so long for your salvation, my soul, not to accomplish it? Has He *"from everlasting"* been going forth to save you, and will He lose you now? What? Has He carried you in His hand, as His precious jewel, and will He now let you slip away between His fingers? Did He choose you before the mountains were brought forth or the channels of the deep were dug, and will He reject you now? Impossible! I am sure He would not have loved you so long if He was not a changeless Lover. If He could grow weary of you, He would have been tired of you long before now. If He had not loved you with a love as deep as hell and as strong as death, He would have turned from you long ago. Oh, joy above all joys, to know that you are His everlasting and inalienable inheritance, given to Him by His Father before the earth ever was! Everlasting love will be the pillow for your head tonight.

*The barrel of meal wasted not, neither did the cruse of oil fail,
according to the word of the LORD, which he spake by Elijah.*
—1 Kings 17:16

ee the faithfulness of divine love. Observe that this
woman had daily needs. She had to feed herself and
her son during a time of famine; now, in addition, the
prophet Elijah needed to be fed. But though the need was
three times as great, the meal did not run out, for she had a
constant supply. Each day she went to the barrel, but each
day the amount in it remained the same. You, dear reader,
also have daily needs. Because they come so frequently, you
are inclined to fear that the barrel of meal will one day be
empty, and the jar of oil will fail you. Rest assured that, according to the Word of God, this will not be the case. Each
day, though it brings its troubles, will also bring its help.
Though you would live to outnumber the years of Methu-
selah, and your needs would be as numerous as the sands of
the seashore, God's grace and mercy will last through all
your necessities, and you will never know a real lack. For
three long years during this widow's lifetime, the heavens
never saw a cloud, and the stars never wept a holy tear of
dew upon the wicked earth. Famine, desolation, and death
made the land a howling wilderness, but this woman was
never hungry; she was always joyful in abundance. So will
it be for you. You will see the sinner's hope perish, for he
trusts in his own strength. You will see the proud Pharisee's confidence waver, for he builds his hope on the sand.
You will even see your own schemes blasted and withered,
but you will find that your place of defense will be in the
Rock of your salvation. Your bread will be given to you,
and your water supply will be secure. It is better to have
God for your guardian than to own the Bank of England.
You might spend the wealth of the Indies, but you can
never exhaust the infinite riches of God.

Now we have received…the spirit which is of God; that we might
know the things that are freely given to us of God.
—1 Corinthians 2:12

ear reader, have you received the Spirit of God, the
Holy Spirit, in your soul? The necessity of the work
of the Holy Spirit in the heart may be clearly seen
from this fact: all that has been done by God the Father and
by God the Son will be of no value to us unless the Spirit
reveals these things to our souls. What effect does the doctrine of election have on any man until the Spirit of God
enters into him? Election is a dead letter in my consciousness until the Spirit of God calls me *"out of darkness into his*
marvellous light" (1 Pet. 2:9). Then, through my calling, I
see my election, and knowing myself to be called by God, I
know I have been chosen in the eternal purpose. A covenant
was made with the Lord Jesus Christ by His Father; but of
what good is that covenant to us until the Holy Spirit brings
us its blessings and opens our hearts to receive them? There
hang the blessings on the nail—Christ Jesus—but being
short of stature, we cannot reach them. The Spirit of God
takes them down and hands them to us, and thus they become actually ours. Covenant blessings in themselves are
like the manna in the skies, far out of mortal reach; but the
Spirit of God opens the windows of heaven and scatters the
living bread around the camp of the spiritual Israel. Christ's
finished work is like wine stored in the wine vat; through
unbelief we can neither draw nor drink. The Holy Spirit
dips our hearts into this precious wine, and then we drink;
but without the Spirit, we are as truly dead in sin as though
the Father never had elected us, and as though the Son had
never bought us with His blood. The Holy Spirit is absolutely necessary to our well-being. Let us walk lovingly
toward Him and tremble at the thought of grieving Him.

He is precious.
—1 Peter 2:7

s all the rivers run into the sea, so all delights center on our Beloved. The glance of His eyes outshines the sun. The beauty of His face is fairer than the choicest flowers. No fragrance is like the breath of His mouth. Gems of the earth and pearls from the sea are worthless things when compared to His preciousness. Peter told us that Jesus is precious, but he did not and could not tell us how precious, nor could any of us compute the value of God's unspeakable gift. Words cannot express the preciousness of the Lord Jesus to His people or fully tell how essential He is to their satisfaction and happiness. Believer, have you not found in the midst of plenty a sore famine if your Lord has been absent? The sun was shining, but Christ had hidden Himself, and all the world was black to you; or it was night, and since the *"bright and morning star"* (Rev. 22:16) was gone, no other star could yield so much as a ray of light to you. What a howling wilderness this world is without our Lord! If He hides Himself from us, the flowers of our garden wither. Our pleasant fruits decay, the birds suspend their songs, and a tempest overturns our hopes. All earth's candles cannot make daylight if the Sun of Righteousness is eclipsed. He is the Soul of our souls, the Light of our light, the Life of our lives. Dear reader, what would you do in the world without Him, when you wake up and look ahead to the day's battle? What would you do at night, when you come home jaded and weary, if there were no door of fellowship between you and Christ? Blessed is His name! He will not allow us to try our lot without Him, for Jesus never forsakes His own. Yet let the thought of what life would be without Him enhance His preciousness.

Unto me, who am less than the least of all saints, is this grace given, that
I should preach among the Gentiles the unsearchable riches of Christ.
—Ephesians 3:8

The apostle Paul felt it was a great privilege to be allowed to preach the Gospel. He did not look on his calling as a drudgery, but he fulfilled it with intense delight. Yet while Paul was thankful for his calling, his success in it greatly humbled him. The fuller a vessel becomes, the deeper it sinks in the water. Idlers may indulge a fond conceit of their abilities, because they are untried; but the earnest worker soon learns his own weakness. If you seek humility, try hard work. If you would know your nothingness, attempt some great thing for Jesus. If you would feel how utterly powerless you are apart from the living God, attempt the great work of proclaiming *"the unsearchable riches of Christ,"* and you will know, as you never knew before, what a weak, unworthy thing you are. Although the apostle thus knew and confessed his weakness, he was never perplexed as to the subject of his ministry. From his first sermon to his last, Paul preached Christ, and nothing but Christ. He lifted up the cross and extolled the Son of God who bled thereon. Follow his example in all your personal efforts to spread the glad tidings of salvation, and let "Christ and Him crucified" (see 1 Corinthians 2:2) be your ever-recurring theme. The Christian should be like those lovely spring flowers that, when the sun is shining, open their golden cups, as if to say, "Fill us with your beams!" but when the sun is hidden behind a cloud, they close their cups and droop their heads. Likewise, the Christian should feel the sweet influence of Jesus. Jesus must be his sun, and he must be the flower that yields itself to the Sun of Righteousness. Oh, to speak of Christ alone is the subject that is both *"seed to the sower, and bread to the eater"* (Isa. 55:10). This is the live coal for the lips of the speaker and the master key to the heart of the hearer.

He saw the Spirit of God descending like a dove.
—Matthew 3:16

s the Spirit of God descended on the Lord Jesus, the Head, so He also, in part, descends on the members of Christ's body, the church. His descent is to us after the same fashion as that in which it fell upon our Lord. There is often an exceptional rapidity about it. Before we are completely aware of what is happening, we are impelled onward and heavenward beyond all expectation. Yet it is not done with earthly haste, for the wings of the dove are as soft as they are swift. Quietness seems to be essential to many spiritual operations. The Lord is in the still small voice; and, like the dew, His grace is distilled in silence. The dove has always been the chosen symbol of purity, and the Holy Spirit is holiness itself. Where He comes, everything that is pure, lovely, and of good report abounds, and sin and uncleanness depart. Peace also reigns where the holy Dove comes with power. He bears the olive branch that shows that the waters of divine wrath are assuaged. Gentleness is a sure sign of the sacred Dove's transforming power; hearts touched by His benign influence are meek and lowly from that point on. Harmlessness follows as a matter of course. Eagles and ravens may hunt their prey; the turtledove can endure wrong, but it cannot inflict it. We must be harmless as doves. The dove is a fitting picture of love; its voice is full of affection. Thus, the soul visited by the blessed Spirit abounds in love for God, in love for other Christians, and in love for sinners. Above all, it abounds in love for Jesus. The brooding of the Spirit of God on *"the face of the deep"* (Gen. 1:2) first produced order and life. In our hearts, He causes and fosters new life and light. Blessed Spirit, as You rested on our dear Redeemer, even so rest on us from this time forward and forever.

They shall be abundantly satisfied with the fatness of thy house.
—Psalm 36:8

The queen of Sheba was amazed at the sumptuousness of Solomon's table. She was overwhelmed when she saw the provision of a single day. She marveled equally at the number of servants who feasted at the royal table. But what is this compared with the hospitality of the God of grace? Hundreds of thousands of His people are fed daily; hungry and thirsty, they bring large appetites with them to the banquet, but not one of them leaves unsatisfied. There is enough for each, enough for all, enough forevermore. Though the host that feeds at Jehovah's table is as countless as the stars of heaven, each one receives his portion of meat. Think how much grace one saint requires, so much that nothing but the Infinite One could supply him for one day; yet the Lord spreads His table, not for one, but for many saints; not for one day, but for many years; not for many years only, but for generation after generation. Observe the full feasting spoken of in the text. The guests at mercy's banquet are satisfied—no, they are *"abundantly satisfied."* They are filled not with ordinary fare, but with *"fatness,"* the unique abundance of God's own house. Such feasting is guaranteed by a faithful promise to all those children of men who put their trust under the shadow of Jehovah's wings. I once thought that if I could just get the leftover meat at God's back door of grace, I would be satisfied—like the woman who said, *"The dogs eat of the crumbs which fall from their masters' table"* (Matt. 15:27). But no child of God is ever served with scraps and leftovers. Like Mephibosheth, they all eat from the king's own table. In matters of grace, we all have Benjamin's portion; we all have many times more than we could have expected. Although our needs are great, we are often amazed at the marvelous abundance of grace that God gives to us to enjoy.

Say unto my soul, I am thy salvation.
—Psalm 35:3

hat does this sweet prayer teach me? It will be my evening's petition, but first let it serve as an instructive meditation. The text informs me that David had his doubts; otherwise, why would he pray, *"Say unto my soul, I am thy salvation,"* if he were not sometimes plagued with doubts and fears? Let me, then, be encouraged, for I am not the only saint who has to complain of weakness of faith. If David doubted, I do not need to conclude that I am not a Christian because I have doubts. The text reminds me that David was not content while he had doubts and fears. Instead, he went immediately to the mercy seat to pray for assurance, which he valued as much as fine gold. I, too, must seek an abiding sense of my acceptance in the Beloved. I must have no joy when His love is not shed abroad in my soul. When my Bridegroom is gone from me, my soul must and will fast. I also learn that David knew where to obtain full assurance. He went to his God in prayer, crying, *"Say unto my soul, I am thy salvation."* I must spend much time alone with God if I expect to have a clear sense of Jesus' love. If my prayers cease, my eye of faith will grow dim. Much in prayer, much in heaven; slow in prayer, slow in progress. I notice that David would not be satisfied unless his assurance had a divine source. *"Say unto my soul."* Lord, please speak to me! Nothing short of a divine testimony in the soul will ever satisfy the true Christian. Moreover, David could not rest unless his assurance had a vivid personality about it. *"Say unto my soul, I am thy salvation."* Lord, if You say this to all the saints, it would mean nothing, unless You said it to me. Lord, I have sinned; I do not deserve Your smile. I hardly dare to ask, but oh, say to my soul, even to my soul, *"I am thy salvation."* Let me have a present, personal, unfailing, indisputable sense that I am Yours and that You are mine.

Before destruction the heart of man is haughty.
—Proverbs 18:12

I t is an old, familiar saying that "coming events cast their shadows before them." The writer of Proverbs teaches us that a haughty heart is the prophetic prelude to evil. Pride forecasts destruction even more reliably than a change of mercury in the barometer predicts rain. When men have ridden the high horse, destruction has always overtaken them. Let David's aching heart show that there is an eclipse of a man's glory when he focuses on his own greatness. (See 2 Samuel 24:10.) Nebuchadnezzar, the mighty builder of Babylon, was reduced to creeping on the earth, devouring grass like an ox, until his nails had grown like birds' claws and his hair like eagles' feathers. (See Daniel 4:33.) Pride turned the boaster into a beast, just as once before it had made an angel into a devil. God hates haughty looks and never fails to bring them down. All the arrows of God are aimed at proud hearts. Christian, is your heart haughty this evening? For pride can get into the Christian's heart as well as into the sinner's; it can delude him into dreaming that he is *"rich, and increased with goods, and [in] need of nothing"* (Rev. 3:17). Are you glorying in your grace or your talents? Are you proud of yourself because you have a holy expression and sweet experiences? If so, then, take note, reader: destruction is coming to you also. Your flaunting poppies of self-conceit will be pulled up by the roots, your mushroom graces will wither in the burning heat, and your self-sufficiency will become as straw for the dunghill. If we forget to live at the foot of the cross in deepest lowliness of spirit, God will not forget to make us suffer under His rod. Destruction will come to you, O self-exalted believer. The destruction of your joys and of your comforts will come, even though there can be no destruction of your soul. Therefore, *"he that glorieth, let him glory in the Lord"* (1 Cor. 1:31).

It is better to trust in the LORD than to put confidence in man.
—Psalm 118:8

ndoubtedly, the reader has been tried with the temptation to rely on things that are seen, instead of resting alone on the invisible God. Christians often look to man for help and counsel and mar the noble simplicity of their reliance on their God. Does this evening's portion meet the eye of a child of God who is anxious about earthly concerns? Then I would reason with him for a while. You say that you trust in Jesus, and only in Jesus, for your salvation. Then why are you troubled? "Because of my great care," you answer. Is it not written, *"Cast thy burden upon the LORD"* (Ps. 55:22)? Does Scripture not also say, *"Be careful for nothing; but in every thing by prayer and supplication with thanksgiving let your requests be made known unto God"* (Phil. 4:6)? Can you not trust God for your material needs? "Oh, I wish I could," you say. If you cannot trust God for earthly needs, how can you dare to trust Him for spiritual needs? Can you trust Him for your soul's redemption and not rely on Him for a few lesser mercies? Is God not enough for your needs, or is His all-sufficiency too limited? Do you need another eye besides the One who sees every secret thing? Is His heart faint? Is His arm weary? If so, then seek another God; but if He is infinite, omnipotent, faithful, true, and all-wise, why do you waste your time seeking another confidence? Why do you comb the earth to find another foundation, when God is strong enough to bear all the weight that you can ever build upon Him? Christian, just as you would not dilute your wine with water, do not alloy the gold of your faith with the dross of human confidence. Wait only on God, and let your hope come from Him. Do not covet Jonah's gourd, but rest in Jonah's God. Let the sandy foundations of earthly trust be the choice of fools; but like the one who foresees the storm, build your house upon the Rock of Ages.

She called his name Benoni [son of sorrow]: *but his father called him Benjamin* [son of my right hand].
—Genesis 35:18

To every matter there is a bright as well as a dark side. Rachel was overwhelmed with the sorrow of her difficult childbirth, which led to her death; Jacob, though weeping at the loss of his wife, could see the mercy of the child's birth. It is well for us if, while the flesh mourns over trials, our faith triumphs in divine steadfastness. Samson's lion yielded honey, and so will our adversities, if we look at them in the right way. The stormy sea feeds multitudes with its fish; the wild forest blooms with beautiful flowers; the stormy wind sweeps away the pestilence, and the biting frost loosens the soil. Dark clouds distill bright drops, and black earth grows colorful flowers. A vein of good is to be found in every mine of evil. Sad hearts have an unusual ability to discover the most disadvantageous point of view from which to gaze upon a trial. If there were only one swamp in the world, they would soon be up to their necks in it; and if there were only one lion in the desert, they would hear it roar. We all have a little tendency to act this way. We are likely, at times, to cry as Jacob did, *"All these things are against me"* (Gen. 42:36). Faith's way of walking is to cast all care upon the Lord and then to anticipate good results from the worst calamities. Like Gideon's men, faith does not fret over the broken pitcher but rejoices that the lamp blazes forth all the more. Out of the rough oyster shell of difficulty, faith extracts the rare pearl of honor; from the deep ocean caves of distress, it uplifts the priceless coral of experience. When the flood of prosperity ebbs, faith finds treasures hidden in the sand; and when the sun of delight goes down, faith turns her telescope of hope to the starry promises of heaven. When death itself appears, faith points to the light of resurrection beyond the grave, thus making our dying Benoni to be our living Benjamin.

Abide in me.
—John 15:4

ommunion with Christ is a certain cure for every ill. Whether it is bitter sorrow or excessive pleasure, close fellowship with the Lord Jesus will remove the pain from the one and the imbalance from the other. Live near to Jesus, Christian, and it is matter of secondary importance whether you reside on the mountain of honor or in the valley of humiliation. Living near to Jesus, you are covered with the wings of God; underneath you are the *"everlasting arms"* (Deut. 33:27). Let nothing keep you from that hallowed fellowship, which is the choice privilege of a soul wedded to the Lord. Do not be content with an interview now and then, but always seek to retain His company. Only in His presence will you find either comfort or safety. Jesus should not be a friend who calls upon us now and then, but One with whom we walk continuously. Do you have a difficult road before you? O traveler to heaven, see that you do not go without your Guide. Do you have to pass through the fiery furnace? Do not enter it unless, like Shadrach, Meshach, and Abednego, you have the Son of God as your Companion. Do you have to battle the Jericho of your own sins? Then do not attempt the warfare until, like Joshua, you have seen the Captain of the Lord's host with His sword drawn in His hand. Are you called to meet the Esau of your many temptations? Do not meet him until at Jabbok's brook you have laid hold on the angel and have prevailed. In every case, in every condition, you will need Jesus. When the iron gates of death open, you will need Him most of all. Keep close to your soul's Husband. Lean your head on His breast, and ask to be refreshed with the spiced wine of His pomegranate. Then you will be found by Him at the end, without *"spot, or wrinkle, or any such thing"* (Eph. 5:27). Since you have lived with Him and lived in Him here, you will abide with Him forever.

Man…is of few days, and full of trouble.
—Job 14:1

Before we fall asleep, it may be of great service to us to remember the truth of this evening's text; it could lead to our being set free from earthly things. There is nothing very pleasant in recalling that we are not immune to adversity, but it may humble us and prevent our boasting like the psalmist in our morning's portion, *"In my prosperity I said, I shall never be moved"* (Ps. 30:6). It may keep us from sinking our roots too deeply into this soil from which we are so soon to be transplanted into the heavenly garden. Let us recall the frail claim we hold on our earthly blessings. If we would remember that all the trees of the earth are marked for the woodsman's ax, we would not be so ready to build our nests in them. We should love with the love that expects death and that counts on separations. Our dear relatives are but loaned to us, and the hour when we must return them to the Lender's hand may be even at the door. The same is certainly true of our worldly goods. Do not riches take wings and fly away? Our health is equally precarious. As frail flowers of the field, we must not think that we will bloom forever. There is a time appointed for weakness and sickness when we will have to glorify God by our suffering and not by earnest activity. There is no single point at which we can hope to escape from the sharp arrows of affliction; out of our few days, there is not one secure from sorrow. Man's life is a cask full of bitter wine; he who looks for joy in it had better seek for honey in an ocean of brine. Beloved reader, do not *"set your affection on things…on the earth"* (Col. 3:2), but seek those things that are above. Here the moth devours, and *"thieves break through and steal"* (Matt. 6:19), but there all joys are perpetual and eternal. The path of trouble is the way home. Lord, make this thought a pillow for many weary heads!

Thou shalt be called, Sought out.
—Isaiah 62:12

The surpassing grace of God is seen very clearly in that we were not only sought, but *"sought out."* Men seek for something that has been lost on the floor of the house, but in such a situation, there is only seeking, not seeking out. The loss is more perplexing and the search more persevering when a thing is sought out. We were mingled with the mire. It is as if we were like some precious piece of gold that had fallen into a sewer. Men gather together to carefully inspect the mass of abominable filth, and they continue to stir and rake and search among the heap until the treasure is found. Or, to use another example, we were lost in a maze. We wandered here and there, and when mercy came after us with the Gospel, it did not find us at the first coming. It had to search for us and seek us out, for like lost sheep, we were so desperately lost. We had wandered into a strange country, and it did not seem possible that even the Good Shepherd would be able to follow our devious wanderings. Glory be to unconquerable grace: we were sought out! No gloom could hide us; no filthiness could conceal us. We were found and brought home. Glory be to infinite love: God the Holy Spirit restored us! If the lives of some of God's people could be written, they would fill us with holy astonishment. Strange and marvelous are the ways that God used in their cases to find His own. Blessed be His name! He never relinquishes the search until the chosen are sought out. They are not a people sought today and cast away tomorrow. Almightiness and wisdom combined will make no failures. They will be called, *"Sought out."* That any should be sought out is matchless grace, but that we should be sought out is grace beyond degree! We can find no reason for it but God's own sovereign love. We can only lift up our hearts in wonder and praise the Lord that this night we wear the name *"Sought out."*

To whom belongest thou?
—1 Samuel 30:13

No neutrality can exist in Christianity. We are either ranked under the banner of Prince Immanuel to serve and fight His battles, or we are followers of the black prince, Satan. *"To whom belongest thou?"* Reader, let me assist you in your response. Have you been born again? If you have, you belong to Christ, but without the new birth, you cannot be His. In whom do you trust? Those who believe in Jesus are the sons of God. Whose work are you doing? You are sure to serve your master, for he whom you serve is admittedly your lord. What company do you keep? If you belong to Jesus, you will fraternize with those who wear the sign of the Cross. As the saying goes, Birds of a feather flock together. What is your conversation? Is it heavenly, or is it earthly? What have you learned of your Master? Servants learn much from their masters to whom they are apprenticed. If you have served your time with Jesus, it will be said of you, as it was of Peter and John, *"They took knowledge of them, that they had been with Jesus"* (Acts 4:13). We press the question, *"To whom belongest thou?"* Answer honestly before you give sleep to your eyes. If you are not Christ's, you are in a hard service. Run away from your cruel master! Enter into the service of the Lord of Love, and you will enjoy a life of blessedness. If you are Christ's, let me advise you to do four things. You belong to Jesus; therefore, *obey Him.* Let His Word be your law; let His wish be your will. Since you belong to the Beloved, *love Him.* Let your heart embrace Him; let your whole soul be filled with Him. Because you belong to the Son of God, *trust Him.* Do not rest anywhere but on Him. You belong to the King of Kings, so *be decided for Him.* Do not waver in your loyalty. Although you are not branded outwardly, live your life so that all will know to whom you belong.

*Then he put forth his hand, and took her, and pulled her
in unto him into the ark.*
—Genesis 8:9

Worn out from her wanderings, the dove finally returns to the ark as her only resting place. How heavily she flies—she will drop—she will never reach the ark! But she struggles on. Noah has been watching for the dove all day long, and he is ready to receive her. She has just enough strength to reach the edge of the ark. She can hardly alight upon it. She is ready to drop when Noah puts forth his hand and pulls her in to him. Notice these words: *"pulled her in unto him."* She did not fly right in herself, for she was too fearful or too weary to do so. She flew as far as she could, and then he reached out his hand and pulled her in to safety. This act of mercy was shown to the wandering dove; she was not scolded for her wanderings. Just as she was, she was pulled into the ark. So you, seeking sinner, with all your sin, will be received. *Only return*—these are God's two gracious words. What? Nothing else? No, "only return." The dove had no olive branch in her mouth this time. She had nothing at all but herself and her wanderings. But the message is still "only return." She does return, and Noah pulls her in. Fly, wanderer; fly, fainting one, dove as you are. Although you think you are black as the raven with the mire of sin, fly back, back to the Savior. Every moment you wait only increases your misery. Your attempts to plume yourself and make yourself fit for Jesus are all vanity. Come to Him just as you are. *"Return, thou backsliding Israel"* (Jer. 3:12). God does not say, "Return, thou repenting Israel" (though undoubtedly there is such an invitation), but He says, *"thou backsliding"* one. As a backslider with all your backslidings, return, return, return! Jesus is waiting for you! He will stretch forth His hand and pull you in. He will pull you in to Himself, your heart's true home.

I will take heed to my ways.
—Psalm 39:1

ellow pilgrim, do not say in your heart, "I will go here and there, and I will not sin," for you are never so far from the danger of sinning as to boast of security. The road is very muddy; it will be hard to pick your path so as not to soil your garments. This world is full of corruption; you will need to watch often if, in handling it, you are to keep yourself clean. At every turn in the road, there is a thief ready to rob you of your jewels. There is a temptation in every blessing and a snare in every joy. If you ever reach heaven, it will be a miracle of divine grace to be ascribed entirely to your Father's power. Be on your guard. When a man carries an explosive in his hands, he should be careful not to go near an open flame. You, too, must take care that you do not enter into temptation. Even your daily activities are sharp tools; you must watch how you handle them. There is nothing in this world to foster a Christian's faith, but everything tries to destroy it. How quick you should be to look to God so that He may keep you! Your prayer should be, "Hold me up, and I will be safe." Having prayed, you must also watch; guard every thought, word, and action with holy jealousy. Do not expose yourselves unnecessarily to danger, but if you are called to go where the darts are flying, never venture forth without your shield. If even once the devil finds you without protection, he will rejoice that his hour of triumph has come, and he will soon make you fall down wounded by his arrows. Though you cannot be slain, you can be wounded. Be sober; be vigilant. Danger may come in the hour when everything seems to be the most secure. Therefore, take heed to your ways, and pray diligently. No one ever fell into error through being too watchful. May the Holy Spirit guide us in all our ways so that we may always please the Lord.

He did it with all his heart, and prospered.
—2 Chronicles 31:21

his is no unusual occurrence; it is the general rule of the moral universe that men who do their work with all their hearts prosper, while those who go to their labor leaving half their hearts behind are almost certain to fail. God does not give harvests to idle men except harvests of thistles. Neither is He pleased to send wealth to those who will not dig in the field to find its hidden treasure. It is universally acknowledged that if a man desires to prosper, he must be diligent in business. It is the same in religion as it is in other things. If you want to prosper in your work for Jesus, let it be heart-work, and let it be done with all your heart. Put as much force, energy, heartiness, and sincerity into Christ's work as you do into your business, for His cause deserves far more. The Holy Spirit helps our infirmities, but He does not encourage our idleness; He loves active believers. Who are the most useful people in the Christian church? Those who do what they undertake for God with all their hearts. Who are the most successful Sunday school teachers? The most talented? No, they are the most zealous; workers whose hearts are on fire are the ones who see their Lord riding forth prosperously in the majesty of His salvation. (See Psalm 45:4.) Wholeheartedness shows itself in perseverance. There may be failure at first, but the diligent worker will say, "It is the Lord's work, and it must be done. My Lord has commanded me to do it, and in His strength, I will accomplish it." Christian, are you serving your Master with all your heart? Remember the earnestness of Jesus! Think what heart-work was His! He could say, *"The zeal of thine house hath eaten me up"* (John 2:17). When He sweat great drops of blood, it was no light burden He had to carry on those blessed shoulders; when He poured out His heart, it was no weak effort He was making for the salvation of His people. After Jesus gave Himself so passionately, can we afford to be lukewarm?

Keep back thy servant also from presumptuous sins.
—Psalm 19:13

uch was the prayer of David, the *"man after [God's] own heart"* (Acts 13:22). If holy David needed to pray this way, how much more do we, babes in grace, need to do so! It is as if he said, "Keep me back, or I will rush headlong over the precipice of sin." Our evil natures, like an ill-tempered horse, are prone to run away. May the grace of God put the bridle on them and hold them in, so that we do not rush into mischief. What might the best of us not do if it were not for the boundaries that the Lord sets upon us both in providence and in grace? The psalmist's prayer is directed against the worst form of sin—that which is done with deliberation and willfulness. Even the holiest need to be "kept back" from the vilest transgressions. It is a solemn thing to find the apostle Paul warning saints against the most loathsome sins. *"Mortify therefore your members which are upon the earth; fornication, uncleanness, inordinate affection, evil concupiscence, and covetousness, which is idolatry"* (Col. 3:5). What! Do saints need to be warned against such sins as these? Yes, they do. The whitest robes, unless their purity is preserved by divine grace, will be defiled by the blackest spots. Experienced Christian, do not boast in your experience; you will trip if you look away from Him who *"is able to keep you from falling"* (Jude 24). You whose love is fervent, whose faith is constant, whose hopes are bright, do not say, "We will never sin." Instead, cry, *"Lead us not into temptation"* (Matt. 6:13). There is enough kindling in the heart of the best of men to light a fire that will burn to the lowest hell, unless God quenches the sparks as they fall. Who would have dreamed that righteous Lot could have been found drunken and committing uncleanness? Hazael said, *"Is thy servant a dog, that he should do this great thing?"* (2 Kings 8:13). We are very likely to ask the same self-righteous question. May infinite wisdom cure us of the foolishness of self-confidence.

Blessed are the peacemakers: for they shall be called
the children of God.
—Matthew 5:9

his is the seventh of the beatitudes, and seven represented the number of perfection among the Hebrews.
It may be that the Savior placed the blessing of the
peacemaker seventh on the list because that person most
nearly approaches the perfect man in Christ Jesus. He who
would have perfect blessedness, as far as it can be enjoyed
on earth, must attain to this seventh benediction and become a peacemaker. There is a significance also in the position of the text. The verse that precedes it speaks of the
blessedness of *"the pure in heart: for they shall see God"* (Matt.
5:8). It is important to understand that we are to be first
pure, then peaceable. Our peaceable nature is never to be an
acceptance of sin or a permissiveness of evil. We must set
our faces like flints against everything that is contrary to
God and His holiness. Once purity in our souls is a settled
matter, we can go on to peaceableness. No less than the
preceding verse does the verse that follows seem to have
been put there on purpose. However peaceable we may be
in this world, we will be misrepresented and misunder-
stood. That should not surprise us, considering that the
Prince of Peace, by His very peacefulness, brought fire upon
the earth. He Himself, though He loved mankind and did no
wrong, was *"despised and rejected of men; a man of sorrows, and*
acquainted with grief" (Isa. 53:3). Lest, therefore, the peaceable in heart should be surprised when they meet with
enemies, it is added in the following verse, *"Blessed are they*
which are persecuted for righteousness' sake: for theirs is the king-
dom of heaven" (Matt. 5:10). Thus, the peacemakers are not
only pronounced to be blessed, but they are surrounded
with blessings. Lord, give us grace to climb to this seventh
beatitude! Purify our minds that we may be first pure, then
peaceable. Fortify our souls so that our peaceableness may
not lead us into cowardice or despair when, for Your sake,
we are persecuted.

As the Father hath loved me, so have I loved you.
—John 15:9

As the Father loves the Son, in the same manner Jesus loves His people. What is divine love like? God loved Jesus without beginning, and, in the same way, Jesus loves His people. *"I have loved thee with an everlasting love"* (Jer. 31:3). You can trace the beginning of human affection; you can easily find the beginning of your love for Christ, but His love for us is a stream whose source is hidden in eternity. God the Father loves Jesus without any change. Christian, be comforted in knowing that there is no change in Christ's love for those who rest in Him. Yesterday you may have been on the mountaintop, and you said, "He loves me!" Today you may be in the valley of humiliation, but He loves you still the same. On the high elevations, you heard His voice, which spoke so sweetly with the musical sounds of love; now, at sea level or even in the sea, when all His waves and billows roll over you, His heart is faithful to His ancient choice. The Father loves the Son without any end, and this is how the Son loves His people. Believer, you do not need to fear the loosing of the silver cord, for His love for you will never cease. Rest confident that even down to the grave, Christ will go with you, and that up again from it, He will be your Guide to the celestial hills. Moreover, the Father loves the Son without any measure, and the Son bestows that same immeasurable love on His chosen ones. The whole heart of Christ is dedicated to His people. He *"loved [us], and gave himself for [us]"* (Gal. 2:20). His is a love that surpasses knowledge. We have indeed an immutable Savior, a precious Savior, one who loves without measure, without change, without beginning, and without end, even as the Father loves Him! There is much food here for those who know how to digest it. May the Holy Spirit lead us into its marrow and fatness.

And she did eat, and was sufficed, and left.
—Ruth 2:14

Whenever we are privileged to eat of the bread that Jesus gives, we are, like Ruth, satisfied with the full and sweet meal. When Jesus is the Host, no guest leaves the table hungry. Our heads are satisfied with the precious truth that Christ reveals. Our hearts are content with Jesus, as the altogether lovely object of affection. Our hopes are satisfied, for whom have we in heaven but Jesus? Our desires are satiated, for what can we wish for more than to know Christ and to *"be found in him"* (Phil. 3:9)? Jesus fills our consciences until they are at perfect peace, our judgment with persuasion of the certainty of His teachings, our memories with recollections of what He has done, and our imaginations with the prospects of what He is yet to do. As Ruth was *"sufficed, and left,"* so it is with us. We have drunk deeply of Christ, and we have thought that we could take in all of Him; but when we have done our best, we have had to leave a vast remainder. We have sat at the table of the Lord's love, and said, "Nothing but the infinite can ever satisfy me. I am such a great sinner that I must have infinite merit to wash my sin away." But we have had our sins cleansed and found that there was merit to spare; we have had our hunger relieved at the feast of sacred love and found that there was an abundance of spiritual food remaining. Certain sweet things in the Word of God we have not enjoyed yet, and we are obliged to leave for a while; for we are like the disciples to whom Jesus said, *"I have yet many things to say unto you, but ye cannot bear them now"* (John 16:12). Yes, there are graces to which we have not attained, places of fellowship nearer to Christ that we have not reached, and heights of communion that our feet have not climbed. At every banquet of love there are many baskets of fragments left. Let us praise the generosity of our glorious heavenly Boaz.

Husbands, love your wives, even as Christ also loved the church.
—Ephesians 5:25

hat a golden example Christ gives to His disciples! Few teachers could venture to say, "If you want to practice my teaching, imitate my life." But since the life of Jesus is the exact transcript of perfect virtue, He can point to Himself as the paragon of holiness, as well as the teacher of it. The Christian should take nothing short of Christ for his model. Under no circumstances should we be content unless we reflect the grace that was in Him. The Christian husband is to look at the portrait of Christ Jesus, and he is to paint his life according to that copy. The true Christian is to be a husband in the same way that Christ was to His church. The love of a husband is special. The Lord Jesus cherishes the church and has a special affection for her that is set upon her above the rest of mankind: *"I pray for them: I pray not for the world"* (John 17:9). The church is the favorite of heaven and the treasure of Christ, the crown of His head, the bracelet of His arm, the breastplate of His heart, the very center and core of His love. A husband should love his wife with a constant love, for thus Jesus loves His church. He does not vary in His affection. He may change in His display of affection, but the affection itself is still the same. A husband should love his wife with an enduring love, for nothing *"shall be able to separate us from the love of God, which is in Christ Jesus our Lord"* (Rom. 8:39). A true husband loves his wife with a hearty love that is fervent and intense. It is not mere lip service. Beloved, what more could Christ have done to prove His love than He has done? Jesus has a delighted love toward His spouse. He prizes her affection and delights in her with sweet satisfaction. Believer, you are amazed by Jesus' love. You admire it, but are you imitating it? In your domestic relationships is the rule and measure of your love to be *"even as Christ also loved the church"*?

Canst thou bind the sweet influences of Pleiades,
or loose the bands of Orion?
—Job 38:31

If we are inclined to boast of our abilities, the grandeur of nature may soon show us how puny we are. We cannot move the least of all the twinkling stars or quench even one of the beams of the morning. We speak of power, but the heavens laugh us to scorn. When the Pleiades, a magnificent cluster of stars, shine forth in the spring with new joy, we cannot restrain their influences, and when Orion reigns aloft, and the year is bound in winter's fetters, we cannot relax the icy bands. The seasons revolve according to divine appointment. The whole race of men cannot change their schedule. Lord, what is man? In the spiritual, as in the natural world, man's power is limited on all sides. When the Holy Spirit sheds abroad His delights in the soul, nothing can take away that joy. All the cunning and malice of men are ineffective in halting the life-giving power of the Comforter. When He deigns to visit a church and revive it, the most inveterate enemies cannot resist the good work; they may ridicule it, but they can no more restrain it than they can push back the spring when the Pleiades rule the hour. God wills it, and so it must be. On the other hand, if the Lord in sovereignty or in justice binds up a man so that his soul is in bondage, who can give him liberty? God alone can remove the winter of spiritual death from an individual or a people. He looses the bands of Orion, and no one but He can do that. What a blessing it is that He can do it! Oh, that He would perform the wonder tonight! Lord, end my winter, and let my spring begin. In spite of all my desires to do so, I cannot raise my soul out of her death and dullness, but all things are possible with You. I need celestial influences, the clear shinings of Your love, the beams of Your grace, the light of Your countenance—these are the Pleiades to me. I suffer from sin and temptation—these are my wintry signs, my terrible Orion. Lord, work wonders in me and for me. Amen.

Father, I will that they also, whom thou hast given me,
be with me where I am.
—John 17:24

Death, why do you touch the tree whose spreading branches offer rest from weariness? Why do you snatch away the excellent of the earth, in whom is all our delight? If you must use your ax, use it on the trees that yield no fruit; then we might thank you. But why do you fell the good cedars of Lebanon? Oh, hold back your ax, and spare the righteous. But no, it must not be. Death smites the best of our friends; the most generous, the most prayerful, the holiest, the most devoted must die. Why? Because Jesus prayed, *"Father, I will that they also, whom thou hast given me, be with me where I am"* (John 17:24). It is His prayer that bears them on eagles' wings to heaven. Every time a believer mounts from this earth to paradise, it is an answer to Christ's prayer. A good old saint remarked, "Many times Jesus and His people pull against one another in prayer. You bend your knee in prayer and say, 'Father, I desire that Your saint would be here with me where I am.' Christ says, *'Father, I will that they also, whom thou hast given me, be with me where I am.'"* Thus the disciple is at cross-purposes with his Lord. The soul cannot be in both places; the beloved one cannot be with Christ and with you, too. Now, which pleader will win the day? If you had your choice, if the King stepped from His throne and said, "Here are two supplicants praying in opposition to one another; which one should be answered?" Oh, I am sure, though it would be agony, you would jump to your feet and say, "Jesus, not my will, but Yours be done." You would give up your prayer for your loved one's life if you realized the thoughts that Christ was praying in the opposite direction: *"Father, I will that they also, whom thou hast given me, be with me where I am."* Lord, You may have them. By faith we let them go.

I tell you that, if these should hold their peace,
the stones would immediately cry out.
—Luke 19:40

But could the stones cry out? They most certainly could if He who opens the mouth of the dumb commanded them to lift up their voice. If they were able to speak, they would have much to testify in praise of Him who created them by the word of His power. They could extol the wisdom and power of their Maker who called them into being. Will we not speak well of Him who made us new creatures and out of stones raised up children of Abraham? The old rocks could tell of chaos and order and of the handiwork of God in successive stages of Creation's drama. Cannot we talk of God's decrees, of God's great work in ancient times, and all that He did for His church in the days of old? If the stones were to speak, they could tell of their breaker who took them from the quarry and made them fit for the temple. Cannot we tell of our glorious Breaker, who broke our hearts with the hammer of His Word so that He might build us into His temple? If the stones could cry out, they would magnify their builder, who polished them and fashioned them into a palace. Will we not talk of our Architect and Builder, who has put us in our places in the temple of the living God? If the stones could cry out, they might have a long, long story to tell by way of a memorial. A great stone has often been set up as a memorial before the Lord. We, too, can testify of the great things God has done for us. They are our Ebenezers, our stones of help and pillars of remembrance. The broken stones of the law cry out against us, but Christ Himself, who has rolled away the stone from the door of the tomb, speaks for us. Stones might well cry out, but we will not let them. We will hush their noise with ours. All our days, we will break forth into sacred song and bless the majesty of the Most High, glorifying Him who is called *"the shepherd, the stone of Israel"* (Gen. 49:24).

In that hour Jesus rejoiced in spirit.
—Luke 10:21

he Savior was *"a man of sorrows"* (Isa. 53:3), but every thoughtful mind has discovered the fact that down deep in His innermost soul, He carried an inexhaustible treasury of refined and heavenly joy. Of all the human race, there was never a man who had a deeper, purer, or more abiding peace than our Lord Jesus Christ. He was *"anointed…with the oil of gladness above* [His] *fellows"* (Ps. 45:7). His vast benevolence must, from the very nature of things, have afforded Him the deepest possible delight, for benevolence is joy. There were a few remarkable seasons when this joy manifested itself. *"In that hour Jesus rejoiced in spirit, and said, I thank thee, O Father, Lord of heaven and earth"* (Luke 10:21). Christ had His songs, even though darkness surrounded Him and though His face was marred and His countenance had lost the glow of earthly happiness. Sometimes, it was still lit up with a matchless splendor of unparalleled satisfaction, as He thought about the final reward and in the midst of the congregation sang His praise to God. In this, the Lord Jesus is a blessed picture of His church on earth. At this hour the church expects to walk along a thorny road in sympathy with her Lord. Through much tribulation, she is forcing her way to the crown. To bear the cross is her calling, and to be scorned and counted a stranger by her mother's children is her lot; yet the church has a deep well of joy, of which none can drink but her own children. There are stores of wine, oil, and corn hidden in the midst of our Jerusalem, on which the saints of God are evermore sustained and nurtured. Sometimes, as in our Savior's case, we have our seasons of intense delight, for *"there is a river, the streams whereof shall make glad the city of God"* (Ps. 46:4). Exiles though we are, we still rejoice in our King; yes, in Him we exceedingly rejoice, while in His name we set up our banners.

The Son of man.
—John 3:13

ow constantly our Master used the title, the *"Son of man"!* If He had chosen, He could have always spoken of Himself as the Son of God, *"Wonderful, Counsellor, The mighty God, The everlasting Father, The Prince of Peace"* (Isa. 9:6). But behold the lowliness of Jesus! He prefers to call Himself the *"Son of man."* Let us learn a lesson of humility from our Savior. Let us never court great titles or proud degrees. There is here, however, a far sweeter thought. Jesus loved mankind so much that He delighted to honor it; since it is a high honor, indeed, the greatest dignity of mankind, that Jesus is the Son of Man. He desires to display this name so that He may, as it were, hang royal stars upon the breast of humanity and show forth the love of God to Abraham's seed. *"Son of man"*—whenever He said those words, He placed a halo around the head of Adam's children. Yet there is perhaps a more precious thought that remains. Jesus Christ called Himself the *"Son of man"* in order to express His oneness and sympathy with His people. He thus reminds us that He is the One whom we may approach without fear. We may take all our griefs and troubles to Him, for, as a Man, He knows them by experience. In that He Himself has suffered as the *"Son of man,"* He is able to help and to comfort us. All hail, blessed Jesus! Inasmuch as You are forever using the sweet name that acknowledges that You are a Brother and a close relative, it is to us a dear token of Your grace, Your humility, and Your love.

Oh, see how Jesus trusts Himself
Unto our childish love,
As though by His free ways with us
Our earnestness to prove!
His sacred name a common word
On earth He loves to hear;
There is no majesty in Him
Which love may not come near.

When he cometh in the glory of his Father with the holy angels.
—Mark 8:38

If we have been partakers with Jesus in His shame, we will share in the radiance that will surround Him when He appears again in glory. Are you, beloved one, with Christ Jesus? Does a vital union knit you together with Him? Then you are today with Him in His shame. You have taken up His cross and gone with Him outside *"the camp, bearing his reproach"* (Heb. 13:13). Without a doubt, you will be with Him when the cross is exchanged for the crown. But judge yourself this evening. For if you are not with Him by being born again, neither will you be with Him when He comes in His glory. If you back away from the dark, painful side of communion with Him, you will not understand its bright, happy period, when the King will come again, *"and all the holy angels with him"* (Matt. 25:31). What! Are angels with Him? And yet He did not take up the angels; He took up the seed of Abraham. Are the holy angels with Him? Come, my soul; if you are indeed His own beloved, you cannot be far from Him. If His friends and His neighbors are called together to see His glory, what are you doing if you are married to Him? Will you be distant from Him? Though it is a Day of Judgment, yet you cannot be far from that heart which, having admitted angels into intimacy, has admitted you into union. Has He not said to you, *"I will betroth thee unto me in righteousness, and in judgment, and in lovingkindness"* (Hosea 2:19)? Have not His own lips said, *"I am married unto you"* (Jer. 3:14)? He delights in you. If the angels, who are but friends and neighbors, will be with Him, it is abundantly certain that His own beloved, in whom is all His delight, will be near Him and sit at His right hand. Here is a morning star of hope for you; it is of such exceeding brilliance that it may well light up the darkest and most desolate experience.

And she said, Truth, Lord: yet the dogs eat of the crumbs
which fall from their masters' table.
—Matthew 15:27

his woman gained comfort in her misery by thinking great thoughts of Christ. The Master had talked about the children's bread. "Now," she reasoned, "since You are the Master of the table of grace, I know that You are a generous Host. There is sure to be abundance of bread on Your table. There will be more than enough food for the children—enough that there will be crumbs to throw on the floor for the dogs. The children will still have plenty even though the dogs are fed." She thought of Jesus as One who had such an abundance to give that all she needed would be just a crumb in comparison. Remember that what she really wanted was to have the devil cast out of her daughter. It was a very great thing to her, but she had such high esteem of Christ that she said, "It is nothing to Him; it is but a crumb for Christ to give. My sins are many, but it is nothing for Jesus to take them all away. The weight of my guilt presses me down as a giant's foot crushes a worm, but it is no more than a grain of dust to Him. He has already borne its curse *'in his own body on the tree'* (1 Pet. 2:24). It will be a small thing for Him to give me full remission, although it will be an infinite blessing for me to receive it." The woman opened her soul's mouth very wide, expecting great things of Jesus, and He filled it with His love. Dear reader, do the same. She confessed what Christ laid at her door, but she laid hold of Him and drew arguments even out of His hard words. She believed great things of Him, and thus she persuaded Him. She won the victory by believing in Him. Her case is an example of prevailing faith. If we would conquer like her, we must imitate her tactics. This is the royal road to comfort. Great thoughts of your sin alone will drive you to despair, but great thoughts of Christ will pilot you into the haven of peace.

I will accept you with your sweet savour.
—Ezekiel 20:41

he merits of our great Redeemer are a sweet savor to the Most High. Whether we speak of the active or passive righteousness of Christ, there is an equal fragrance. There was a sweet aroma in His active life by which He honored the law of God. He made every precept glitter like a precious jewel in the pure setting of His own person. In His passive obedience, with unmurmuring submission, He endured hunger and thirst, cold and nakedness. He sweat great drops of blood in Gethsemane, gave His back to the smiters, and His cheeks to those who plucked out His hair. Then He was nailed to the cruel cross so that He might suffer the wrath of God on our behalf. These things are sweet before the Most High. Because of the way that He lived and the way that He died, because of His substitutionary sufferings and His vicarious obedience, the Lord our God accepts us. What a preciousness there is in Him to overcome our lack of preciousness! What a sweet fragrance to remove our bad aroma! What a cleansing power in His blood to take away sin such as ours! What glory in His righteousness to make such unacceptable creatures be *"accepted in the beloved"* (Eph. 1:6)! Believer, how sure and unchanging our acceptance must be since it is in Him! Never doubt your acceptance in Jesus. You cannot be accepted without Christ; but when you have received His merit, you cannot be unaccepted. Despite all your doubts, fears, and sins, Jehovah's gracious eye never looks on you in anger. Although He sees sin in you, in yourself, when He looks at you through Christ, He sees no sin. You are always accepted in Christ and are always blessed and dear to the Father's heart. Therefore, lift up a song, and as you see the smoking incense of the merit of the Savior rising before the sapphire throne, let the incense of your praise rise also.

I called him, but he gave me no answer.
—Song of Solomon 5:6

rayer sometimes waits like a petitioner at the gate until the King comes forth to fill the heart with the blessings that it seeks. The Lord, when He has given great faith, has been known to try it by long delays. He has permitted His servants' voices to echo in their ears as from a brazen sky. They have knocked at the golden gate, but it has remained immovable, as though it were rusted on its hinges. Like Jeremiah, they have cried, *"Thou hast covered thyself with a cloud, that our prayer should not pass through"* (Lam. 3:44). Thus have true saints continued for a long time in patient waiting without receiving a reply. This was not because their prayers were not intense or because they were unaccepted; it was because God who is a Sovereign gives according to His own pleasure. If it pleases Him for our patience to be exercised, He will do as He desires with His own! Beggars must not be choosers regarding the time, place, or form of their answers. But we must be careful not to mistake delays in prayer as denials. God's long-dated bills will be punctually honored. We must not allow Satan to shake our confidence in the God of truth by pointing to our unanswered prayers. Unanswered petitions are not unheard. God keeps a file for our prayers; they are not blown away by the wind but are treasured in the King's archives. There is a registry in the court of heaven in which every prayer is recorded. Tried believer, your Lord has a tear-bottle in which the costly drops of sacred grief are stored and a book in which your holy groanings are numbered. In due time, your suit will prevail. Can you not be content to wait a little? Will not your Lord's time be better than your time? Soon He will appear, to your soul's joy, and make you put away the sackcloth and ashes of long waiting. He will clothe you with the scarlet and fine linen of your heart's desire.

Let us search and try our ways, and turn again to the LORD.
—Lamentations 3:40

he spouse who loves her absent husband longs for his return. A protracted separation from her spouse causes a partial death to her spirit. It is the same with souls who love the Savior. They must see His face. They cannot bear that He should be away and not be in fellowship with them. A disapproving glance or an uplifted finger is grievous to loving children who never want to offend their tender father; they are happy only when they see his smile. Beloved, it was the same with you at one time. A Scripture, a correction, a touch of the rod of affliction, and you went to your Father's feet, crying, "Show me why You are angry with me." Is it so now? Are you content to follow Jesus from a distance? Can you contemplate ending your communion with Christ without alarm? Can you bear to have your Beloved walking contrary to you because you are walking contrary to Him? Have your sins separated you and your God, and is your heart at rest? Let me warn you in kindness: it is a grievous thing when we can live contentedly without the present enjoyment of the Savior's face. Let us realize what an evil thing it is to have little love for our own dying Savior, little joy in our precious Jesus, little fellowship with the Beloved! Hold a true Lent in your souls, while you sorrow over your hardness of heart. But do not stop with sorrow! Remember where you first received salvation. Go at once to the cross. There, and only there, can your spirit be made alive. No matter how hard, how unfeeling, how dead we may have become, let us go again in all our rags and poverty and defilement of our natural condition. Let us clasp that cross and look into His eyes. Let us bathe in that fountain filled with blood. Then we will have our first love restored to us. Once again we will experience the simplicity of our faith and the tenderness of our hearts.

And Rizpah the daughter of Aiah took sackcloth, and spread it for her upon the rock, from the beginning of harvest until water dropped upon them out of heaven, and suffered neither the birds of the air to rest on them by day, nor the beasts of the field by night.
—2 Samuel 21:10

If the love of a woman for her slain sons could make her continue her mournful vigil for so long a period, will we grow weary of considering the sufferings of our blessed Lord? Rizpah drove away the birds of prey, and will we not chase from our meditations those worldly and sinful thoughts that defile both our minds and the sacred themes on which we are focused? Away, birds of evil! Leave the sacrifice alone! Unsheltered and alone, Rizpah bore the heat of summer, the night dews, and the rain. Sleep was chased from her weeping eyes: her heart was too full for slumber. Behold how she loved her children! Will Rizpah's example endure, or will we begin to complain at the first little inconvenience or trial? Are we such cowards that we cannot bear to suffer with our Lord? Showing unusual courage, she chased away even the wild beasts. Will we not be ready to encounter every foe for Jesus' sake? Her children were slain by hands other than hers, yet she wept and watched. What should we do who have by our sins crucified our Lord? Our obligations are boundless; our love should be fervent and our repentance thorough. To watch with Jesus should be our business, to protect His honor our occupation, to abide by His cross our solace. Those ghastly corpses might well have frightened Rizpah, especially at night, but in our Lord, at whose cross we are sitting, there is nothing revolting, but everything attractive. Never was living beauty so enchanting as in our dying Savior. Jesus, we will watch with You. Graciously reveal Yourself to us. Then we will not sit in sackcloth, but in a royal pavilion.

It is time to seek the LORD.
—Hosea 10:12

his month of April is said to derive its name from the Latin verb *aperio*, which means to open. All the buds and blossoms are now opening, and we have arrived at the gates of the flowery season. Reader, if you are yet unsaved, may your heart, in accord with the universal awakening of nature, be opened to receive the Lord. Every blossoming flower warns you that *"it is time to seek the LORD."* Do not be out of tune with nature, but let your heart bud and bloom with holy desires. Do you tell me that the warm blood of youth leaps in your veins? Then I entreat you, give your vigor to the Lord. It was my unspeakable happiness to be called in early youth, and I could gladly praise the Lord for it every day. Salvation is priceless; let it come when it may, but oh, an early salvation has a double value in it. Young men and women, since you may perish before you reach your prime, now is the time to seek the Lord. You who are experiencing the first signs of aging, quicken your pace. That hollow cough and hectic flush are warnings that you must not take lightly. It is indeed *"time to seek the LORD."* Did I observe a little gray mingled with your once luxurious, dark tresses? Years are swiftly passing, and death is drawing nearer with its hasty march. Let each return of spring inspire you to set your house in order. Dear reader, if you are now advanced in age, let me entreat and implore you to delay no longer. There is a day of grace for you now—be thankful for that, but it is a limited season and grows shorter every time the clock ticks. Here in your silent room, on this first night of another month, I speak to you as best I can by paper and ink. From my inmost soul, as God's servant, I lay before you this warning, *"It is time to seek the LORD."* Do not neglect that work. It may be your last call from destruction, the final syllable from the lips of grace.

He shall see his seed, he shall prolong his days, and the pleasure
of the LORD shall prosper in his hand.
—Isaiah 53:10

ll you who love the Lord, plead for the speedy fulfillment of the promise of today's text. It is easy
work to pray when our desires are grounded in and
based on God's own promise. How can He who gave the
Word refuse to keep it? Unchangeable truth cannot demean
itself by a lie, and eternal faithfulness cannot degrade itself
by neglect. God must bless His Son; His covenant binds
Him to it. What the Spirit prompts us to ask from Jesus is
that which God decrees to give to Him. Whenever you are
praying for the kingdom of Christ, let your eyes behold the
dawning of the blessed day that is drawing near, when the
Crucified One will receive His crown in the place where
men rejected Him. Be encouraged, you who prayerfully
work and toil for Christ with little apparent success. It will
not always be so. Better times are ahead for you. Your eyes
cannot see the blissful future. Borrow the telescope of faith,
wipe the misty breath of your doubts from the glass, look
through it, and see the coming glory. Reader, do you make
this your constant prayer? Remember that the same Christ
who told us to say, *"Give us this day our daily bread"* (Matt.
6:11), first gave us this petition: *"Hallowed be thy name. Thy
kingdom come. Thy will be done in earth, as it is in heaven"* (vv.
9–10). Do not let your prayers be all about your own sins,
your own needs, your own imperfections, or your own trials. Instead, let them climb the starry ladder and reach
Christ Himself. Then, as you draw near to the blood-
sprinkled mercy seat, offer this prayer continually: "Lord,
extend the kingdom of Your dear Son." Such a petition, fervently presented, will elevate the spirit of all your devotions. Remember that you prove the sincerity of your
prayer by working to promote the Lord's glory.

All we like sheep have gone astray; we have turned every one to his own way; and the LORD hath laid on him the iniquity of us all.
—Isaiah 53:6

This confession of sin is common to all the elect people of God. We have all fallen; therefore, in common chorus, from the first who entered heaven to the last who will enter there, we can all say, *"All we like sheep have gone astray."* The confession, while unanimous, is also unique and individual: *"We have turned every one to his own way."* There is a particular sinfulness about every person. All are sinful, but each one has some special aggravation not found in others. It is the mark of genuine repentance that it naturally associates itself with other penitents, but it also takes up a position of individuality. *"We have turned every one to his own way"* is a confession that each person has sinned against light in a way unique to himself or sinned with an intensity that he does not perceive in others. This confession is also unreserved. There is not a word to detract from its force or a syllable by way of excuse. The confession is a giving up of all pleas of self-righteousness. It is the declaration of those who are consciously guilty— guilty with severity, guilty without excuse. They stand with their weapons of rebellion broken in pieces and cry, *"All we like sheep have gone astray; we have turned every one to his own way."* Yet we hear no mournful wailing attending this confession of sin, for the next sentence makes it almost a song: *"The LORD hath laid on him the iniquity of us all."* It is the most grievous sentence of the three, but it overflows with comfort. It is strange that where misery was concentrated, mercy reigned; where sorrow reached her climax, weary souls find rest. The bruised Savior is the Healer of bruised hearts. See how the lowliest repentance gives place to assured confidence through simply gazing at Christ on the cross!

Come ye, and let us go up to the mountain of the LORD.
—Isaiah 2:3

It is exceedingly beneficial to our souls to rise above this present evil world to something nobler and better. The cares of this world and the deceitfulness of riches are likely to choke everything that is good within us and cause us to grow fretful, despondent, and perhaps proud and carnal. It is good for us to cut down these thorns and briers, for heavenly seed sown among them is not likely to yield a harvest. Where will we find a better sickle with which to cut them down than communion with God and the things of the kingdom? In the valleys of Switzerland, many of the inhabitants become sickly because the air is close and stagnant; but up yonder, on the mountains, you find a hardy race, who breathe the clear, fresh air as it blows from the virgin snows of the Alpine summits. It would be good if those who live in the valley could frequently leave their homes among the marshes and the fever mists and inhale the bracing mountain air. It is to such an exploit of climbing that I invite you this evening. May the Spirit of God assist us to leave the mists of fear and the fevers of anxiety and all the ills that gather in this valley of earth. Let us ascend the mountains of anticipated joy and blessedness. May God the Holy Spirit cut the cords that keep us here below and assist us to climb! Too often, we sit like chained eagles fastened to the rock. Unlike the eagle, though, we begin to love our chain and would, perhaps, if it really came to the test, loathe to have it snapped. May God grant us grace so that, if we cannot escape from the chains of our flesh, He would enable our spirits to be set free. Leaving our fleshly bodies behind, like Abraham left behind his servants when he was called to offer Isaac as a sacrifice, may our souls reach the top of the mountain. May we there enjoy communion with the Most High.

Before honour is humility.
—Proverbs 15:33

Humiliation of soul always brings a blessing with it. If we empty our hearts of self, God will fill them with His love. He who desires close communion with Christ should remember the word of the Lord, *"To this man will I look, even to him that is poor and of a contrite spirit, and trembleth at my word"* (Isa. 66:2). If you would climb to heaven, stoop. Do we not say of Jesus, "He descended so that He might ascend"? So must you. You must grow downward so that you may grow upward, for the sweetest fellowship with heaven is to be had by humble souls, and by them alone. God will deny no blessing to a thoroughly humbled spirit. *"Blessed are the poor in spirit: for theirs is the kingdom of heaven"* (Matt. 5:3), which includes all of its riches and treasures. The whole treasury of God will be given as a gift to the soul that is humble enough to be able to receive it without growing proud because of it. God blesses us all up to the full measure and extremity that it is safe for Him to do so. If you do not receive a blessing, it is because it is not safe for you to have one. If our heavenly Father were to let your unhumbled spirit win a victory in His holy war, you would steal the crown for yourself; meeting with a new enemy, you would fall a victim. So you are kept low for your own safety. When a man is sincerely humble and never ventures to touch as much as a grain of the praise, there is scarcely any limit to what God will do for him. Humility makes us ready to be blessed by the God of all grace and equips us to deal efficiently with our fellowmen. True humility is a flower that will adorn any garden. This is a sauce with which you may season every dish of life, and you will find an improvement in every case. Whether it is in prayer or praise or in work or suffering, the genuine salt of humility cannot be used in excess.

In the name of the LORD I will destroy them.
—Psalm 118:12

Our Lord Jesus, by His death, did not purchase a right to only a part of us, but to our entire being. In His crucifixion and death, He contemplated our entire sanctification—spirit, soul, and body—so that in this triple kingdom, He Himself might reign supreme without a rival. It is the business of the newborn nature that God has given to the regenerated to assert the rights of the Lord Jesus Christ. My soul, since you are a child of God, you must conquer each part of yourself that is not submitted to Christ; you must surrender all your powers and passions to the silver scepter of Jesus' gracious reign. You must never be satisfied until He who is King by purchase becomes King by gracious coronation and reigns supreme in your life. Seeing then that sin has no right to any part of us, we go about a good and lawful warfare when we seek, in the name of God, to drive it out. My body, you are a member of Christ. Will you tolerate your subjection to the prince of darkness? My soul, Christ has suffered for your sins and redeemed you with His most precious blood. Will you permit your memory to become a storehouse of evil or your passions to be firebrands of iniquity? Will you surrender your judgment to be perverted by error or your will to be chained by sin? No, my soul, you are Christ's, and sin has no right to you. Be courageous concerning this, Christian! Do not be discouraged as though your spiritual enemies could never be destroyed. You are able to overcome them, though not in your own strength; the weakest of them would be too much for you in that. But you can and will overcome them through the blood of the Lamb. Do not ask, "How will I banish them, for they are greater and mightier than I?" but go to the strong for strength, wait humbly on God, and the mighty God of Jacob will surely come to your rescue. Then you will sing of victory through His grace.

Deliver me from bloodguiltiness, O God, thou God of my salvation: and my tongue shall sing aloud of thy righteousness.
—Psalm 51:14

In this solemn confession, it is pleasing to observe that David plainly named his sin. He did not call it manslaughter or speak of it as an indiscretion by which an unfortunate accident occurred to a worthy man, but he called it by its true name, bloodguiltiness. He did not actually kill the husband of Bathsheba, but he planned in his heart that Uriah should be slain; therefore, he stood before the Lord as a murderer. Learn in confession to be honest with God. Do not give fair names to foul sins; call them what you will, they will smell no sweeter. See your sins as God sees them; with all openness of heart, acknowledge their real character. Observe that David was evidently oppressed with the heinousness of his sin. It is easy to use words, but it is harder to feel their meaning. The Fifty-first Psalm is the portrait of a contrite spirit. Let us seek to have the same brokenness of heart; for however excellent our words may be, if our hearts are not conscious that we are deserving of hell because of our sins, we cannot expect to find forgiveness. Our text has in it an earnest prayer that is addressed to the God of salvation. It is His prerogative to forgive; it is His very name and nature to save those who seek His face. Better still, the text calls Him the *"God of my salvation"* (emphasis added). Yes, blessed is His name! While I am continuing to go to Him through Jesus' blood, I can rejoice in the *"God of my salvation."* The psalmist ended with a commendable vow: if God would deliver him, he would sing—no, more than that, he would *"sing aloud."* Who can sing in any other style in the face of such great mercy! But notice the subject of the song: God's righteousness. We must sing of the finished work of a precious Savior; and he who knows the most of forgiving love will sing the loudest.

I will fear no evil: for thou art with me.
—Psalm 23:4

How independent of outward circumstances the Holy Spirit can make the Christian! What a bright light may shine within us when it is all dark without! How firm, how happy, how calm, how peaceful we may be, when the world shakes to and fro and the pillars of the earth are removed! Even death itself, with all its terrible influences, has no power to suspend the music of a Christian's heart. Instead, it makes that music become sweeter, clearer, and more heavenly, until the last kind act that death can do is to let the earthly strain melt into the heavenly chorus, the earthly joy into eternal bliss! Let us have confidence, then, in the blessed Spirit's power to comfort us. Dear reader, are you facing poverty? Do not fear; the divine Spirit can give you, in your need, a greater abundance than the rich have in their wealth. You do not know what joys may be stored up for you in the cottage around which grace will plant the roses of content. Are you conscious of a growing failure of your bodily powers? Do you expect to suffer long nights of languishing and days of pain? Oh, do not be sad! That bed may become a throne to you. Little do you know how every pang that shoots through your body may be a refining fire to consume your dross—a beam of glory to light up the secret parts of your soul. Are your eyes growing dim? Jesus will be your light. Do your ears fail you? Jesus' name will be your soul's best music, and His person your dear delight. Socrates said, "Philosophers can be happy without music." Christians can be happier than philosophers when all outward causes of rejoicing are withdrawn. In You, my God, my heart will triumph, come what may of troubles without! By Your power, O blessed Spirit, my heart will be exceedingly glad, though all things fail me here below.

Thy gentleness hath made me great.
—Psalm 18:35

hese words may be translated, "Thy goodness hath made me great." David gratefully ascribed all his personal greatness not to his own goodness but to the goodness of God. "Thy providence" is another reading, and providence is nothing more than goodness in action. Goodness is the bud, and providence is the flower; goodness is the seed, and providence is the harvest. Some render it, "Thy help," which is another word for providence. Providence is the firm ally of the saints, aiding them in the service of their Lord. Two other renderings are, "Thy humility" and "Thy condescension hath made me great." The word _condescension_ combines the ideas mentioned so far, including that of humility. The verse means that God's humbling of Himself is the cause of our being made great. We are so little that if God would manifest His greatness without reaching out to us in love, we would be trampled under His feet. But God, who must stoop to view the skies and bow to see what angels do, lowers His eyes even further to look at the lowly and contrite and make them great. There are yet other translations. For instance, the Septuagint reads, "Thy discipline"—His fatherly correction—"hath made me great." The Chaldee paraphrase reads, "Thy word hath increased me." The idea remains the same. David ascribed all his own greatness to the loving goodness of his Father in heaven. May this sentiment be echoed in our hearts this evening while we cast our crowns at Jesus' feet and cry, _"Thy gentleness hath made me great."_ How marvelous our experience of God's gentleness has been! How gentle are His corrections! How gentle His forbearance! How gentle His teachings! How gentle His entreaties! Meditate on this theme, believer. Let gratitude be awakened, let humility be deepened, and let love be rekindled before you fall asleep tonight.

For there stood by me this night the angel of God.
—Acts 27:23

torms and long darkness, coupled with imminent risk of shipwreck, had brought the crew of the vessel into a sad situation. One man alone among them remained perfectly calm, and, by his word, the rest were reassured. Paul was the only man who had heart enough to say, *"Sirs, be of good cheer"* (Acts 27:25). Veteran Roman soldiers and brave old mariners were on board, yet their poor Jewish prisoner had more spirit than they had combined. He had a secret Friend who kept his courage up. The Lord Jesus dispatched a heavenly messenger to whisper words of consolation in the ear of His faithful servant; therefore, Paul wore a shining countenance and spoke like a man at ease. If we fear the Lord, we may look for timely interventions when our circumstances are at their worst. Angels are not kept from us by storms or hindered by darkness. They do not consider it a humiliation to visit the poorest of the heavenly family. If angels' visits are few and far between during ordinary times, they are frequent in our storm-tossed nights. Friends may abandon us when we are under pressure, but our encounters with the inhabitants of the angelic world will be more abundant. In the strength of their encouraging words, brought to us from the throne by way of Jacob's ladder, we will be strong to do great things for God. Dear reader, is this an hour of distress for you? Then ask for special help. Jesus is the Angel of the covenant, and if His presence is earnestly sought, it will not be denied. Those who, like Paul, have had the angel of God standing by them throughout a night of storm, when anchors would no longer hold and rocks were close at hand, remember what that presence brings in heart-cheer.

> O angel of my God, be near,
> Amid the darkness, hush my fear;
> Loud roars the wild tempestuous sea,
> Your presence, Lord, shall comfort me.

Look upon mine affliction and my pain; and forgive all my sins.
—Psalm 25:18

It is well for us when prayers about our sorrows are linked with pleas concerning our sins—when, being under God's hand, we are not wholly absorbed with our pain, but remember our offenses against God. It is well, also, to take both sorrow and sin to the same place. It was to God that David carried his sorrow, and it was to God that David confessed his sin. Notice that we must take our sorrows to God. You may give even your little sorrows to God, for He counts the hairs of your head; your great sorrows you may commit to Him, for He holds the ocean in the hollow of His hand. Go to Him, whatever your present trouble may be, and you will find Him willing and able to relieve you. But we must take our sins to God, too. We must carry them to the cross so that the blood may fall upon them, to purge away their guilt and to destroy their defiling power. The special lesson of the text is this: in the right spirit, we are to go to the Lord with our sorrows and our sins. Note that all David asked concerning his sorrow was, *"Look upon mine affliction and my pain."* But the next petition is vastly more precise, definite, decided, plain: *"Forgive all my sins."* Many sufferers would have put it, "Remove my affliction and my pain, and look at my sins." But David did not say this. He cried, "Lord, as for my affliction and my pain, I will not dictate to Your wisdom. Lord, look at them. I will leave them to You. I would be glad to have my pain removed, but do as You desire. But as for my sins, Lord, I know what I want to happen to them. I must have them forgiven; I cannot endure to lie under their curse for a moment longer." A Christian considers sorrow to be lighter on the scale than sin; he can bear it if his troubles continue, but he cannot support the burden of his transgressions.

The king's garden.
—Nehemiah 3:15

he mention of the king's garden by Nehemiah brings to mind the Paradise that the King of Kings prepared for Adam. Sin had utterly ruined that fair abode of all delights and had driven out the children of men to till the ground, which yielded thorns and briers to them. My soul, remember the Fall, for it was your fall. Weep much because the Lord of love was so shamefully mistreated by the head of the human race, of which you are a member, as undeserving as any. Behold how dragons and demons dwell on this fair earth, which once was a garden of delights. See yonder another King's garden, which the King waters with His bloody sweat. It is Gethsemane, whose bitter herbs are far sweeter to renewed souls than even Eden's luscious fruits. There the mischief of the serpent in the first Garden was undone. There the curse was lifted from the earth and borne by the woman's promised Seed. My soul, think much about the agony and the passion; resort to the Garden of the olive press and view your great Redeemer rescuing you from your lost estate. This is the Garden of Gardens indeed, wherein the soul may see the guilt of sin and the power of love, two sights that surpass all others. Is there no other King's garden? Yes, my heart, you are, or should be. How do the flowers flourish? Do any choice fruits appear? Does the King walk within and rest in the arbor of your spirit? Be sure that the plants are trimmed and watered and the mischievous foxes hunted out. Come, Lord, and let the heavenly wind blow at Your coming so that the spices of Your garden may flow abroad. Nor must I forget the King's garden of the church. O Lord, send prosperity to it. Rebuild her walls, nourish her plants, ripen her fruits, and from the huge wilderness, reclaim the barren waste and make of it a King's garden.

And he shall put his hand upon the head of the burnt offering; and it
shall be accepted for him to make atonement for him.
—Leviticus 1:4

ur Lord's being made sin for us is shown here by the very significant transfer of sin to the bullock, which was made by the elders of the people. The laying of the hand was not a mere touch of contact, for in other places of Scripture the original word for *"put"* has the meaning of leaning heavily, as in the expression, *"Thy wrath lieth hard upon me"* (Ps. 88:7). Surely this is the very essence and nature of faith, which not only brings us into contact with the great Substitute, but also teaches us to lean on Him with all the burden of our guilt. Jehovah placed on the head of the Substitute all the offenses of His covenant people, but each one of the chosen is brought personally to ratify this solemn covenant act, when by grace he is enabled by faith to lay his hand upon the head of the *"Lamb slain from the foundation of the world"* (Rev. 13:8). Believer, do you remember that rapturous day when you first obtained pardon through Jesus, the Sin-bearer? Can you not make glad confession and join with the writer in saying, "My soul recalls its day of deliverance with delight. Laden with guilt and full of fear, I saw my Savior as my Substitute, and I laid my hand on Him. Oh, how timidly I did so at first, but then my courage grew, and confidence was confirmed until I leaned my soul entirely on Him. Now it is my unceasing joy to know that my sins are no longer counted against me, but they are laid on Him. Jesus, like the good Samaritan, has said of all my future sinfulness, like the debts of the wounded traveler, 'Charge that to My account'"? Blessed discovery! Eternal solace of a grateful heart!

> My numerous sins transferr'd to Him,
> Shall never more be found,
> Lost in His blood's atoning stream,
> Where every crime is drown'd!

Say ye to the righteous, that it shall be well with him.
—Isaiah 3:10

It is always well with the righteous! If the prophet had said, "Say ye to the righteous, that it is well with him in his prosperity," we would have been thankful for so great a blessing, for prosperity can also bring danger. It is a gift from heaven to be secured from the enticements of wealth. If it had been written, "It is well with him when under persecution," we would have been thankful for so sustaining an assurance, for persecution is hard to bear. But when no time is mentioned, all time is included. God's *shall*s must be understood always in their largest sense. From the beginning to the end of the year, from the first gathering of evening shadows until the daystar shines, in all conditions and under all circumstances, it will be well with the righteous. It is so well with him that we could not imagine it to be better, for he is well fed; he feeds upon the flesh and blood of Jesus. He is well clothed; he wears the imputed righteousness of Christ. He is well housed; he dwells in God. He is well married; his soul is joined in the bonds of marriage union to Christ. He is well provided for; the Lord is his Shepherd. He is well endowed; heaven is his inheritance. It is well with the righteous—well upon divine authority. The mouth of God speaks the comforting assurance. Beloved, if God declares that all is well, ten thousand devils may declare it to be ill, but we laugh them all to scorn. Blessed be God for a faith that enables us to believe God when the creatures contradict Him! It is, says the Word, at all times well with you, righteous one; then, beloved, if you cannot see it, believe in God's Word instead of your sight. Yes, believe it on divine authority more confidently than if your eyes and your feelings told it to you. Whom God blesses is blessed indeed, and what His lips declare is a truth that is steadfast and sure.

Lift them up for ever.
—Psalm 28:9

God's people need lifting up. They are very heavy by nature. They have no wings, or, if they have, they are like the dove of old that lay among the pots; and they need divine grace to make them mount on wings covered with silver and feathers of yellow gold. By nature *"sparks fly upward"* (Job 5:7), but the sinful souls of men fall downward. O Lord, *"lift them up for ever"!* David himself said, *"Unto thee, O LORD, do I lift up my soul"* (Ps. 25:1), and he here felt the necessity that other men's souls should be lifted up as well as his own. When you ask this blessing for yourself, do not forget to seek it for others. There are three ways in which God's people need to be lifted up. They need to be elevated in character. Lift them up, O Lord; do not permit Your people to be like the world's people. The world lies in the wicked one; lift them out of it. The world's people are looking after silver and gold, seeking their own pleasures and the gratification of their lusts; but, Lord, lift Your people up above all this. Keep them from being "muckrakers," as John Bunyan called the man who was always scraping after gold. Set their hearts upon their risen Lord and their heavenly heritage. Moreover, believers need to be prospered in conflict. In battle, if they seem to fall, O Lord, be pleased to give them the victory. If the enemy's foot is upon their necks for a moment, help them to grasp the sword of the Spirit and eventually win the battle. Lord, lift up Your children's spirits in the day of conflict. Do not let them sit in the dust, mourning forever. Do not allow the adversary to vex them sorely and make them fret. But if they have been persecuted like Hannah (see 1 Samuel 1:2–20), let them sing of the mercy of a delivering God. We may also ask our Lord to lift them up on the Last Day. Lift them up by taking them home, lift their bodies from the tomb, and raise their souls to Your eternal kingdom in glory.

And [Moses'] hands were steady until the going down of the sun.
—Exodus 17:12

he prayer of Moses was so mighty that everyone depended on it. The petitions of Moses defeated the enemy more than the fighting of Joshua. Yet both were needed. In the soul's conflict, force and fervor, decision and devotion, valor and vehemence must join their forces, and all will be well. You must wrestle with your sin, but the major part of the wrestling must be done alone in private with God. Prayers like Moses' hold up the token of the covenant before the Lord. The rod was the symbol of God's working with Moses, the symbol of God's government in Israel. Learn, O interceding saint, to hold up the promise and the oath of God before Him. The Lord cannot deny His own declarations. Hold up the rod of promise, and you will have what you will. When Moses grew weary, his friends assisted him. At any time your prayer weakens, let faith support one hand and holy hope uplift the other. Then prayer seating itself upon the Stone of Israel, the Rock of our salvation, will persevere and prevail. Beware of faintness in devotion; if Moses felt it, who can escape? It is far easier to fight with sin in public than to pray against it in private. It is said that Joshua never grew weary in the fighting, but Moses did grow weary in the praying. The more spiritual an exercise, the more difficult it is for flesh and blood to maintain it. Let us cry, then, for special strength, and may the Spirit of God, who helps our infirmities, as He helped Moses, enable us like him to continue with our hands steady *"until the going down of the sun."* May we remain steadfast until the evening of life is over, until we come to the rising of a better sun, in the land where prayer is swallowed up in praise.

We would see Jesus.
—John 12:21

he constant cry of the world is, "Who will show us any good?" People seek satisfaction in earthly comforts, enjoyments, and riches. But the convicted sinner knows of only one good: *"Oh that I knew where I might find him!"* (Job 23:3). When a person is truly awakened to feel his guilt, if you could pour the gold of India at his feet, he would say, "Take it away. I want to find Him!" It is a blessed thing for a man when he has brought his desires into focus so that they all center on one object. When he has fifty different desires, his heart resembles a pool of stagnant water, spread out into a marsh, breeding disease and pestilence. But when all his desires are brought into one channel, his heart becomes like a river of pure water, flowing swiftly to fertilize the fields. Happy is he who has one desire, if that one desire is set on Christ, even though it may not yet have been realized. If Jesus is the soul's desire, it is a blessed sign of divine work within. Such a man will never be content with mere laws. He will say, "I want Christ; I must have Him. Rules are of no use to me; I need Him! Do not offer me these. You offer me the empty pitcher, while I am dying of thirst. Give me water, or I will die. Jesus is my soul's desire. I would see Jesus!" Is this your condition, my reader, at this moment? Do you have but one desire, and is it Christ? Then you are not far from the kingdom of heaven. Have you but one wish in your heart, and that one wish is that you would be washed from all your sins in Jesus' blood? Can you really say, "I would give all I have to be a Christian. I would give up everything I have and hope for, if I could only feel that I have an interest in Christ"? Then, despite all your fears, be of good cheer. The Lord loves you, and you will come out into daylight soon. Rejoice *"in the liberty wherewith Christ hath made us free"* (Gal. 5:1).

And thou saidst, I will surely do thee good.
—Genesis 32:12

hen Jacob was on the other side of the brook Jabbok, and Esau was coming toward him with armed men, Jacob earnestly sought God's protection. As his primary argument, Jacob pleaded, *"And thou saidst, I will surely do thee good."* Oh, the force of that plea! He was holding God to His word: *"Thou saidst."* The attribute of God's faithfulness is a splendid horn of the altar on which to lay hold, but the promise is a mightier anchor still because it contains something more: *"Thou saidst, I will surely do thee good."* Has God said it, and will He not do it? *"Let God be true, but every man a liar"* (Rom. 3:4). Will God be untrue? Will He not keep His word? Will not every word that comes from His lips stand fast and be fulfilled? Solomon, at the opening of the temple, used this same mighty plea. He asked God to remember the word that He had spoken to his father David and to bless that place. When a man gives a promissory note, his honor is pledged. He signs his name, and he must pay the debt when the time comes; otherwise, he loses credit. It will never be said that God dishonors His bills. The reputation of the Most High has never been impeached and never will be. He is punctual to the moment: He is never before His time, but He is never behind it. Search God's Word through, and compare it with the experience of God's people. You will find the two agree from the first to the last. Many patriarchs have said with Joshua, *"Not one thing hath failed of all the good things which the* LORD *your God spake concerning you; all are come to pass"* (Josh. 23:14). If you have a divine promise, you do not need to plead it with an *if;* you may claim it with certainty. The Lord meant to fulfill the promise, or He would not have given it. God does not give His words merely to quiet us and to keep us hopeful for a while, with the intention of putting us off in the end. When He speaks, it is because He means to do as He has said.

The Amen.
—Revelation 3:14

he word *"Amen"* solemnly confirms that which went before. Jesus is the great Confirmer. The Amen in all His promises is forever unchanging. Sinner, I would comfort you with this reflection. Jesus Christ said, *"Come unto me, all ye that labour and are heavy laden, and I will give you rest"* (Matt. 11:28). If you come to Him, He will say "Amen" in your soul; His promise will be true to you. Jesus fulfilled the words of the prophet, *"A bruised reed shall he not break"* (Isa. 42:3). O poor, broken, bruised heart, if you come to Him, He will say "Amen" to you, and that will be as true in your soul as in hundreds of cases in years past. Christian, is it not comforting to you also that there is not a word that has gone out of the Savior's lips that He has ever retracted? The words of Jesus will stand when heaven and earth pass away. If you take hold of but half a promise, you will find it to be true. Beware of him whom Bunyan called "Clip-promise," who destroys much of the comfort of God's Word. He does not doubt the promise, but he clips the edge of it. He suggests that the promise will not all be fulfilled, only a part of it. But Jesus is *"yea, and...Amen"* (2 Cor. 1:20) in all His offices. He was a Priest to pardon and cleanse once, and He is Amen as Priest still. He was a King to rule and reign for His people and to defend them with His mighty arm, and He is an Amen King, the same still. He was a Prophet of old to foretell good things to come, and His lips are sweet and drip with honey still. He is an Amen Prophet. He is Amen as to the merit of His blood, and He is Amen as to His righteousness. That sacred robe will remain fair and glorious although nature will decay. He is Amen in every single title that He bears; your Husband, never seeking a divorce; your Friend, sticking closer than a brother; your Shepherd, with you in death's dark vale. He is your help and your deliverer; your castle and your high tower; the horn of your strength, your confidence, your joy, your all in all, and in everything, your *"yea, and...Amen."*

Fight the LORD'S battles.
—1 Samuel 18:17

he sacramental host of God's elect is warring still on earth, and Jesus Christ is the Captain of their salvation. He has said, *"Lo, I am with you alway, even unto the end of the world"* (Matt. 28:20). Listen to the shouts of war! Now let the people of God stand fast in their ranks, and let no man's heart fail him. It is true that just now in England the battle is turned against us, and unless the Lord Jesus lifts His sword, we do not know what may become of the church of God in this land. But let us be of good courage and act like men. There never was a day when Protestantism seemed to tremble more in the scales than now that a fierce effort is being made to restore the antichrist to his ancient seat. We greatly need a bold voice and a strong hand to preach and publish the old Gospel for which martyrs bled and confessors died. The Savior is, by His Spirit, still on earth; let this truth encourage us. He is always in the midst of the fight; therefore, the results of the battle are not in doubt. And as the conflict rages, what a sweet satisfaction it is to know that the Lord Jesus, in His office as our great Intercessor, is powerfully interceding for His people! O anxious gazer, do not look so much at the battle below, for there you will be enshrouded in smoke and amazed with garments rolled in blood. Instead, lift your eyes yonder where the Savior lives and pleads, for while He intercedes, the cause of God is safe. Let us fight as if it all depended on us, but let us look up and know that it all depends on Him. Now, by the lilies of Christian purity, by the roses of the Savior's atonement, and *"by the roes, and by the hinds of the field"* (Song 2:7), we charge you who are lovers of Jesus to do valiantly in the holy war, for truth and righteousness, for the kingdom and crown jewels of your Master. Onward! *"For the battle is not yours, but God's"* (2 Chron. 20:15).

Who is even at the right hand of God.
—Romans 8:34

He who was once despised and rejected of men now occupies the honorable position of a beloved and honored Son. The right hand of God is the place of majesty and favor. Our Lord Jesus is His people's Representative. When He died for them, they had rest; He rose again for them, and they had liberty; when He sat down at His Father's right hand, they had favor, honor, and dignity. The raising and elevation of Christ is the elevation, the acceptance, and enshrinement, the glorifying of all His people, for He is their Head and Representative. This sitting at the right hand of God, then, is to be viewed as the acceptance of the person of the Surety, the reception of the Representative, and therefore, the acceptance of our souls. O believer, see in this your sure freedom from condemnation. *"Who is he that condemneth?"* (Rom. 8:34). Who will condemn those who are in Jesus at the right hand of God? The right hand is the place of power. Christ at the right hand of God has all power in heaven and in earth. Who will fight against the people who have such power vested in their Captain? O my soul, what can destroy you if Omnipotence is your helper? If the shield of the Almighty covers you, what sword can smite you? Rest secure. If Jesus is your all-prevailing King and has trampled your enemies underneath His feet; if sin, death, and hell are all vanquished by Him; and if you are represented in Him, by no possibility can you be destroyed.

> Jesu's tremendous name
> Puts all our foes to flight:
> Jesus, the meek, the angry Lamb,
> A Lion is in fight.
>
> By all hell's host withstood;
> We all hell's host o'erthrow;
> And conquering them, through Jesu's blood
> We still to conquer go.

Thou shalt not be afraid for the terror by night.
—Psalm 91:5

What is this terror? It may be the cry of fire or the noise of thieves or imagined appearances or the shriek of sudden sickness or death. We live in the world of death and sorrow; therefore, we may look for trouble in the nighttime as well as during the glare of the broiling sun. Nor should this alarm us, for no matter what the terror is, the promise is that the believer will not be afraid. Why should he be fearful? Let us make it more personal: why should we be afraid? God our Father is here, and He will be here all through the lonely hours. He is an almighty Watcher, a sleepless Guardian, a faithful Friend. Nothing can happen without His direction, for even hell itself is under His control. Darkness is not dark to Him. He has promised to be a wall of fire around His people: who can break through such a barrier? Unbelievers may well be afraid, for they have an angry God above them, a guilty conscience within them, and a yawning hell below them. But we who rest in Jesus are saved from all these through rich mercy. If we give way to foolish fear, we will dishonor our profession of faith and lead others to doubt the reality of godliness. We ought to be afraid of being afraid, lest we vex the Holy Spirit by foolish distrust. Down, then, dismal foreboding and groundless apprehension. God has not forgotten to be gracious or shut up His tender mercies. It may be night in the soul, but there does not need to be any terror, for the God of love does not change. Children of light may walk through darkness, but they are not cast away. No, they are enabled to prove their adoption by trusting in their heavenly Father as hypocrites cannot do.

> Though the night be dark and dreary,
> Darkness cannot hide from Thee;
> Thou art He, who, never weary,
> Watchest where Your people be.

Lo, in the midst of the throne…stood a Lamb as it had been slain.
—Revelation 5:6

Why should our exalted Lord appear in His wounds in glory? The wounds of Jesus are His glories, His jewels, His sacred ornaments. To the eye of the believer, Jesus is more than beautiful; He is *"white and ruddy"* (Song 5:10)—white with innocence and ruddy with His own blood. We see Him as the lily of matchless purity and as the rose crimsoned with His own blood. Christ is lovely upon Olivet and Tabor, and by the sea, but oh, there never was such a matchless Christ as He who hung upon the cross! There we behold all His beauties in perfection, all His attributes developed, all His love drawn out, all His character expressed. Beloved, the wounds of Jesus are far fairer in our eyes than all the splendor and pomp of kings. The thorny crown is more than an imperial diadem. It is true that He no longer bears the scepter of reed, but there was a glory in it that never flashed from a scepter of gold. Jesus appears as a slain Lamb as He woos our souls and redeems them by His complete atonement. Nor are these the only ornaments of Christ. They are the trophies of His love and of His victory. He has divided *"the spoil with the strong"* (Isa. 53:12). He has redeemed for Himself a great multitude whom no man can number, and these scars are the memorials of the fight. If Christ thus loves to retain the thought of His sufferings for His people, how precious should his wounds be to us!

> Behold how every wound of His
> A precious balm distills,
> Which heals the scars that sin had made,
> And cures all mortal ills.
>
> Those wounds are mouths that preach His grace;
> The ensigns of His love;
> The seals of our expected bliss
> In paradise above.

The flowers appear on the earth; the time of the singing of birds is come, and the voice of the turtle is heard in our land.
—Song of Solomon 2:12

he season of spring is sweet. The long, dreary winter helps us to appreciate spring's gentle warmth, and its promise of summer enhances its present delights. After periods of depression of spirit, it is delightful once again to see the light of the Sun of Righteousness. Then our slumbering graces rise from their lethargy like the crocus and the daffodil from their beds of earth. Our hearts are made merry with delightful notes of gratitude, far more melodious than the warbling of birds. The comforting assurance of peace, infinitely more appealing than the turtledove's note, is heard within the soul. Now is the time for the soul to seek communion with her Beloved. Now she must rise from her native sordidness and come away from her old associations. If we do not hoist the sail when the breeze is favorable, we will be to blame. Times of refreshing should not pass over us and leave us unchanged. When Jesus Himself visits us in tenderness and entreats us to arise, can we be so foolish as to refuse His request? He has risen so that He may draw us after Him. By His Holy Spirit, He now has revived us so that we may, in newness of life, ascend into the heavenlies and hold communion with Him. Let our wintry state suffice for coldness and indifference; when the Lord creates a spring within, let our sap flow with vigor and our branches blossom with high resolve. O Lord, if it is not springtime in my chilly heart, I pray that You would make it so, for I am thoroughly weary of living at a distance from You. When will You bring the long and dreary winter to an end? Come, Holy Spirit, and renew my soul. Renew me, restore me, and have mercy on me. This very night I earnestly implore the Lord to take pity on His servant and send me a happy revival of spiritual life.

If any man hear my voice, and open the door, I will come in to him.
—Revelation 3:20

What is your desire this evening? Is it set on heavenly things? Do you long to enjoy the high doctrine of eternal love? Do you desire liberty in very close communion with God? Do you aspire to know the heights, depths, lengths, and breadths of God? Then you must draw near to Jesus. You must get a clear view of Him in His preciousness and completeness. You must see Him in His work, in His offices, and in His person. He who understands Christ receives an anointing from the Holy One, by which He knows all things. Christ is the great master key of all the chambers of God. There is no treasury of God that will not open and yield up all its wealth to the soul that lives near to Jesus. Are you saying, "Oh, that He would dwell in my heart. If only He would make my heart His dwelling place forever"? Open the door, beloved, and He will come into your soul. He has been knocking for a long time, and all with the purpose that He might dine with you and you with Him. He dines with you because you have invited Him into your heart, and you dine with Him because He brings the provision. He could not commune with you if it were not in your heart, you providing the house; and you could not fellowship with Him if He did not bring provision with Him, because you have a bare cupboard. Fling wide, then, the entrance to your soul. He will come with the love that you long to feel. He will come with the joy into which you cannot work your poor depressed spirit. He will bring the peace that now you do not have. He will come with His flagons of wine and sweet apples of love and cheer you until you have no other sickness but that of "love o'erpowering, love divine." Only open the door to Him, drive out His enemies, give Him the keys of your heart, and He will dwell there forever. Oh, wondrous love, that brings such a Guest to dwell in such a heart!

Blessed is he that watcheth.
—Revelation 16:15

"*I die daily*" (1 Cor. 15:31), said the apostle Paul. This was the life of the early Christians. They went everywhere with their lives in their hands. In this day, we are not called to pass through the same fearful persecutions. If we were, the Lord would give us grace to bear the test; but the tests of the Christian life, at the present moment, though outwardly not as terrible, are yet more likely to overcome us than even those of the fiery age. If we have to bear the ridicule of the world, that is not so hard. Its flattery, its soft words, its oily speeches, its fawning, and its hypocrisy are far worse. Our danger is that we would grow rich and become proud, that we would give ourselves up to the trends of this present evil world and lose our faith. If wealth is not our trial, worldly care is just as dangerous. If we cannot be torn in pieces by the roaring lion, we may be hugged to death by the bear. The devil does not care which it is, as long as he destroys our love for Christ and our confidence in Him. I fear that the Christian church is far more likely to lose her integrity in these soft and silken days than in those rougher times. We must be awake now, for we travel on enchanted ground, and we are most likely to fall asleep, to our own undoing, unless our faith in Jesus is a reality and our love for Jesus a vehement flame. Many in these days of easy profession are likely to prove to be tares, and not wheat; hypocrites with fair masks on their faces, but not the true-born children of the living God. Christian, do not think that these are times in which you can dispense with watchfulness or with holy ardor. You need these things more than ever, and may God the eternal Spirit display His omnipotence in you so that you may be able to say, in all these softer things, as well as in the rougher, "*We are more than conquerors through him that loved us*" (Rom. 8:37).

The LORD is King for ever and ever.
—Psalm 10:16

esus Christ makes no despotic claim of divine right, for He is really and truly the Lord's anointed! *"It pleased the Father that in him should all fulness dwell"* (Col. 1:19). God has given to Him all power and all authority. As the Son of Man, He is now Head over all things to His church, and He reigns over heaven, earth, and hell with the keys of life and death. Certain princes have delighted to call themselves kings by the popular will, and certainly our Lord Jesus Christ is such in His church. If it could be put to the vote whether He should be King in the church, every believing heart would crown Him. Oh, that we could crown Him more gloriously than we do! We would consider no expense to be wasted that would glorify Christ. Suffering would be pleasure, and loss would be gain, if thereby we could surround His brow with brighter crowns and make Him more glorious in the eyes of men and angels. Yes, He shall reign. Long live the King! All hail to You, King Jesus! Go forth, virgin souls who love your Lord. Bow at His feet, and strew His way with the lilies of your love and the roses of your gratitude: "Bring forth the royal diadem, and crown Him Lord of all." Moreover, our Lord Jesus is King in Zion by right of conquest. He has taken and carried by storm the hearts of His people, and He has slain their enemies who held them in cruel bondage. In the Red Sea of His own blood, our Redeemer has drowned the Pharaoh of our sins. Will He not be King in Jeshurun? He has delivered us from the iron yoke and heavy curse of the law: shall not the Liberator be crowned? We are His portion, whom He has taken out of the hand of the Amorite with His sword and with His bow. Who will snatch His conquest from His hand? All hail, King Jesus! We gladly acknowledge Your gentle reign! Rule in our hearts forever, lovely Prince of Peace.

All the house of Israel are impudent and hardhearted.
—Ezekiel 3:7

re there any exceptions? No, not one. Even the favored race is described as *"impudent and hardhearted."* If the best are so bad, then what must the worst be? Come, my heart; consider how much you have a share in this universal accusation, and while considering, be ready to accept your part of the guilt. The first charge is impudence, an arrogant spirit, a lack of holy shame, or an unhallowed boldness in evil. Before my conversion, I could sin and feel no compunction, hear of my guilt and yet remain unhumbled, and even confess my iniquity and manifest no inward humiliation on account of it. For a sinner to go to God's house and pretend to pray to Him and praise Him argues a brash disrespect of the worst kind! Alas, since the day of my new birth, I have doubted my Lord to His face, murmured unblushingly in His presence, worshipped before Him in a slovenly manner, and sinned without bewailing myself concerning it! If my head were not as hard as flint, I would have a far holier fear and a far deeper contrition of spirit. Woe is me! I am one of the impudent house of Israel. The second charge is hard-heartedness, and I must not venture to plead innocent here. Once I had nothing but a heart of stone, and although through grace I now have a new and fleshy heart, much of my former stubbornness remains. I am not affected by the death of Jesus as I should be; neither am I moved as much as I should be by the ruin of my fellowmen, the wickedness of the times, the chastisement of my heavenly Father, and my own failures. Oh, that my heart would melt at the recital of my Savior's sufferings and death! Would to God I were rid of this base millstone within me, this hateful body of death. Blessed be the name of the Lord! The disease is not incurable! The Savior's precious blood is the universal solvent, and it will effectively soften me, even me, until my heart melts as wax before the fire.

The LORD taketh pleasure in his people.
—Psalm 149:4

ow comprehensive is the love of Jesus! There is no part of His people's interests that He does not consider, and there is nothing that concerns their welfare that is not important to Him. Not merely does He think of you, believer, as an immortal being, but as a mortal being, too. Do not deny it or doubt it: *"The very hairs of your head are all numbered"* (Matt. 10:30). *"The steps of a good man are ordered by the LORD: and he delighteth in his way"* (Ps. 37:23). It would be a sad thing for us if this mantle of love did not cover all our concerns, for what mischief might be worked in us in that part of our business that did not come under our gracious Lord's inspection! Believer, rest assured that the heart of Jesus cares about your daily affairs. The breadth of His tender love is such that you may resort to Him in all matters; for in all your afflictions, He is afflicted, and as a father pities his children, so He pities you. The daily concerns of all His saints are borne in the broad heart of the Son of God. Oh, what a heart is His that does not merely understand His people but also comprehends the diverse and innumerable concerns of all those persons! Do you think, O Christian, that you can measure the love of Christ? Think of what His love has brought you: justification, adoption, sanctification, eternal life! The riches of His goodness are unsearchable; you will never be able to name them or even conceive them. Oh, the breadth of the love of Christ! Will such a love as this have half our hearts? Will it have a cold love in return? Will Jesus' marvelous lovingkindness and tender care meet with but faint response and delayed acknowledgment? Tune your harp, my soul, to a glad song of thanksgiving! Go to your rest rejoicing, for you are no desolate wanderer, but a beloved child, watched over, cared for, supplied, and defended by your Lord.

How precious also are thy thoughts unto me, O God!
—Psalm 139:17

ivine omniscience affords no comfort to the ungodly mind, but to the child of God it overflows with consolation. God is always thinking about us. He never turns aside His mind from us, and He always has us before His eyes. This is precisely as we would have it, for it would be dreadful to exist for a moment beyond the observation of our heavenly Father. His thoughts are always tender, loving, wise, prudent, and far-reaching. They bring to us countless benefits; therefore, it is a choice delight to remember them. The Lord has always thought about His people: hence, their election and the covenant of grace by which their salvation is secured. He always will think about them: hence, their final perseverance by which they will be brought safely to their final rest. In all our wanderings, the vigilant gaze of the eternal Watcher is always fixed upon us; we never roam beyond the Shepherd's eye. In our sorrows, He observes us incessantly, and not one of our pains escapes His attention. In our toils, He marks all our weariness and writes in His book all the struggles of His faithful ones. These thoughts of the Lord encompass us in all our paths and penetrate the innermost region of our being. Not a nerve or tissue, valve or vessel, of our bodily organization is uncared for; all the details of our little world are thought about by the great God. Dear reader, is this truth precious to you? Then hold to it. Never be led astray by those philosophic fools who preach an impersonal God and talk of self-existent, self-governing matter. The Lord lives and thinks about us; this is a truth far too precious for us to be lightly robbed of it. The notice of a nobleman is valued so highly that he who has it counts his fortune made; but what is it to be thought of by the King of Kings! If the Lord thinks of us, all is well, and we may rejoice forevermore.

I am the rose of Sharon.
—Song of Solomon 2:1

Whatever beauty there may be in the natural world, Jesus Christ possesses all that in the spiritual world in a tenfold degree. Among flowers, the rose is considered to be the sweetest, but Jesus is infinitely more beautiful in the garden of the soul than the rose can be in the gardens of earth. He takes first place as the fairest among ten thousand. He is the sun, and all others are the stars; the heavens and the day are dark in comparison with Him, for the King in His beauty transcends all. *"I am the rose of Sharon."* This was the best and rarest of roses. Jesus is not *"the rose"* alone; He is *"the rose of Sharon"*—the best of the best. He is positively lovely and superlatively the loveliest. There is variety in His charms. The rose is delightful to the eye, and its scent is pleasant and refreshing. Similarly, each of the senses of the soul—whether taste, feeling, hearing, sight, or spiritual smell—find appropriate gratification in Jesus. Even the remembrance of His love is sweet. Take the rose of Sharon, and pull it leaf from leaf; set aside the leaves in the jar of memory, and you will find each leaf fragrant long afterward, filling the house with perfume. Christ satisfies the highest taste of the most educated spirit to the fullest degree. The greatest amateur in perfumes is quite satisfied with the rose. When the soul has arrived at its highest elevation of true taste, it will still be content with Christ; no, it will be all the better able to appreciate Him. Heaven itself possesses nothing that excels the rose of Sharon. What symbol can fully express His beauty? Human speech and earthborn things fail to tell of Him. Earth's choicest charms combined inadequately depict His abounding preciousness. Blessed rose, bloom in my heart forever!

These all died in faith.
—Hebrews 11:13

ehold the epitaph of all those blessed saints who passed away before the coming of our Lord! It does not matter how they died, whether of old age or by violent means. This one point in which they all agree is the worthiest to record: *"These all died in faith."* In faith they lived. It was their comfort, their guide, their motive, and their support; and, in the same spiritual grace, they died, ending their life-song in the sweet strain in which they had so long continued. They did not die resting in the flesh or on their own achievements. They never wavered from their first acceptance of God's will, but they held to the way of faith to the end. Faith is as precious to die by as to live by. Dying in faith has distinct reference to the past. They believed the promises that had gone before and were assured that their sins were blotted out through the mercy of God. Dying in faith has to do with the present. These saints were confident of their acceptance with God. They enjoyed the rays of His love and rested in His faithfulness. Dying in faith looks into the future. They fell *"asleep in Christ"* (1 Cor. 15:18), affirming that the Messiah would surely come, and that when He would in the last days appear on the earth, they would rise from their graves to behold Him. To them the pains of death were but the birth pangs of a better state. Take courage, my soul, as you read this epitaph. Your life's journey is one of faith through grace, and sight seldom cheers you; this has also been the pathway of the brightest and the best. Faith was the orbit in which these stars of the first magnitude moved during all the time of their shining here; you will be happy if that it is also your path. Look anew tonight to Jesus, the Author and Finisher of your faith, and thank Him for giving you the same precious faith that belonged to the souls who are now in glory.

A very present help.
—Psalm 46:1

Covenant blessings are not meant to be only looked at; they are intended to be appropriated. Even our Lord Jesus is given to us for our present use. Believer, do you make use of Christ as you should? When you are in trouble, why do you not tell Him all your grief? Does He not have a sympathizing heart, and can He not comfort and relieve you? No, you are going about to all your friends, except for your best Friend, and you are telling your tale everywhere except to the heart of your Lord. Are you burdened with this day's sins? Here is a fountain filled with blood: use it, saint; use it. Has a sense of guilt returned to you? The pardoning grace of Jesus may be proved again and again. Come to Him at once for cleansing. Do you deplore your weakness? He is your strength; why not lean on Him? Do you feel naked? Come here, soul; put on the robe of Jesus' righteousness. Do not stand looking at it, but wear it. Strip off your own righteousness and your own fears, too. Put on the fair white linen, for it was meant to wear. Do you feel sick? Pull the night-bell of prayer, and call up the Beloved Physician! He will give the medicine that will revive you. You are poor, but then you have *"a kinsman..., a mighty man of wealth"* (Ruth 2:1). Will you not go to Him and ask Him to give you of His abundance, when He has given you the promise that you will be a joint heir with Him? All that He is and all that He has, He has made available to you. There is nothing Christ dislikes more than for His people to make a display of Him and not to use Him. He loves to be employed by us. The more burdens we put on His shoulders, the more precious He will be to us.

> Let us be simple with Him, then,
> Not backward, stiff, or cold,
> As though our Bethlehem could be
> What Sinai was of old.

Being born again, not of corruptible seed, but of incorruptible.
—1 Peter 1:23

Peter most earnestly exhorted the scattered saints to love each other *"with a pure heart fervently"* (1 Pet. 1:22). He wisely based his argument, not on the law or human nature or philosophy, but on that high and divine nature that God has implanted in His people. Just as some wise tutor of princes might labor to instill and foster in them a kingly spirit and dignified behavior, finding arguments in their position and descent, so, looking upon God's people as heirs of glory, princes of the royal blood, descendants of the King of Kings, earth's truest and oldest aristocracy, Peter said to them, "See that you love one another because of your noble birth, being born of incorruptible seed; because of your pedigree, being descended from God, the Creator of all things; and because of your immortal destiny, for you will never pass away, though the glory of the flesh will fade, and even its existence will cease." (See 1 Peter 2:22–25.) It would be well if, in the spirit of humility, we recognized the true dignity of our regenerated nature and lived up to it. What is a Christian? If you compare him with a king, he adds priestly sanctity to royal dignity. The king's royalty often lies only in his crown, but with a Christian it is infused into his inmost nature. He is as much above his fellows through his new birth as a man is above the beast that perishes. Surely he should carry himself, in all his dealings, as one who is not of the crowd, but chosen out of the world, distinguished by sovereign grace, described as *"a peculiar people"* (1 Pet. 2:9). Therefore, the Christian cannot grovel in the dust as others do or live after the manner of the world's citizens. Let the dignity of your nature and the brightness of your prospects, believers in Christ, constrain you to cleave to holiness and to *"abstain from all appearance of evil"* (1 Thess. 5:22).

He that handleth a matter wisely shall find good:
and whoso trusteth in the LORD, happy is he.
—Proverbs 16:20

Wisdom is man's true strength; under its guidance, he best accomplishes his life's goals. Handling matters wisely gives man the richest enjoyment and presents the noblest occupation for his talents. By walking in wisdom, a person finds good in the fullest sense. Without wisdom, a man is like a wild colt, running here and there, wasting strength that otherwise might be profitably employed. Wisdom is the compass by which man is to steer across the trackless expanse of life; without it he is a derelict vessel, the sport of winds and waves. A man must be prudent in such a world as this, or he will find no good; instead, he will encounter unnumbered difficulties. The pilgrim will sorely wound his feet among the briers of the forest of life if he does not choose his steps with the utmost caution. He who is in a wilderness infested with robbers must handle matters wisely if he desires to journey safely. If, trained by the great Teacher, we follow where He leads, we will find good, even while in this dark abode. There are heavenly fruits to be gathered on this side of Eden's arbors and songs of paradise to be sung amid the groves of earth. But where will this wisdom be found? Many have dreamed of it, but they have not possessed it. Where will we learn it? Let us listen to the voice of the Lord, for He has declared the secret. He has revealed to the sons of men wherein true wisdom lies, and we have it in the text, *"Whoso trusteth in the LORD, happy is he."* The true way to handle a matter wisely is to trust in the Lord. This is the sure guide to the most intricate mazes of life; follow it and find eternal bliss. He who trusts in the Lord has a diploma for wisdom granted by inspiration. He is happy now, and he will be even happier above. Lord, in this sweet evening, walk with me in the garden and teach me the wisdom of faith.

All the days of my appointed time will I wait.
—Job 14:14

A little stay on earth will make heaven more heavenly. Nothing makes rest as sweet as work does; nothing renders security as pleasant as exposure to danger does. The bitter tonics of earth will give a relish to the new wine that sparkles in the golden bowls of glory. Our battered armor and scarred countenances will render more illustrious our victory above, when we are welcomed to the seats of those who have overcome the world. We would not have full fellowship with Christ if we did not for a while sojourn below, for He was baptized with a baptism of suffering among men; we must be baptized with the same if we wish to share His kingdom. Fellowship with Christ is so honorable that the worst sorrow is a light price by which to procure it. Another reason for our lingering here is for the good of others. We would not wish to enter heaven until our work is done, and it may be that we are yet ordained to minister light to souls trapped in the darkness of sin. Our prolonged stay here is doubtless for God's glory. A tried saint, like a well-cut diamond, glitters much in the King's crown. Nothing reflects as much honor on a workman as a protracted and severe trial of his work, and its triumphant endurance of the ordeal without giving way in any part. We are God's workmanship, in whom He will be glorified by our afflictions. It is for the honor of Jesus that we endure the trials of our faith with sacred joy. Let each man surrender his own longings to the glory of Jesus, and feel, "If my lying in the dust would elevate my Lord by as much as an inch, let me still lie among the pots of earth. If to live on earth forever would make my Lord more glorious, it would be my heaven to be shut out of heaven." Our time is fixed and settled by eternal decree. Let us not be anxious about it, but wait with patience until the gates of pearl open.

Jesus saith unto him, Rise, take up thy bed, and walk.
—John 5:8

Like many others, the crippled man had been waiting for a miracle to happen and for a sign to be given. Wearily, he watched the pool, but no angel came or came for him; yet, thinking it was his only chance, he waited still. He did not know that there was One near him whose word could heal him in a moment. Many are in the same plight. They are waiting for some extraordinary emotion, remarkable impression, or heavenly vision. They wait in vain and watch for nothing. Even supposing that, in a few cases, remarkable signs are seen, yet these are rare, and no one has a right to look for them in his own situation—especially no one who feels his inability to avail himself of the moving of the water even if it did come. It is very sad to realize that tens of thousands are now waiting on the use of means, ordinances, vows, or resolutions, and they have waited in vain, utterly in vain, longer than one can imagine. Meanwhile these poor souls forget the present Savior, who invites them to look to Him and be saved. He could heal them immediately, but they prefer to wait for an angel or a miracle. To trust God is the sure way to every blessing, and He is worthy of the most implicit confidence; but unbelief makes them prefer the cold porches of Bethesda to the warm bosom of His love. Oh, that the Lord may turn His eye upon the multitudes who are in this situation tonight. May He forgive the slights that they put upon His divine power. In His sweet, constraining voice, may He call them to rise from their beds of despair and in the energy of faith to take up their beds and walk. O Lord, hear our prayers for everyone who is in this situation tonight. At this calm hour of sunset and before the day breaks, may they look and live. Dear reader, is there anything in this passage that speaks to you?

Acquaint now thyself with him.
—Job 22:21

If we desire to properly acquaint ourselves with God and be at peace, we must know Him as He has revealed Himself—not only in the unity of His essence and existence, but also in the plurality of His persons. *"God said, Let us make man in our image"* (Gen. 1:26). Do not let man be content until he knows something of the *"us"* from whom his being was derived. Endeavor to know the Father; bury your head in His bosom in deep repentance, and confess that you are not worthy to be called His child. Receive the kiss of His love. Let the ring that is the token of His eternal faithfulness be on your finger. Sit at His table, and let your heart be made merry in His grace. Then press forward and seek to know much of the Son of God, who is the brightness of His Father's glory; yet, in unspeakable condescension of grace, He became Man for our sakes. Know Him in the unique complexity of His nature: eternal God, yet suffering, finite man. Follow Him as He walks the waters with the footsteps of deity and as He sits on the well in the weariness of humanity. Do not be satisfied unless you know much of Jesus Christ as your Friend, your Brother, your Husband, your All. Do not forget the Holy Spirit. Endeavor to obtain a clear view of His nature and character, His attributes, and His works. Behold that Spirit of the Lord, who first of all moved upon chaos and brought forth order; who now visits the chaos of your soul and creates the order of holiness. Behold Him as the Lord and Giver of spiritual life, the Illuminator, the Instructor, the Comforter, and the Sanctifier. Behold Him as, in holy power, He descends on the head of Jesus, and then afterward rests on you who are as the skirts of His garments. Such an intelligent, scriptural, and experiential belief in the Trinity in Unity is yours if you truly know God. Such knowledge brings peace indeed!

Come, my beloved, let us go forth into the field;...
let us see if the vine flourish.
—Song of Solomon 7:11–12

he church was about to engage in earnest labor and desired her Lord's company in it. She did not say, "I will go," but *"Let us go."* It is a blessing to work when Jesus is at our side! It is the business of God's people to be trimmers of God's vines. Like our first parents, we are put into the garden of the Lord for usefulness; therefore, let us go forth into the field. Observe that the church, when she is thinking rightly, desires to enjoy communion with Christ in all her many labors. Some imagine that they cannot serve Christ actively and still have fellowship with Him. They are mistaken. True, it is very easy to fritter away our inward life in outward activities and complain to the Spouse, *"They made me the keeper of the vineyards; but mine own vineyard have I not kept"* (Song 1:6). There is no reason, however, why this should be the case except through our own folly and neglect. Certainly, a believer may do nothing, yet grow quite as lifeless in spiritual things as those who are the busiest. Mary was not praised for sitting still, but for sitting at Jesus' feet. Even so, Christians are not to be praised for neglecting duties under the pretense of having secret fellowship with Jesus. It is not sitting, but sitting at Jesus' feet that is commendable. Do not think that activity is in itself evil. It is a great blessing and a means of grace to us. Paul called it a grace given to him to be allowed to preach, and every form of Christian service may become a personal blessing to those engaged in it. Those who have the most fellowship with Christ are not recluses or hermits, who have much time to spare, but indefatigable laborers who are toiling for Jesus, and who, in their labors, have Him side by side with them, so that they are *"workers together"* (2 Cor. 6:1) with God. Let us remember that in anything we have to do for Jesus, we can do it and should do it in close communion with Him.

The only begotten of the Father, full of grace and truth.
—John 1:14

Believer, you can give your testimony that Christ is the *"only begotten of the Father,"* as well as *"the first begotten of the dead"* (Rev. 1:5). You can say, "He is divine to me, even if He is human to all the world. He has done for me what no one but God could do. He has subdued my stubborn will, melted my hardened heart, opened *'gates of brass, and cut the bars of iron in sunder'* (Ps. 107:16). He has turned my mourning into laughter and my desolation into joy. He has led my captivity captive and made my heart *'rejoice with joy unspeakable and full of glory'* (1 Pet. 1:8). Let others think as they will of Him, to me He must be the *'only begotten of the Father.'"* Blessed be His name! And He is full of grace. Oh, if it had not been for Him, I would never have been saved. He drew me when I struggled to escape from His grace; and, when at last I came to His mercy seat, trembling like a condemned criminal, He said, "Your sins, which are many, are all forgiven: be of good cheer." And He is full of truth. His promises have all been true; not one has failed. I bear witness that no servant ever had such a master as I have. No brother has had a kinsman as He has been to me. No spouse has had a husband as Christ has been to my soul. No sinner has had a better Savior; no mourner has had a better comforter than Christ has been to my spirit. I desire no one besides Him. In life, He is my life; in death, He will be the death of death. In poverty, Christ is my riches; in sickness, He makes my bed. In darkness, He is my star; in brightness, He is my sun. He is the manna of the camp in the wilderness, and He will be the new corn of the host when they come to Canaan. Jesus is all grace and no wrath to me, all truth and no falsehood. He is full of truth and grace, infinitely full. My soul, this night, with all your strength, bless *"the only begotten."*

Only be thou strong and very courageous.
—Joshua 1:7

God's tender love for His servants makes Him concerned for the state of their emotions. He wants them to be of good courage. Some consider it a small thing for a believer to be troubled with doubts and fears, but God does not think so. From this text, it is clear that our Master would not have us entangled with fears. He wants us to be free of cares, doubts, and cowardice. Our Master takes our unbelief more seriously than we do. When we are despondent, we are subject to a grievous disease that should not be ignored, but should be taken immediately to the Beloved Physician. Our Lord does not want to see our countenance sad. It was a law of Ahasuerus that no one could come into the king's court dressed in mourning; this is not the law of the King of Kings, for we may come mourning as we are. Still, He would have us put on *"the garment of praise for the spirit of heaviness"* (Isa. 61:3), for there are many reasons to rejoice. The Christian should be of a courageous spirit, so that he may glorify the Lord by enduring trials in a heroic manner. If he is fearful and fainthearted, it will dishonor his God. Besides, what a bad example it is. This disease of doubtfulness and discouragement is an epidemic that soon spreads among the Lord's flock. One downcast believer makes twenty souls sad. Moreover, unless your courage is kept up, Satan will be too much for you. Let your spirit be joyful in God your Savior. *"The joy of the LORD is your strength"* (Neh. 8:10), and no fiend of hell will make headway against you. But cowardice throws down the banner. Moreover, labor is light to a man of cheerful spirit, and success waits on cheerfulness. The man who toils, rejoicing in his God and believing with all his heart, has guaranteed success. He who sows in hope will reap in joy; therefore, dear reader, *"be thou strong and very courageous."*

*Fear not to go down into Egypt; for I will there make of thee
a great nation: I will go down with thee into Egypt;
and I will also surely bring thee up again.*
—Genesis 46:3–4

acob must have shuddered at the thought of leaving the land of his father and having to live among heathen strangers. It was a new scene and likely to be a trying one. Who could venture among couriers of a foreign monarch without anxiety? Yet the way was evidently appointed for him; therefore, he resolved to go. This is frequently the position of believers now: they are called to perils and temptations altogether untried. At such seasons let them imitate Jacob's example by offering sacrifices of prayer to God and seeking His direction. Do not let them take a step until they have waited on the Lord for His blessing. Then they will have Jacob's companion to be their Friend and Helper. How blessed to feel assured that the Lord is with us in all our ways and condescends to go down into our humiliation and banishment with us! Even beyond the ocean our Father's love beams like the sun in its strength. We cannot hesitate to go where Jehovah promises His presence; even the valley of the shadow of death grows bright with the radiance of this assurance. Marching onward with faith in their God, believers will have Jacob's promise. They will be brought up again, whether it is from the troubles of life or the rooms of death. Jacob's seed came out of Egypt in due time, and so will all the faithful pass unscathed through the tribulation of life and the terror of death. Let us exercise Jacob's confidence. *"Fear not"* is the Lord's command and His divine encouragement to those who at His bidding are launching upon new seas. The divine presence and preservation forbid so much as one unbelieving fear. Without our God, we would fear to move; but when He commands us to go, it would be dangerous to delay. Reader, go forward, and do not fear.

Thou art my portion, O LORD.
—Psalm 119:57

Look at your possessions, believer, and compare your portion with the lot of your fellowmen. Some make their living in the field. They are rich, and their harvests yield them a golden increase. But what are harvests compared with your God, who is the God of harvests? What are bursting granaries compared with Him, who is the Husbandman who feeds you with the bread of heaven? Some do their work in the city. Their wealth is abundant and flows to them in constant streams, until they become a very reservoir of gold. But what is gold compared with your God? You could not live on it; your spiritual life could not be sustained by it. Apply it to a troubled conscience, and could it reduce its pain? Apply it to a discouraged heart, and see if it could stop a single groan or lessen one's grief. But you have God, and in Him you have more than gold or riches could ever buy. Some obtain their livelihood through that which most men love—applause and fame; but ask yourself, is God not more important to you than that? What if thousands of trumpets loudly blared your praise? Would this prepare you to cross the Jordan or cheer you in the face of judgment? No, there are griefs in life that wealth cannot alleviate; and there is the deep need at your dying hour for which no riches can provide. But when you have God for your portion, you have more than all else put together. In Him every need is met, whether in life or in death. With God for your portion, you are rich indeed; for He will supply your needs, comfort your heart, assuage your grief, guide your steps, be with you in the dark valley, and then take you home to enjoy Him forever. *"I have enough"* (Gen. 33:9), Esau said; that statement is the best a worldly man can say. However, Jacob replied, *"God hath dealt graciously with me, and...I have* [all things, more than] *enough"* (v. 11), which is a note too high for carnal minds to understand.

He shall gather the lambs with his arm,
and carry them in his bosom.
—Isaiah 40:11

Who is He of whom such gracious words are spoken? He is the Good Shepherd. Why does He carry the lambs close to His heart? Because He has a tender heart, and any weakness at once melts His heart. The sighs, the ignorance, the feebleness of the little ones of His flock elicit His compassion. It is His office, as a faithful High Priest, to consider the weak. Besides, He purchased them with His blood, so they are His property. He must and will care for that which cost Him so dearly. Then He is responsible for each lamb, bound by covenant engagements not to lose one. Moreover, they are all a part of His glory and reward. But how may we understand the expression, "He will carry them"? Sometimes He carries them by not permitting them to endure many trials. Providence deals tenderly with them. Often they are "carried" by being filled with an unusual degree of love, so that they bear up and stand fast. Though their knowledge may not be deep, they have great sweetness in what they do know. Frequently He carries them by giving them a very simple faith, which takes the promise just as it stands, and believingly, they run straight to Jesus with every trouble. The simplicity of their faith gives them an unusual degree of confidence, which lifts them above the world. He carries the lambs in His bosom. Here is boundless affection. Would He put them next to His heart if He did not love them so much? Here is tender nearness; they are so near that they could not possibly be nearer. Here is hallowed familiarity; there are precious love-passages between Christ and His weak ones. Here is perfect safety; next to His heart, who can hurt them? The enemy must hurt the Shepherd first. Here is perfect rest and sweetest comfort. Surely we are not sufficiently aware of the infinite tenderness of Jesus!

Made perfect.
—Hebrews 12:23

here are two kinds of perfection that the Christian needs: the perfection of justification in the person of Jesus and the perfection of sanctification brought about in him by the Holy Spirit. At present, corruption remains, even in the hearts of the regenerate; experience soon teaches us this. Within us are still lusts and evil imaginations. But I rejoice to know that the day is coming when God will finish the work that He has begun, and He will present my soul, not only perfect in Christ, but perfect through the Spirit, *"not having spot, or wrinkle, or any such thing; but that it should be holy and without blemish"* (Eph. 5:27). Can it be true that this poor, sinful heart of mine is to become holy even as God is holy? Can it be that this spirit, which often cries, *"O wretched man that I am! who shall deliver me from the body of this death?"* (Rom. 7:24), will get rid of sin and death—that I will have no evil things to harass my ears and no unholy thoughts to disturb my peace? Oh, happy hour! May it come quickly! When I cross the Jordan, the work of sanctification will be finished; but not until that moment will I even claim perfection in myself. Then my spirit will have its last baptism in the Holy Spirit's fire. I long to die to receive that last and final purification that will usher me into heaven. Not even an angel will be purer than I; for I will be able to say, "I am clean," in a double sense, through Jesus' blood and through the Spirit's work. Oh, how we should extol the power of the Holy Spirit in making us fit to stand before our Father in heaven! Yet do not let the hope of perfection hereafter make us content with imperfection now. If it does this, our hope cannot be genuine; for a good hope is a purifying thing, even now. The work of grace must be abiding in us now, or it cannot be perfected then. Let us pray to *"be filled with the Spirit"* (Eph. 5:18), so that we may increasingly bring forth the fruits of righteousness.

And he said, Thus saith the LORD, Make this valley full of ditches.
For thus saith the LORD, Ye shall not see wind, neither shall ye see
rain; yet that valley shall be filled with water, that ye may drink,
both ye, and your cattle, and your beasts.
—2 Kings 3:16–17

he armies of the three kings were famishing from a lack of water. God was about to send it, and in these words the prophet announced the coming blessing. Here was a case of human helplessness. All the valiant men could not procure a drop of water from the skies or find any in the wells of earth. In the same way, the people of the Lord are often at their wits' end; they see their own inadequacy and discover where their help is to be found. Still the people were to prepare by faith for the divine blessing; they were to dig the trenches in which the precious liquid would be held. The church must by her varied agencies, efforts, and prayers make herself ready to be blessed; she must make the pools, and the Lord will fill them. This must be done in faith, in the full assurance that the blessing is about to descend. Soon there was a wonderful bestowal of the needed blessing. The shower did not pour from the clouds as it did in Elijah's case, but, in a silent and mysterious manner, the pools were filled. The Lord has His own sovereign methods of action. He is not tied to manner and time as we are, but He does as He pleases among the sons of men. It is ours to receive from Him thankfully and not to dictate to Him. We must also notice the remarkable abundance of the supply: there was enough to meet everyone's needs. And so it is in the gospel blessing. All the needs of the congregation and of the entire church will be met by divine power in answer to prayer; above all this, victory will be speedily given to the armies of the Lord. What am I doing for Jesus? What trenches am I digging? O Lord, make me ready to receive the blessing that You are so willing to bestow.

Thou art my servant; I have chosen thee.
—Isaiah 41:9

If we have received the grace of God in our hearts, its practical effect has been to make us God's servants. We may be unfaithful servants—we certainly are unprofitable ones—yet, blessed be His name, we are His servants, wearing His badge, feeding at His table, and obeying His commands. We were once the servants of sin, but He who made us free has now taken us into His family and taught us obedience to His will. We do not serve our Master perfectly, but we would if we could. As we hear God's voice saying to us, *"Thou art my servant,"* we can answer with David, *"I am thy servant;...thou hast loosed my bonds"* (Ps. 116:16). But the Lord calls us not only His servants, but also His chosen ones: *"I have chosen thee."* We have not chosen Him first, but He has chosen us. If we are God's servants, we were not always so; the change must be ascribed to sovereign grace. The eye of sovereignty singled us out, and the voice of unchanging grace declared, *"I have loved thee with an everlasting love"* (Jer. 31:3). Long before time began or space was created, God had written on His heart the names of His elect people. He had predestined them to be conformed to the image of His Son and ordained them heirs of all the fullness of His love, His grace, and His glory. What comfort is here! Has the Lord loved us so long, and will He yet cast us away? He knew how stiff-necked we would be. He understood that our hearts were evil, yet He made the choice. Oh, our Savior is no fickle Lover! He does not feel enchanted for a while with some gleams of beauty from His church's eye, and then afterward cast her off because of her unfaithfulness. No, He married her in old eternity; and it is written of Jehovah, *"He hateth putting away"* (Mal. 2:16). The eternal choice is a bond on our gratitude and on His faithfulness, which neither can disown.

Afterward.
—Hebrews 12:11

How happy are tried Christians, *"afterward"!* There is no calm deeper than that which follows a storm. Who has not rejoiced in bright sunshine after a rain? Victory banquets are for well-exercised soldiers. After killing the lion, we eat the honey. After climbing the Hill of Difficulty, we sit down in the shade to rest. After traversing the Valley of Humiliation and fighting with the devil, we see the Shining One appear with the healing branch from the Tree of Life. Our sorrows, like the passing keels of the vessels on the sea, leave a silver line of holy light behind them *"afterward."* It is peace—sweet, deep peace—that follows the horrible turmoil that once reigned in our tormented, guilty souls. See, then, the happy estate of a Christian! He has his best things last, and, in this world, he receives his worst things first. But even his worst things are *"afterward"* good things; harsh plowings yield joyful harvests. Even now he grows rich by his losses, he rises by his falls, he lives by dying, and he becomes full by being emptied. If, then, his grievous afflictions yield him so much *"peaceable fruit"* (Heb. 12:11) in this life, what will the full vintage of joy be *"afterward"* in heaven? If his dark nights are as bright as the world's days, what will his days be? If even his starlight is more splendid than the sun, what must his sunlight be? If he can sing in a dungeon, how sweetly will he sing in heaven? If he can praise the Lord in the fires, how will he extol Him before the eternal throne? If evil is good to him now, what will the overflowing goodness of God be to him then? Oh, blessed *"afterward"!* Who would not be a Christian? Who would not bear the present cross for the crown that comes *"afterward"?* But herein is work for patience, for the rest is not for today, nor the triumph for the present, but *"afterward."* Wait, O soul, and *"let patience have her perfect work"* (James 1:4).

And [Elijah] requested for himself that he might die.
—1 Kings 19:4

It was a remarkable thing that Elijah—the man for whom God had ordained an infinitely better lot, who was never to die, who would be carried to heaven in a chariot of fire and be translated so that he would not see death—would thus pray, *"O LORD, take away my life; for I am not better than my fathers"* (1 Kings 19:4). We have here a memorable proof that God does not always answer prayer in-kind, though He always does in effect. He gave Elijah something better than what he asked for, and thus God really heard and answered Elijah's prayer. It was unusual that the lion-hearted Elijah would be so depressed by Jezebel's threat as to ask to die, and it was blessedly kind on the part of our heavenly Father that He did not take His despondent servant at his word. There is a limit to the doctrine of the prayer of faith. We are not to expect that God will give us everything for which we choose to ask. We know that sometimes we ask and do not receive, because we *"ask amiss"* (James 4:3). If we ask for what is not promised, if we contradict the spirit that the Lord would have us cultivate, if we ask contrary to His will or to the decrees of His providence, if we ask merely for the gratification of our own comfort and without an eye to His glory, we must not expect that we will receive. Yet, when we ask in faith, without doubting, if we do not receive the precise thing for which we asked, we will receive an equivalent, and more than an equivalent for it. As one remarked, "If the Lord does not pay in silver, He will in gold; and if He does not pay in gold, He will in diamonds." If He does not give you precisely what you ask for, He will give you what is tantamount to it, and what you will greatly rejoice to receive in place of what you asked for. Be then, dear reader, much in prayer, and make this evening a season of earnest intercession. But be careful what you ask for.

I drew them with cords of a man, with bands of love.
—Hosea 11:4

ur heavenly Father often draws us with the cords of love; but oh, how hesitant we are to run toward Him! How slowly we respond to His gentle impulses! He wants us to exercise a simpler faith in Him, but we have not yet attained Abraham's level of trust in God. We do not leave our worldly cares with God, but, like Martha, we burden ourselves with much serving. Our meager faith brings leanness to our souls; we do not open our mouths wide, even though God has promised to fill them. (See Psalm 81:10.) Does He not this evening invite us to trust Him? Can we not hear Him say, "Come, My child, and trust Me. The veil is rent. Enter into My presence and boldly approach the throne of My grace. I am worthy of your full confidence; cast your cares on Me. Shake off the dust of your cares, and put on your beautiful garments of joy"? But though we are called with tones of love for the blessed exercise of this comforting grace, we do not respond. At other times, He draws us to closer communion with Himself. We have been sitting on the doorstep of God's house; He invites us to come into the banqueting hall and dine with Him, but we decline the honor. There are secret rooms not yet opened to us; Jesus invites us to enter them, but we hold back. Shame on our cold hearts! We are but poor lovers of our sweet Lord Jesus, not fit to be His servants, much less to be His brides. Yet He has exalted us to be bone of His bone and flesh of His flesh, married to Him by a glorious marriage covenant. Herein is love! But it is a love that accepts no denial. If we do not obey the gentle invitations of His love, He will send affliction to drive us into closer intimacy with Himself. He will do whatever it takes to draw us closer to Him. What foolish children we are to refuse those bands of love and so bring upon our backs that scourge of small cords, which Jesus knows how to use to our benefit!

There is corn in Egypt.
—Genesis 42:2

Famine pinched all the nations, and it seemed inevitable that Jacob and his family would suffer great need. But the God of providence, who never forgets the objects of electing love, had stored a granary for His people by giving the Egyptians warning of the scarcity and leading them to store up the grain during their years of plenty. Little did Jacob expect deliverance from Egypt, but the corn in store for him was there. Believer, though all things are apparently against you, rest assured that God has made a reservation on your behalf; in the list of your griefs there is a saving clause. Somehow He will deliver you, and somewhere He will provide for you. The place from which your rescue will arise may be a very unexpected one, but help will assuredly come during your time of critical need, and you will magnify the name of the Lord. If men do not feed you, ravens will; if the earth does not yield wheat, heaven will drop manna. Therefore, be of good courage, and rest quietly in the Lord. God can make the sun rise in the west if He pleases, and He can make your source of distress the channel of delight. The corn in Egypt was all in the hands of the beloved Joseph; he opened or closed the granaries at will. And so the riches of providence are all in the absolute power of our Lord Jesus, who will dispense them liberally to His people. Joseph was abundantly ready to provide for his own family; and Jesus is unceasing in His faithful care for His children. Our business is to go after the help that is provided for us: we must not sit still in despondency, but rouse ourselves. Prayer will soon bring us into the presence of our royal Brother. Once we are before His throne, we have only to ask and we will receive. His provisions are not exhausted; there is corn still. His heart is not hard; He will give the corn to us. Lord, forgive our unbelief, and this evening cause us to draw largely from Your fullness and receive *"grace for grace"* (John 1:16).

Behold, thou art fair, my beloved.
—Song of Solomon 1:16

rom every point of view, our Well Beloved is most fair. Our various experiences are meant by our heavenly Father to furnish fresh viewpoints from which we may see the loveliness of Jesus. How beneficial are our trials when they carry us aloft where we may gain clearer sights of Jesus than ordinary life could afford us! We have seen Him *"from the top of Amana, from the top of Shenir and Hermon"* (Song 4:8), and He has shone upon us as the sun in his strength; but we have also seen Him *"from the lions' dens, from the mountains of the leopards"* (v. 8), and He has lost none of His loveliness. From the languishing of a sick bed, from the borders of the grave, we have turned our eyes to our soul's Spouse, and He has never been otherwise than *"all fair"* (v. 7). Many of His saints have looked on Him from the gloom of dungeons and from the fiery flames of the stake, yet they have never uttered a bad word about Him; instead, they have died extolling His surpassing charms. Oh, noble and pleasant employment to be forever gazing at our sweet Lord Jesus! Is it not unspeakably delightful to view the Savior in all His offices and to perceive Him matchless in each—to shift the kaleidoscope, as it were, and to find fresh combinations of unequaled graces? In the manger and in eternity, on the cross and on His throne, in the Garden and in His kingdom, among thieves or in the midst of angels, He is everywhere *"altogether lovely"* (Song 5:16). Examine carefully every little act of His life and every trait of His character, and He is as lovely in the minute as in the majestic. Judge Him as you will, you cannot censure; weigh Him as you please, and He will not be found wanting. Eternity will not discover the shadow of a spot in our Beloved, but rather, as ages revolve, His hidden glories will shine forth with yet more inconceivable splendor. His unutterable loveliness will more and more fill all celestial minds with rapturous joy.

Thou hast bought me no sweet cane with money.
—Isaiah 43:24

orshippers at the temple were accustomed to bringing presents of sweet perfumes to be burned on the altar of God. Yet Israel, in the time of her backsliding, became stingy and brought only a few offerings of thankfulness to her Lord. This was an evidence of coldness of heart toward God and His house. Reader, does this ever occur with you? Might not the complaint of the text be occasionally, if not frequently, brought against you? Those who are poor in pocket, if rich in faith, will be accepted even though their gifts are small; but, poor reader, do you give in fair proportion to the Lord, or is the widow's mite kept back from the sacred treasury? The rich believer should be thankful for the gifts entrusted to him, but he should not forget his large responsibility, for where *"much is given...much* [will be] *required"* (Luke 12:48). But, rich reader, are you mindful of your obligations and giving to the Lord according to the benefits you have received? Jesus gave His blood for us; what will we give to Him? We are His, and all that we have is His, for He has purchased us for Himself. Can we act as if we were our own? Oh, for more consecration and more love! Blessed Jesus, how good it is of You to accept our sweet cane bought with money! Nothing is too costly as a tribute to Your unrivalled love, yet You receive with favor the smallest sincere token of affection! You receive our poor forget-me-nots and love-tokens as though they were intrinsically precious, though indeed they are but as the bunch of wildflowers that the child brings to his mother. May we never grow miserly toward You. From this hour, may we never hear You complain again of our withholding the gifts of our love. We will give You the firstfruits of our increase and pay tithes of all to You. Then we will confess *"of thine own have we given thee"* (1 Chron. 29:14).

Only let your conversation be as it becometh the gospel of Christ.
—Philippians 1:27

he word *"conversation"* does not merely mean our talk, but the whole course of our lives and behavior in the world. The Greek word signifies the actions and the privileges of citizenship. Thus, as citizens of the New Jerusalem, we are commanded to let our actions be such as become the Gospel of Christ. What sort of conversation is this? In the first place, the Gospel is very simple. So Christians should be simple and plain in their habits. Our manner, our speech, our dress, and our whole behavior should reflect a simplicity that is the very soul of beauty. The Gospel is pre-eminently true. It is gold without dross, and the Christian's life will be lusterless and valueless without the jewel of truth. The Gospel is a very fearless Gospel. It boldly proclaims the truth, whether men like it or not. We must be equally faithful and unflinching. But the Gospel is also very gentle. Mark this spirit in its Founder: *"a bruised reed shall he not break"* (Isa. 42:3). Some people who profess to be Christians are sharper than a thornbush; such people are not like Jesus. Let us seek to win others by the gentleness of our words and actions. The Gospel is very loving. It is the message of the God of love for a lost and fallen race. Christ's last command to His disciples was, *"Love one another"* (John 13:34). Oh, for more real, hearty unity and love for all the saints and for more tender compassion toward the souls of the worst and vilest of men! We must not forget that the Gospel is holy. It never excuses sin: it pardons it, but only through the Atonement. If our lives are to resemble the Gospel, we must shun, not merely the grosser vices, but everything that would hinder our perfect conformity to Christ. For His sake, for our own sakes, and for the sakes of others, we must strive day by day to let our conversation be more in accordance with His Gospel.

*And they rose up the same hour, and returned to Jerusalem…and
they told what things were done in the way,
and how he was known of them.*
—Luke 24:33, 35

When the two disciples had reached Emmaus and were refreshing themselves at the evening meal, the mysterious stranger who had so enchanted them upon the road took bread and broke it. He made Himself known to them, and then He vanished out of their sight. They had urged Him to abide with them, because the day was nearly over; but now, although it was much later, their love was a lamp, yes, even wings to their feet. They forgot the darkness. Their weariness was all gone, and immediately they journeyed back the sixty furlongs to tell the glad news of a risen Lord, who had appeared to them by the way. They reached the Christians in Jerusalem and were received by a burst of joyful news before they could tell their own tale. These early Christians were all on fire to speak of Christ's resurrection and to proclaim what they knew of the Lord. They shared their experiences. This evening let their example impress us deeply. We, too, must give our witness concerning Jesus. John's account of the empty tomb needed to be supplemented by Peter's, and Mary could add something further still; combined, we have a full testimony from which nothing can be left out. Each of us has unique gifts and special manifestations, but the one objective God has in view is the perfecting of the whole body of Christ. We must, therefore, bring our spiritual possessions, lay them at the apostles' feet, and distribute unto all from what God has given to us. Hold back no part of the precious truth, but speak what you know and testify to what you have seen. Do not allow the labor involved, darkness, or possible unbelief of your friends hinder you in any way. Get up, march to the place of duty, and tell what great things God has shown to your soul.

Continue in the faith.
—Acts 14:22

Perseverance is the badge of true saints. The Christian life is more than a beginning in the ways of God. It is also a continuance in the faith as long as life lasts. It is the same for a Christian as it was with the great Napoleon. He said, "Conquest has made me what I am, and conquest must maintain me." So, under God, dear friend in the Lord, conquest has made you what you are, and conquest must sustain you. Your motto must be, "Excelsior" [still higher]. A true conqueror, who will be crowned at the last, is the one who continues until war's trumpet is blown no more. Perseverance is, therefore, the target of all our spiritual enemies. The world does not object to your being a Christian for a time, if it can tempt you to cease your pilgrimage and settle down to buy and sell in Vanity Fair. The flesh will seek to ensnare you and to prevent your pressing on to glory. The flesh says, "It is weary work being a pilgrim; come, give it up. Am I always to be mortified? Am I never to be indulged? Give me at least a vacation from this constant warfare." Satan will make many fierce attacks on your perseverance; it will be the mark for all his arrows. He will strive to hinder you in service. He will insinuate that you are doing no good and that you need to rest. He will endeavor to make you weary of suffering. He will whisper, *"Curse God, and die"* (Job 2:9). Or he will attack your steadfastness by asking, "What is the good of being so zealous? Be quiet like the rest; sleep as the others are, and let your lamp go out as the other virgins do." Or he will attack your doctrinal sentiments by asking, "Why do you hold to these denominational creeds? Sensible people are becoming more liberal; they are removing the old landmarks. Get with the times." Therefore, Christian, wear your shield close to your armor, and cry mightily to God so that by His Spirit you may endure to the end.

*What is thy servant, that thou shouldest look upon
such a dead dog as I am?*
—2 Samuel 9:8

If Mephibosheth was thus humbled by David's kindness, what will we be in the presence of our gracious
Lord? The more grace we have, the less we will think
of ourselves, for grace, like light, reveals our impurity.
Eminent saints have scarcely known to what to compare
themselves; their sense of unworthiness has been so clear
and keen. "I am," said holy Rutherford, "a dry and withered
branch, a piece of dead carcass, dry bones, and not able to
step over a straw." In another place he wrote, "Except as to
open outbreakings, I want nothing of what Judas and Cain
had." The lowliest objects in nature appear to the humbled
mind to have a preference above itself, because they have
never contracted sin. A dog may be greedy, fierce, or filthy,
but it has no conscience to violate, no Holy Spirit to resist.
A dog may be a worthless animal, yet by a little kindness, it
is soon won to love its master and is faithful to death. But
we forget the goodness of the Lord and do not respond to
His call. The term *"dead dog"* is the most expressive of all
terms of contempt, but it is not too strong to use to express
the self-abhorrence of instructed believers. They do not
pretend to be modest; they mean what they say. They have
weighed themselves in the balances of the sanctuary and
realized the vanity of their natures. At best, we are but clay,
animated dust, mere walking hills; but viewed as sinners,
we are monsters indeed. Let it be published in heaven as a
miracle that the Lord Jesus would set His heart's love upon
such as we. Dust and ashes though we are, we must and
will magnify the *"exceeding greatness of his power"* (Eph.
1:19). Could not His heart find rest in heaven? Must He
come to these tents of Kedar for a spouse and choose a bride
on whom the sun had looked? (See Song of Solomon 1:5–6.)
O heavens and earth, break forth into song, and give all
glory to our sweet Lord Jesus.

This I recall to my mind, therefore have I hope.
—Lamentations 3:21

emory is frequently the slave of despair. Despondent minds call to remembrance every dark prediction from the past and focus on every gloomy aspect of the present; thus memory, clothed in sackcloth, presents to the mind a cup of mingled gall and wormwood. There is, however, no need for this. Wisdom can readily transform memory into an angel of comfort. That same recollection that in its left hand brings so many gloomy omens may be trained to bear in its right a wealth of hopeful signs. She need not wear a crown of iron. She may encircle her brow with a ribbon of gold, all spangled with stars. Thus it was in Jeremiah's experience. In the previous verse, memory had brought him to deep humiliation of soul: *"My soul hath them still in remembrance, and is humbled in me"* (v. 20). Now this same memory restored him to life and comfort. *"This I recall to my mind, therefore have I hope."* Like a two-edged sword, his memory first killed his pride with one edge, and then slew his despair with the other. As a general principle, if we desire to exercise our memories more wisely, we might, in our very darkest distress, strike a match that would instantaneously kindle the lamp of comfort. There is no need for God to create a new thing upon the earth in order to restore believers to joy. If they would prayerfully rake the ashes of the past, they would find light for the present; and if they would turn to the Book of Truth and the throne of grace, their candle would soon shine as before. May we remember the lovingkindness of the Lord and rehearse His deeds of grace. Let us open the volume of recollection that is so richly illuminated with memorials of mercy, and we will soon be happy. Thus memory may be, as Coleridge called it, "the bosom-spring of joy." When the Divine Comforter bends it to His service, memory may be chief among earthly comforters.

Cursed be the man before the LORD, that riseth up
and buildeth this city Jericho.
—Joshua 6:26

Since the man who rebuilt Jericho was cursed, much more damned are those who labor to restore false religions among us. In our fathers' days, the gigantic walls of unrighteousness fell by the power of their faith, the perseverance of their efforts, and the blast of their gospel trumpets. Now there are some who want to rebuild accursed, so-called religious systems on their old foundations. O Lord, be pleased to thwart these unrighteous endeavors, and pull down every stone upon which they build. It should be a serious business with us to be thoroughly purged of every error that may have a tendency to foster an ungodly spirit. Then, when we have made a clean sweep at home, we should seek in every way to oppose sin's all-too-rapid spread abroad in the church and in the world. This last can be done in secret through fervent prayer and in public through giving a strong testimony. With judicious boldness, we must warn those who are inclined to believe false teachings. We must instruct the young in gospel truth and alert them to the sinful practices of religion in past times. We must aid in spreading the light more thoroughly through the land, for false teachers, like owls, hate daylight. Are we doing all we can for Jesus and the Gospel? If not, our negligence plays into the hands of the enemy. What are we doing to distribute the Bible? Are we spreading abroad good, sound gospel writings? Luther once said, "The devil hates goose quills," and, undoubtedly, he has good reason: ready writers, by the Holy Spirit's blessing, have done the devil's kingdom much damage. If the thousands who read this brief word tonight will do all they can to hinder the rebuilding of this accursed Jericho, the Lord's glory will speed among the sons of men. Reader, what can you do? What will you do?

Henceforth we should not serve sin.
—Romans 6:6

hristian, what do you have to do with sin? Has it not cost you enough already? Burned child, will you play with fire? When you have already been between the jaws of the lion, will you step into his den a second time? Have you not had enough of the old serpent? Did he not poison all your veins once, and will you play upon the hole of the asp and put your hand on the serpent's den a second time? Oh, do not be so foolish! Did sin ever bring you real pleasure? Did you find solid satisfaction in it? If so, go back to your old drudgery and wear the chain again, if it pleases you. But inasmuch as sin never gave you what it promised to bestow, but deluded you with lies, do not be snared a second time by the old fowler. Be free, and let the remembrance of your ancient bondage forbid you to enter the net again! It is contrary to the intentions of eternal love, which all have an eye to your purity and holiness; therefore, do not run counter to the purposes of your Lord. Another thought should restrain you from sin. Christians can never sin cheaply; they pay a heavy price for iniquity. Transgression destroys peace of mind, obscures fellowship with Jesus, hinders prayer, and brings darkness over the soul; therefore, do not be the slave of sin. There is yet a higher argument: each time you *"serve sin,"* you have crucified the Lord *"afresh, and put him to an open shame"* (Heb. 6:6). Can you bear that thought? Oh, if you have fallen into any special sin during this day, it may be that my Master has sent this warning this evening to bring you back before you have backslidden very far. Turn to Jesus anew; He has not forgotten His love for you. His grace is still the same. With weeping and repentance, come to His footstool, and you will be once more received into His heart. You will be set upon a rock again, and He will direct your steps.

Who healeth all thy diseases.
—Psalm 103:3

umbling as is the statement, yet the fact is certain that we are all more or less suffering under the disease of sin. What a comfort it is to know that we have a Great Physician who is both willing and able to heal us! Let us think about Him for a while tonight. His cures are very speedy; there is life in a look at Him. His cures are radical; He strikes at the center of the disease. Hence, His cures are sure and certain. He never fails, and the disease never returns. There is no relapse where Christ heals. There is no fear that His patients will be merely patched up for a season; He makes them new people. He gives them a new heart also and puts a right spirit within them. He is well skilled in all diseases. Physicians generally have some specialty. Although they may know a little about almost all our aches and pains, there is usually one area of medicine that they have studied above all others. But Jesus Christ is thoroughly acquainted with the whole of human nature. He is as much at home with one sinner as with another; never yet has He met with an out-of-the-way case that was difficult for Him. He has had extraordinary complications of strange diseases to deal with, but He has known exactly with one glance of His eye how to treat the patient. He is the only universal Doctor; and the medicine He gives is the only true remedy, healing in every instance. Whatever our spiritual malady may be, we should go at once to this Divine Physician. There is no brokenness of heart that Jesus cannot bind up. His blood *"cleanseth us from all sin"* (1 John 1:7). If we think of the countless number who have been delivered from all sorts of diseases through the power and virtue of His touch, we will joyfully put ourselves in His hands. We trust Him, and sin dies; we love Him, and grace lives; we wait for Him, and grace is strengthened; we see Him as He is, and grace is perfected forever.

He will make her wilderness like Eden.
—Isaiah 51:3

see a vision of a howling wilderness, a great and terrible desert like the Sahara. I see nothing in it to relieve the eye. Everywhere I look, I am wearied with a vision of hot, arid sand, strewn with ten thousand bleaching skeletons of wretched men who have died in anguish, having lost their way in the merciless wasteland. What an appalling sight! How horrible! It is a sea of sand without end and without an oasis, a cheerless graveyard for a forlorn race! But behold and wonder! Suddenly I see, springing up from the scorching sand, a plant of renown. As it grows, it buds. The bud expands. It is a rose, and at its side, a lily bows its modest head. Miracle of miracles! As the fragrance of these flowers is diffused, the wilderness is transformed into a fruitful field; all around, it blossoms exceedingly. The glory of Lebanon is given to it, the excellency of Carmel and Sharon. Do not call it the Sahara; call it Paradise. Do not speak of it any longer as the valley of death's shadow; for where the skeletons lay bleaching in the sun, behold a resurrection is proclaimed. The dead spring up and become a mighty army, full of eternal life. Jesus is that plant of renown, and His presence makes all things new. Each individual's salvation is no less than a miracle. Yonder I see you, dear reader, cast out, an unswaddled, unwashed infant, defiled with your own blood and left to be food for beasts of prey. But a jewel has been thrown into your heart by a divine hand, and for its sake, you have been pitied and tended by divine providence. You are washed and cleansed from your defilement. You are adopted into heaven's family. The fair seal of love is on your forehead, and the ring of faithfulness is on your hand. Now, you are a prince unto God, though once you were an orphan who had been cast away. Highly value the matchless power and grace that changes deserts into gardens and makes the barren heart sing for joy.

Good Master.
—Matthew 19:16

I f the young man in the Gospel used this title in speaking to our Lord, how much more aptly may I address Him this way! He is indeed my Master in both senses, a ruling Master and a teaching Master. I delight to run His errands and to sit at His feet. I am both His servant and His disciple, and I count it my highest honor to acknowledge both relationships. If He would ask me why I call Him *"good,"* I would have a ready answer. It is true that *"there is none good but one, that is, God"* (Matt. 19:17), but then He is God, and all the goodness of deity shines forth in Him. In my experience, I have found Him good, so good, indeed, that all the good I have has come to me through Him. He was good to me when I was dead in sin, for He raised me by His Spirit's power. He has been good to me in all my needs, trials, struggles, and sorrows. There could never be a better Master, for His service is freedom, and His rule is love. I wish I were one-thousandth part as good a servant. When He teaches me as my Rabbi, He is unspeakably good. His doctrine is divine, His manner is gracious, and His spirit is gentleness itself. No error mingles with His instruction; the golden truth that He brings forth is pure, and all His teachings lead to goodness, sanctifying as well as edifying the disciple. Angels find Him a good Master and delight to pay their homage at His footstool. The ancient saints proved Him to be a good Master, and each of them rejoiced to sing, "I am Your servant, Lord!" My own humble testimony must certainly be to the same effect. I will give this witness before my friends and neighbors, for possibly they may be led by my testimony to seek my Lord Jesus as their Master. Oh, that they would do so! They would never regret so wise a choice. If they would but take His easy yoke, they would find themselves in so royal a service that they would enlist in it forever.

He humbled himself.
—Philippians 2:8

Jesus is the great Teacher of true humility. Daily we need to learn of Him. See the Master taking a towel and washing His disciples' feet! Follower of Christ, will you not humble yourself? See Him as the Servant of servants, and surely you cannot be proud! Is not this sentence the summary of His biography: *"He humbled himself"*? While on earth, was He not always stripping off first one robe of honor and then another, until, naked, He was nailed to the cross? Did He not empty His inmost self, pouring out His lifeblood, giving up all for us, until they laid Him penniless in a borrowed grave? How low was our dear Redeemer brought! How then can we be proud? Stand at the foot of the cross, and count the purple drops by which you have been cleansed. Wear the crown of thorns. Observe His scourged shoulders, still gushing with the crimson stream of His blood. See His hands and feet given up to the rough iron, and His whole self to mockery and scorn. Notice the bitterness, the anguish, and the pain of inward grief showing themselves in His outward frame. Hear the chilling cry, *"My God, my God, why hast thou forsaken me?"* (Matt. 27:46). And if you do not lie prostrate on the ground before that cross, you have never seen it. If you are not humbled in the presence of Jesus, you do not know Him. You were so lost that nothing could save you but the sacrifice of God's only begotten Son. Think of that, and as Jesus stooped for you, bow yourself in lowliness at His feet. A sense of Christ's amazing love for us has a greater tendency to humble us than even a consciousness of our own guilt. May the Lord bring us in contemplation to Calvary. Then our position will no longer be that of a pompous man of pride, but we will assume the humble place of one who loves much because he has had much forgiven. Pride cannot live beneath the cross. Let us sit there and learn our lesson, and then rise and put it into practice.

Received up into glory.
—1 Timothy 3:16

We have seen our beloved Lord in the days of His flesh, humiliated and painfully distressed; for He was *"despised and rejected of men; a man of sorrows, and acquainted with grief"* (Isa. 53:3). He whose brightness is as the morning wore the sackcloth of sorrow as His daily dress: shame and reproach were His clothing. Yet now, inasmuch as He has triumphed on the bloody tree over all the powers of darkness, our faith beholds our King returning *"from Edom, with dyed garments"* (Isa. 63:1), robed in the splendor of victory. How glorious must He have been in the eyes of angels, when a cloud received Him out of mortal sight, and He ascended to heaven! Now He wears the glory that He had with God before the earth ever was, and yet another glory above all—that which He has well earned in the fight against sin, death, and hell. As Victor, He wears the illustrious crown. Listen to how the song swells high! It is a new and sweeter song: *"Worthy is the Lamb that was slain"* (Rev. 5:12), for He has *"redeemed us to God by [His] blood"* (v. 9). He wears the glory of an Intercessor who can never fail, of a Prince who can never be defeated, of a Conqueror who has vanquished every foe, of a Lord who has the heart's allegiance of every subject. Jesus wears all the glory that the pomp of heaven can bestow upon Him, which ten thousand times ten thousand angels can minister to Him. You cannot with your utmost stretch of imagination conceive His exceeding greatness; yet there will be a further revelation of it when He will descend from heaven in great power, with all the holy angels: *"Then shall he sit upon the throne of his glory"* (Matt. 25:31). Oh, the splendor of that glory! It will delight His people's hearts. Nor will that be the end of our praise, for eternity will sound His praise, *"Thy throne, O God, is for ever and ever"* (Ps. 45:6)! Reader, if you wish to rejoice in Christ's glory in the future, He must be glorious in your sight right now. Is He so?

He that loveth not knoweth not God.
—1 John 4:8

The distinguishing mark of a Christian is his confidence in the love of Christ, and his commitment to love Christ in return. First, faith sets her seal upon the man by enabling the soul to say with the apostle, Christ *"loved me, and gave himself for me"* (Gal. 2:20). Then love adds its signature and stamps upon the heart gratitude and love for Jesus in return. *"We love him, because he first loved us"* (1 John 4:19). In those grand days of the early church, a heroic period of the Christian faith, this double mark was clearly seen in all believers in Jesus. They were people who knew the love of Christ and rested on it as a man leans on a staff whose dependability he has proven. The love that they felt toward the Lord was not a quiet emotion that they hid within themselves in a secret room in their souls. They did not speak of it only in their private meetings when they gathered on the first day of the week and sang hymns in honor of Christ Jesus, the Crucified One. Instead, it was a passion of such fervid, all-consuming energy that it was visible in all their actions, spoken of in their daily conversation, and unmistakably seen in their eyes, even in their casual glances. Love for Jesus was a flame that fed on the core and heart of their being; therefore, from its own force, it burned its way into the outer man and shone there. Zeal for the glory of King Jesus was the seal and mark of all genuine Christians. Because of their dependence on Christ's love, they dared much; because of their love for Christ, they did much, and it is the same now. The children of God are ruled in their inmost powers by love: the love of Christ drives them. They rejoice that divine love is set upon them. They feel it shed abroad in their hearts by the Holy Spirit, who is given to them. Then, by force of gratitude, they love the Savior with a pure, fervent heart. Reader, do you love Him? Before you sleep, give an honest answer to this weighty question!

Are they Israelites? so am I.
—2 Corinthians 11:22

We have a personal claim here, and one that needs proof. The apostle knew that his claim was indisputable, but many persons have no right to the title who still claim to belong to Israel. If we confidently declare, "I, too, am an Israelite," let us say it only after having searched our hearts in the presence of God. But if we can give proof that we are following Jesus, if we can say from the heart, "I trust Him wholly, trust Him only, trust Him simply, trust Him now, and trust Him forever," then the position that the saints of God hold belongs to us; we possess all their privileges. We may be the very least in Israel, *"less than the least of all saints"* (Eph. 3:8); yet since the mercies of God belong to the saints as saints, and not as advanced saints or well-taught saints, we may put in our plea, and say, "Are they Israelites? I am, too; therefore, the promises are mine, grace is mine, and glory will be mine." The claim, rightfully made, is one that will yield untold comfort. When God's people are rejoicing that they are His, what happiness it brings if I can say, "So am I!" When they speak of being pardoned, justified, and *"accepted in the beloved"* (Eph. 1:6), how joyful to respond, "Through the grace of God, so am I." But this claim has not only its enjoyments and privileges, but also its conditions and duties. We must share with God's people in cloudy times as well as in sunshine. When we hear them spoken of with contempt and ridicule for being Christians, we must come boldly forward and say, "I am a Christian, too." When we see them working for Christ, giving their time, their talents, their whole hearts to Jesus, we must be able to say, "I will give of myself as well." Let us prove our gratitude by our devotion and live as those who, having claimed a privilege, are willing to take the responsibility connected with it.

Be zealous.
—Revelation 3:19

If you desire to see souls converted; if you want to hear the cry that *"the kingdoms of this world are become the kingdoms of our Lord"* (Rev. 11:15); if you would place crowns upon the head of the Savior and lift His throne high, then be filled with zeal. For, under God, the way of the world's conversion must be by the zeal of the church. Every Christlike characteristic will be utilized, but zeal will be employed first; prudence, knowledge, patience, and courage will follow in their places, but zeal must lead the way. It is not the extent of your knowledge, though that is useful; it is not the extent of your talent, though that is not to be despised; it is your zeal that will do great exploits. This zeal is the fruit of the Holy Spirit. It draws its vital force from the continued operations of the Holy Spirit in the soul. If our inner lives dwindle, if our hearts beat slowly before God, we will not know zeal. But if all is strong and vigorous within, then we cannot but feel a loving eagerness to see the kingdom of Christ come and His will done on earth, even as it is in heaven. A deep sense of gratitude will nourish Christian zeal. Looking to the hole of the pit from which we were rescued, we find abundant reasons why we should spend and be spent for God. And zeal is also stimulated by the thought of the eternal future. It looks with tearful eyes down to the flames of hell, and it cannot sleep. It looks up with longing for the glories of heaven, and it cannot but rouse itself. It feels that time is short compared with the work to be done; therefore, it devotes all that it has to the cause of its Lord. And it is always strengthened by the remembrance of Christ's example. He was clothed with zeal as with a cloak. How swift the chariot wheels of duty went with Him! He knew no loitering by the way. Let us prove that we are His disciples by manifesting the same spirit of zeal.

*Thou shalt see now whether my word shall
come to pass unto thee or not.*
—Numbers 11:23

God promised Moses that for the space of a whole month He would feed the vast host in the wilderness with flesh. Moses, suddenly overtaken by unbelief, looked to the outward means and was at a loss to know how the promise could be fulfilled. He looked to the creature instead of to the Creator. But does the Creator expect the creature to fulfill His promise for Him? No. He who makes the promise always fulfills it by His own unaided omnipotence. If He speaks, it is done—done by Himself. His promises do not depend for their fulfillment on the cooperation of the puny strength of man. We can see at once the mistake that Moses made. Yet how often we do the same! God has promised to supply our needs, and we look to the creature to do what God has promised to do; then, because we perceive the creature to be weak and feeble, we indulge in unbelief. Why do we look in that direction at all? Will you look to the North Pole to gather fruits ripened in the sun? In truth, that would be no more foolish than looking to the weak for strength or to the creature to do the Creator's work. Let us, then, put the question on the right footing. The visible means for the performance of the promise is not a sufficient basis for faith; the all-sufficiency of the invisible God is the only solid foundation for faith. He will most surely do as He has said He would. After clearly seeing that the burden lies with the Lord and not with the creature, will we dare to indulge in mistrust? The question of God comes home mightily to us: *"Is the LORD'S hand waxed short?"* (Num. 11:23). May it happen, too, in His mercy, that with the question there may flash upon our souls that blessed declaration, *"Thou shalt see now whether my word shall come to pass unto thee or not."*

Search the scriptures.
—John 5:39

he Greek word for *search* signifies a strict, close, diligent, curious search, such as men make when they are
seeking gold, or hunters demonstrate when they are
earnestly pursuing game. We must not rest content with
having given a superficial reading to a chapter or two, but
with the candle of the Spirit, we must deliberately seek out
the hidden meaning of the Word. Holy Scripture requires
searching—much of it can be learned only by careful study.
There is milk for babies, but also meat for strong men. The
rabbis wisely say that a mountain of matter hangs on every
word, yes, upon every verse of Scripture. Tertullian ex-
claimed, "I adore the fullness of the Scriptures." No man
who merely skims the Book of God can profit thereby; we
must dig and mine until we obtain the hidden treasure. The
door of the Word opens only with the key of diligence. The
Scriptures demand searching. They are the writings of
God, bearing the divine stamp and sanction. Who will dare
to treat them lightly? He who despises them despises the
God who wrote them. God forbid that any of us should allow our Bibles to become swift witnesses against us on the
Great Judgment Day. The Word of God will repay searching. God does not tell us to sift a mountain of chaff in order
to find a grain of wheat in it here and there, but the Bible is
winnowed corn. We have but to open the granary door and
find it. Scripture grows upon the student. It is full of surprises. Under the teaching of the Holy Spirit, to the
searching eye, it glows with splendor of revelation, like a
vast temple paved with gold and roofed with rubies, emer-
alds, and all manner of gems. There is nothing like the
truth of Scripture. Last, the Scriptures reveal Jesus: *"They
are they which testify of me"* (John 5:39). No more powerful
motive can be urged upon Bible readers than this: he who
finds Jesus finds life, heaven, and all things. Happy is he
who, searching the Bible, discovers his Savior.

They are they which testify of me.
—John 5:39

esus Christ is the Alpha and Omega of the Bible. He is the constant theme of its sacred pages; from first to last they testify of Him. At the creation we at once discern Him as one of the sacred Trinity. We catch a glimpse of Him in the promise of the woman's Seed. We see Him typified in the ark of Noah. We walk with Abraham, as He sees Messiah's day. We dwell in the tents of Isaac and Jacob, feeding on the gracious promise. We hear the venerable Israel talking of Shiloh, and in the numerous types of the law, we find the Redeemer abundantly foreshadowed. Prophets and kings, priests and preachers, all look one way—they all stand as the cherubs did over the ark, desiring to look within and to read the mystery of God's great propitiation. Even more clearly, in the New Testament, we find our Lord the one pervading subject. It is not an ingot here and there or some gold dust thinly scattered. Here you stand on a solid floor of gold; for the whole substance of the New Testament is Jesus crucified, and even its closing sentence is bejeweled with the Redeemer's name. We should always read Scripture in this light. We should consider the Word to be like a mirror into which Christ looks down from heaven. Then we, looking into it, see His face reflected as in a mirror. It is true that the reflection is dim, but still it is a blessed preparation for seeing Him as we will see Him face-to-face. The Bible contains Jesus Christ's letters to us, perfumed by His love. Its pages are the garments of our King, and they all smell of myrrh, aloes, and cassia. Scripture is the royal chariot in which Jesus rides, and it is paved with love for the daughters of Jerusalem. The Scriptures are the swaddling clothes of the holy child Jesus; unroll them and you find your Savior. The essence of the Word of God is Christ.

There brake he the arrows of the bow, the shield,
and the sword, and the battle.
—Psalm 76:3

ur Redeemer's glorious cry of *"It is finished"* (John 19:30) was the death knell of all the adversaries of His people. It signified the breaking of *"the arrows of the bow, the shield, and the sword, and the battle."* The Hero of Golgotha used His cross as an anvil and His woes as a hammer, dashing to pieces bundle after bundle of our sins, those poisoned *"arrows of the bow."* He trampled on every indictment and destroyed every accusation. What glorious blows the mighty Breaker gives with a hammer far weightier than the fabled weapon of Thor! The diabolical darts were reduced to fragments, and the infernal shields were broken like potters' vessels! Jesus drew the dreadful sword of satanic power from its sheath of hellish workmanship. He snapped it across His knee, as a man breaks a bundle of dry wood and casts it into the fire. Beloved, no sin of a believer can now be an arrow to wound him mortally. No condemnation can now be a sword to kill him, for the punishment of our sin was borne by Christ. A full atonement was made for all our iniquities by our blessed Substitute and Surety. Who can accuse us now? Who can condemn us? *"It is Christ that died, yea rather, that is risen again"* (Rom. 8:34). Jesus has emptied the quivers of hell, has quenched every fiery dart, and has broken off the head of every arrow of wrath. The ground is strewn with the splinters and relics of the weapons of hell's warfare, which are visible to us only to remind us of our former danger and of our great deliverance. Sin no longer has dominion over us. Jesus has made an end of it and put it away forever. O enemy, your efforts to destroy have come to an end. Talk of all the wondrous works of the Lord. Make mention of His name, and do not keep silent either by day or when the sun goes to its rest at night. Bless the Lord, O my soul.

Who hath saved us, and called us with an holy calling.
—2 Timothy 1:9

The apostle used the perfect tense when he wrote, *"Who hath saved us,"* which indicates that the action had already been completed. Believers in Christ Jesus are saved. They are not looked on as persons who are in a hopeful state in which they may ultimately be saved, but they are already saved. Salvation is not a blessing to be enjoyed on the deathbed and to be sung of in a future state above; it is a matter promised to be obtained, received, and enjoyed now. The Christian is perfectly saved in God's purpose. God has ordained him unto salvation, and that purpose is complete. He is saved also because of the price that has been paid for him. *"It is finished"* (John 19:30) was the cry of the Savior before He died. The believer is also perfectly saved in His covenant Head, for as he fell in Adam, so he lives in Christ. This complete salvation is accompanied by a holy calling. Those whom the Savior saved on the cross are in due time effectively called by the power of God the Holy Spirit to holiness. They leave their sins, and they endeavor to be like Christ. They choose holiness, not out of any compulsion, but from the influence of a new nature, which leads them to rejoice in holiness just as naturally as before they delighted in sin. God neither chose them nor called them because they were holy, but He called them so that they might be holy, and holiness is the beauty produced by His workmanship in them. The Christlike qualities that we see in a believer are as much the work of God as the Atonement itself. Thus the fullness of the grace of God is brought out very sweetly. Salvation must be of grace, because the Lord is the Author of it. What motive but grace could move Him to save the guilty? Salvation must be of grace, because the Lord works in such a way that our righteousness is forever excluded. The believer's privilege is a present salvation; the evidence that he is called to it is his holy life.

Remove far from me vanity and lies.
—Proverbs 30:8

O my God, be not far from me.
—Psalm 38:21

Here we have two great lessons—what to pray for and what to pray against. The happiest state of a Christian is the holiest state. As there is the most heat nearest to the sun, so there is the most happiness nearest to Christ. No Christian enjoys comfort when his eyes are fixed on empty pursuits; he finds no satisfaction unless his soul is made alive in the ways of God. The world may find happiness elsewhere, but he cannot. I do not blame ungodly men for rushing to their pleasures. Why should I? Let them have their fill. That is all they have to enjoy. A converted wife who despaired of her husband's salvation was always very kind to him, for she said, "I fear that this is the only world in which he will be happy; therefore, I have made up my mind to make him as happy in it as I can." Christians must seek their delights in a higher sphere than the empty frivolities or sinful enjoyments of the world. Vain pursuits are dangerous to renewed souls. We have heard of a philosopher who, while he looked up to the stars, fell into a pit; but how deeply do they fall who look down. Their fall is fatal. No Christian is safe when his soul is lazy and his God is far from him. Every Christian is always safe on the great matter of his standing in Christ, but he is not safe on his experience in holiness and communion with Jesus in this life. Satan does not often attack a Christian who is living near to God. It is when the Christian departs from God, becomes spiritually starved, and endeavors to feed on self-conceit that the devil discovers his advantage. He may sometimes stand foot-to-foot with the child of God who is active in his Master's service, but the battle is generally short. He who slips as he goes down into the Valley of Humiliation, every time he takes a false step invites Apollyon to assail him. Oh, for grace to walk humbly with our God!

O Lord, to us belongeth confusion of face...because
we have sinned against thee.
—Daniel 9:8

A deep sense and clear sight of sin, its hideousness, and the punishment that it deserves should make us bow low before the throne. We have sinned as Christians. It should not be so! Favored as we have been, we have been ungrateful. Privileged beyond most, we have not brought forth fruit in proportion. Who is there, although he may long have been engaged in Christian warfare, that will not blush when he looks back upon the past? As for our days before we were saved, may they be forgiven and forgotten. Yet, since then, though we have not sinned as before, we have sinned against light and against love—light that has really penetrated our minds and love in which we have rejoiced. Oh, the atrocity of the sin of a pardoned soul! An unpardoned sinner sins cheaply compared with the sin of one of God's own elect, who has had communion with Christ and leaned his head on Jesus' bosom. Look at David. Many will talk about his sin, but I trust you will look at his repentance. Hear his broken bones as each one of them moans out its sorrowful confession! See his tears as they fall on the ground, and hear the deep sighs with which he accompanies the softened music of his harp! We have sinned. Let us, therefore, seek the spirit of repentance. Look again at Peter. We speak much of Peter's denying his Master. Remember, it is written, Peter *"wept bitterly"* (Matt. 26:75). Have we no denials of our Lord to be lamented with tears? These sins of ours, before and after conversion, would send us to the place of inextinguishable fire if it were not for the sovereign mercy that has made us different. It has snatched us like burning wood from the fire. My soul, bow down under a sense of your natural sinfulness, and worship your God. Admire the grace that saves you, the mercy that spares you, and the love that pardons you!

He…openeth, and no man shutteth.
—Revelation 3:7

Jesus is the Keeper of the gates of paradise. Before every believing soul, He sets an open door, which no man or devil is able to close. What joy it will be to find that faith in Him is the golden key to the everlasting doors. My soul, do you carry this key in your heart, or are you trusting in some deceitful burglar, who will fail you in the end? Hear this parable of the preacher, and remember it. The great King has made a banquet, and He has proclaimed to all the world that no one will enter but those who bring with them the fairest flower that blooms. The spirits of men advance to the gate by thousands, and each one brings the flower that he esteems to be the queen of the garden; but they are all driven from the royal presence and cannot enter into the festive halls. Some bear in their hands the deadly nightshade of superstition or the flaunting poppies of false religions or the hemlock of self-righteousness, but these are not dear to the King. The bearers of these flowers are shut out of the pearly gates. My soul, have you gathered the rose of Sharon? Do you wear the lily of the valley in your bosom constantly? If so, when you come up to the gates of heaven, you will know its value, for you need only to show this choicest of flowers, and the Porter will open the heavenly door for you. He will not deny you admission for one moment, for the Porter always opens the door when He sees that rose. You will find your way with the rose of Sharon in your hand up to the throne of God Himself, for heaven itself possesses nothing that excels its radiant beauty. Of all the flowers that bloom in paradise, there is none that can rival the lily of the valley. My soul, by faith get Calvary's bloodred rose into your hand, by love wear it, by communion preserve it, by daily watchfulness make it your all in all, and you will be blessed beyond all bliss and happy beyond all dreams. Jesus, be mine forever. Be my God, my heaven, and my all.

The LORD is my light and my salvation; whom shall I fear? the
LORD is the strength of my life; of whom shall I be afraid?
—Psalm 27:1

he LORD *is my light and my salvation."* Here is personal interest: *"my light"* and *"my salvation."* The soul is assured of it and therefore declares it boldly. At the new birth, divine light is poured into the soul as the precursor of salvation; where there is not enough light to reveal our own darkness and to make us long for the Lord Jesus, there is no evidence of salvation. After conversion, our God is our joy, comfort, guide, teacher, and in every sense our light. He is light within, light around, light reflected from us, and light to be revealed to us. Notice that it is not said that the Lord merely gives light, but that He is light; nor that He gives salvation, but that He is salvation. He, then, who by faith lays hold upon God, has all covenant blessings in his possession. This truth established, the argument drawn from it is then put in the form of a question: *"Whom shall I fear?"* This question provides its own answer. The powers of darkness are not to be feared, for the Lord, our light, destroys them. The damnation of hell is not to be dreaded, for the Lord is our salvation. This is a very different challenge from that of boastful Goliath. It rests not on the conceited strength of the *"arm of flesh"* (2 Chron. 32:8), but on the real power of the omnipotent I AM. (See Exodus 3:14.) *"The Lord is the strength of my life."* Here is a third glowing epithet; it shows that the writer's hope was fastened with a threefold cord that could not be broken. We may well accumulate terms of praise where the Lord lavishes deeds of grace. Our lives derive all their strength from God; if He deigns to make us strong, we cannot be weakened by all the schemes of the adversary. *"Of whom shall I be afraid?"* The bold question looks into the future as well as the present. *"If God be for us, who can be against us?"* (Rom. 8:31)—either now or in the time to come!

Then Israel sang this song, Spring up, O well; sing ye unto it.
—Numbers 21:17

he well of Beer in the wilderness was famous because it was the subject of a promise: *"That is the well whereof the* LORD *spake unto Moses, Gather the people together, and I will give them water"* (Num. 21:16). The people needed water, and it was promised by their gracious God. We need fresh supplies of heavenly grace, and in the covenant the Lord has pledged Himself to give all we require. The well became the cause of a song. Before the water gushed forth, cheerful faith prompted the people to sing; and as they saw the crystal fount bubbling up, the music grew even more joyous. In like manner, we who believe the promise of God should rejoice in the prospect of divine revivals in our souls. As we experience them, our holy joy should overflow. Are we thirsting? Let us not complain, but sing. Spiritual thirst is bitter to bear, but we need not bear it. The promise indicates a well; let us be of good heart and look for it. In addition, the well was the center of prayer. *"Spring up, O well."* What God has promised to give, we must seek after, or we show that we have neither desire nor faith. This evening let us ask that the Scripture we have read and our devotional exercises may not be empty formalities; instead, may they be a channel of grace to our souls. Oh, that God the Holy Spirit would work in us with all His mighty power, filling us with all the fullness of God! Last, the well was the object of effort. *"The nobles of the people digged it...with their staves"* (v. 18). The Lord wants us to be active in obtaining grace. Our staves are ill adapted for digging in the sand, but we must use them to our utmost ability. Prayer must not be neglected; the assembling of ourselves together must not be forsaken; ordinances must not be slighted. The Lord will give us His peace most abundantly, but not as a reward for idleness. Let us, then, rouse ourselves to seek Him in whom are all our fresh springs.

I am come into my garden, my sister, my spouse.
—Song of Solomon 5:1

The heart of the believer is Christ's garden. He bought it with His precious blood, and He enters it and claims it as His own. A garden implies separation. It is not public property; it is not a wilderness. It is walled around or hedged in. Would that we could see the wall of separation between the church and the world made broader and stronger. It makes one sad to hear Christians saying, "Well, there is no harm in this; there is no harm in that," thus getting as near to the world as possible. Grace is at a low ebb in the soul that can even raise the question of how far it may go in worldly conformity. A garden is a place of beauty. It far surpasses the wild, uncultivated lands. The genuine Christian must seek to be more excellent in his life than the best moralist, because Christ's garden should produce the best flowers in all the world. Even the best is poor compared with what Christ deserves; let us not put Him off with withering, dwarfed plants. The rarest, richest, choicest lilies and roses should bloom in the place that Jesus calls His own. The garden is a place of growth. The saints are not to remain undeveloped, always mere buds and blossoms. We should *"grow in grace, and in the knowledge of our Lord and Saviour Jesus Christ"* (2 Pet. 3:18). Growth should be rapid where Jesus is the Gardener and where the Holy Spirit is the dew from above. A garden is a place of retirement. The Lord Jesus Christ would have us reserve our souls as a place in which He can manifest Himself in ways that He does not reveal Himself to the world. Oh, that Christians were more reserved, that they would keep their hearts more closely guarded for Christ! We often worry and trouble ourselves, like Martha, with much serving, so that we do not have the room for Christ that Mary had, and we do not sit at His feet as we should. May the Lord grant the sweet showers of His grace to water His garden this day.

My beloved is mine, and I am his: he feedeth among the lilies. Until
the day break, and the shadows flee away, turn, my beloved, and be
thou like a roe or a young hart upon the mountains of Bether.
—Song of Solomon 2:16–17

Surely if there is a joyous verse in the Bible it is this: *"My beloved is mine, and I am his."* This thought is so peaceful, so full of assurance, so overrunning with happiness and contentment that it might well have been written by the same hand that penned the Twenty-third Psalm. Although the prospect is exceedingly fair and lovely—earth cannot show its superior—it is not entirely a sunlit landscape. There is a cloud in the sky that casts a shadow over the scene. Listen, *"Until the day break, and the shadows flee away."* There is a word, too, about the *"mountains of Bether,"* or the "mountains of division," and to our love, anything like division is bitterness. Beloved, this may be your present state of mind: you do not doubt your salvation; you know that Christ is yours, but you are not feasting with Him. You understand that you are of vital concern to Him, so that you have no shadow of a doubt of your being His and of His being yours, but still His left hand is not under your head, and His right hand does not embrace you. A shade of sadness is cast over your heart, perhaps by affliction, certainly by the temporary absence of your Lord, so even while exclaiming, *"I am his,"* you are forced to fall to your knees and to pray, *"Until the day break, and the shadows flee away, turn, my beloved."* "Where is He?" asks the soul. And the answer comes, *"He feedeth among the lilies."* If we would find Christ, we must be in communion with His people, and we must come to the ordinances with His saints. Oh, for an evening glimpse of Him! Oh, to dine with Him tonight!

Straightway they forsook their nets, and followed him.
—Mark 1:18

When Simon and Andrew heard the call of Jesus, they obeyed at once without question. If we would always, promptly and with resolute zeal, put into practice what we hear on the spot or at the first suitable occasion, our attention to the means of grace and our reading of good books could not fail to enrich us spiritually. He will not lose his loaf who has taken care to eat it immediately. Neither can he be deprived of the benefit of a doctrine who has already acted on it. Most readers and hearers become motivated to change; but, sadly, the proposal is a blossom that has not been rooted; therefore, no fruit comes of it. They wait, they waver, and then they forget, until, like the ponds on nights of frost, when the sun shines by day, they are thawed only in time to be frozen again. That fatal tomorrow is bloodred with the death of fair resolutions; it is the slaughterhouse of the innocents. We are very concerned that this little book of evening devotions would not be fruitless, and we pray that readers may not be readers only, but *"doers of the word"* (James 1:22). The practice of truth is the most profitable reading of it. Should the reader be impressed with any duty while perusing these pages, let him hurry to fulfill it before the holy glow has departed from his soul. Let him leave his nets, and all that he has, rather than be found rebellious to the Master's call. Do not give place to the devil by delay! Move while opportunity and renewal are in happy conjunction. Do not be caught in your own nets, but break the cords of worldliness. Come away to where glory calls you. Happy is the writer who finds readers who are resolved to carry out his teachings; his harvest will be a hundredfold, and his Master will receive great honor. Would to God that such might be the reward from these brief meditations and hurried hints. Grant it, O Lord, to your servant!

Nevertheless the foundation of God standeth sure.
—2 Timothy 2:19

he foundation on which our faith rests is this: *"God was in Christ, reconciling the world unto himself, not imputing their trespasses unto them"* (2 Cor. 5:19). The great fact on which genuine faith relies is that *"the Word was made flesh, and dwelt among us"* (John 1:14), and that *"Christ also hath once suffered for sins, the just for the unjust, that he might bring us to God"* (1 Pet. 3:18); *"Who his own self bare our sins in his own body on the tree"* (1 Pet. 2:24), for *"the chastisement of our peace was upon him; and with his stripes we are healed"* (Isa. 53:5). In one word, the great pillar of the Christian's hope is substitution. His hope is in the vicarious sacrifice of Christ for the guilty, Christ being made *"sin for us…that we might be made the righteousness of God in him"* (2 Cor. 5:21), Christ offering up a true and proper expiatory and substitutionary sacrifice in the room, place, and stead of as many as the Father gave to Him, who are known to God by name and who are recognized in their own hearts by their trusting in Jesus. This is the cardinal fact of the Gospel. If this foundation were removed, what could we do? But it stands as firm as the throne of God. We know it; we rest on it; we rejoice in it; and our delight is to hold it, to meditate on it, and to proclaim it, while we desire to be moved by gratitude for it in every part of our lives and conversation. In these days a direct attack has been made on the doctrine of the Atonement. Men cannot bear substitution. They gnash their teeth at the thought of the Lamb of God bearing the sin of man. But we, who know by experience the preciousness of this truth, will proclaim it confidently and unceasingly in defiance of them. We will neither dilute it nor change it, nor fritter it away in any shape or fashion. It will still be Christ, a sure Substitute, who bears human guilt and suffering in the stead of men. We cannot or dare not give it up, for it is our life. Despite every controversy, we feel that *"nevertheless the foundation of God standeth sure."*

That those things which cannot be shaken may remain.
—Hebrews 12:27

Many things in our possession at the present moment can be shaken, and it ill becomes a Christian to set much store by them, for there is nothing stable under these rolling skies; change is written on all things. Yet we have certain *"things which cannot be shaken,"* and I invite you this evening to think about them. If the things that can be shaken would all be taken away, you may derive real comfort from the things that cannot be shaken, which will remain. Whatever your losses have been, or may be, you enjoy present salvation. You are standing at the foot of His cross, trusting alone in the merit of Jesus' precious blood. No rise or fall of the markets can interfere with your salvation in Him. No breaking of banks, no failures, no bankruptcies can touch that. You are a child of God this evening. God is your Father. No change of circumstances can ever rob you of that. Although by losses, you are brought to poverty and stripped bare, you can say, "He is my Father still. In my Father's house are many mansions; therefore, I will not be troubled." You have another permanent blessing, namely, the love of Jesus Christ. He who is God and Man loves you with all the strength of His affectionate nature—nothing can affect that. The fig tree may not blossom, and the flocks may *"be cut off from the fold"* (Hab. 3:17). These things do not matter to the one who can sing, *"My beloved is mine, and I am his"* (Song 2:16). We cannot lose our best portion and richest heritage. Whatever troubles come, let us act like adults. Let us show that we are not such little children as to be cast down by what may happen in this poor, fleeting state of time. Our country is Immanuel's land, and our hope is above the sky; therefore, calm as the summer's ocean, we will see the wreck of everything earthborn, yet rejoice in the God of our salvation.

Waiting for the adoption.
—Romans 8:23

Even in this world, saints are God's children, but people cannot recognize them to be so unless they observe certain moral characteristics in them. The adoption is not manifested, and the children are not yet openly declared. Among the Romans a man might adopt a child and keep the matter private for a long time, but there was a second adoption that took place in public. Then the child was brought before the constituted authorities, and his former garments were removed. The father who was adopting the child gave him clothing suitable to the child's new station in life. *"Beloved, now are we the sons of God, and it doth not yet appear what we shall be"* (1 John 3:2). We are not yet arrayed in the apparel that befits the royal family of heaven. We are wearing in this flesh and blood just what we wore as the sons of Adam. But we know that when the *"firstborn among many brethren"* (Rom. 8:29) appears, *"we shall be like him; for we shall see him as he is"* (1 John 3:2). Can you not imagine that a child taken from the lowest ranks of society and adopted by a Roman senator would say to himself, "I long for the day when I will be publicly adopted. Then I will remove these coarse, plebeian garments and be robed as becomes my senatorial rank"? Because he is happy in what he has received, for that very reason, he longs to get the fullness of what is promised to him. So it is with us today. We are waiting until we will put on our proper garments and will be manifested as the children of God. We are young nobles and have not yet worn our crowns. We are young brides, and the marriage day has not yet come. But because of the love our Spouse shows us, we are led to long and sigh for the bridal morning. Our very happiness makes us long for more; our joy, like a swollen spring, wants to well up like a geyser, leaping to the skies, and it heaves and groans within our spirits for lack of space and room by which to manifest itself to men.

Shadrach, Meshach, and Abednego, answered and said…, Be it known unto thee, O king, that we will not serve thy gods.
—Daniel 3:16, 18

The story of the bold courage and marvelous deliverance of the three Hebrew children, or rather champions, well illustrates firmness and steadfastness in upholding the truth while facing the teeth of tyranny and the very jaws of death. It motivates believers to imitate their example. Let young Christians especially learn, both in matters of faith in religion and matters of uprightness in business, never to sacrifice their consciences. Lose all rather than to lose your integrity, and when all else is gone, still hold fast to a clear conscience as the rarest jewel that can adorn the human heart. Do not be guided by a will-o'-the-wisp kind of policy, but by the North Star of divine authority. Follow the right path at all costs. When you see no present advantage, *"walk by faith, not by sight"* (2 Cor. 5:7). Honor God by trusting Him even when it comes to matters of loss for the sake of principle. See whether He will be your debtor! See if He does not even in this life prove His Word that *"godliness with contentment is great gain"* (1 Tim. 6:6), and that those who seek *"first the kingdom of God, and his righteousness* [will have] *all these things…added unto* [them]*"* (Matt. 6:33). Should it happen that, in the providence of God, you suffer a loss by following your conscience, you will find that if the Lord does not pay you back in the silver of earthly prosperity, He will fulfill His promise in the gold of spiritual joy. Remember that a man's life does not consist *"in the abundance of the things which he possesseth"* (Luke 12:15). To wear a guileless spirit, to have a heart void of offense, and to have the favor and smile of God are greater riches than the mines of Ophir could yield or the business of Tyre could earn. *"Better is a dinner of herbs where love is, than a stalled ox and hatred therewith"* (Prov. 15:17). An ounce of heartsease is worth a ton of gold.

The dove found no rest for the sole of her foot.
—Genesis 8:9

eader, can you find rest apart from the ark, Christ Jesus? Then be assured that your religion is vain. Are you satisfied with anything short of a conscious knowledge of your union and interest in Christ? Then woe to you. If you profess to be a Christian, yet find full satisfaction in worldly pleasures and pursuits, your profession is false. If your soul can stretch itself, find the bed long enough, and the coverlet wide enough to cover it in the chambers of sin, then you are a hypocrite. You are far from any right thoughts of Christ or perception of His preciousness. On the other hand, if you could indulge in sin without receiving any punishment, but you feel that sin in itself would be a punishment; and if you could have the whole world and live in it forever, but you feel that would be true misery, for your God is what your soul craves; then be of good courage: you are a child of God. With all your sins and imperfections, let this thought comfort you: if your soul finds no rest in sin, you are not as the sinner is! If you are still crying for and craving after something better, Christ has not forgotten you, for you have not quite forgotten Him. The believer cannot do without his Lord. Words are inadequate to express his thoughts of Him. We cannot live on the sands of the wilderness. We need the manna that drops from on high. Our skin bottles of creature confidence cannot yield us a drop of moisture, but we drink of the Rock that follows us, and that Rock is Christ. (See 1 Corinthians 10:4.) When you feed on Him, your soul can sing, "He has satisfied my *'mouth with good things; so that* [my] *youth is renewed like the eagle's'"* (Ps. 103:5). But if you do not have Him, your bursting wine vat and well-filled barn can give you no sort of satisfaction. Instead, lament over them in the words of wisdom, *"Vanity of vanities; all is vanity"* (Eccl. 1:2).

Having escaped the corruption that is in the world through lust.
—2 Peter 1:4

Banish forever all thoughts of indulging the flesh if you want to live in the power of your risen Lord. It is immoral for a man who is alive in Christ to dwell in the corruption of sin. *"Why seek ye the living among the dead?"* (Luke 24:5), asked the angel of the women who came to Jesus' tomb. Should the living dwell in a tomb? Should divine life be buried in the mausoleum of fleshly lust? How can we partake of the cup of the Lord and yet drink from the cup of Satan? Surely, believer, you are delivered from open lusts and sins. Have you also escaped from the more secret and deceptive traps of the satanic fowler? Have you come forth from the lust of pride? Have you escaped from slothfulness? Have you made a clean break from carnal security? Are you seeking day by day to live above worldliness, the pride of life, and the ensnaring vice of greed? Remember, it is for this that you have been enriched with the treasures of God. If you are indeed the chosen of God and beloved by Him, do not permit all the lavish treasure of grace to be wasted on you. Follow after holiness; it is the Christian's crown and glory. An unholy church is useless to the world and has no esteem among men. It is an abomination; it is hell's laughter and heaven's abhorrence. The worst evils that have ever come upon the world have been brought by an unholy church. O Christian, the vows of God are upon you. You are God's priest: act as such. You are God's king: reign over your lusts. You are God's chosen: do not associate with the devil. Heaven is your portion: live like a heavenly spirit, and you will prove that you have true faith in Jesus. There cannot be faith in the heart unless there is holiness in the life.

> Lord, I desire to live as one
> Who bears a blood-bought name,
> As one who fears but grieving Thee,
> And knows no other shame.

Let every man abide in the same calling wherein he was called.
—1 Corinthians 7:20

ome people have the foolish notion that the only way they can live for God is by becoming ministers, missionaries, or Bible teachers. Think of how many would be shut out from any opportunity of magnifying the Most High if this were the case! Beloved, it is not your calling; it is earnestness. It is not your position; it is grace that will enable us to glorify God. God is most surely glorified in that cobbler's stall, where the godly worker, as he plies the awl, sings of the Savior's love. He is glorified far more there than in many churches where official religiousness performs its scanty duties. The name of Jesus is glorified by the poor, unlearned peddler, as he drives his horse and blesses his God or speaks to his fellow laborer by the roadside, as much as by the popular clergyman who, throughout the country, like Boanerges, is thundering out the Gospel. God is glorified by our serving Him in our proper vocations. Take care, dear reader, that you do not forsake the path of duty by leaving your occupation, and take care that you do not dishonor your profession while in it. Think little of yourselves, but do not think too little of your calling. Every lawful trade may be sanctified by the Gospel to the noblest ends. Turn to the Bible, and you will find the most menial forms of labor connected either with the most daring deeds of faith or with persons whose lives have been illustrious for holiness. Therefore, do not be discontented with your calling. Whatever God has made your position or your work, abide in that, unless you are quite sure that He calls you to something else. Let your first care be to glorify God to the utmost of your power where you are. Fill your present sphere to His praise, and if He needs you in another place, He will show it to you. This evening, lay aside distressing ambition, and embrace peaceful contentment.

But Aaron's rod swallowed up their rods.
—Exodus 7:12

This incident is an instructive example of the sure victory of the divine handiwork over all opposition. Whenever a divine principle is cast into the heart, though the devil may fashion a counterfeit and produce swarms of opponents, as surely as God is in the work, it will swallow up all its foes. If God's grace takes possession of a man, the world's magicians may throw down all their rods. Every rod may be as cunning and poisonous as a serpent, but Aaron's rod will swallow up their rods. The sweet attractions of the Cross will woo and win the man's heart, and he who once lived only for this deceitful earth will now have an eye for the upper spheres and a wing to mount into heavenly heights. When grace has won the day, the person who once was concerned only with earthly matters now seeks the world to come. The same fact is to be observed in the life of the believer. What a host of foes our faith has had to meet! Our old sins—the devil threw them down before us, and they turned to serpents. What a great number of sins there were! But the Cross of Jesus destroys them all. Faith in Christ makes short work of all our sins. Then the devil has launched forth another host of serpents in the form of worldly trials, temptations, and unbelief; but faith in Jesus is more than a match for them and overcomes them all. The same absorbing principle shines in the faithful service of God! When one has an enthusiastic love for Jesus, his difficulties are surmounted, his sacrifices become pleasures, and his sufferings are honors. But if religion is thus a consuming passion in the heart, it follows that there are many persons who profess religion but do not have it; for what they have will not bear this test. Examine yourself, dear reader, on this point. Aaron's rod proved its heaven-given power. Is your religion doing so? If Christ is anything, He must be everything. Do not rest until love and faith in Jesus are the master passions of your soul!

Howbeit in the business of the ambassadors of the princes of Babylon,
who sent unto him to inquire of the wonder that was done in the
land, God left him, to try him, that he might know
all that was in his heart.
—2 Chronicles 32:31

ezekiah was growing so inwardly great and priding himself so much on the favor of God that self-righteousness crept in. Because of his carnal security, the grace of God was, in its more active operations, withdrawn for a time. This explains his difficulties with the Babylonians; for if the grace of God would leave the best Christian, there is enough of sin in his heart to make him the worst of transgressors. If left to yourselves, you who are warmest for Christ would cool down like Laodicea into sickening lukewarmness. (See Revelation 3:16.) You who are sound in the faith would be white with the leprosy of false doctrine. You who now walk before the Lord in excellency and integrity would reel to and fro and stagger with a drunkenness of evil passion. Like the moon, we borrow our light; bright as we are when grace shines on us, we are darkness itself when the Sun of Righteousness withdraws Himself. Therefore, let us cry to God never to leave us. Lord, do not take Your Holy Spirit from us! Do not withdraw Your indwelling grace! Have You not said, *"I the LORD do keep it; I will water it every moment: lest any hurt it, I will keep it night and day"* (Isa. 27:3)? Lord, keep us everywhere. Keep us when we are in the valley, so that we will not complain about Your humbling hand. Keep us when we are on the mountain, so that we will not become dizzy from being lifted up. Keep us in our youth, when our passions are strong; keep us in our old age, when becoming conceited by our wisdom, we might prove greater fools than the young and foolish. Keep us when we come to die, lest, at the very end, we would deny You! Keep us living, keep us dying, keep us laboring, keep us suffering, keep us fighting, keep us resting, keep us everywhere, for everywhere we need You, O our God!

*Ah Lord GOD! behold, thou hast made the heaven and the earth
by thy great power and stretched out arm, and there is
nothing too hard for thee.*
—Jeremiah 32:17

t the very time when the Chaldeans surrounded Jerusalem, when the sword, famine, and pestilence had desolated the land, Jeremiah was commanded by God to purchase a field and have the deed of transfer legally sealed and witnessed. This was a strange purchase for a rational man to make. Prudence could not justify it, for there was scarcely a chance that Jeremiah could ever enjoy the possession. But it was enough for Jeremiah that his God had commanded him, for he knew well that God will be justified by all His children. He reasoned in this manner: "Lord God, You can make this plot of ground of use to me. You can rid this land of these oppressors. You can make me sit under my vine and my fig tree on the property that I have bought, for You made the heavens and the earth. There is nothing too hard for You." This gave a majesty to the early saints, for they dared to do at God's command things that human reason would condemn. Whether it was Noah who built a ship on dry land; Abraham who offered up his only son; Moses who despised the treasures of Egypt; or Joshua who besieged Jericho in seven days, using no weapons except for the blasts of rams' horns—they all acted on God's command, contrary to the dictates of earthly reason. And the Lord gave them a rich reward as the result of their obedient faith. Would to God that we had in the religion of these modern times a more potent infusion of this heroic faith in God! If we would venture more on the revealed promises of God, we would enter a world of miracles to which as yet we are strangers. Let Jeremiah's place of confidence be ours. Nothing is too hard for the God who created the heavens and the earth!

*They heard the voice of the LORD God
walking in the garden in the cool of the day.*
—Genesis 3:8

My soul, now that the *"cool of the day"* has come, go to a quiet place and listen to the voice of your God. He is always ready to speak with you when you are prepared to hear. If you find that communion with God is slow in coming, the problem is not on His part but altogether on your own. For He stands at the door and knocks, and if His people will only open to Him, He will rejoice to enter. Yet in what state is my heart, which is my Lord's garden? May I venture to hope that it is well trimmed and watered and is bringing forth fruit fit for Him? If not, He will have much about which to reprove me. Yet I still ask Him to come to me, for nothing can so certainly bring my heart into a right condition as the presence of the Sun of Righteousness, who brings *"healing in his wings"* (Mal. 4:2). Come, therefore, O Lord my God; my soul invites You earnestly and waits for You eagerly. Come to me, O Jesus, my Well Beloved, and plant fresh flowers in my garden, such as I see blooming in perfection in Your matchless character. Come, O my Father. You are the Husbandman; deal with me in Your tenderness and prudence. Come, O Holy Spirit, and let Your dew fall on my whole nature, as the herbs are now moistened with the evening dews. Oh, that God would speak to me! *"Speak, LORD; for thy servant heareth"* (1 Sam. 3:9). Oh, that He would walk with me! I am ready to give up my whole heart and mind to Him, and every other thought is hushed. I only ask what He delights to give. I am sure that He will, in His grace, have fellowship with me, for He has given me His Holy Spirit to be with me forever. Sweet is the cool twilight, when every star seems like the eye of heaven and the cool wind is as the breath of divine love. My Father, my Elder Brother, my sweet Comforter, speak now in lovingkindness, for You have *"opened mine ear, and I* [am] *not rebellious"* (Isa. 50:5).

Unto thee will I cry, O LORD my rock; be not silent to me: lest, if thou be silent to me, I become like them that go down into the pit.
—Psalm 28:1

A cry is a natural expression of sorrow and a suitable utterance when all other modes of appeal fail us; but the cry must be directed to the Lord alone, for to cry to man is to waste our entreaties on the air. When we consider the readiness of the Lord to hear, and His ability to aid, we will see good reason for directing all our appeals immediately to the God of our salvation. It will be useless to call to the rocks to *"fall on us, and hide us"* (Rev. 6:16) in the Day of Judgment; but our Rock attends to our cries. *"Be not silent to me."* Those who go through merely the motions of prayer may be content without answers to their prayers, but genuine suppliants cannot be. They are not satisfied with the ability of prayer to calm the mind and subdue the will; they must go further and obtain actual replies from heaven, or they cannot rest. They long to receive those replies at once; they dread even a little of God's silence. God's voice is often so terrible that it shakes the wilderness, but His silence is equally terrible to an eager suppliant. When God seems to close His ear, we must not close our mouths. Instead, we must cry with more earnestness. For when our note grows shrill with eagerness and grief, He will not deny us a hearing for long. What a dreadful situation we would be in if the Lord were to become forever silent to our prayers! *"Lest, if thou be silent to me, I become like them that go down into the pit."* Deprived of the God who answers prayer, we would be in a more pitiable plight than the dead in their graves and would soon sink to the same level as the lost in hell. We *must* have answers to prayer. Ours is an urgent case of dire necessity. Surely the Lord will speak peace to our agitated minds, for He never can find it in His heart to permit His own elect to perish.

If we suffer [with Christ], *we shall also reign with him.*
—2 Timothy 2:12

e must not imagine that we are suffering for Christ and with Christ, if we are not in Christ. Beloved friend, are you trusting in Jesus alone? If not, no matter what you may have to mourn over on earth, you are not suffering with Christ. Such suffering offers no hope of reigning with Him in heaven. Neither are we to conclude that all of a Christian's sufferings are sufferings with Christ; to suffer with Christ, the Christian must be called by God to suffer. If we are rash and imprudent, and then run into situations for which neither providence nor grace has prepared us, we ought to consider whether we are sinning rather than communing with Jesus. If we let passion take the place of judgment and allow self-will to reign instead of scriptural authority, we are attempting to fight the Lord's battles with the devil's weapons. If we are injured in the fight, we must not be surprised. Again, when troubles come upon us as a result of sin, we must not imagine that we are suffering with Christ. When Miriam spoke evil of Moses, and the leprosy defiled her, she was not suffering for God. Moreover, suffering that God accepts must have God's glory as its purpose. If I suffer in order to make a name for myself or to win applause, I will receive no other reward than that of the hypocritical Pharisee. It is essential that love for Jesus and love for His elect always be the chief motive for all our patience. We must manifest the Spirit of Christ in meekness, gentleness, and forgiveness. Let us search our hearts to see if we truly suffer with Jesus. If we do thus suffer, what is *"our light affliction"* (2 Cor. 4:17) compared with reigning with Him? Oh, it is very blessed to be in the furnace of affliction with Christ, and it is such an honor to stand in the face of scorn and ridicule with Him. If there were no future reward, we might consider ourselves happy in this present honor. Yet when the reward is so eternal, so infinitely more than we had any right to expect, will we not take up the cross with zeal and go on our way rejoicing?

He that hath clean hands, and a pure heart; who hath not lifted up his soul unto vanity, nor sworn deceitfully.
—Psalm 24:4

Outward practical holiness is a very precious evidence of grace. It is to be feared that many who profess Christ have perverted the doctrine of justification by faith in such a way as to treat good works with contempt. Such people will receive everlasting contempt on the Last Great Day. If our hands are not clean, let us wash them in Jesus' precious blood, so that we may lift up pure hands to God. *"Clean hands"* will not suffice unless they are connected with *"a pure heart."* True religion is a work of the heart. We may wash the outside of the cup and the plate as long as we please. However, if the inward parts are filthy, we are filthy altogether in the sight of God, for our hearts are more truly ourselves than are our hands. The very life of our being lies in the inner nature, and that is why we have an imperative need for inward purity. It is the pure in heart who will see God; all others are but blind bats. The man who is born for heaven *"hath not lifted up his soul unto vanity."* All men have their joys by which their souls are lifted up. The worldly person lifts up his soul to carnal delights, which are mere empty vanities. However, the believer loves more substantial things. Like Jehoshaphat, he is lifted up in the ways of the Lord. He who is content with husks will be counted among the swine. Does the world satisfy you? Then you have your reward and portion in this life; make much of it, for you will know no other joy. *"Nor sworn deceitfully."* Believers in Christ are people of honor still. The Christian's word is his only oath; however, it is as good as the oaths of twenty others. False speaking will shut anyone out of heaven, for a liar will not enter into God's house, no matter what his profession of faith or deeds may be. Reader, does today's text condemn you, or do you hope to *"ascend into the hill of the LORD"* (Ps. 24:3)?

Trust ye in the LORD for ever: for in the LORD JEHOVAH
is everlasting strength.
—Isaiah 26:4

Since we have such a God on whom to rely, let us rest on Him with all our weight. Let us resolutely drive out all unbelief and endeavor to get rid of doubts and fears, which disturb our comfort so much. There is no excuse for fear when God is the foundation of our trust. A loving parent would be extremely grieved if his child could not trust him. How ungenerous and unkind is our conduct when we put so little confidence in our heavenly Father, who has never failed us and never will. It would be a good thing if doubting were banished from the household of God. However, it is to be feared that old Unbelief is as nimble nowadays as when the psalmist asked, *"Is his mercy clean gone for ever? doth his promise fail for evermore?"* (Ps. 77:8). David had not spent much time experimenting with the mighty sword of the giant Goliath, yet he said, "There is none like it." (See 1 Samuel 21:9.) He had tested it once in the hour of his youthful victory, and it had proven itself to be of the right metal; therefore, he praised it from that time forward. In the same way, we should speak well of our God, for there is no one like Him in heaven or on earth. *"To whom then will ye liken me, or shall I be equal? saith the Holy One"* (Isa. 40:25). There is no rock like the rock of Jacob, as our enemies themselves will affirm. Instead of allowing doubts to live in our hearts, let us take the whole detestable crew, as Elijah did the prophets of Baal, and slay them at the brook (1 Kings 18:40). Let us kill them at the sacred stream that wells forth from our Savior's wounded side. We have been in many trials, but we have never yet been in a place where we could not find in our God all that we needed. Let us, then, be encouraged to *"trust...in the LORD for ever,"* assured that His *"everlasting strength"* will be, as it has been, our help and support.

How many are mine iniquities and sins?
—Job 13:23

Have you ever really weighed and considered how great the sin of God's people is? Think how heinous your own sin is, and you will find that not only does a sin here and there tower up like a high, rugged mountain, but also your iniquities heap upon each other, as in the old Greek myth of the giants who piled Mount Pelion upon Mount Ossa, mountain upon mountain. What an accumulation of sin there is in the life of one of the most sanctified of God's children! If you were to try to multiply the sin of only one person by the multitude of the redeemed, *"which no man could number"* (Rev. 7:9), you would have some idea of the great mass of the guilt of the people for whom Jesus shed His blood. However, we can arrive at a more adequate idea of the magnitude of sin by considering the greatness of the remedy provided for it: the blood of Jesus Christ, God's only and well-beloved Son. God's Son! Angels cast their crowns before Him. All the choral symphonies of heaven surround His glorious throne; He is *"over all, God blessed forever. Amen"* (Rom. 9:5). Yet He took on Himself the form of a servant and was scourged and pierced, bruised and torn, and finally slain, since nothing but the blood of the incarnate Son of God could make atonement for our offenses. No human mind can adequately estimate the infinite value of the divine sacrifice. For as great as is the sin of God's people, the Atonement, which takes it away, is immeasurably greater. Therefore, even when sin swells like a black flood and the remembrance of the past is bitter, the believer can still stand before the blazing throne of the great and holy God and cry, *"Who is he that condemneth? It is Christ that died, yea rather, that is risen again"* (Rom. 8:34). While the recollection of his sin fills him with shame and sorrow, at the same time, he uses it to reveal the brightness of God's mercy. Guilt is the dark night in which the fair star of divine love shines with serene splendor.

When I passed by thee,…I said unto thee…, Live.
—Ezekiel 16:6

aved one, consider gratefully this command of mercy in our text. Note first that this command of God is majestic. We perceive a sinner with nothing in him but sin, and expecting nothing but wrath. However, the eternal Lord passes by in His glory. He looks, He pauses, and He pronounces the solitary but royal word, *"Live."* There speaks a God. Who but He could thus venture to deal with life and dispense it with a single syllable? Second, this command is manifold. When He says, *"Live,"* His command includes many things. It is judicial life. The sinner is ready to be condemned, but the mighty One says, *"Live,"* and so he rises pardoned and absolved. It is spiritual life. Before we knew Jesus, our eyes could not see Him, and our ears could not hear His voice. Yet Jehovah said, *"Live,"* and we were *"quickened, who were dead in trespasses and sins"* (Eph. 2:1). Moreover, it is glory life, which is the perfection of spiritual life. *"I said unto thee…, Live."* This last word rolls on through all the years of time until death comes, and in the midst of the shadows of death, the Lord's voice is still heard: *"Live."* On the morning of the resurrection to life, this same word will be echoed by the archangel: *"Live."* As holy spirits rise to heaven to be blessed forever in the glory of their God, it will be in the power of this very word, *"Live."* Third, it is an irresistible command. Saul of Tarsus was on the road to Damascus to arrest the children of the living God. He heard a voice from heaven and saw a light brighter than the sun, and he cried out, *"Lord, what wilt thou have me to do?"* (Acts 9:6). Fourth, it is a command of free grace. When sinners are saved, God saves them solely to glorify His free, unpurchased, unsought grace. Christians, recognize your position: you are debtors to grace. Since God has commanded you to live, show your gratitude by living earnest, Christlike lives.

*Lead me in thy truth, and teach me: for thou art the God
of my salvation; on thee do I wait all the day.*
—Psalm 25:5

hen the believer has begun with trembling feet to walk in the way of the Lord, he still asks to be led onward like a little child upheld by his parent's helping hand, and he craves to be further instructed in the alphabet of truth. Experiential instruction is the refrain of David's prayer in Psalm 25:4–5. David knew much, but he felt his ignorance and still desired to be in the Lord's school. Four times in these two verses he applied for a scholarship in the college of grace. It would be a good thing if believers would inquire into the good old ways of God's truth and earnestly ask the Holy Spirit to give them sancti-fied understanding and teachable spirits, instead of follow-ing their own devices and cutting out new paths of thought for themselves. *"For thou art the God of my salvation."* The triune Jehovah is the Author and Perfecter of salvation for His people. Is He the God of your salvation? Do you find in the Father's election, in the Son's atonement, and in the Spirit's quickening, all the grounds of your eternal hopes? If so, you may use these means of grace as the basis for ob-taining further blessings. If the Lord has ordained to save you, surely He will not refuse to instruct you in His ways. It is a happy thing when we can address the Lord with the confidence that David manifested in our text; it gives us great power in prayer and comfort in trial. *"On thee do I wait all the day."* Patience is the fair handmaiden and daugh-ter of faith; we cheerfully wait when we are certain that we will not wait in vain. It is our duty and privilege to wait on the Lord in service, in worship, in expectancy, and in trust all the days of our lives. Our faith will be tried faith; and if it is true faith, it will bear continued trial without yielding. We will not grow weary of waiting on God if we will remember how long and how graciously He once waited for us.

And God divided the light from the darkness.
—Genesis 1:4

A believer has two principles at work within him. In his natural state, he was subject to one principle alone, which was darkness. However, now light has entered, and the two principles are in disagreement. Note the apostle Paul's words in the seventh chapter of Romans: *"I find then a law, that, when I would do good, evil is present with me. For I delight in the law of God after the inward man: but I see another law in my members, warring against the law of my mind, and bringing me into captivity to the law of sin which is in my members"* (vv. 21–23). How is this state of things brought about? *"God divided the light from the darkness."* Darkness, by itself, is quiet and undisturbed; however, when the Lord sends in light, there is conflict, for the one is in opposition to the other. This conflict will not cease until the believer is altogether light in the Lord. Since there is this division within the individual Christian, there is certain to be division outside of him, as well. As soon as the Lord gives light to anyone, he proceeds to separate himself from the darkness around him. He withdraws from a merely worldly religion of outward ceremony, for nothing short of the Gospel of Christ will now satisfy him. He withdraws from those who are worldly and from frivolous amusements, and he seeks the company of believers, for *"we know that we have passed from death unto life, because we love the brethren"* (1 John 3:14). The light gathers light to itself, and the darkness gathers darkness to itself. What God has divided, let us never try to unite. As Christ went *"without the camp, bearing his reproach"* (Heb. 13:13), let us come out from among the ungodly and be God's own people. Christ was *"holy, harmless, undefiled, separate from sinners"* (Heb. 7:26). As He was, so are we to be—nonconformists to the world, dissenting from all sin, and distinguished from the rest of mankind by our likeness to our Master.

And the evening and the morning were the first day.
—Genesis 1:5

he evening was *"darkness"* (Gen. 1:5) and the morning was *"light"* (v. 5). Yet the two together are called by the name that is given to the light alone—*"day."* This is rather remarkable, but it has an exact analogy in spiritual experience. There is darkness and light in every believer, yet the believer is not to be called a "sinner," even though there is sin in him. He is to be called a "saint," because he possesses some degree of holiness. This should be a very comforting thought to those who are mourning over their weaknesses, and who ask, "Can I be a child of God while there is so much darkness in me?" Yes, you can; for you, like the day, take your name not from the evening, but from the morning. You are spoken of in the Word of God as if you are even now perfectly holy, as you will be soon. You are called a child of light, even though there is still darkness in you. You are named after what is the predominate quality in the sight of God, which will one day be the only principle remaining in you. Observe that the evening comes first. Naturally, in the order of time, we are darkness first, and the gloom is often first in our mournful understanding, driving us to cry out in deep humiliation, *"God be merciful to me a sinner"* (Luke 18:13). The place of the morning is second; it dawns when grace overcomes nature. John Bunyan's saying, "That which is last, lasts forever," is a blessed adage. What is first yields in due season to what is last, but nothing comes after what is last. Therefore, although you are naturally darkness, when you become light in the Lord, no evening will follow. *"Thy sun shall no more go down"* (Isa. 60:20). The first day in this earthly life was an evening and a morning; but the second day, when we will be with God forever, will be a day with no evening. It will be one, sacred, high, eternal noon.

*Tell ye your children of it, and let your children tell their children,
and their children another generation.*
—Joel 1:3

In this simple way, by God's grace, a living testimony for truth is always to be kept alive in the land—the beloved of the Lord are to hand down their witness for the Gospel and the covenant to their heirs; these, in turn, are to hand it down to their descendants. This is our first duty. We are to begin with the family. He who does not begin his ministry at home is a bad preacher. The unsaved are to be sought by all means, and the *"highways and hedges"* (Luke 14:23) are to be searched, but home has a prior claim. Woe to those who reverse the order of the Lord's arrangement. Teaching our children God's ways is a personal duty; we cannot delegate it to Sunday school teachers or other friendly helpers. They can assist us, but they cannot deliver us from our sacred obligation; proxies and sponsors are wicked instruments under these conditions. Mothers and fathers must, like Abraham, instruct their households in the fear of God and talk with their offspring concerning the wondrous works of the Most High. Parental teaching is a natural duty. Who are best able to look to a child's well-being as those who are the authors of his physical being? To neglect the instruction of our offspring is worse than foolish. Family religion is necessary for the family itself, for the nation, and for the church of God. One of the most effective means of preventing unbelief and doctrinal error is the instruction of children in the faith. However, this means is all but being neglected. Parents must realize the importance of this matter. It is a pleasant duty to talk to our sons and daughters about Jesus, and even more so because it has often proven to be an accepted work. God has saved children through their parents' prayers and admonitions. May every house into which this book comes honor the Lord and receive His smile of approval.

His heavenly kingdom.
—2 Timothy 4:18

The city of the great King—heaven—is a place of active service. Redeemed spirits serve Him day and night in His temple. They never cease to fulfill the good pleasure of their King. They always rest, as far as ease and freedom from care are concerned, and they never rest, in the sense of laziness or inactivity. Jerusalem the Golden is the place of communion with all the people of God. We will sit in eternal fellowship with Abraham, Isaac, and Jacob. We will have exalted conversation with the noble host of the elect, all of whom are reigning with Him who by His love and powerful arm has brought them safely home. We will not sing solos but will praise our King in chorus. Heaven is a place of realized victory. Christian, whenever you have achieved a victory over your lusts—whenever, after hard struggling, you have laid a temptation dead at your feet—you have had in that hour a foretaste of the joy that awaits you. The Lord will shortly tread Satan under your feet, and you will find yourself more than a conqueror through Him who loved you (Rom. 8:37). Paradise is a place of security. When you enjoy the *"full assurance of faith"* (Heb. 10:22), you have the pledge of that glorious security that will be yours when you are a perfect citizen of the heavenly Jerusalem. O my sweet home, Jerusalem, happy harbor of my soul! Thanks, even now, to Him whose love has taught me to long for you; but louder thanks in eternity, when I will possess you.

> My soul has tasted of the grapes
> And now it longs to go
> Where my dear Lord His vineyard keeps
> And all the clusters grow.
>
> Upon the true and living vine,
> My famish'd soul would feast,
> And banquet on the fruit divine,
> An everlasting guest.

When I cry unto thee, then shall mine enemies turn back:
this I know; for God is for me.
—Psalm 56:9

It is impossible for any human words to express the full meaning of this delightful statement, *"God is for me."* He was for us before the universe was made. He was for us when He gave His well-beloved Son for us. He was for us when He struck the Only Begotten and laid the full weight of His wrath on Him; He was for us—though He was "against" Him. He was for us when we were ruined in the Fall; He loved us despite all. He was for us when we were rebels, defying Him with clenched fists. He was for us when He led us to humbly seek His face. He has been for us in many struggles; we have been summoned to encounter a multitude of dangers, and we have been assailed by internal and external temptations. How could we have remained unharmed to this hour if He had not been for us? He is for us with the infinity of His being, the omnipotence of His love, and the infallibility of His wisdom. He is for us, arrayed in all His divine attributes. He is eternally and unchangeably for us. He will be for us when the blue skies are rolled up like a worn-out garment; He will be for us throughout eternity. Because He is for us, our prayers will always secure His help. *"When I cry unto thee, then shall mine enemies turn back."* This is not an uncertain hope, but a well-grounded assurance: *"this I know."* I will direct my prayer to God and will look to Him for the answer, assured that it will come and that my enemies will be defeated, *"for God is for me."* O believer, how happy you are with the King of Kings on your side! How safe you are with such a Protector! How sure is your cause, when it is pleaded by such an Advocate! *"If God be for us, who can be against us?"* (Rom. 8:31).

As it began to dawn…, came Mary Magdalene…to see the sepulchre.
—Matthew 28:1

Let us learn from Mary Magdalene how to obtain fellowship with the Lord Jesus. Notice how she sought Him. She sought the Savior very early in the morning. If you cannot wait for Christ and be patient in the hope of having fellowship with Him at some later time, you will never have fellowship at all; for the heart that is prepared for communion is a hungering and thirsting heart. She sought Him also with very great boldness. Other disciples fled from the sepulchre, *"for they trembled and were amazed"* (Mark 16:8); but Mary, it is said, *"stood"* (John 20:11) at the sepulchre. If you want to have Christ with you, seek Him boldly. Let nothing hold you back. Defy the world. Press on when others flee. Mary also sought Christ faithfully: she stood *"at the sepulchre"* (v. 11). Some find it hard to stand by a living Savior, but she stood by a dead one. Let us seek Christ as she did, cleaving to the very least thing that has to do with Him, remaining faithful even though all others might forsake Him. Note further that she sought Jesus earnestly: she stood *"weeping"* (v. 11). Her tears moved the Savior and made Him come forth and show Himself to her. If you desire Jesus' presence, weep for it! If you cannot be happy unless He comes and says to you, "You are My beloved," you will soon hear His voice. Last, she sought *only* the Savior. What did she care about angels? She turned away from them; her search was only for her Lord. If Christ is your one and only love, if your heart has cast out all rivals, you will not lack the comfort of His presence for long. Mary Magdalene sought Jesus in these ways because *"she loved much"* (Luke 7:47). Let us rouse ourselves to the same intensity of affection. If our hearts, like Mary's, are full of Christ, then our love, like hers, will be satisfied with nothing short of Himself. O Lord, reveal Yourself to us this evening!

He appeared first to Mary Magdalene.
—Mark 16:9

esus probably *"appeared first to Mary Magdalene"* not only because of her great love and persevering seeking, but also because she had been a special example of Christ's delivering power. We can learn from Mary's experience that the greatness of our sin before conversion should not make us think that we cannot be especially favored with the very highest degree of fellowship with the Lord. Mary had left everything else to continually tend to the Savior's needs. He was her first and chief object. Many who were on Christ's side did not take up Christ's cross; she did. She spent her substance on meeting His needs. If we want to see much of Christ, let us serve Him. Who are they who sit most often under the banner of His love and drink most deeply from the cup of communion? I am sure that they are those who give most, serve best, and remain closest to the bleeding heart of their dear Lord. But notice *how* Christ revealed Himself to this sorrowing one. It was by a word: *"Mary"* (John 20:16). Mary needed only one word, spoken in Christ's voice, for her to recognize Him at once. Her heart acknowledged allegiance by another word, for it was too full to say anything else. That one word would naturally be the most fitting for the occasion. It implied obedience. She said, *"Master"* (v. 16). There is no state of mind in which this confession of allegiance will be too cold. No, when your spirit glows most with heavenly fire, then you will say, *"I am thy servant....Thou hast loosed my bonds"* (Ps. 116:16). If you can say, "Master," if you feel that His will is your will, then you are standing in a happy, holy place. If He had not said, *"Mary,"* she could not have said, *"Rabboni"* (John 20:16). See, then, from all this, how Christ honors those who honor Him, how love draws our Beloved, how just one word of His will turn our weeping to rejoicing, how His presence brings sunshine to our hearts.

Thou shalt arise, and have mercy upon Zion: for the time to favour her, yea, the set time, is come. For thy servants take pleasure in her stones, and favour the dust thereof.
—Psalm 102:13–14

A selfish man in trouble is exceedingly hard to comfort, because the springs of his comfort lie entirely within himself; when he is sad, all his springs are dry. But a Christian who is full of love and generosity has other springs from which to supply himself with comfort besides those that lie within. First, he can go to God and find abundant help there; he can discover reasons for comfort in things relating to the world at large, to his country, and, above all, to the church. David was exceedingly sorrowful in the psalm from which our text comes. He wrote, *"I am like an owl of the desert. I watch, and am as a sparrow alone upon the house top"* (Ps. 102:6–7). His only comfort was in the thought that God would *"arise, and have mercy upon Zion."* Even though David was sad, Zion would prosper. No matter how low his own condition was, Zion would arise. Christian, learn to comfort yourself in God's gracious dealings toward the church. Should not what is so dear to your Master also be dear above all else to you? Even though your way may be dark, can you not encourage your heart with the triumphs of His Cross and the advancement of His truth? Our own personal troubles will be forgotten when we look not only at what God has done and is doing for Zion, but also on the glorious things He will do for His church. Believer, try this prescription whenever you are sad of heart and heavy in spirit: forget yourself and your little concerns, and seek the welfare and prosperity of Zion. When you bend your knee in prayer to God, do not limit your petition to the narrow circle of your own life, tried though it might be. Send out earnest prayers for the church's prosperity. *"Pray for the peace of Jerusalem"* (Ps. 122:6), and your own soul will be refreshed.

Let not one of them escape.
—1 Kings 18:40

When the prophet Elijah had received the answer to his prayer, and the fire from heaven had consumed the sacrifice in the presence of all the people, he called on the assembled Israelites to seize the priests of Baal. Then he sternly cried, *"Let not one of them escape."* He took them all down to the brook Kishon and slew them there. We must do the same with our sins. They are all doomed; not one must be preserved. Your favorite sin must die. Do not spare it, even though it cries and begs. Strike it down, even though it is as dear to you as Isaac was to Abraham. Strike, for God struck at sin when it was laid on His own Son. With stern, unflinching purpose, you must condemn to death the sin that was once the idol of your heart. Do you ask how you are to accomplish this? Jesus will be your power. Grace to overcome sin was given to you in the covenant of grace. You have strength to win the victory in the crusade against inward lusts, because Christ Jesus has promised to be with you *"even unto the end"* (Matt. 28:20). If you want to triumph over darkness, place yourself in the presence of the Sun of Righteousness. No place is as well suited for the discovery of sin and recovery from its power and guilt as the immediate presence of God. Job didn't know how to get rid of sin half as well as he did when the eyes of his faith rested on God. Then he abhorred himself and repented *"in dust and ashes"* (Job 42:6). The fine gold of the Christian often becomes dim. We need the sacred fire to consume the dross. Let us run to our God. He is a consuming fire, but He will not consume our spirits, only our sins. Let the goodness of God move us to a sacred jealousy and a holy revenge against our iniquities, which are hateful in His sight. Go forth to battle in His strength, and utterly destroy the accursed crew of sins—*"let not one of them escape."*

Neither shall one thrust another; they shall walk
every one in his path.
—Joel 2:8

Locusts always keep their ranks. Although their number is legion, they do not crowd each other, throwing their columns into confusion. This remarkable fact of nature shows how thoroughly the Lord has infused the spirit of order into His universe. The smallest animate creatures are as much controlled by it as are the revolving planets or the angelic messengers. It would be wise for believers to be ruled by the same influence in their spiritual lives. First, regarding Christian graces, no one virtue should usurp the sphere of another or drain the lifeblood of the rest for its own support. Affection must not smother honesty, courage must not elbow meekness out of the field, modesty must not jostle energy, and patience must not slaughter resolution. Second, regarding our duties, one must not interfere with another; public usefulness must not injure private piety; church work must not push family worship into a corner. It is wrong to offer God one duty stained with the blood of another. Each thing is beautiful in its season, but not otherwise. It was to the Pharisee that Jesus said, *"These ought ye to have done, and not to leave the other undone"* (Matt. 23:23). Third, the same rule applies to our personal positions. We must take care to know our place, take it, and keep to it. We must minister as the Spirit has given us ability and not intrude on our fellow servant's domain. Our Lord Jesus taught us not to covet the high positions, but to be willing to be least among our brothers and sisters. May an envious, ambitious spirit be far from us. Let us feel the force of the Master's command and do as He instructs us, keeping rank with the rest of the host. Tonight, let us examine whether or not we are keeping the *"unity of the Spirit in the bond of peace"* (Eph. 4:3). Let our prayer be that, in all the churches of the Lord Jesus, peace and order may prevail.

A bruised reed shall he not break,
and smoking flax shall he not quench.
—Matthew 12:20

hat is weaker than a bruised reed or smoking flax? If a wild duck merely lands on a reed that grows in a swamp or marsh, the reed will snap. If someone's foot brushes against it, it will become bruised or broken. Every wind that flits across the river moves it back and forth. One can conceive of nothing more frail or brittle, or whose existence is more in jeopardy, than a bruised reed. Now consider smoking flax—what is it? It is true that it has a spark within it. However, it is almost smothered; an infant's breath might blow it out. Nothing has a more precarious existence than its flame. Weak things are being described in our text, yet Jesus says of them, "The smoking flax I will not quench; the bruised reed I will not break." Some of God's children have been made strong to do mighty works for Him. God has His Samsons here and there who can pull up Gaza's gates and carry them to the top of the hill. He has a few mighty believers who are lion-like, but the majority of His people are a timid, trembling race. They are like starlings, frightened at every passerby; they are a fearful little flock. If temptation comes, they are taken like birds in a snare; if trial threatens, they are ready to faint. Their frail little boat is tossed up and down by every wave; they drift along like a seabird on the crest of the billows. They are weak things, without strength, without wisdom, and without foresight. Yet, weak as they are, and *because* they are so weak, this promise is made especially to them. Herein is grace and graciousness! Herein is love and lovingkindness! How it reveals to us the compassion of Jesus—so gentle, tender, and considerate. We never need to shrink back from His touch. We never need to fear a harsh word from Him. Although He may well chide us for our weakness, He does not rebuke us. Bruised reeds will receive no blows from Him, and smoking flax will receive no quenching frowns.

And now what hast thou to do in the way of Egypt,
to drink the waters of Sihor?
—Jeremiah 2:18

By many miracles, mercies, and extraordinary deliverances, Jehovah had proved Himself worthy of Israel's trust. Yet they broke down the hedges with which God had enclosed them as a sacred garden; they forsook their own true and living God and followed after false gods. The Lord constantly reproved them for their unfaithfulness, and our text contains one instance of God's reasoning with them. "Why are you going to Egypt to drink the waters of the muddy river?" It may be translated, "Why do you wander afar and leave your own cool stream from Lebanon? Why do you forsake Jerusalem and turn aside to Noph and Tahpanhes? Why are you so strangely set on mischief that you cannot be content with the good and healthful but want to follow after what is evil and deceitful?" Is there not in our text a word of reproof and warning to the Christian? O true believer, called by grace and washed in the precious blood of Jesus, you have tasted better drink than the muddy river of this world's pleasures can give you. You have had fellowship with Christ; you have obtained the joy of seeing Jesus and leaning your head upon His chest. Do the novelties, the songs, the honors, and the merriment of this earth bring you contentment after you have experienced these things? After you have you eaten the bread of angels, can you live on husks? Good Rutherford once said, "I have tasted of Christ's own manna, and I have lost my taste for the brown bread of this world's joys." The same thing should be true of you. If you are wandering after the waters of Egypt, return quickly to the one living Fountain. The waters of Sihor may be sweet to the Egyptians, but they will prove only bitter to you. This evening, Jesus asks you, "What do you have to do with them?" What will you answer Him?

Why go I mourning?
—Psalm 42:9

Can you answer this question, believer? Can you find any reason why you are so often mourning instead of rejoicing? Why yield to gloomy apprehension? Who told you that the night would never end in day? Who told you that the sea of circumstances would ebb out until there was nothing left but long, muddy stretches of horrible poverty? Who told you that the "winter of your discontent" would proceed from frost to frost; from snow, ice, and hail to deeper snow and an even worse blizzard of despair? Do you not know that day follows night, that flood comes after ebb, that spring and summer follow winter? Then hope! Always hope, for God will not fail you. Do you not know that your God loves you in the midst of all your troubles? Mountains, when hidden in darkness, are as real as they are in daylight. In the same way, God's love is as true to you now as it was in your brightest moments. No father disciplines continuously. Your Lord hates the rod as much as you do; He only cares to use it for the reason that should make you willing to receive it, namely, that it is for your lasting good. You will yet climb Jacob's ladder with the angels and behold Him who sits at the top of it—your covenant God. You will yet, amid the splendors of eternity, forget the trials of time—or only remember them to bless the God who led you through them and worked your lasting good by them. Come and sing in the midst of tribulation. Rejoice even while you are passing through the furnace of affliction. Make the wilderness blossom like the rose. Cause the desert to ring with your exulting joys. These light afflictions will soon be over; then, forever with the Lord, your bliss will never diminish.

> Faint not nor fear, His arms are near,
> He changes not, and you are dear;
> Only believe and you will see,
> That Christ is all in all to thee.

Behold the man!
—John 19:5

I f there is one place where our Lord Jesus most fully became the joy and comfort of His people, it is where He plunged deepest into the depths of woe. Come, gracious souls, and *"behold the man"* in the Garden of Gethsemane. See His heart brimming so full of love that He cannot hold it in—and so full of sorrow that it must find release. See the bloody sweat as it drips from every pore of His body and falls to the ground. *"Behold the man"* as they drive the nails into His hands and feet. Look up, repenting sinners, and see the sorrowful image of your suffering Lord on the cross. Notice how the ruby drops of blood stand on the crown of thorns and adorn, as if priceless gems, the diadem of the King of Misery. *"Behold the man"* when all His bones are out of joint, and He is poured out like water and brought into the dust of death. God forsook Him and hell surrounded Him. Look and see: did anyone else ever sorrow as He sorrowed? All you who pass by, draw near and look upon this spectacle of grief—unique, unparalleled, a wonder to men and angels. Behold the Emperor of Woe, who has no equal or rival in His agonies! Gaze on Him, you mourners, for if there is no consolation in a crucified Christ, there is no joy on earth or in heaven. If there is no hope in the ransom-price of His blood, there is no joy in the harps of heaven, and the right hand of God will never know any pleasures. If we would sit more often at the foot of the cross, we would be less troubled with our doubts and sorrows. If we see His sorrows, we will be ashamed to mention our sorrows. If we but gaze into His wounds, our wounds will be healed. If we want to live right, it must be by the contemplation of His death. If we want to rise to dignity, it must be by considering His humiliation and sorrow.

The blood of Jesus Christ his Son cleanseth us from all sin.
—1 John 1:7

cleanseth," says the text—not "shall cleanse." There are multitudes who think they can wait until they are on their deathbeds before they ask God's pardon for their sins. Oh, how infinitely better to have cleansing now than to depend on the bare possibility of forgiveness when the time comes for me to die! Others imagine that a sense of pardon is only obtainable after many years of Christian experience. But forgiveness of sin is a *present* thing—a privilege for this day, a joy for this very hour. The moment a sinner trusts in Jesus, he is fully forgiven. The text is written in the present tense, indicating continuance; it was *"cleanseth"* yesterday, it is *"cleanseth"* today, and it will be *"cleanseth"* tomorrow. It will always be so with you, Christian, until you cross the river. You may come to this fountain every hour, for it cleanses still. Notice, likewise, the completeness of the cleansing: *"The blood of Jesus Christ his Son cleanseth us from all sin"*—not only from *"sin,"* but from *"all sin."* Reader, I cannot express the exceeding sweetness of this word *"all,"* but I pray that God the Holy Spirit may give you a taste of it. Our sins against God are manifold. Yet whether the debt is little or great, the same receipt can discharge one as well as the other. The blood of Jesus Christ is as blessed and divine a payment for the transgressions of blaspheming Peter as it is for the shortcomings of loving John. Our iniquity is gone, all gone at once, and all gone forever. Blessed completeness! What a sweet theme for us to dwell on as we drift off to sleep.

> Sins against a holy God;
> Sins against His righteous laws;
> Sins against His love, His blood;
> Sins against His name and cause;
> Sins immense as is the sea—
> From them all He cleanses me.

His camp is very great.
—Joel 2:11

My soul, consider the mightiness of the Lord, who is your glory and defense. He is a man of war; Jehovah is His name. All the forces of heaven are at His command. Legions wait at His door; cherubim and seraphim, watchers and holy ones, principalities and powers—all are attentive to His will. If our eyes were not blinded by the limitations of our flesh, we would see horses of fire and chariots of fire surrounding the Lord's beloved. (See 2 Kings 6:17.) The powers of nature are all subject to the absolute control of the Creator: stormy winds and tempests, lightning and rain, snow and hail, and the soft dews and cheering sunshine come and go at His decree. He looses the bands of Orion and binds the sweet influences of the Pleiades (Job 38:31). Earth, sea, air, and the places under the earth are the barracks for Jehovah's great armies. Space is His camp, light is His banner, and flame is His sword. When He goes forth to war, famine ravages the land, pestilence smites the nations, hurricanes sweep the sea, tornadoes shake the mountains, and earthquakes make the solid ground tremble. As for animate creatures, they all acknowledge His dominion; from the *"great fish"* (Jonah 1:17) that swallowed the prophet down to all manner of flies that plagued the field of Zoan (Ps. 78:43, 45), all are His servants. The palmerworm, the caterpillar, and the cankerworm are squadrons of His great army, for His *"camp is very great."* My soul, see to it that you are at peace with this mighty King. Even more than that, be sure to enlist under His banner, for to war against Him is foolishness, but to serve Him is glory. Jesus, *"Emmanuel... God with us"* (Matt. 1:23), is ready to receive recruits for the army of the Lord. If I am not already enlisted, let me go to Him before I sleep and beg to be accepted through His merits. If I am already a soldier of the Cross, as I hope I am, let me be of good courage, for the enemy is powerless compared with my Lord, whose *"camp is very great."*

In their affliction they will seek me early.
—Hosea 5:15

Losses and adversities are frequently the means that the Great Shepherd uses to fetch home His wandering sheep. Like fierce dogs, they worry the wanderers back to the fold. Lions cannot be tamed if they are too well fed; their stomachs must be deprived, and they must be brought down from their great strength, before they will submit to the tamer's hand. We have often seen the Christian rendered obedient to the Lord's will by lack of bread and difficult trials. When *"rich, and increased with goods"* (Rev. 3:17), many believers carry their heads much too proudly and speak exceedingly boastfully. Like David, they flatter themselves, saying, "My mountain stands strong; *'I shall never be moved'* (Ps. 30:6–7)." When the Christian grows wealthy, is in good repute, and has good health and a happy family, he too often admits Mr. Carnal Security as a guest at his table. If he is a true child of God, a rod of correction will be prepared for him. Wait awhile, and you may see his wealth melt away as if it were only a dream. There goes a portion of his estate—how soon the acres change hands. That debt, that unpaid bill—how fast his losses roll in; where will they end? It is a blessed sign of divine life if, when these embarrassments occur one after another, he begins to be distressed about his backsliding and goes back to his God. Blessed are the waves that wash the seaman upon the rock of salvation! Losses in business are often sanctified to our souls' enrichment. If the chosen soul will not come to the Lord full-handed, he will come empty-handed. If God, in His grace, finds no other means of making us honor Him among men, He will cast us into the deep; if we fail to honor Him on the pinnacle of riches, He will bring us into the valley of poverty. Yet do not faint, heir of sorrow, when you are thus rebuked. Instead, recognize the loving hand that disciplines, and say, *"I will arise and go to my father"* (Luke 15:18).

That he may set him with princes.
—Psalm 113:8

ur spiritual privileges are of the highest order. *"With princes"* is the place of select society. *"Truly our fellowship is with the Father, and with his Son Jesus Christ"* (1 John 1:3). Speaking of select society, there is none like this! *"Ye are a chosen generation, a royal priesthood,...a peculiar people"* (1 Pet. 2:9). *"Ye are come unto...the general assembly and church of the firstborn, [whose names] are written in heaven"* (Heb. 12:22–23). The saints have an audience with the King; princes have admittance to royalty, while common people must stand afar off. The child of God has free access to the inner courts of heaven. *"For through him we both have access by one Spirit unto the Father"* (Eph. 2:18). *"Let us therefore come boldly,"* said the apostle, *"unto the throne of grace"* (Heb. 4:16). Among princes there is abundant wealth, but what is the abundance of princes compared to the riches of believers? *"For all things are yours;...and ye are Christ's; and Christ is God's"* (1 Cor. 3:21, 23). *"He that spared not his own Son, but delivered him up for us all, how shall he not with him also freely give us all things?"* (Rom. 8:32). Princes have special power. A prince of heaven's empire has great influence; he wields a scepter in his own domain. He sits on Jesus' throne, for He *"hath made us kings and priests unto God"* (Rev. 1:6). We *"shall reign for ever and ever"* (Rev. 22:5). We reign over the united kingdom of time and eternity. Princes also have special honor. We may look down upon all earthly dignity from the eminence upon which grace has placed us. For what is human grandeur to this: He *"hath raised us up together, and made us sit together in heavenly places in Christ Jesus"* (Eph. 2:6)? We share the honor of Christ. Compared to this, earthly splendors are not worth a thought. Communion with Jesus is a richer gem than any that ever glittered in a royal crown. Union with the Lord is a coronet of beauty outshining all the brilliance of imperial splendor.

Who shall lay any thing to the charge of God's elect?
—Romans 8:33

hat a blessed challenge is the question of our text! How unanswerable it is! Every sin of the elect was laid on the great Champion of our salvation and was carried away by the Atonement. There is no sin in God's book against His people. He sees no sin in Jacob or iniquity in Israel; they are justified in Christ forever. When the guilt of sin was taken away, the punishment of sin was also removed. For the Christian, there is no stroke from God's angry hand—not so much as a single frown of punitive justice. The believer may be disciplined by his Father, but God the Judge has nothing to say to the Christian except, "I have absolved you; you are acquitted." For the Christian, there is no penal death in this world, much less any *"second death"* (Rev. 2:11). He has been completely freed from all the punishment, as well as the guilt, of sin. The power of sin has been removed, too. It may stand in our way and agitate us with perpetual warfare, but sin is a conquered foe to every soul who is in union with Jesus. There is no sin that a Christian cannot overcome if he will only rely on his God to do it. Those who wear the white robes in heaven *"overcame...by the blood of the Lamb"* (Rev. 12:11), and we may do the same. No lust is too mighty, no besetting sin too strongly entrenched; we can overcome through the power of Christ. Christian, believe that your sin is a condemned thing. It may kick and struggle, but it is doomed to die. God has written "condemned" across its forehead. Christ has crucified it, *"nailing it to his cross"* (Col. 2:14). Go now and put it to death. May the Lord help you to live to His praise. For sin—with all its guilt, shame, and fear—is gone.

> Here's pardon for transgressions past,
> It matters not how black their cast;
> And, O my soul, with wonder view,
> For sins to come here's pardon, too.

Who went about doing good.
—Acts 10:38

hese are few words, yet they are an exquisite depiction of the Lord Jesus Christ. There are not many lines, but they are the strokes of a master's pencil. Of the Savior, and only of the Savior, is our text true in the fullest, broadest, and most unqualified sense. He *"went about doing good."* From this description, it is evident that He did good personally. The writers of the Gospels constantly told us that He touched the leper with His own hand; that He anointed the eyes of the blind; and that in cases where He was asked only to speak a word of healing at a distance, He usually did not comply, but went Himself to the sickbed and personally worked the cure. His example is a lesson to us: if we want to do good, we should do it personally. Give charity with your own hands; a kind look or word will enhance the value of the gift. Speak to a friend about the state of his soul; your loving appeal will have more influence than a whole library of tracts. Our Lord's method of doing good also shows His incessant activity. He not only did good close to home, but He also *"went about"* on His errands of mercy. Throughout the whole land of Judea, scarcely a village or a hamlet was not gladdened by the sight of Him. How His example reproves the slow, loitering manner in which many Christians serve the Lord! Let us *"gird up the loins"* (1 Pet. 1:13) of our minds and *"be not weary in well doing"* (2 Thess. 3:13). Does not the text imply that Jesus Christ went out of His way to do good? He *"went about doing good."* He was never deterred by danger or difficulty. He sought out the objects of His gracious intentions. So must we. If old plans will not serve, we must try new ones. Fresh measures sometimes achieve more than regular methods. Christ's perseverance and unity of purpose are also implied in our text. The practical application of our theme for today may be summed up in these words: *"Christ…[left] us an example, that [we] should follow his steps"* (1 Pet. 2:21).

All that the Father giveth me shall come to me.
—John 6:37

his declaration concerns, first, the doctrine of election. There are some whom the Father gave to Christ. It also concerns the doctrine of effectual calling. Those who are given must and will come. However obstinately they may set themselves against it, they will be brought out of darkness into God's marvelous light. Our text also teaches us the indispensable necessity of faith, for even those who are given to Christ are not saved until they come to Jesus. Even they must come, for there is no other way to heaven but by the Door, Christ Jesus. All whom the Father gives to our Redeemer must come to Him; therefore, no one can enter heaven unless he first comes to Christ. Oh, the power and majesty that rest in the words *"shall come"*! Christ does not say that they have the power to come or that they may come if they will, but that they *"shall come."* By His messengers, His Word, and His Spirit, the Lord Jesus sweetly and graciously compels men to come in, so that they may eat of His marriage supper. He does this, not by any violation of the free will of man, but by the power of His grace. I may exercise power over another man's will, yet that other man's will may be perfectly free, because the constraint is exercised in a manner that is harmonious with the laws of the human mind. Jehovah Jesus knows how—by irresistible arguments addressed to the understanding, by mighty reasons appealing to the affections, and by the mysterious influence of His Holy Spirit operating on all the powers and passions of the soul—to subdue the whole man. In this way, whereas the man was once rebellious, he now yields cheerfully to Christ's rule, conquered by sovereign love. How will those whom God has chosen be known? They will be known by this result: they willingly and joyfully accept Christ and come to Him with simple and genuine faith, resting on Him as all their salvation and all their desire. Reader, have you thus come to Jesus?

Him that cometh to me I will in no wise cast out.
—John 6:37

N o limit is set on the duration of this promise. It does not say, "I will not cast out a sinner at his first coming," but *"I will in no wise cast out."* The original words in the Greek may be translated, "I will not, not cast out" or "I will never, never cast out." This means that Christ will not reject a believer the first time he comes, and that, as He will not reject him at the first, so He will not reject him to the last. Suppose the believer sins after coming? *"If any man sin, we have an advocate with the Father, Jesus Christ the righteous"* (1 John 2:1). Suppose the believer backslides? *"I will heal their backsliding, I will love them freely: for mine anger is turned away from him"* (Hos. 14:4). Yet the believer may fall under temptation. *"God is faithful, who will not suffer you to be tempted above that ye are able; but will with the temptation also make a way to escape, that ye may be able to bear it"* (1 Cor. 10:13). The believer may also fall into sin, as David did. Yes, but He will purge him with hyssop, and he will be clean; He will wash him, and he will be whiter than snow (Ps. 51:7). *"I will cleanse them from all their iniquity"* (Jer. 33:8).

> Once in Christ, in Christ forever,
> Nothing from His love can sever.

"I give unto [My sheep] *eternal life,"* He says, *"and they shall never perish, neither shall any man pluck them out of my hand"* (John 10:28). What do you say to this, O trembling, feeble mind? Is it not a precious mercy that, when you come to Christ, you do not come to one who will treat you well for a little while and then send you away, but One who will receive you and make you His bride, so that you will be His forever? Do not receive *"the spirit of bondage again to fear,"* but receive *"the Spirit of adoption, whereby* [you will] *cry, Abba, Father"* (Rom. 8:15). Oh, the grace of these words: *"I will in no wise cast out"*!

And these are the singers…: for they were employed
in that work day and night.
—1 Chronicles 9:33

It was good that the sacred songs in the temple never ceased. The singers continuously praised the Lord, whose mercy endures forever. As mercy did not cease to rule either by day or by night, neither did music quiet its holy ministry. My heart, there is a sweet lesson for you in the ceaseless song of Zion's temple. You, too, are a constant debtor. See to it that your gratitude, like love, never fails. God's praise is constant in heaven, which is to be your final dwelling place; learn to practice the eternal hallelujah. As the sun scatters its light around the earth, its beams awaken grateful believers to sing their morning hymns, so that, by the priesthood of the saints, perpetual praise is kept up at all hours. These praises wrap our globe in a cloak of thanksgiving and encircle it with a golden belt of song. The Lord always deserves to be praised for what He is in Himself, for His works of creation and providence, for His goodness toward His creatures, and especially for the incomparable act of redemption and all the marvelous blessings that flow from it. It is always beneficial to praise the Lord. It cheers the day and brightens the night; it lightens work and softens sorrow. It sheds a sanctifying radiance over earthly gladness that makes it less liable to blind us with its glare. Have we not something to sing about at this moment? Can we not weave a song out of our present joys, our past deliverances, or our future hopes? Earth yields her summer fruits: the hay is housed, the golden grain invites the sickle, and the sun, lingering long to shine upon a fruitful earth, shortens the interval of darkness, so that we may lengthen our hours of devout worship. Let us be stirred by our love for Jesus to close the day with a psalm of sanctified gladness.

Thou crownest the year with thy goodness.
—Psalm 65:11

All year round, every hour of every day, God is richly blessing us. Both when we are asleep and when we are awake, His mercy attends us. The sun may not shine, but our God never ceases to shine on His children with beams of love. Like a river, His lovingkindness is always flowing with a fullness as inexhaustible as His own nature. Like the atmosphere that constantly surrounds the earth and is always ready to support the life of man, the benevolence of God surrounds all His creatures. In it, as in their element, they live, move, and have their being. As the sun on summer days makes us glad with rays that are warmer and brighter than at other times; as rivers are at certain seasons swollen by the rain; and as the atmosphere itself is sometimes fresher, more invigorating, or milder than previously, so it is with the mercy of God. It has its golden hours, its days of surplus, when the Lord magnifies His grace before the sons of men. Among His blessings, the joyous days of harvest are a special season of abundant favor. It is the glory of autumn that the ripe gifts of providence are then abundantly bestowed. It is the season of realization, whereas all that came before was but hope and expectation. Great is the joy of harvest. Happy are the reapers who fill their arms with the generosity of heaven. The psalmist tells us that the harvest is the crowning of the year. Surely these crowning mercies call for crowning thanksgiving! Let us offer thanks by inward expressions of gratitude. Let our hearts be warmed. Let our spirits remember and meditate on the goodness of the Lord. Then let us praise Him, glorifying and magnifying His name, from whose bounty all this goodness flows. Let us glorify God by yielding our gifts to His purposes. A practical proof of our gratitude is a special thank offering to the Lord of the harvest.

So she gleaned in the field until even.
—Ruth 2:17

Let me learn from Ruth, the gleaner. As she went out to gather ears of corn, so I must go out into the fields of prayer, meditation, doctrine, and the hearing of the Word, in order to gather spiritual food. The gleaner gathers her portion ear by ear; her gains are little by little. I must be content to search for single truths, if there is no greater abundance of them. Every ear helps to make a bundle, and every gospel lesson assists in making us *"wise unto salvation"* (2 Tim. 3:15). The gleaner keeps her eyes open. If she were to stumble along the fields while daydreaming, she would have no load to carry home in the evening. I must be watchful while engaging in religious disciplines, so that they will not become unprofitable to me. I fear I have lost much already. Oh, that I may rightly estimate my opportunities and glean with greater diligence! The gleaner stoops for all she finds, and so must I. Haughty spirits criticize and object, but humble minds glean and receive benefit. A humble heart is a great help toward profitably hearing the Gospel. The soul-saving *"engrafted word"* (James 1:21) is not received except with meekness. A stiff back makes for bad gleaning. Pride is a vile robber, not to be endured for a moment. What the gleaner gathers, she holds. If she were to drop one ear to find another, the result of her day's work would be meager. She is as careful to retain as to obtain, so that in the end her gains are great. How often do I forget all that I hear; a second truth pushes the first out of my head, and so my reading and hearing end in much ado about nothing! Do I have the proper conviction of the importance of storing up the truth? A hungry stomach makes the gleaner wise. If there is no corn in her hand, there will be no bread on her table. She labors under a sense of necessity; therefore, she walks nimbly, and her grasp is firm. I have an even greater need. Lord, help me to be convinced of this need, so that it may urge me onward to glean in fields that yield so plenteous a reward to diligence.

But as he went.
—Luke 8:42

he context of our text is that Jesus is moving through the crowd toward the house of Jairus, to raise the ruler's dead daughter. However, Jesus is so abounding in goodness that He works another miracle while traveling on the road. Even while this *"rod of Aaron"* (Num. 17:8) bears the blossom of a latent miracle, it yields the ripe almonds of a perfect work of mercy. It is enough for us, if we have one purpose, to go and accomplish it right away. It would be imprudent for us to expend our energies along the way. If we were rushing to rescue a drowning friend, we could not afford to exhaust our strength on another in similar danger. It is enough for a tree to yield one kind of fruit, and for a man to fulfill his own particular calling. But our Master knows no limitation of power or boundary of mission. He is so prolific in grace that, like the sun that shines as it turns in its orbit, His path is radiant with lovingkindness. He is a swift arrow of love that not only reaches its ordained target but also perfumes the air through which it flies. Power is always emanating from Jesus, as sweet scents waft from flowers; it always will be flowing from Him, as water from a sparkling fountain. What delightful encouragement this truth affords us! If our Lord is so ready to heal the sick and bless the needy, then do not be slow to put yourself in His path, so that He may smile on you. Do not be slack in asking, since He gives so abundantly. Pay close attention to His Word now, and at all times, so that Jesus may speak through it to your heart. Frequent the place where He may be found, in order to obtain His blessing. When He is present to heal, will He not heal you? Surely, He is present even now, for He always comes to hearts that need Him. Do you not need Him? He knows how much you need Him! Son of David, turn Your eyes and look upon the distress that is now before You, and make Your petitioner whole.

*I smote you with [blight] and with mildew and with hail
in all the labours of your hands.*
—Haggai 2:17

How destructive hail is to standing crops, beating the precious grain to the ground! How grateful we ought to be when the corn is spared so terrible a ruin. Let us offer thanksgiving to the Lord. Even more to be dreaded are those mysterious destroyers—disease and mildew. These spoilers turn an ear of corn into a mass of blackness; they render it putrid or dry it up—all in a manner so beyond human control that the farmer is compelled to cry, "This is the hand of God!" Innumerable, minute fungi cause the damage. If it were not for the goodness of God, the rider on the black horse would soon scatter famine over the land. Infinite mercy spares the food of men; however, in view of the active agents that are ready to destroy the harvest, we are very wisely taught to pray, *"Give us this day our daily bread"* (Matt. 6:11). The curse is widespread; we are in constant need of blessing. When blight and mildew come, they are often chastisements from heaven, and men must learn to recognize and heed God's correction. Spiritually, mildew is not an uncommon evil. When our work is most promising, this blight appears. Perhaps we had hoped for many conversions, but instead were met by a general apathy, an abounding worldliness, or a cruel hardness of heart. There may be no obvious sin in those for whom we are laboring, but rather a deficiency of sincerity and decision that sadly disappoints our desires. From these experiences, we learn that we must depend on the Lord and pray that no blight may fall on our work. Spiritual pride or sloth may soon bring on us the dreadful evil, and only the Lord of the harvest can remove it. Mildew may even attack our own hearts, shriveling our prayers and devotion. May it please the great Husbandman to avert so serious a calamity. Shine, blessed Sun of Righteousness, and drive the blights away!

Shall your brethren go to war, and shall ye sit here?
—Numbers 32:6

amily relationships have their obligations. The Reubenites and Gadites would have been unbrotherly if they had claimed the land that had been conquered, but had left the rest of the people to fight for their own land (Joshua 1:12–16). We in the church have received much by means of the efforts and sufferings of the saints in years past. If we do not make some repayment to the church of Christ by giving her our best energies, we are unworthy to be enrolled in her ranks. Others are combating the errors of the age manfully or excavating perishing ones from amid the ruins of the Fall. If we fold our hands in idleness, we must be warned, lest the curse of Meroz falls upon us. (See Judges 5:23.) The Master of the vineyard says, *"Why stand ye here all the day idle?"* (Matt. 20:6). What is the idler's excuse? Personal service for Jesus becomes all the more the duty of everyone because it is cheerfully and abundantly offered by some. The efforts of devoted missionaries and fervent ministers shame us if we sit in laziness. Shrinking from trial is the temptation of those who are *"at ease in Zion"* (Amos 6:1). They would be happy to escape the cross, yet wear the crown. To them, the question of this evening's meditation is very applicable. If the most precious of God's servants are tried in the fire, can we expect to escape the crucible? If a diamond must be distressed while it is being cleaved, cut, and polished, are we to be made perfect without suffering? Do we expect the wind to cease from blowing simply because our ship is at sea? Why should we be treated better than our Lord? If the Firstborn felt the rod, why shouldn't His younger brothers and sisters? It is cowardly pride that would choose a soft pillow and bed for a soldier of the Cross. Far wiser is the person who first submits to the divine will and then grows to be pleased with it through the operations of grace. He will learn to gather lilies at the foot of the cross and, like Samson, to find honey in the lion. (See Judges 14:1–9.)

Let the whole earth be filled with his glory; Amen, and Amen.
—Psalm 72:19

This is an enormous request. To intercede for a whole city requires us to stretch our faith, and there are times when prayer for one person is enough to stagger us. But how far-reaching was the psalmist's intercession! How comprehensive! How sublime! *"Let the whole earth be filled with his glory."* This prayer does not exempt a single country, no matter how crushed it may be by the foot of superstition. It does not exclude a single nation, no matter how barbarous it may be. This prayer was spoken for the cannibal as well as for the civilized person—for all regions and races. It encompasses the entire circumference of the earth and omits no child of Adam. We must be up and doing for our Master, or we cannot honestly offer such a prayer. We are not praying this prayer with a sincere heart if we are not endeavoring, as God helps us, to extend the kingdom of our Master. Are there not some who neglect both intercession and work? Reader, is the prayer of our text also your prayer? Turn your eyes to Calvary. See the Lord of Life nailed to the cross, with the crown of thorns on His brow, with His bleeding head, hands, and feet. What! Can you look upon this miracle of miracles—the death of the Son of God—without feeling within your heart a marvelous adoration that language could never express? When you perceive that the blood has been applied to your conscience and know that He has blotted out your sins, you are not a true believer unless you fall to your knees and cry out, *"Let the whole earth be filled with his glory; Amen, and Amen."* How can you bow before the Crucified One in loving homage, then not wish to see your Monarch take His rightful place as Master of the world? Shame on you if you can pretend to love your Prince, but not desire to see Him as the Universal Ruler. Your piety is worthless unless it leads you to wish that the same mercy that has been extended to you may bless the whole world. Lord, it is harvesttime. Put in Your sickle and reap.

Satan hindered us.
—1 Thessalonians 2:18

From the first hour that goodness came into conflict with evil, it has never ceased to be true in spiritual experience that Satan hinders us. From all points of the compass, all along the battle lines—in the front and in the rear—at the dawn of day and in the midnight hour, Satan hinders us. If we toil in a field, he seeks to break the plow. If we build a wall, he works to knock down the stones. If we desire to serve God in suffering or in conflict, Satan hinders us. He hinders us everywhere. He hindered us when we first came to Jesus Christ. We had fierce conflicts with Satan when we first looked to the cross and lived. Now that we are saved, he endeavors to hinder the perfection of our personal characters. You may be congratulating yourself, saying, "I have walked consistently this far; no one can challenge my integrity." Beware of boasting, for your character will yet be tested. Satan will direct his schemes against the very character quality for which you are the most famous. If you have been a firm believer up to this point, your faith will be attacked before long. If you have been as meek as Moses, expect to be tempted to speak unadvisedly. The birds will peck at your ripest fruit, and the wild boar will dash his tusks at your choicest vines. Satan is sure to hinder us when we are earnest in prayer. He impedes our prayers and weakens our faith so that, if possible, we may miss the blessing. Satan is no less vigilant in obstructing Christian ministry. There never has been a revival of religion without a revival of his opposition. As soon as Ezra and Nehemiah began to work, Sanballat and Tobiah were stirred up to hinder them. (See Nehemiah 1–6; 8, especially 4:7–8.) What are we to do about these attacks of the enemy? We are not to be alarmed when Satan hinders us, for it is proof that we are on the Lord's side and are doing the Lord's work. In His strength, we will win the victory and triumph over our adversary.

All things are possible to him that believeth.
—Mark 9:23

Many professing Christians are constantly filled with doubt and fear. They forlornly think that this state of affairs is inevitable for a believer. This kind of thinking is a mistake, for *"all things are possible to him that believeth."* It is possible for us to reach a state in which a doubt or a fear will be to us as a migratory bird—flitting across the soul but never lingering there. When you read of the exalted and sweet communion enjoyed by favored saints, you sigh and murmur in your heart, "It is a pity that these blessings are not for me." O spiritual climber, if you will only have faith, you will yet stand on the sunny pinnacle of the temple, for *"all things are possible to him that believeth."* You hear of the exploits that holy men and women have done for Jesus—what they have enjoyed of Him, how much they have been like Him, and how they have been able to endure great persecution for His sake—and you say, "I am but a worm; I can never attain to that." However, there is nothing that one saint was that you cannot be. There is no height of grace, no attainment of spirituality, no clearness of assurance, no post of duty that is not open to you if you have the power to believe. Lay aside your sackcloth and ashes, and rise to the dignity of your true position. You are little in God's kingdom because you allow this to be the case, not because there is any necessity for it. It is not fitting that you should grovel in the dust, O child of the King. Ascend! The golden throne of assurance is waiting for you. The crown of communion with Jesus is ready to adorn your head. Wrap yourself in scarlet and fine linen, and eat sumptuously every day. For, if you believe, you may eat the choicest of wheat. Your land will flow with milk and honey, and your soul will be satisfied as with the richest and most abundant food. Gather golden sheaves of grace, for they await you in the fields of faith. *"All things are possible to him that believeth."*

He appeared first to Mary Magdalene,
out of whom he had cast seven devils.
—Mark 16:9

Mary of Magdala was the victim of a dreadful evil. She was not possessed by only one demon but by seven. These frightful inmates caused much pain and defilement to the poor body in which they had found a lodging. Hers was a hopeless, horrible case. She could not help herself, nor could any human help avail. Yet Jesus passed her way. Unsought by the poor demoniac, and probably even resisted by her, He uttered the word of power, and Mary of Magdala became a striking example of the healing power of Jesus. All seven demons left her, never to return—forcibly ejected by the Lord of all. What a blessed deliverance! What a happy change! She went from delirium to delight, from despair to peace, from hell to heaven! Mary immediately became a constant follower of Jesus, hanging on His every word, following His itinerant steps, sharing His difficult life. She also became His generous helper. She was the first among the group of healed and grateful women who followed Jesus to minister to Him out of her substance. When Jesus was lifted up in crucifixion, Mary stayed to share in His shame. We first find her looking at Him from afar, and then drawing near to the foot of the cross. She could not die on the cross with Jesus, but she stood as near to it as she could. When His blessed body was taken down, she watched to see how and where it was laid. She was the faithful and watchful believer—last at the tomb where Jesus slept in death, first at the grave from which He arose. Her holy faithfulness made her a favored witness of her beloved *"Rabboni"* (John 20:16)—who graciously called her by name and made her His messenger of good news to Peter and the other frightened disciples. Thus grace found her when she was a deranged demoniac and made her into a minister; grace cast demons out of her, granted her to see angels, delivered her from Satan, and united her forever to the Lord Jesus. May I also be such a miracle of grace!

The Son of man hath power on earth to forgive sins.
—Matthew 9:6

Note one of the Great Physician's mightiest skills: He has the power to forgive sin! While He lived here on earth—before the ransom had been paid, before His blood had been sprinkled on the mercy seat—He had the power to forgive sin. Therefore, does He not have the power to forgive sin now that He has died? What power must dwell in Him who, to the last penny, has faithfully discharged the debts of His people! He has boundless power now that He has accomplished what was needed to pay for our transgressions and has made an end of sin (Dan. 9:24). If you doubt this truth, think of Him rising from the dead. See Him in ascending splendor raised to the right hand of God. Hear Him interceding before the eternal Father, pointing to His wounds, urging the merit of His sacred suffering. What power to forgive He has! He *"hast ascended on high"* and *"hast received gifts for men"* (Ps. 68:18). He is exalted on high to give repentance and remission of sins (Acts 5:31). The most crimson of sins are removed by the crimson of His blood. At this moment, dear reader, whatever your sinfulness, Christ has power to pardon—power to pardon *you*, and millions like you. A word from Him will grant it. He has nothing more to accomplish in order to win your pardon; all the atoning work is done. He can, in answer to your tears, forgive your sins today and cause you to know that He has done so. At this very moment, He can breathe into your soul a peace with God *"which passeth all understanding"* (Phil. 4:7), which will spring from perfect forgiveness of your many iniquities. Do you believe this? I trust that you believe it. May you experience now the power of Jesus to forgive sin. Waste no time in appealing to the Physician of souls, but hurry to Him with words like these: "Jesus, Master, hear my cry! Save me; heal me with a word."

> Fainting at Your feet I lie,
> You my whisper'd plaint have heard.

Everlasting consolation.
—2 Thessalonians 2:16

"*onsolation.*" There is music in this word. Like David's harp, it chases away the evil spirit of melancholy (1 Sam. 16:23). It was a distinguished honor to Barnabas to be called *"the son of consolation"* (Acts 4:36). Indeed, this word is one of the illustrious names of One greater than Barnabas, for the Lord Jesus is *"the consolation of Israel"* (Luke 2:25). *"Everlasting consolation"*—this is the best part of all, for an eternity of comfort is our crown and glory. What is this *"everlasting consolation"*? It includes a sense of pardoned sin. A Christian has received in his heart the witness of the Spirit that his iniquities are *"blotted out...as a cloud"* and his transgressions *"as a thick cloud"* (Isa. 44:22). If sin is pardoned, is that not an *"everlasting consolation"*? Next, the Lord gives His people an abiding sense of acceptance in Christ. The Christian knows that God looks upon him as standing in union with Jesus. Union with the risen Lord is a consolation of the most abiding kind; it is, in fact, everlasting. Even if sickness sidelines us, have we not seen hundreds of believers as happy in the weakness of disease as they would have been in bodily strength and robust health? Even if death's arrows pierce us to the heart, our comfort does not die. Have not our ears very often heard the songs of dying saints while they have rejoiced as the living love of God was poured out into their hearts? Yes, a sense of acceptance in the Beloved is an *"everlasting consolation."* Moreover, the Christian has a conviction of his security. God has promised to save those who trust in Christ. The Christian does trust in Christ. He believes that God will be as good as His Word and will save him. He believes that he is safe by virtue of his being bound up with the person and work of Jesus.

The bow shall be seen in the cloud.
—Genesis 9:14

he rainbow, the symbol of God's covenant with Noah, is a type of the Lord Jesus, who is God's witness to the people. When may we expect to see the sign of the covenant? The rainbow can only be seen painted against the backdrop of clouds. When a sinner's conscience is dark with clouds, when he remembers his past sin, mourns over it, and repents before God, Jesus Christ is revealed to him as the covenant Rainbow, displaying all the glorious colors of the divine character as a testimony to the sinner's peace with God. When a believer's trials and temptations surround him, it is sweet for him to think about the Lord Jesus Christ—to remember how He lived, bled, rose, and is even now interceding for His people. God's Rainbow is placed over the cloud of our sins, our sorrows, and our afflictions, to prophesy deliverance. A cloud alone does not produce a rainbow; there must also be raindrops to reflect the light of the sun. In the same way, sorrow for sin must not only threaten to fall on us, but must really fall on us, if we are to see God's Rainbow. Note that Christ would not have been our Redeemer if the vengeance of God had been merely a threatening cloud. Punishment had to fall in terrible drops upon our Surety. Until there is *real* anguish in the sinner's conscience, Christ cannot be his Savior. Until the conviction that the sinner experiences becomes grievous, he cannot see Jesus. But there must also be a sun, for clouds and drops of rain do not create rainbows unless the sun also shines. Beloved, our God, who is as the sun to us, always shines, but we do not always see Him—clouds hide His face. Yet no matter what drops may be falling or what clouds may be threatening, if He shines, there will be a rainbow at once. It is said that when we see a rainbow, the rain showers are over. Certainly, when Christ comes, our troubles leave. When we see Jesus, our sins vanish and our doubts and fears subside. When Jesus walks the waters of the sea, how profound the calm is!

And I will remember my covenant.
—Genesis 9:15

ote the form of this promise. God did not say, "When you look upon the rainbow, and *you* remember My covenant, then I will not destroy the earth." The promise does not depend on our memories, which are fickle and frail; instead, it gloriously rests on God's memory, which is infinite and unchanging. *"The bow shall be in the cloud; and I will look upon it, that I may remember the everlasting covenant"* (v. 16). It is not my remembering God and my laying hold of His covenant, but it is God's remembering me and His covenant's laying hold of me that is the basis of my safety. Glory to God! All the fortresses of salvation are secured by divine power. Even the minor towers, which we may think are left to man to defend, are guarded by almighty strength. Even the remembrance of the covenant is not left to our memories. We might forget, but our Lord cannot forget the saints whom He has engraved on the palms of His hands (Isa. 49:16). It is with us as it was with Israel in Egypt. The blood was put on the tops and the two sides of the doorframes. The Lord did not say, "When you see the blood, I will pass over you," but, "When I see the blood, I will pass over you." (See Exodus 12:22–23.) My looking to Jesus brings me joy and peace, but it is God's looking to Jesus that secures my salvation and that of all His elect. It is impossible for God to look at Christ, our bleeding Surety, and then to be angry with us for sins already punished in Jesus. No, it is not even left to us to be saved by remembering the covenant. There is no mismatched combination of linen and wool in Christ's sacrifice—not a single thread of mankind mars the fabric of salvation. Salvation is not of man or by man but of the Lord alone. We should remember the covenant, and we will do so, through divine grace. However, the hinge of our safety does not hang there. It is God's remembering us, not our remembering Him, that is our security. This is why the covenant is an *"everlasting covenant"* (Gen. 9:16).

I know their sorrows.
—Exodus 3:7

he child is comforted as he sings, "This my father knows." Will we not be comforted as we realize that our dear Friend and tender Soul-husband knows all about us? First, He is the Physician. If He knows all, there is no need for the patient to know. Calm down, you silly, fluttering heart; stop your prying, peeking, and mistrusting! What you do not know now, you will know later on. Meanwhile, Jesus, the beloved Physician, knows your soul in its adversity. Why does the patient need to analyze all the medicine or evaluate all the symptoms? This is the Physician's work, not mine. It is my business to trust and His to prescribe. If I cannot read His handwriting on the prescription, I will not become uneasy. I will rely on His unfailing skill to make everything clear in the results that are obtained, however mysteriously they are accomplished. Second, He is the Master, and His knowledge is to serve us instead of our own knowledge. We are to obey, not to judge: *"The servant knoweth not what his lord doeth"* (John 15:15). Should the architect explain his plans to every unskilled laborer on the project? If he knows his own intent, is that not enough? The clay on the potter's wheel cannot guess what shape it is being made into, but if the potter understands his art, what does it matter if the clay is ignorant? My Lord must no longer be cross-examined by one as ignorant as I. Third, He is the Head. All understanding centers in Him. Does an arm exercise judgment? Does a foot have comprehension? All the power to know lies in the head. Why should a member of the body have a brain of its own when the head fulfills every intellectual function for it? Therefore, when a believer is sick, he must place his comfort in the following truth: he may not be able to see the end result, but Jesus knows all. Sweet Lord, be our eyes, soul, and head at all times, and let us be content to know only what You choose to reveal.

And I will give you an heart of flesh.
—Ezekiel 36:26

A *"heart of flesh"* is known, first, by its tenderness concerning sin. To have indulged an impure thought or to have allowed a wild desire to linger, even for a moment, is quite enough to make a heart of flesh grieve before the Lord. A heart of stone (v. 26) will claim that a great iniquity is nothing, but a heart of flesh will not.

> If to the right or left I stray,
> That moment, Lord, reprove;
> And let me weep my life away,
> For having grieved Your love.

Second, a heart of flesh is tender toward God's will. The carnal will is very arrogant; it is hard to subject it to God's will. However, when a heart of flesh is given, the will quivers like an aspen leaf with every breath of heaven and bows like a willow with every breeze of God's Spirit. The natural will is like cold, hard iron, which cannot be hammered into form. Yet the renewed will, like molten metal, is soon molded by the hand of grace. Third, in a heart of flesh, there is a tenderness of the affections. The hard heart does not love the Redeemer, but the renewed heart burns with affection for Him. The hard heart is selfish and coldly demands, "Why should I weep for sin? Why should I love the Lord?" In contrast, the heart of flesh says, "Lord, *'thou knowest that I love thee'* (John 21:15). Help me to love You more!" Many are the privileges of this renewed heart.

> 'Tis here the Spirit dwells,
> 'Tis here that Jesus rests.

The renewed heart is ready to receive every spiritual blessing, and every blessing comes to it. It yields every heavenly fruit to the honor and praise of God. Therefore, the Lord delights in it. A tender heart is the best defense against sin and the best preparation for heaven. A renewed heart stands on its watchtower looking for the coming of the Lord Jesus. Do you have a *"heart of flesh"*?

Ourselves also, which have the firstfruits of the Spirit.
—Romans 8:23

resent possession is declared in this verse. At this present moment, we have the *"firstfruits of the Spirit."* We have repentance, that gem of purest luster; faith, that priceless pearl; hope, that heavenly emerald; and love, that glorious ruby. We already have been made new creations in Christ Jesus by the effective working of God the Holy Spirit. Salvation is considered the firstfruits because it comes first. The sheaf used in the wave offering was the first of the harvest. (See Leviticus 23:10–12.) Similarly, the spiritual life and all the graces that adorn that life are the first operations of the Spirit of God in our souls. The firstfruits were the pledge of the harvest. As soon as an Israelite had plucked the first handful of ripe ears, he looked forward with glad anticipation to harvesting his crop. In the same way, beloved, when God gives us things that are *"pure," "lovely,"* and *"of good report"* (Phil. 4:8) as the work of the Holy Spirit, these are a foretaste of the coming glory. The firstfruits were always holy to the Lord, and our new nature, with all its powers, is a consecrated thing. The new life is not ours that we should ascribe its excellence to our own merits. It is Christ's image and creation and is ordained for His glory. The firstfruits were not the harvest itself, and the works of the Spirit in us at this moment are not the consummation—perfection is yet to come. We must not boast that we have attained perfection, and thereby think that the sheaf for the wave offering is the entire produce of the year. We must *"hunger and thirst after righteousness"* (Matt. 5:6) and long for the day of full redemption. Dear reader, this evening, open your mouth wide, and God will fill it (Ps. 81:10). Let the blessing that you presently possess stir up in you a sacred craving for more grace. Groan within yourself for higher degrees of consecration, and your Lord will grant them to you. He is *"able to do exceeding abundantly above all that we ask or think"* (Eph. 3:20).

This sickness is not unto death.
—John 11:4

From the above words of our Lord, we learn that there is a limit to sickness. There is an *"unto"* within which the ultimate end of sickness is restrained, and beyond which it cannot go. Lazarus had to experience death, but death was not the final outcome of his sickness. In all sickness, the Lord says to the waves of pain, "This far you may go, but no farther." (See Job 38:11.) His steadfast purpose is the instruction—not the destruction—of His people. Wisdom hangs a thermometer at the mouth of the furnace of affliction and regulates the furnace's heat. The limitation on sickness is, first of all, encouragingly comprehensive. The God of providence has limited the time, manner, intensity, repetition, and effects of all our sicknesses. Each throb is decreed, each sleepless hour predestined, each relapse ordained, each depression of spirit foreknown, and each sanctifying result eternally purposed. Nothing great or small escapes the ordaining hand of Him who numbers the hairs of our heads (Matt. 10:30). Second, the limitation on sickness is wisely adapted to our strength, to the intended purpose of the sickness, and to the grace apportioned. Affliction does not come haphazardly. The weight of every stroke of the rod is accurately measured. He who made no mistakes in balancing the clouds and setting the boundaries of the heavens commits no errors in measuring out the ingredients that make up the medicine of souls. We cannot suffer too much or be relieved too late. Third, the limitation is tenderly set. The knife of the heavenly Surgeon never cuts deeper than is absolutely necessary. *"He doth not afflict willingly nor grieve the children of men"* (Lam. 3:33). A mother's heart cries, "Spare my child!" but no mother is more compassionate than our gracious God. When we consider how obstinate we are, it is a wonder that we are not driven with a sharper bit. It is very comforting to know that He who has set the boundaries of our habitation has also set the boundaries of our tribulation.

And they gave him to drink wine mingled with myrrh:
but he received it not.
—Mark 15:23

golden truth is hidden in the fact that the Savior refused the cup of wine and myrrh. The Son of God stood on the heights of heaven before He became man. As He looked down upon our globe, He measured the long descent to the utmost depths of human misery. He added up the sum total of all the agonies that the Atonement would require, but He did not weaken at all. He solemnly determined that, to offer a sufficient atoning sacrifice, He must go the whole way—from the highest to the lowest, from the throne of highest glory to the cross of deepest misery. The cup of wine and myrrh, with its tranquilizing influence, would have kept Him a little within the utmost limits of misery. Therefore, He refused it. He would not stop short of all He had undertaken to suffer for His people. How many of us have longed to relieve our grief, which would have been injurious to us! Reader, have you never prayed, with a petulant and willful eagerness, to be released from difficult service or suffering? Perhaps providence has taken away from you the desire of your eyes with one stroke. Answer this, Christian: if you were to be told, "If you so desire, your loved one will live, but God will be dishonored," could you renounce the temptation and say, *"Thy will be done"* (Matt. 26:42)? Oh, it is sweet to be able to say, "My Lord, if I do not need to suffer for other reasons, but if I can honor You more by suffering, and if the loss of everything earthly that belongs to me will bring You glory, then let it be so. I refuse the comfort, if it stands in the way of Your honor." If only we would thus walk in the footsteps of our Lord—cheerfully enduring trial for His sake, promptly and willingly putting aside thoughts of self and comfort when they would interfere with our finishing the work He has given us to do. Great grace is needed if we are to walk in Christ's footsteps, but great grace is also provided.

Pull me out of the net that they have laid privily for me:
for thou art my strength.
—Psalm 31:4

Our spiritual enemies are of the same nature as the serpent in the Garden of Eden; they seek to ensnare us by subtlety. The prayer of our text supposes the possibility of the believer being caught like a bird. So deftly does the fowler do his work that simple ones are soon surrounded by the net. The text asks that the captive one be delivered even out of Satan's meshes. This is a legitimate prayer, and one that can be granted. From between the jaws of the lion, and out of the belly of hell, eternal love can rescue the saint. A quick yank may be needed to save a believer from the net of temptation, and a mighty pull may be needed to extricate him from the snare of malicious cunning, but the Lord is equal to every emergency. The most skillfully placed nets of the hunter will never be able to hold His chosen ones. Those who are so clever at laying nets, those who tempt others, will themselves be destroyed. *"For thou art my strength."* What inexpressible sweetness may be found in these few words! How joyfully we may encounter struggles, and how cheerfully we may endure sufferings, when we can take hold of divine strength. Divine power will tear apart all the works of our enemies, confound their schemes, and frustrate their deceitful tricks. Happy is the one who has such matchless might engaged on his behalf! Our own strength is of little service when overwhelmed in the nets of base cunning, but the Lord's strength is always available to us. We only have to invoke it, and we will find it close at hand. If, by faith, we are depending on the strength of the mighty God of Israel alone, we may use our holy reliance as a plea in supplication.

> Lord, evermore Your face we seek:
> Tempted we are, and poor, and weak;
> Keep us with lowly hearts, and meek.
> Let us not fall. Let us not fall.

And they fortified Jerusalem unto the broad wall.
—Nehemiah 3:8

ities that are well fortified have broad walls, as Jerusalem had in her glory. The New Jerusalem must, in like manner, be surrounded and preserved by a broad wall of nonconformity to the world and separation from its customs and spirit. The tendency in these days is to break down the holy barrier and to make the distinction between the church and the world merely nominal. Christians no longer keep a strict watch over their attitudes and actions, questionable literature is read everywhere, frivolous pastimes are commonly indulged, and a general laxity threatens to deprive the Lord's own people of the sacred singularity that separates them from sinners. It will be an evil day for the church and the world when the proposed unification is complete, and the *"sons of God"* and the *"daughters of men"* (Gen. 6:2) are as one. Then another flood of wrath will be ushered in. Beloved reader, let it be your aim in heart, word, dress, and action to maintain the *"broad wall,"* remembering that friendship with this world means enmity against God. The broad wall afforded a pleasant meeting place for the inhabitants of Jerusalem, from which they could have an excellent view of the surrounding country-side. This reminds us of the Lord's exceedingly broad commandments, in which we walk at liberty in communion with Jesus, overlooking the scenes of earth and looking out toward the glories of heaven. Although we are separated from the world and deny ourselves all ungodliness and fleshly lusts, we are nevertheless not in prison, nor restricted within narrow bounds. No, we walk at liberty, because we keep His precepts. Come, reader, walk with God in His statutes this evening. As friend met friend upon the city wall, so meet your God in the way of holy prayer and meditation. You have a right to traverse the fortresses of salvation, for you are a freeman of the royal borough, a citizen of the capital of the universe.

I said not unto the seed of Jacob, Seek ye me in vain.
—Isaiah 45:19

We may gain much comfort by considering what God has *not* said. What He has said is inexpressibly full of comfort and delight; what He has not said is hardly less rich in consolation. It was one of these "said nots" that preserved the kingdom of Israel in the days of Jeroboam, the son of Joash. *"The LORD **said not** that he would blot out the name of Israel from under heaven"* (2 Kings 14:27, emphasis added). In our text, we have an assurance that God will answer prayer, because He *"**said not** unto the seed of Jacob, Seek ye me in vain."* You who say bitter things against yourselves should remember that, no matter what your doubts and fears may say, if God has not cut you off from mercy, there is no room for despair. Even the voice of conscience is of little weight if it is not seconded by the voice of God. What God has said, tremble at! But do not allow false ideas to overwhelm you with despondency and sinful despair. Many timid people have been troubled by the suspicion that there may be something in God's decree that shuts them out from hope. Yet here is a complete refutation of that troublesome fear, for no true seeker can be decreed to wrath: *"I have not spoken in secret, in a dark place of the earth: I said not [even in the secret of My unsearchable decree] unto the seed of Jacob, Seek ye me in vain"* (Isa. 45:19). God has clearly revealed that He will hear the prayer of those who call on Him, and that declaration cannot be contravened. He has so firmly, so truthfully, so righteously spoken that there can be no room for doubt. He does not reveal His mind in unintelligible words, but He speaks plainly and positively, *"Ask, and ye shall receive"* (John 26:24). Trembling one, believe these sure truths—that prayer must and will be heard, and that never, even in the secrets of eternity, has the Lord said to any living soul, *"Seek ye me in vain."*

The unsearchable riches of Christ.
—Ephesians 3:8

My Master has riches beyond the count of arithmetic, the measurement of reason, the dream of imagination, or the eloquence of words. They are *"unsearchable"!* You may look, study, and weigh, but Jesus is a greater Savior than you think He is when your thoughts are at their greatest. My Lord is more ready to pardon than you are to sin, more able to forgive than you are to transgress. My Master is more willing to supply your needs than you are to acknowledge them. Never tolerate low thoughts of my Lord Jesus. When you put the crown on His head, you will crown Him only with silver when He deserves gold. My Master has riches of happiness to bestow on you now. He can cause you to lie down in green pastures and lead you beside still waters. There is no music like the music of His flute when He is the Shepherd and you are the sheep, and you lie down at His feet. There is no love like His; neither earth nor heaven can match it. To know Christ and to *"be found in him"* (Phil. 3:9)—this is life, this is joy, this is *"marrow and fatness"* (Ps. 63:5), *"wines on the lees well refined"* (Isa. 25:6)! My Master does not treat His servants in a stingy way. He gives to them as a king gives to another king. He gives them two heavens—a heaven below in serving Him here, and a heaven above in delighting in Him forever. His *"unsearchable riches"* will be best known in eternity. He will give you all you need on your way to heaven. Your place of defense will be the stronghold of rocks; your bread will be given to you, and your waters will be sure (Isa. 33:16). It is there where you will hear the song of those who triumph, the shout of those who feast, and will have a face-to-face view of the glorious and beloved One. *"The unsearchable riches of Christ"!* This is the tune for the musicians of earth and the song for the harpists of heaven. Lord, teach us more and more of Jesus, and we will tell the good news to others.

That Christ may dwell in your hearts by faith.
—Ephesians 3:17

Beyond measure, it is desirable that we, as believers, should keep the person of Jesus constantly in mind, in order to ignite our love for Him and to increase our knowledge of Him. I wish that all my readers were enrolled as diligent scholars in Jesus' college, students of "Corpus Christi" or the body of Christ, resolved to attain a good degree in the learning of the Cross. In order to keep Jesus always near, the heart must be full of Him, welling up with His love, even to overflowing. Therefore, the apostle prayed, *"That Christ may dwell in your hearts."* See how near he wanted Jesus to be! You cannot get a subject closer to you than to have it in your very heart. *"That Christ may dwell"*—not that He may visit you sometimes, as a casual visitor comes into a house and stays for a night, but that He may *"dwell,"* that Jesus may become the Lord and Tenant of your inmost being, never to leave. Observe these words: *"That Christ may dwell in your hearts."* The heart is the best room of the house of mankind. Christ is not to dwell in your thoughts alone, but in your affections; not merely in the mind's meditations, but in the heart's emotions. We should earnestly desire an abiding love for Christ—not a love that flames up, then dies out into the darkness of a few embers; but a constant flame, fed by sacred fuel, like the fire that never went out on the altar of the tabernacle (Lev. 6:12–13). This cannot be accomplished except *"by faith."* Faith must be strong or love will not be fervent. The root of the flower must be healthy, or we cannot expect the bloom to be sweet. Faith is the lily's root, and love is the lily's bloom. Jesus cannot be in your heart's love unless you have a firm hold of Him by your heart's faith. Therefore, pray that you may always trust Christ so that you may always love Him. If love is cold, you may be sure that faith is drooping.

If fire break out, and catch in thorns, so that the stacks of corn, or the standing corn, or the field, be consumed therewith; he that kindled the fire shall surely make restitution.
—Exodus 22:6

What restitution can someone make who scatters around the firebrands of error or the coals of licentiousness and sets men's souls ablaze with the fires of hell? The guilt is beyond estimate, and the results are irretrievable. If such an offender is forgiven, what grief it will cause him in retrospect, since he cannot undo the harm that he has done! An evil example may kindle a flame that years of amended character cannot quench. To burn men's food is bad enough, but how much worse it is to destroy the soul! It may be useful to us to reflect to what extent we may have been guilty of this in the past. It may also be helpful to inquire whether, even in the present, there may not be in us an evil that has a tendency to bring damage to the souls of our relatives, friends, or neighbors. The fire of strife is a terrible evil when it breaks out in a Christian church. Where converts are multiplied and God is glorified, jealousy and envy do the devil's work most effectively. Where the golden grain is being housed to reward the toil of the Great Boaz, the fire of enmity comes in and leaves little else but smoke and a heap of blackness. Woe to those by whom offenses come. May they never come through us. For although we cannot make restitution, we will certainly be the chief sufferers if we are the chief offenders. Those who feed the fire deserve just censure, but he who first kindles it is the most to blame. Discord usually first takes hold of the thorns—it is nurtured among the hypocrites and low-minded Christians in the church. Then it goes among the righteous, blown by the winds of hell. No one knows where it may end. Lord and Giver of peace, make us peacemakers. Never let us aid and abet men of strife or even unintentionally cause the least division among Your people.

If thou believest with all thine heart, thou mayest.
—Acts 8:37

These words may answer your conscience, devout reader, regarding participating in the ordinances of the church. Perhaps you say, "I am afraid to be baptized. It is such a solemn thing to declare that I am dead and buried with Christ. I do not feel at liberty to come to the Lord's Table. I am afraid of eating and drinking damnation on myself by *'not discerning the Lord's body'* (1 Cor. 11:29)." Poor fearful one, Jesus has given you liberty. Do not be afraid. If a stranger came to your house, he would stand at the door or wait in the hall. He would not dream of intruding unasked into your private rooms, for he is not at home. However, your child feels very free to roam around the house. A stranger may not intrude where a child may go. It is this way with the child of God. When the Holy Spirit has enabled you to feel the *"Spirit of adoption"* (Rom. 8:15), you may come to Christian ordinances without fear. The same rule holds true of the Christian's inward privileges. You think, poor seeker, that you are not allowed to *"rejoice with joy unspeakable and full of glory"* (1 Pet. 1:8). If you are permitted to get inside Christ's door or to sit at the end of His table, you will be well contented. Oh, but you will not have fewer privileges than the very greatest. God makes no distinction in His love for His children. A child is a child to Him. He will not make him a hired servant. His child will feast on the fatted calf; he will have music and dancing as much as if he had never gone astray. When Jesus comes into a person's heart, He issues a general license to be *"glad in the LORD"* (Ps. 32:11). No chains are worn in the court of King Jesus. Our admission into full privileges may be gradual, but it is sure. Perhaps you are saying, "I wish I could enjoy the promises and walk at liberty in my Lord's commands." *"If thou believest with all thine heart, thou mayest."* Loose the chains from your neck, *"O captive daughter of Zion"* (Isa. 52:2), for Jesus makes you free.

The people, when they beheld him, were greatly amazed,
and running to him saluted him.
—Mark 9:15

What a great difference there was between Moses and Jesus! After Moses had spent forty days with God on Mount Sinai, he underwent a kind of transfiguration, so that his face shone with great brightness. When he came down from the mountain, he put a veil over his face, for the people could not endure to look upon the glory. This was not the case with our Savior. He was transfigured with a greater glory than that of Moses. (See Mark 9:2–8.) Yet the Bible does not say that the people were blinded by the blaze of His countenance. Rather, they *"were greatly amazed, and running to him saluted him."* The glory of the law repels, but the greater glory of Jesus attracts. Although Jesus is holy and just, so much truth and grace is blended with His purity that sinners run to Him, amazed at His goodness and fascinated by His love. They greet Him, become His disciples, and take Him as their Lord and Master. Reader, it may be that you are even now being blinded by the dazzling brightness of the law of God. You feel its claims on your conscience, but you cannot obey it in your life. It is not that you find fault with the law. On the contrary, it commands your most profound respect. Yet you are not drawn to God by it at all. Instead, your heart is hard, and you are close to desperation over it. Poor heart, turn your eyes from Moses, with all his repelling splendor, and look to Jesus, resplendent with gentler glories. See the blood flowing from His wounds and His head crowned with thorns! He is the Son of God; therefore, He is greater than Moses. Yet He is also the Lord of love and is more tender than the lawgiver. He bore the wrath of God. In His death, He revealed more of God's justice than Sinai did when it was ablaze with God's glory. However, God's justice has been vindicated, and now it is the guardian of believers in Jesus. Sinner, look to the bleeding Savior. As you feel the attraction of His love, run to His arms, and you will be saved.

Into thine hand I commit my spirit: thou hast redeemed me,
O LORD God of truth.
—Psalm 31:5

requently, these words have been used by holy men and women in their hour of departure from this world. We will benefit from considering them this evening. The object of the faithful believer's concern in life and in death is not his body or his estate, but his spirit. His spirit is his most valuable treasure. If this is safe, all is well. What is the state of the body compared to the state of the spirit? The believer commits his spirit into the hands of God. It came from Him; it is His own. He has sustained it, and He is able to preserve it; it is most fitting that He should receive it. All things are safe in Jehovah's hands. What we entrust to the Lord will be secure, both now and in that Day of days toward which we are quickly moving. It is peaceful living and glorious dying to rest in the care of heaven. At all times, we should commit our all to Jesus' faithful hands. Then, even though life may hang by a thread and adversities may multiply as the sands of the sea, our spirits will dwell at ease and delight in *"quiet resting places"* (Isa. 32:18). *"Thou hast redeemed me, O LORD God of truth."* Redemption is a solid basis for confidence. David did not know Calvary as we do, but temporal redemption comforted him. Will not eternal redemption comfort us even more sweetly? Past times of deliverance are strong pleas for present assistance. What the Lord has done in the past, He will do again, for He never changes. He is faithful to His promises and gracious to His saints. He will not turn away from His people.

> Though You slay me I will trust,
> Praise You even from the dust,
> Prove, and tell it as I prove,
> Thine unutterable love.
>
> You may chasten and correct,
> But You never can neglect;
> Since the ransom price is paid,
> On Your love my hope is stay'd.

Sing, O barren.
—Isaiah 54:1

e have yielded some fruit for Christ, and we have a joyful hope that we are plants that His right hand has planted (Ps. 80:15). Yet there are times when we feel very barren. Our prayers are lifeless, our love is cold, and our faith is weak. Each grace in the garden of our hearts languishes and droops. We are like flowers in the hot sun that need a refreshing shower. What are we to do in such a condition? The verse from which our text comes is addressed to those in just such a state: *"Sing, O barren...; break forth into singing, and cry aloud"* (v. 1). But what can I sing about? I cannot talk about the present, and even the past looks full of barrenness. Oh, I can sing of Jesus Christ! I can talk of visits that the Redeemer has paid me in the past. Or I can praise the great love by which He loved His people when He came from the heights of heaven for their redemption. I will go to the cross again. Come, my soul. You were once *"heavy laden"* (Matt. 11:28), but you lost your burden there. Go to Calvary again. Perhaps the very cross that gave you life may also give you fruitfulness. What is my barrenness? It is the platform for His fruit-creating power. What is my desolation? It is the black setting for the sapphire of His everlasting love. I will go in poverty; I will go in helplessness; I will go in all my shame and backsliding. I will tell Him that I am still His child. In confidence in His faithful heart, even I, the barren one, will *"sing...and cry aloud."* Sing, believer, for it will comfort your own heart and the hearts of other desolate ones. Sing on, for now that you are really ashamed of being barren, you will be fruitful soon. Now that God has made you unwilling to be without fruit, He will soon cover you with clusters. The experience of our barrenness is painful, but the Lord's visitations are delightful. A sense of our own poverty drives us to Christ. That is where we need to be, for in Him our fruit is found.

All the days of his separation shall he eat nothing that is made of the vine tree, from the kernels even to the husk.
—Numbers 6:4

Among other vows, Nazarites took a vow that precluded them from drinking wine. (See Numbers 6:2–3.) To keep them from violating the obligation, they were forbidden to drink wine vinegar or strong liquor. To make the rule even clearer, they were not to touch the unfermented juice of grapes or even eat the fruit of grapes—either fresh or dried. In order to completely ensure the integrity of the vow, they were not allowed anything that had to do with the vine. They were, in fact, to avoid the *"appearance of evil"* (1 Thess. 5:22). Surely, their abstinence is a lesson to the Lord's separated ones, teaching them to move away from sin in every form—not merely to avoid sin's more obvious forms, but also its spirit and likeness. Being strict with oneself in regard to walking in God's ways is much despised in these days. However, rest assured, dear reader, that it is both the safest and the happiest way to live. He who yields a point or two to the world is in fearful peril; he who eats the grapes of Sodom will soon drink the wine of Gomorrah. A little crack in the seawall lets in the sea, and the gap quickly grows until a town is completely flooded. Worldly conformity, in any degree, is a snare to the soul and makes the soul increasingly liable to presumptuous sins. The Nazarite who drank grape juice could not be quite sure that it had not undergone a degree of fermentation. Consequently, he could not have a clear conscience that his vow was intact. In the same way, the yielding, compromising Christian cannot maintain a clear conscience; he senses that his inward monitor doubts his integrity. We do not need to wonder about things that are questionable. They are wrong for us. We must not toy with things that are tempting, but quickly flee from them. It is better to be sneered at as a Puritan than to be despised as a hypocrite. Walking before the Lord carefully may involve much self-denial, but it has pleasures of its own that are more than sufficient compensation.

Heal me, O LORD, and I shall be healed.
—Jeremiah 17:14
I have seen his ways, and will heal him.
—Isaiah 57:18

It is the sole prerogative of God to remove spiritual disease. Physical disease may be healed by men in an accessory way. However, even then, the honor is to be given to God, who gives healing power to medicine and grants the human body the power to ward off disease. As for spiritual sicknesses, these are the domain of the Great Physician alone. He claims them as His exclusive right: *"I kill, and I make alive; I wound, and I heal"* (Deut. 32:39). One of the Lord's preeminent titles is Jehovah-Rapha, *"The LORD that healeth thee"* (Exod. 15:26). "I will heal you of your wounds" is a promise that could not come from man, but only from the eternal God. For this reason, the psalmist cried to the Lord, *"O LORD, heal me; for my bones are vexed"* (Ps. 6:2), and, *"Heal my soul; for I have sinned against thee"* (Ps. 41:4). For this reason, also, the godly praise the name of the Lord, saying, "He heals all our diseases." (See Psalm 103:3.) He who made man can restore man, and He who was the Creator of our nature at the beginning can newly create it. What an incomparable comfort it is to know that in the person of Jesus *"dwelleth all the fulness of the Godhead bodily"* (Col. 2:9)! No matter what your disease may be, the Great Physician can heal you. He is God, and there is no limit to His power. Come, then, with the blind eye of darkened understanding. Come with the limping foot of wasted energy or the maimed hand of weak faith. Come with the fever of an angry temper or the chills of shivering despondency. Come just as you are, for He who is God can certainly cure you of your plague. No one can restrain the healing power that proceeds from Jesus our Lord. Legions of demons have been forced to acknowledge the power of the beloved Physician. Never once has He been baffled. All His patients have been cured in the past and will be cured in the future. You will be among them, my friend, if you will only rest in Him tonight.

If we walk in the light, as he is in the light.
—1 John 1:7

W alk…*as he is in the light*"! Can we ever attain to this? Will we ever be able to walk as clearly in the light as He whom we call *"Our Father"* (Matt. 6:9), of whom it is written, *"God is light, and in him is no darkness at all"* (1 John 1:5)? Certainly, this is the model that it set before us, for the Savior Himself said, *"Be ye therefore perfect, even as your Father which is in heaven is perfect"* (Matt. 5:48). Although we may feel that we can never measure up to the perfection of God, we are still to seek it and never be satisfied until we obtain it. When the youthful artist grasps his pencil at the beginning of his training, he can hardly hope to equal Raphael or Michelangelo. However, if he did not have a noble *beau idéal* or archetype in his mind, he would create something only very average and ordinary. Yet what is meant by the statement that the Christian is to *"walk in the light, as* [God] *is in the light"*? I understand this statement to mean likeness, rather than degree. We are as truly in the light, as completely in the light, as sincerely in the light, as honestly in the light as God is, although we cannot be in the light in the same measure that He is. I cannot dwell in the sun; it is too bright a place for me to reside in. However, I can *walk* in the light of the sun. Similarly, although I cannot attain to the perfection of purity and truth that belongs to the Lord of Hosts by nature as the Infinitely Good One, I can *"set the LORD always before me"* (Ps. 16:8). I can strive, by the help of the indwelling Spirit, to conform to His image. That famous old commentator, John Trapp, said, "We may be in the light as God is in the light for *quality,* but not for *equality.*" We are to have the light and to walk in it as truly as God has the light and walks in it. As for equality with God in His holiness and purity, that must be left until we cross the Jordan and enter into the perfection of the Most High. Note that the blessings of sacred fellowship and perfect cleansing are tied to walking in the light. (See 1 John 1:7.)

Trust in him at all times.
—Psalm 62:8

aith is as much the rule of temporal life as it is of spiritual life. We ought to have faith in God for our earthly matters as well as for our heavenly concerns. It is only as we learn to trust in God to supply all our daily needs that we will live above the world. We are not to be idle, for that would show that we do not trust in God, who continually works, but in the devil, who is the father of idleness. We are not to be imprudent or rash, for that would be to trust chance rather than the living God, who is a God of economy and order. Acting in all prudence and uprightness, we are to rely simply and entirely on the Lord at all times. Let me commend to you a life of trusting in God in temporal things. By trusting in God, you will not have to repent for having used sinful means to grow rich. Serve God with integrity. If you achieve no success, at least no sin will be on your conscience. By trusting in God, you will not become guilty of self-contradiction. He who trusts only in his own abilities sails this way today and that way the next, like a boat tossed about by the fickle wind. However, he who trusts in the Lord is like a steamship, which cuts through the waves, defies the wind, and makes one bright, silvery, straightforward track to her desired haven. Be someone who has living principles within him. Never yield to the varying practices of worldly wisdom. Walk in the path of integrity with determined steps, and show that you are invincibly strong in the strength that confidence in God alone can provide. Thus you will be delivered from burdensome care. You will not be troubled by bad news. Your heart will be steadfast, *"trusting in the LORD"* (Ps. 112:7). How pleasant it is to float along the stream of providence! There is no more blessed way of living than living a life of dependence upon a covenant-keeping God. We have no cares, *"for he careth for [us]"* (1 Pet. 5:7). We have no troubles, because we cast our burdens upon the Lord.

Except ye see signs and wonders, ye will not believe.
—John 4:48

A craving for miracles was a symptom of the sickly state of men's minds in our Lord's day. They refused solid nourishment and longed for mere wonders. The Gospel that they so greatly needed, they did not want. The miracles that Jesus did not always choose to give, they eagerly demanded. Many people today must see signs and wonders, or they will not believe. Some have said in their hearts, "I must feel a deep terror in my soul regarding my sins, or I will never believe in Jesus." But what if you never feel it, as you probably never will? Will you go to hell just to spite God, because He will not deal with you as He deals with others? Some say to themselves, "If I had a dream, or if I could feel a sudden shock of something—I don't know what—then I would believe." In this way, undeserving mortals imagine that the Lord is to be dictated to by them! You are beggars at His gate, asking for mercy. Will you draw up rules and regulations as to how He should give that mercy? Do you think that He will submit to this? My Master has a generous spirit, but He has a true royal heart. He spurns all other rule and maintains His sovereignty of action. Dear reader, if the text describes your condition, why do you crave signs and wonders? Is the Gospel not its own sign and wonder? Is it not a miracle of miracles that *"God so loved the world, that he gave his only begotten Son, that whosoever believeth in him should not perish"* (John 3:16)? Surely, this precious offer, *"Whosoever will, let him take the water of life freely"* (Rev. 22:17), and this solemn promise, *"Him that cometh to me I will in no wise cast out"* (John 6:37), are better than signs and wonders! A truthful Savior should be believed. He is truth itself. Why do you ask for proof of the truthfulness of One who cannot lie? The demons themselves declared Him to be the Son of God. (See Mark 3:11.) Will you mistrust Him?

The LORD trieth the righteous.
—Psalm 11:5

All events are under God's control. Consequently, all the trials of our outward lives may be directly traced to the great First Cause. Out of the golden gate of God's ordinance, the armies of trial march forth in order, dressed in their iron armor and armed with weapons of war. All acts of God's providence are doors to trial. Even our mercies, like roses, have their thorns. Men may be drowned in seas of prosperity as well as in rivers of affliction. Our mountains are not too high and our valleys are not too low for temptations; trials lurk on all roads. Everywhere, above and beneath, we are surrounded and attacked by dangers. Yet no showers fall from the threatening clouds without permission; every drop has its order before it hurries to the earth. The trials that come from God are sent to prove and strengthen our Christlike qualities. Therefore, at the same time, they illustrate the power of divine grace, test the genuineness of these qualities, and add to their effectiveness. Our Lord places so high a value on His people's faith that, in His infinite wisdom and abounding love, He will not screen them from the trials by which faith is strengthened. You would never have possessed the precious faith that now supports you if the trial of your faith had not been a trial by fire. You are a tree that never would have rooted as well if the winds of adversity had not rocked you back and forth and made you take firm hold of the precious truths of covenant grace. Worldly ease is a great enemy to faith; it loosens the joints of holy valor and snaps the sinews of sacred courage. A hot-air balloon doesn't rise until the cords holding it to the earth are cut. Affliction does a similar service for believing souls. While the wheat sleeps comfortably in the husk, it is useless to man. It must be threshed out of its resting place before its value can be known. Thus it is good that Jehovah *"trieth the righteous,"* for their trials cause them to grow rich toward God.

Just balances, just weights, a just ephah, and a just hin, shall ye have.
—Leviticus 19:36

eights, scales, and measures are all to be set according to the standard of justice. Surely, no Christian needs to be reminded of this in his business, for if righteousness were banished from the rest of the world, it would find shelter in believing hearts. There are, however, other balances that weigh moral and spiritual things, and these often need examining. Are the balances in which we weigh our own and others' characters accurate? Do we not turn our own ounces of goodness into pounds, and other people's bushels of excellence into pecks? Pay attention to weights and measures, Christian. Are the scales in which we measure our trials and troubles according to standard? Paul, who suffered more than we do, called his afflictions *"light"* (2 Cor. 4:17). Yet we often think that our afflictions are heavy. Surely, something must be amiss with the weights! We must see to this matter, lest we be reported to the heavenly court for unjust dealing. Are the weights with which we measure our doctrinal beliefs fair? The doctrines of grace should have the same weight with us as the precepts of the Word—no more and no less. However, it is to be feared that, with many people, one scale or the other is unfairly weighted. It is important to give a just measure in truth. Christian, be careful in regard to this. The measures by which we estimate our obligations and responsibilities look rather small. When a rich man contributes no more to the cause of God than a poor man contributes, is that *"a just ephah, and a just hin"*? When ministers are half starved because of our selfishness, is that honest dealing? When the poor are despised while ungodly rich men are held in admiration, is that a just balance? Reader, I might lengthen the list, but I prefer to leave it as your evening's work to discover and destroy all unrighteous balances, weights, and measures in your life.

Hast thou entered into the springs of the sea?
—Job 38:16

ome things in nature must remain a mystery to the most intelligent and enterprising investigators. Human knowledge has bounds beyond which it cannot pass. Universal knowledge is for God alone. If this is the case in regard to things that are seen and temporal, I may rest assured that it is even more the case in spiritual and eternal matters. Why, then, have I been torturing my mind with speculations about destiny and will, predestination, and human responsibility? I am no more able to comprehend these deep and mysterious truths than I am to plumb the depths that lie beneath, from which the old ocean draws her watery stores. Why am I so curious to know the reasons for my Lord's providences, the motives of His actions, the purposes of His visitations? Will I ever be able to clasp the sun in my fist and hold the universe in my palm? Yet these things are as a drop in the bucket compared to what the Lord my God is able to do. Let me not strive to understand the infinite, but rather spend my strength in love. What I cannot gain by intellect, I can possess by affection. Let that satisfy me. I cannot penetrate the heart of the sea, but I can enjoy the healthful breezes that sweep over its surface, and I can sail over its blue waves, if I have favorable winds. If I could enter *"the springs of the sea,"* the feat would serve no useful purpose either for me or for others. It would not save a sinking ship or give back a drowned sailor to his weeping wife and children. My solving deep mysteries would not profit me a single bit. The least love for God, and the simplest act of obedience to Him, are better than the most profound knowledge. My Lord, I leave the infinite to You. I pray that You would put far from me any love for the Tree of Knowledge of Good and Evil that would keep me from the Tree of Life.

If ye be led of the Spirit, ye are not under the law.
—Galatians 5:18

He who evaluates his own character and standing from a legalistic point of view not only will despair when he comes to the end of his assessment, but—if he is wise—will also despair at the beginning of it. If we are to be judged on the basis of the law, no one will be acquitted. How blessed to know that we dwell in the domain of grace and not of the law! When we consider our condition before God, we are not to ask, "Am I, in myself, perfect before the law?" but, "Am I perfect in Christ Jesus?" These are very different matters. We do not need to inquire, "Am I without sin through my own merits?" but, "Have I been washed in the fountain provided for sin and uncleanness?" The question is not, "Am I, in myself, well pleasing to God?" but, "Am I *'accepted in the beloved'* (Eph. 1:6)?" When the Christian views his merits from the top of Mount Sinai, he grows alarmed concerning his salvation. He says, "My faith has unbelief in it. It is not able to save me." It would be far better for him to read his merits by the light of Calvary. He should consider the object of his faith rather than his faith itself. Then he could say, "There is no failure in Him; therefore, I am safe." The Christian sighs, "My hope of heaven is marred and dimmed because I am full of anxiety about present things. How can I be accepted?" If he had regarded the ground of his hope, he would have seen that the promise of God stands sure. Whatever our doubts may be, the oath and promise never fail. (See Hebrews 6:17.) Believer, it is always safer for you to be led by the Spirit into gospel liberty than to wear the chains of legalism. Judge yourself by what Christ is rather than by what you are. Satan will try to destroy your peace by reminding you of your sinfulness and imperfections. You can meet his accusations only by faithfully adhering to the Gospel and refusing to wear the yoke of bondage.

There is sorrow on the sea; it cannot be quiet.
—Jeremiah 49:23

We don't know what sorrow there may be on the sea at this moment. We are safe in our quiet rooms, but far away on the salty sea, a hurricane may be cruelly seeking the lives of men. Hear how the fiends of death howl among the rigging, how every timber loosens as the waves beat like battering rams against the vessel! May God help you, poor drenched and wearied ones! My prayer goes up to the great Lord of sea and land, that He will calm the storm and bring you to your desired haven! However, I should do more than just pray. I should also try to help those hardy men who risk their lives so constantly. Have I ever done anything for them? What can I do? How often the tumultuous sea swallows up the sailor! Thousands of corpses lie in the deep, where pearls lie. There is death-sorrow on the sea, which is echoed in the long wail of widows and orphans. The salt of the sea is in the eyes of many mothers and wives. Remorseless billows, you have devoured the love of women and the support of households. What a resurrection there will be from the caverns of the deep when the sea gives up its dead (Rev. 20:13)! Until then, there will be sorrow on the sea. As if in sympathy with the woes of the earth, the sea is continually fretting along a thousand shores, wailing with a sorrowful cry like its own birds, booming with a hollow crash of unrest, raving with noisy discontent, chafing with hoarse wrath, or jangling with the voices of ten thousand murmuring pebbles. The roar of the sea may be joyous to a rejoicing spirit, but to the child of sorrow, the wide, wide ocean is even more forlorn than the wide, wide world. This world is not our rest, and the restless billows tell us so. There is a land where there is *"no more sea"* (Rev. 21:1). Our faces are steadfastly set toward it; we are going to the place of which the Lord has spoken. Until then, we cast our sorrows on the Lord, who walked on the sea long ago, and who makes a way for His people through its depths.

*The exceeding greatness of his power to us-ward who believe,
according to the working of his mighty power, which he wrought in
Christ, when he raised him from the dead.*
—Ephesians 1:19–20

In the resurrection of Christ, as in our salvation, nothing short of divine power was employed. What can we say of those who think that conversion is brought about by the free will of man and is due to his own good character? When we see the dead rise from their graves by their own power, then we can expect to see ungodly sinners turning to Christ of their own free will. The preached or read Word, in itself, does not bring this divine power. All quickening power proceeds from the Holy Spirit. The power that raised Christ from the dead was irresistible. All the soldiers and the high priests could not keep the body of Christ in the tomb. Death itself could not hold Jesus in its chains. The same irresistible power is employed in the believer when he is raised to *"newness of life"* (Rom. 6:4). No sin, no corruption, no demons in hell or sinners on earth can hold back the hand of God's grace when He intends to convert someone. If God omnipotently says, "You will," man cannot say, "I will not." The power that raised Christ from the dead was also glorious. It reflected honor upon God and brought dismay to the hosts of evil. God receives great glory in the conversion of every sinner. The power was everlasting. *"Christ being raised from the dead dieth no more; death hath no more dominion over him"* (Rom. 6:9). Therefore, since we have been raised from the dead in Christ, we do not go back to our dead works or old corruptions. Instead, we live for God. Because He lives, we live also. *"For ye are dead, and your life is hid with Christ in God"* (Col. 3:3). *"As Christ was raised up from the dead by the glory of the Father, even so we also should walk in newness of life"* (Rom. 6:4). Last, note that the new life is united to Jesus. The same power that raised the Head works life in the members. What a blessing to be *"quickened…together with Christ"* (Eph. 2:5)!

And round about the throne were four and twenty seats: and upon the
seats I saw four and twenty elders sitting, clothed in white raiment.
—Revelation 4:4

hese representatives of the saints in heaven are said to be around the throne. In the passage where Solomon spoke of the king sitting at his table (Song 1:12), some scholars translate *"table"* as "a round table." From this translation, some Bible expositors—without stretching the meaning of the text, I believe—have said that this imagery means there is an equality among the saints. This idea is conveyed by the equal nearness of the twenty-four elders. The condition of glorified spirits in heaven is that of nearness to Christ, clear vision of His glory, constant access to His court, and intimate fellowship with Him. There is no difference, in this respect, between one saint and another. All the people of God—apostles, martyrs, ministers, as well as private and obscure Christians—will be seated near the throne, where they will forever gaze upon their exalted Lord and be satisfied in His love. They will all be near to Christ, all be in ecstasy over His love, all be eating and drinking at the same table with Him, all be equally beloved as His favorites and friends, even if they will not all be equally rewarded as servants. Let believers on earth imitate the saints in heaven in their nearness to Christ. Let us on earth be as the elders are in heaven, sitting around the throne. May Christ be the object of our thoughts, the center of our lives. How can we endure to live at such a distance from our Beloved? Lord Jesus, draw us nearer to Yourself. Say to us, *"Abide in me, and I in you"* (John 15:4). Permit us to sing, *"His left hand is under my head, and his right hand doth embrace me"* (Song 2:6).

> O lift me higher, nearer Thee,
> And as I rise more pure and meet,
> O let my soul's humility
> Make me lie lower at Thy feet;
> Less trusting self, the more I prove
> The blessed comfort of Thy love.

Evening wolves.
—Habakkuk 1:8

While I was preparing *Evening by Evening*, the above phrase came to my mind so frequently that, in order to free myself from its unrelenting persistence, I determined to devote a page to it! The evening wolf, infuriated by a day of hunger, was fiercer and more ravenous than he would have been in the morning. This furious creature may represent our doubts and fears after a day of distractions, losses in business, and perhaps ridicule from our fellowmen. How our thoughts howl in our ears, "Where is your God now?" How voracious and greedy they are, swallowing up all suggestions of comfort and remaining as hungry as before. Great Shepherd, slay these *"evening wolves."* Cause Your sheep to lie down in green pastures, undisturbed by insatiable unbelief. The fiends of hell are like the *"evening wolves."* When the flock of Christ is in a cloudy and dark day, and its sun seems to be going down, they are quick to tear and devour. They will hardly ever attack a Christian in the daylight of faith; but in the gloom of soul conflict, they will assault him. O Lord, You have laid down Your life for the sheep. Preserve them from the fangs of the wolf. False teachers, who craftily and industriously hunt for the precious lives of the sheep, and devour them by their falsehoods, are as dangerous and detestable as *"evening wolves."* Darkness is their element, deceit is their character, and destruction is their end. We are most in danger from them when they wear sheepskin. (See Matthew 7:15.) Blessed is the one who is kept from them, for thousands are made the prey of *"grievous* [destructive] *wolves"* (Acts 20:29) that enter within the fold of the church. What a wonder of grace it is when fierce persecutors are converted! Then the wolf dwells with the lamb, and men of cruel, ungovernable dispositions become gentle and teachable. O Lord, convert many of these wolves. We pray for their salvation tonight.

Lead me, O LORD, in thy righteousness because of mine enemies.
—Psalm 5:8

he enmity of the world against the followers of Christ is very bitter. People will forgive a thousand faults in others, but they will magnify the most trivial offenses in the followers of Jesus. Instead of regretting this state of affairs, which will accomplish nothing, let us use it for our benefit. Since so many are waiting for us to stumble, let this circumstance be our special motivation to walk very carefully before God. If we live carelessly, the eagle-eyed world will soon see it. With its hundred tongues, it will spread the story, exaggerated and emblazoned by the zeal of slander. People will shout triumphantly, "Aha! We were right! See how these Christians act. They are all hypocrites!" In this way, much damage will be done to the cause of Christ, and His name will be gravely insulted. The Cross of Christ is, in itself, an offense to the world. Let us be careful not to add any offense of our own. The Cross is *"unto the Jews a stumblingblock"* (1 Cor. 1:23). Let us make sure that we do not put any stumbling blocks where there are enough already. It is *"unto the Greeks foolishness"* (v. 23). Let us not add our folly, and thereby give any excuse for the scorn with which the worldly-wise deride the Gospel. How vigilant we need to be over ourselves! How strict we must be with our consciences! In the presence of adversaries who will misrepresent our best deeds and impugn our motives when they cannot censure our actions, how circumspect we must be! Pilgrims travel as suspect persons through Vanity Fair. Not only are we under surveillance, but also there are more spies than we imagine. The espionage is everywhere, at home and abroad. If we fall into our enemies' hands, we may sooner expect generosity from a wolf or mercy from a fiend than anything like patience with our weaknesses from men who spice their infidelity toward God with scandals against His people. O Lord, lead us always, lest our enemies trip us up!

I will sing of mercy and judgment.
—Psalm 101:1

aith triumphs in trial. When reason is thrust into the inner prison, with her feet secured in the stocks, faith makes the dungeon walls ring with her joyful notes, as she cries, *"I will sing of mercy and judgment: unto thee, O LORD, will I sing"* (Ps. 101:1). Faith pulls the black mask from the face of trouble and discovers the angel underneath. Faith looks up at the cloud and sees that

> 'Tis big with mercy and will break
> In blessings on her head.

There is a theme for a song even in the judgments of God toward us. First, the trial is not as heavy as it might have been. Second, the trouble is not as severe as we deserve to bear. Third, our affliction is not as crushing as the burden that others have to carry. Faith sees that even her worst sorrow is not given to her as a punishment. There is not a drop of God's wrath in it; it is all sent in love. Faith discerns love gleaming like a jewel on the breast of an angry God. Faith says of her grief, "This is a badge of honor, for the child must undergo the rod." Then she sings of the sweet result of her sorrows, because they are for her spiritual benefit. Faith says, *"Our light affliction, which is but for a moment, worketh for us a far more exceeding and eternal weight of glory"* (2 Cor. 4:17). Therefore, Faith rides on its black horse, conquering and going forth to conquer, trampling down carnal reason and fleshly-mindedness, and singing songs of victory amid the thickest of the fray.

> All I meet I find assists me
> In my path to heavenly joy:
> Where, though trials now attend me,
> Trials never more annoy.

> Blest there with a weight of glory,
> Still the path I'll ne'er forget,
> But, exulting, cry, it led me
> To my blessed Savior's seat.

This man receiveth sinners.
—Luke 15:2

Note the graciousness of the fact that Jesus receives sinners. This Man, who towers above all other men, who is *"holy, harmless* [innocent], *undefiled, separate from sinners"* (Heb. 7:26)—*this* Man receives sinners. This Man, who is none other than the eternal God, before whom angels cover their faces (Isa. 6:2)—*this* Man receives sinners. Only the language of angels could describe such a mighty example of humility for the sake of love. It is not remarkable that any of us would be willing to seek lost men, women, and children, because they are of our own race. However, that He, the offended God, against whom the transgression has been committed, would take upon Himself the form of a servant and bear the sin of many, and would then be willing to receive the vilest of the vile—that is marvelous! *"This man receiveth sinners,"* not so that they may remain sinners, but so that He may pardon their sins, justify them, cleanse their hearts by His purifying Word, and preserve their souls by the indwelling of the Holy Spirit. He receives them so that He may enable them to serve Him, to show forth His praise, and to have communion with Him. He receives sinners into His heart's love. He takes them from the dunghill and wears them as jewels in His crown. He plucks them as brands from the fire and preserves them as costly monuments of His mercy. None are so precious in Jesus' sight as the sinners for whom He died. Jesus does not receive sinners at some outdoor receiving area or courtyard where He charitably shows them hospitality, as men might do for beggars who pass by. Instead, He opens the golden gates of His royal heart and receives the sinner right into Himself! Yes, He admits the humble penitent into personal union with Himself and makes Him a member of His body—of His own flesh and bones. There was never such a reception as this! This fact is still very certain this evening: He is still receiving sinners. I pray that sinners will receive Him.

I acknowledged my sin unto thee, and mine iniquity have I not hid. I said, I will confess my transgressions unto the LORD; and thou forgavest the iniquity of my sin.
—Psalm 32:5

David's grief over his sin was bitter. Its effects were visible on his body: his bones wasted away (Ps. 32:3), and his vigor was turned into the *"drought of summer"* (v. 4). He could find no remedy until he had made a full confession of his sin before the throne of heavenly grace. He told us that, for a time, he kept silent, and his heart became more and more filled with grief (vv. 3–4). Like a mountain lake whose outlet is blocked up, his soul was swollen with torrents of sorrow. He made excuses, and he tried to divert his thoughts, but it was no use. His anguish gathered like a festering sore. Since he would not use the scalpel of confession, his spirit was full of torment and knew no rest. At last it came to this: he must return to his God in humble penitence or die outright. So he ran to the mercy seat and there unrolled the volume of his iniquities before the all-seeing One, acknowledging all the evil of his ways in language such as you read in the Fifty-first Psalm and other penitential psalms. Having done this, a work so simple and yet so difficult on his pride, he immediately received the sign of divine forgiveness. The bones that had been broken were caused to rejoice, and he came forth singing of the blessedness of the man whose transgression is forgiven (v. 1). See the value of a grace-worked confession of sin! It is to be prized above all cost, for in every case where there is genuine, gracious confession, mercy is freely given. This is not because the repentance and confession deserve mercy; the mercy is given for Christ's sake. May God be blessed, for there is always healing for the broken heart. The fountain is continuously flowing to cleanse us from our sins. Truly, O Lord, *"thou art a God ready to pardon"* (Neh. 9:17)! Therefore, we will acknowledge our iniquities to You.

A people near unto him.
—Psalm 148:14

The dispensation of the old covenant was one of distance. Even when God appeared to His servant Moses, He said, *"Draw not nigh hither: put off thy shoes from off thy feet"* (Exod. 3:5). When He manifested Himself on Mount Sinai to His own chosen and separated people, one of the first commands He gave was, *"Set bounds about the mount"* (Exod. 19:23). In the sacred worship of both the tabernacle and the temple, the thought of distance was always prominent. Into the inner court, none but the priests might dare to intrude, while into the innermost place or the Holy of Holies, the high priest entered only once a year. It was as if the Lord in those early ages wanted to teach man that sin was so utterly loathsome to Him that He had to treat men as lepers put outside the camp. When He came nearest to them, He still made them feel the width of the separation between a holy God and an impure sinner. Yet when the Gospel came, we were placed on quite another footing. The word "Go" was exchanged for "Come," distance was succeeded by nearness, and we who formerly were afar off were brought near by the blood of Jesus Christ. Incarnate Deity has no wall of fire around Him. *"Come unto me, all ye that labour and are heavy laden, and I will give you rest"* (Matt. 11:28) is the joyful proclamation of God as He appears in human flesh. Now He does not teach the leper his leprosy by setting him at a distance, but by Himself suffering the penalty of the leper's defilement. What a state of safety and privilege this nearness to God through Jesus is! Do you know it by experience? If you know it, are you living in the power of it? This nearness is marvelous, yet it is to be followed by a dispensation of even greater nearness, when it will be said, *"The tabernacle of God is with men, and he will dwell with them"* (Rev. 21:3). Make the time of this greater nearness come quickly, O Lord!

Am I a sea, or a whale, that thou settest a watch over me?
—Job 7:12

This was a strange question for Job to ask of the Lord. He felt he was too insignificant to be so strictly watched and chastened, and he hoped that he was not so unruly as to need to be restrained. The inquiry was natural from one surrounded by such insupportable miseries. Nevertheless, the question is such that it leaves the questioner open to receiving a very humbling answer. It is true that man is not the ocean, but he is even more troublesome and unruly than the sea. The sea obediently respects its own boundaries. It does not go beyond its limit, even though its limit may be only a sandbar. Mighty as it is, it obeys the divine *"Hitherto"* (Job 38:11). Even when it is raging at the height of a storm, it respects God's word. However, self-willed man defies heaven and oppresses earth. There is no end to his rebellious rage. The sea, obedient to the moon, ebbs and flows with ceaseless regularity, and thus fulfills an active as well as a passive obedience. Yet man is restless beyond his domain. He sleeps far inside the lines of duty, being lazy when he should be active. He will neither come nor go at the divine command, but sullenly prefers to do what he should not do and to leave undone what is required of him. Every drop in the ocean, every beaded bubble, every bit of foam, and every shell and pebble feel the power of God's law, and they yield or move at once. If only our nature were but one thousandth as much conformed to the will of God! We call the sea fickle and false, but how constant it is! From our fathers' days, and from ancient days before them, the sea has remained where it was, beating on the same cliffs, to the same tune. We know where to find it. It does not forsake its bed, and its ceaseless boom does not change. Yet where is man—vain, fickle man? Can the wise man guess by what foolishness he will next be seduced from his obedience? We need more watching than the billowy sea, for we are far more rebellious. Lord, rule us for Your own glory. Amen.

Encourage him.
—Deuteronomy 1:38

od uses His people to encourage one another. He did not say to the angel, "Gabriel, my servant Joshua is about to lead my people into Canaan. Go and encourage him." God never works needless miracles. If His purposes can be accomplished by ordinary means, He will not use miraculous methods. Gabriel would not have been half as well equipped for the work of encouraging Joshua as Moses was. A brother's sympathy is more precious than an angel's message. The angel, who was swift of wing, would have known the Master's commands but might not have been familiar with the people's character. The angel had never experienced the hardness of the road or seen the fiery serpents; neither had he led the stiff-necked multitude in the wilderness, as Moses had done. We should be glad that God usually works *for* man *by* man. It forms a bond of brotherhood. When we are mutually dependent on one another, we are more completely blended into one family. Beloved, take the text as God's message to you. Work to help others, and especially strive to encourage them. Speak in an encouraging way to the young person who is anxiously seeking God, and lovingly try to move stumbling blocks out of his way. When you find a spark of grace in his heart, kneel down and blow it into a flame. Allow the young believer to discover the roughness of the road by degrees, but tell him of the strength that dwells in God, of the sureness of the promise, and of the delights of communion with Christ. Aim to comfort the sorrowful and to encourage the despondent. *"Speak a word in season to him that is weary"* (Isa. 50:4), and encourage those who are fearful to go on their way with gladness. God encourages you by His promises; Christ encourages you as He points to the heaven He has won for you; and the Spirit encourages you as He works in you *"to will and to do of his good pleasure"* (Phil. 2:13). Imitate divine wisdom, and encourage others, according to this evening's text.

And they follow me.
—John 10:27

e should follow our Lord as unhesitatingly as sheep follow their shepherd, for He has a right to lead us wherever He pleases. We are not our own; we are *"bought with a price"* (1 Cor. 6:20). Therefore, let us recognize the rights of the redeeming blood. The soldier follows his captain, and the servant obeys his master. How much more should we follow our Redeemer, to whom we are purchased possessions. We are not true to our profession of faith as followers of Christ if we question the commands of our Leader and Commander. Submission is our duty; being argumentative is our folly. Our Lord might often say to us, as He did to Peter, *"What is that to thee? follow thou me"* (John 21:22). Wherever Jesus leads us, He goes before us. Even if we do not know where we are going, we know with whom we go. With such a Companion, we do not need to dread the perils of the road. The journey may be long, but His *"everlasting arms"* (Deut. 33:27) will carry us to the end. The presence of Jesus is the assurance of eternal salvation. Because He lives, we also will live. We should follow Christ in simplicity and faith, because the paths in which He leads us all end in glory and immortality. It is true that they may not be smooth paths. They may be covered with sharp, unyielding trials, but they lead to the *"city which hath foundations, whose builder and maker is God"* (Heb. 11:10). *"All the paths of the LORD are mercy and truth unto such as keep his covenant"* (Ps. 25:10). Let us put full trust in our Leader. We know that, come prosperity or adversity, health or sickness, popularity or contempt, His purpose will be worked out. That purpose will be pure, unmingled good for every heir of mercy. We will find that it is sweet to go up the exposed side of the hill with Christ. When rain and snow blow into our faces, His dear love will make us far more blessed than those who sit at home and warm their hands at the world's fire. Into the dens of lions or to the hills of leopards, we will follow our Beloved. Precious Jesus, draw us, and we will run after You.

For this child I prayed.
—1 Samuel 1:27

evout souls delight to look on the mercies that they have obtained in answer to prayer, for they can see God's special love in them. When we can name our blessings *Samuel,* that is, "asked of God," they will be as dear to us as Hannah's child was to her. Hannah's husband had another wife, Peninnah, who had many children. However, her children came as common blessings unsought in prayer. Hannah's one, heaven-given child was far dearer, because he was the fruit of earnest pleadings. The cup of prayer puts sweetness into the medicine it brings. When we have prayed for the conversion of our children, how doubly sweet it is for us when they are saved, for we see our own petitions fulfilled in them! It is even better to rejoice over our children as the fruit of our intercession than as the fruit of our bodies. Have we sought the Lord for one of the *"best* [spiritual] *gifts"* (1 Cor. 12:31)? When it comes to us, it will be wrapped up in the gold cloth of God's faithfulness and truth, and thus will be doubly precious. Have we prayed for success in the Lord's work? How joyful the prosperity is that comes flying upon the wings of prayer! It is always best to receive blessings into our house in the legitimate way—by the door of prayer. Then they are blessings indeed, and not temptations. Even when prayer is not quickly answered, the blessings grow all the richer because of the delay. When Jesus was a boy, He was all the more lovely in the eyes of Mary when she found Him after having sought Him sorrowfully. (See Luke 2:42–51.) We should dedicate to God what we gain by prayer, as Hannah dedicated Samuel. The gift came from heaven; let it be given back to heaven. Prayer brought it, and gratitude sang over it. Now let devotion consecrate it. It will be a special occasion for saying, "I have only given to You what is already Yours." (See 1 Chronicles 29:14.) Reader, does prayer invigorate or weary you? Which is it?

In the evening withhold not thine hand.
—Ecclesiastes 11:6

Opportunities are plentiful in the evening. People return to their homes after work, and the zealous soulwinner finds time to go about telling of the love of Jesus. Am I engaged in evening work for Jesus? If not, let me no longer withhold my hand from a service that requires abundant labor. Sinners are perishing for lack of knowledge. He who delays may find the hems of his clothes crimson with the blood of souls. (See Jeremiah 2:34.) Jesus submitted both of His hands to the nails when He died on the cross. How can I keep back one of mine from His blessed work? Night and day, He toiled and prayed for me. How can I give a single hour to pampering my flesh with luxurious ease? Get up, idle heart. Stretch out your hands to work, or lift them up in prayer. Heaven and hell are in earnest. Let me be earnest, also, and sow good seed this evening for the Lord my God. The evening of life also has a claim on us. Life is so short that a morning of humanity's vigor and an evening of decline are the sum of it. To some people, life seems long, but a nickel is a great sum of money to a poor man. Life is so brief that no one can afford to lose a day. It has been well said that if a great king were to present us with a huge pile of gold and tell us to take as much of it as we could count in a day, we would make a long day of it. We would begin early in the morning and not stop even when it was evening. Winning souls is a far nobler work. Then why do we withdraw from it so soon? Some people are spared for a long evening of vigorous old age. If that is the case with me, let me use the talents that I still retain and serve my blessed and faithful Lord to my last hour. By His grace, I will die in the harness. I will lay down my charge only when I lay down my body. Those who are elderly may instruct the young, comfort the fainthearted, and encourage the despondent. If evening has less vigorous heat, it should have more calm wisdom. Therefore, in the evening, I will not withhold my hand.

Gather not my soul with sinners.
—Psalm 26:9

ear made David pray this prayer, for something whispered to him, "Perhaps, after all, you may be gathered with the wicked." Although marred by unbelief, this kind of fear springs mainly from holy anxiety arising from the recollection of past sin. Even the pardoned man will inquire, "What if, in the end, my sins are remembered, and I am left off the list of the saved?" He remembers his present unfruitfulness—so little grace, so little love, so little holiness. Looking toward the future, he considers his weaknesses and the many temptations that surround him, and he fears that he may fall and become prey to the enemy. A sense of sin and present evil, as well as his prevailing corruptions, compel him to pray, in fear and trembling, *"Gather not my soul with sinners."* Reader, if you have prayed this prayer, and if your character is described in the psalm from which it is taken, you do not need to be afraid that you will be gathered with sinners. Do you have the two virtues that David had—walking in integrity outwardly and trusting in the Lord inwardly? Are you resting in Christ's sacrifice, and can you approach the altar of God with humble hope? If so, rest assured that you will never be gathered with the wicked, for that calamity is impossible. At the Judgment, like will be gathered with like. *"Gather ye together first the tares, and bind them in bundles to burn them: but gather the wheat into my barn"* (Matt. 13:30). Therefore, if you are like God's people, you will be with God's people. You cannot be gathered with the wicked, for you were too dearly bought. You are redeemed by the blood of Christ, and you are His forever. Where He is, His people must be. You are loved too much to be cast away with reprobates. Will one who is dear to Christ perish? Impossible! Hell cannot hold you. Heaven claims you. Trust in your Surety, and do not fear!

When my heart is overwhelmed: lead me to the rock
that is higher than I.
—Psalm 61:2

ost of us know what it means to be overwhelmed in heart. It is like being emptied, as when someone thoroughly washes and rinses a dish and then turns it upside down to dry. Or it is like being thrown on one's side and submerged, like a ship mastered by a storm. Discoveries of inward corruption will overwhelm our hearts, when the Lord permits the great depths of our depravity to become troubled and to cast up mire and dirt. Disappointment and heartbreak will also overwhelm us, when billow after billow rolls over us, and we are like a broken shell that is hurled to and fro by the surf. May God be blessed, for at such seasons we are not without an all-sufficient solace. Our God is the Harbor of weather-beaten sails, the Lodging of forlorn pilgrims. He is higher than we are—His mercy is higher than our sins, and His love is higher than our thoughts. It is pitiful to see men putting their trust in something lower than themselves. Yet our confidence is fixed on an exceedingly high and glorious Lord. He is a Rock, since He does not change; and He is a high Rock, because the storms that overwhelm us roll far beneath at His feet. He is not disturbed by them, but rules them at His will. If we get under the shelter of this great Rock, we may defy the hurricane. All is calm under the protection of this towering cliff. Sadly, such is the confusion into which the troubled mind is often thrown, that we need piloting to this divine shelter! That is why we have the prayer of our text. O Lord, our God, by Your Holy Spirit, teach us the way of faith and lead us into Your rest. The wind blows us out to sea, and the helm does not respond to our feeble hands. You, and You alone, can steer us safely over the bar between the sunken rocks and into the fair haven. How dependent we are on You—we need You to bring us to You. To be wisely directed and steered into safety and peace is Your gift, and Yours alone. This night, be pleased to deal well with Your servants.

Jesus said unto him, If thou canst believe.
—Mark 9:23

A certain man had a demon-possessed son, who was afflicted with a spirit that made him mute. The father had witnessed the futile attempts of Jesus' disciples to heal his child (see Mark 9:18), and so he had little or no faith in Christ. Therefore, when Jesus told him to bring his son to Him, he answered, *"If thou canst do any thing, have compassion on us, and help us"* (v. 22). Now, there was an *"if"* in his question, but the poor fearful father had put the *"if"* in the wrong place. Without commanding the man to retract the *"if,"* Jesus Christ kindly put it in its rightful position. "Truly," He seemed to say, "there should be no 'if' about My power or My willingness. The 'if' lies somewhere else." He told the father, *"**If thou** canst believe, all things are possible to him that believeth"* (v. 23, emphasis added). When the man heard these words, his trust was strengthened, and he offered a humble prayer for an increase of faith. Instantly, Jesus spoke the word, and the demon was cast out, with an injunction never to return. There is a lesson from this incident that we need to learn. Like this man, we often realize that there should be an "if" somewhere, but we are perpetually blundering by putting it in the wrong place. We make "if" statements, such as the following: "If Jesus can help me…." "If He can give me grace to overcome temptation…." "If He can give me pardon…." "If He can make me successful…." If *He* can? No, if *you* can believe, He both can and will. You have misplaced your "if." If you can confidently trust in Him, then, as all things are possible for Christ, all things will be possible for you. Faith stands in God's power and is robed in God's majesty. It wears the royal apparel and rides on the King's horse, for faith is a grace that the King delights to honor. Equipping itself with the glorious might of the all-working Spirit, faith becomes, in the omnipotence of God, mighty to work, to dare, and to suffer. *"All things"*—without limit—*"are possible to him that believeth."* My soul, can you believe your Lord tonight?

I sleep, but my heart waketh.
—Song of Solomon 5:2

Paradoxes abound in Christian experience. Our text provides us with an example of one: the spouse was asleep, yet she was awake. The only one who can solve the believer's riddle is the one who has plowed with the heifer of his experience. (See Judges 14:11–18.) I would like to emphasize two points in this evening's text: a mournful sleepiness and a hopeful wakefulness. *"I sleep."* Through the sin that dwells in us, we may become lax in holy duties, slothful in religious disciplines, lackluster in spiritual joys, and altogether slack and careless. Yet this is a shameful condition for one in whom the quickening Spirit dwells; it is dangerous to the highest degree. Even wise virgins sometimes sleep, but it is high time for all to shake off the shackles of sloth. It is to be feared that many believers lose their strength, as Samson lost his hair, while sleeping on the lap of carnal security. With a world perishing around us, to sleep is cruel. With eternity so near-at-hand, it is madness. Yet none of us is as awake as we should be. A few thunderclaps would do us all good. It may be that, unless we soon rouse ourselves, we will have them in the form of war, pestilence, or personal losses and bereavements. Oh, that we might leave forever the bed of fleshly ease and go forth with flaming torches to meet the coming Bridegroom! *"My heart waketh."* This is a happy sign. Life has not been extinguished, although it has been sadly smothered. When our renewed hearts struggle against our natural heaviness, we should be grateful to sovereign grace for keeping a little vitality within *"the body of this death"* (Rom. 7:24). Jesus will hear our hearts, help our hearts, and visit our hearts, for the voice of the wakeful heart is really the voice of our Beloved, saying, *"Open to me"* (Song 5:2). Holy zeal will surely open the door.

> Oh, lovely attitude! He stands
> With melting heart and laden hands;
> My soul forsakes her every sin;
> And lets the heavenly stranger in.

Who of God is made unto us wisdom.
—1 Corinthians 1:30

an's intellect seeks rest and, by nature, seeks it apart from the Lord Jesus Christ. Even when they are converted, intellectuals are apt to look upon the simplicities of the Cross of Christ with insufficient reverence and love. They are snared in the old net in which the Greeks were taken; they desire to mix philosophy with revelation. The temptation for someone of refined thought and high education is to depart from the simple truth of *"Christ cruci-fied"* (1 Cor. 1:23) and to invent a more "intellectual" doctrine. This temptation led the early Christian churches into Gnosticism and seduced them with all sorts of heresies. This is the root of Neology and other fine things that, in days gone by, were fashionable in Germany, and are now so ensnaring to certain members of the clergy. Whoever you are, good reader, and whatever your education may be, if you are the Lord's, be assured that you will find no rest in philosophizing theology. You may receive this dogma of one great thinker or that dream of another profound reasoner; however, what the chaff is to the wheat, these ideas are to the pure Word of God. When it is best guided, all that reason can learn is merely the ABCs of truth. Even then, its findings lack certainty. In contrast, all the fullness of wisdom and knowledge is treasured up in Christ Jesus. All attempts on the part of Christians to be content with systems that Unitarian and theologically liberal thinkers would approve of will fail. True heirs of heaven must come back to the great but simple reality that *"Christ Jesus came into the world to save sinners"* (1 Tim. 1:15). Jesus satisfies the most elevated intellect when He is received in faith. Apart from Him, the minds of the redeemed will find no rest. *"The fear of the LORD is the beginning of knowledge"* (Prov. 1:7). *"A good understanding have all they that do his commandments"* (Ps. 111:10).

Howl, fir tree, for the cedar is fallen.
—Zechariah 11:2

When the crash of a falling oak is heard in the forest, it is a sign that the woodsman is at work. Every tree in the forest may tremble, for fear that tomorrow the sharp edge of the ax will find it out. We are all like trees marked for the ax. The fall of one should remind us that, whether we are as great as the cedar or as humble as the fir, the appointed hour is quickly creeping up on every one of us. I trust that we have not become callous toward death by hearing about it often. May we never be like the birds in the church steeple, which build their nests when the funeral bells are tolling and sleep quietly when the solemn peals are startling the air. May we regard death as the weightiest of all events and be sobered by its approach. It is foolish to spend our time on frivolous matters while our eternal destiny hangs on a thread. The sword is out of its sheath—let us not trifle with it. The sword is polished, and the edge is sharp—let us not play with it. He who does not prepare for death is more than an ordinary fool; he is a madman. When the voice of God is heard among the trees of the garden, let fig tree, sycamore, elm, and cedar alike hear the sound of it. Be ready, servant of Christ, for your Master comes without delay. He will come when an ungodly world least expects Him. See to it that you are faithful in His work, for a grave will soon be dug for you. Be ready, parents. See to it that your children are brought up in the fear of God, for they will soon be without their fathers and mothers. Be ready, you who are engaged in business. Make sure that your affairs are in order and that you serve God with all your hearts. The days of your earthly service will soon be over, and you will be called to give account for what you did while in the body, whether good or evil. May we all prepare for the tribunal of the great King with a circumspection that will be rewarded with the gracious commendation, *"Well done, good and faithful servant"* (Matt. 25:23).

My beloved put in his hand by the hole of the door,
and my [heart was] moved for him.
—Song of Solomon 5:4

Knocking was not enough, for my heart was too full of sleep, too cold and ungrateful, for me to rise and open the door. Yet the touch of His grace has caused my soul to awaken. Oh, the longsuffering of my Beloved! He waited for me when He found Himself shut out, and me asleep on the bed of laziness! Oh, the greatness of His patience, to knock and knock again, and to add His voice to His knocking, urging me to open to Him! How could I have refused Him! You base heart—blush, and be ashamed! Yet the greatest kindness of all is that He becomes His own doorman and unlocks the door Himself. Most blessed is the hand that graciously lifts the latch and turns the key. Now I see that nothing but my Lord's own power can save me, for I am a corrupt mass of wickedness. The church's ordinances fail to help me, and even the Gospel has no effect on me, until He stretches out His hand to help. I also now perceive that His hand is effective where everything else is unsuccessful. He can open when nothing else will. May His name be blessed! I feel His gracious presence even now. Well may my heart be moved for Him, when I think of all that He has suffered for me, and of my unkind response. I have allowed my affections to wander. I have set up rivals. I have grieved Him. Sweetest and dearest of all beloveds, I have treated You as an unfaithful wife treats her husband. Oh, my cruel sins, my cruel self. What can I do? Tears are a poor representation of my repentance. My whole heart boils with indignation at myself. What a wretch I am, to treat my Lord, my All in All, my Exceeding Great Joy, as though He were a stranger. Jesus, You freely forgive, but that is not enough. Prevent my unfaithfulness in the future. Kiss away these tears; but then purge my heart and bind it to Yourself seven times over, so that it never wanders again.

Go again seven times.
—1 Kings 18:43

uccess is certain when the Lord has promised it. You may have pleaded in prayer month after month, without any evidence of an answer. However, it is not possible that the Lord will be deaf to His people when they are in earnest about a matter that concerns His glory. Elijah the prophet continued to wrestle with God on Mount Carmel, even when he did not receive an immediate answer to his prayer. Never for a moment did he give in to fear that he would not be served in Jehovah's courts. Six times, Elijah's servant returned to him, unable to report any sign of progress. However, on each occasion, Elijah merely told him, *"Go again."* We must not even consider giving in to unbelief, but hold to our faith even to *"seventy times seven"* (Matt. 18:22). Faith sends expectant hope to look from the top of Mount Carmel. If nothing can be seen, she sends again and again. Far from being crushed by repeated disappointment, Faith is animated to intercede more fervently with her God. She is humbled, but not discouraged. Her groans are deeper, and her sighs more vehement, but she never relaxes her hold. It would be more agreeable to flesh and blood to have a speedy answer, but believing souls have learned to be submissive, and to find it good to wait *for* as well as *upon* the Lord. Delayed answers often cause the heart to search itself, and so lead to contrition and spiritual reformation. Deadly blows are thus struck at our corruption, and our hearts are cleansed of idolatry. The great danger is that people might give up and miss the blessing. Reader, do not fall into that sin, but continue in prayer and watching. At last the little cloud was seen, the sure forerunner of torrents of rain. It will be the same with you. The *"token for good"* (Ps. 86:17) will surely be given, and you will rise as a prevailing prince to enjoy the mercy you have sought. Elijah was a man of *"like passions as we are"* (James 5:17). His power with God did not lie in his own merits. If his believing prayer availed much, why not yours? Plead the precious blood with unceasing persistence, and you will receive what you ask for.

I found him whom my soul loveth:
I held him, and would not let him go.
—Song of Solomon 3:4

Does Christ receive us when we come to Him, regardless of all our past sinfulness? Does He ever chide us for having tried all other refuges first? Is there no one on earth like Him? Is He the best of all the good, the fairest of all the fair? Oh, then let us praise Him! Daughters of Jerusalem, glorify Him with timbrel and harp! Cast down your idols, and lift up the Lord Jesus. Let the standards of haughtiness and pride be trampled underfoot, but let the Cross of Jesus, at which the world frowns and scoffs, be lifted on high. Oh, for a throne of ivory for our King Solomon! Let Him be set on high forever. Let my soul sit at His footstool, kiss His feet, and wash them with my tears. Oh, how precious Christ is! How can it be that my thoughts have not often turned to Him? How can I go elsewhere for joy or comfort when He is so full, so rich, so satisfying? Fellow believer, make a covenant with your heart that you will never depart from Him, and ask your Lord to ratify it. Ask Him to set you as a signet ring on His finger, and as a bracelet on His arm. Ask Him to fasten you around Himself, as a bride adorns herself with jewels, and as a bridegroom clothes himself with finery (Isa. 61:10). I want to live in Christ's heart. In the clefts of that rock, my soul would eternally abide. *"The sparrow hath found an house, and the swallow a nest for herself, where she may lay her young, even thine altars, O LORD of hosts, my King, and my God"* (Ps. 84:3). I want to make my nest, my home, in You. May the *"soul of thy turtledove"* (Ps. 74:19) never leave You again. May I nestle close to You, O Jesus, my true and only rest.

> When my precious Lord I find,
> All my ardent passions glow;
> Him with cords of love I bind,
> Hold and will not let Him go.

A living dog is better than a dead lion.
—Ecclesiastes 9:4

Life is a precious thing. In its humblest form, it is superior to death. This truth is especially certain regarding spiritual things. It is better to be the least in the kingdom of heaven than to be the greatest outside of it. The lowest degree of grace is superior to the noblest development of the unregenerate nature. When the Holy Spirit implants divine life in the soul, it is a precious deposit, which none of the refinements of education can equal. The thief on the cross excels Caesar on his throne; Lazarus among the dogs (see Luke 16:19–31) is better than Cicero among the senators; and the most uneducated Christian is, in the sight of God, superior to Plato. Life is the badge of nobility in the realm of spiritual things. Those without it are only coarser or finer specimens of the same lifeless material, needing to be made alive, for they are *"dead in trespasses and sins"* (Eph. 2:1). A living, loving, gospel sermon, however unlearned in matter and unpolished in style, is better than the finest discourse devoid of anointing and power. A living dog keeps better watch than a dead lion and is of more service to his master. Similarly, the poorest spiritual preacher is infinitely to be preferred to the exquisite orator who has no wisdom but that of words, no energy but that of sound. The same holds true of our prayers and other religious exercises. If we are quickened in them by the Holy Spirit, they are acceptable to God through Jesus Christ, even though we may think that they are worthless. In contrast, our "grand performances," in which our hearts are absent, are—like dead lions—as decaying flesh in the sight of the living God. Oh, we need living groans, living sighs, living despondency, rather than lifeless songs and dead calm. Anything is better than death. The snarls of the dog of hell will at least keep us awake. Yet what greater curse can a person have than dead faith? Quicken us, quicken us, O Lord!

The LORD will give grace and glory.
—Psalm 84:11

t is the nature of Jehovah to be bounteous. He delights in giving. His gifts are precious beyond measure and are as freely given as the light of the sun. He gives grace to His elect because He wills it, to His redeemed because of His covenant, to the called because of His promise, to believers because they seek it, to sinners because they need it. He gives grace abundantly, seasonably, constantly, readily, sovereignly—doubly enhancing the value of the blessing by the way in which He gives it. He freely gives grace, in all its forms, to His people. He generously and unceasingly pours into their souls comforting, preserving, sanctifying, directing, instructing, and assisting grace. He will always give grace bountifully, no matter what may happen to us. We may become sick, but the Lord will give grace. We may experience poverty, but grace will surely be provided. Death must come, but grace will light a candle at the darkest hour. Reader, how blessed it is, as the seasons come and go, and as the leaves begin to fall again, to enjoy such an unfading promise as this: *"The LORD will give grace and glory."* The little conjunction *"and"* in this verse is a diamond rivet that binds the present with the future, for grace and glory always go together. God has married them, and no one can divorce them. The Lord will never deny glory to someone when He has freely granted that person the right to live in His grace. Indeed, glory is nothing more than grace in its Sunday best, grace in full bloom, grace like autumn fruit—ripe and perfected. No one can tell how soon we may have glory! It may be that before this month of October has ended, we will see the Holy City. However, whether the interval is long or short, we will be glorified before long. The Lord will surely give glory to His chosen—the glory of heaven, the glory of eternity, the glory of Jesus, the glory of the Father. Glory is the exceptional promise of a faithful God!

> Two golden links of one divine chain:
> Who owns grace will surely glory gain.

A man greatly beloved.
—Daniel 10:11

hild of God, do you hesitate to claim this title? Has your unbelief made you forget that you are greatly beloved, too? You must have been greatly beloved to have been bought *"with the precious blood of Christ, as of a lamb without blemish and without spot"* (1 Pet. 1:19). When *"God...gave his only begotten Son"* (John 3:16) for you, did that not mean that you were greatly beloved? You lived in sin. Not only that, but you reveled in it. You must have been greatly beloved for God to have been so patient with you. You were called by grace and led to a Savior. You were made a child of God and an heir of heaven. Does all of that not prove God's very great and superabundant love for you? Since that time, whether your path has been rough with troubles or smooth with mercies, it has been full of proofs that you are greatly beloved. If the Lord has disciplined you, He has not done so in anger. If He has made you poor, you have still been rich in grace. The more unworthy you feel, the more evidence you have that nothing but inexpressible love could have led the Lord Jesus to save a soul such as yours. The more sinful you feel, the clearer is the demonstration of the abounding love of God in that He chose you, called you, and made you an heir of bliss. Now, since there is such love between God and us, let us live in the influence and sweetness of it, and use the privilege of our position. Let us not approach our Lord as though we were strangers or as though He were unwilling to hear us, for we are greatly beloved by our loving Father. *"He that spared not his own Son, but delivered him up for us all, how shall he not with him also freely give us all things?"* (Rom. 8:32). Come boldly, believer, for despite the whisperings of Satan and the doubts of your own heart, you are greatly beloved. Meditate on the exceeding greatness and faithfulness of divine love this evening, and go to sleep in peace.

He himself hath suffered being tempted.
—Hebrews 2:18

This is a well-known concept, yet it tastes sweet to the weary heart: Jesus was tempted in the same ways I am. You probably have heard this truth many times, but have you really grasped it? He was tempted to commit the very same sins into which we fall. Do not disassociate Jesus from our common humanity. You are going through a dark place, but Jesus has already gone through it. You are waging a fierce battle, but Jesus has stood toe-to-toe with the same enemy. Let us be encouraged. Christ carried the load before we did, and the bloodstained footsteps of the King of Glory may be seen along the road that we are now traveling. Yet there is something even sweeter than the knowledge that Jesus was tempted in the same way that we are: although Jesus was tempted, He never sinned; therefore, it is not necessary for us to sin. Jesus was a man, and if one Man endured these temptations and did not sin, then in His power, the members of His body may also refrain from sin. Some who are just beginning the Christian life think that they cannot be tempted without sinning. However, they are mistaken. There is no sin in *being* tempted, only in *yielding* to temptation. This truth is comforting for those who are being severely tempted. There is still more to encourage them if they will reflect on the fact that the Lord Jesus, though tempted, gloriously triumphed. As He overcame, His followers will also surely overcome, for Jesus is the representative Man for His people. The Head has triumphed, and the members share in the victory. Fears are needless, for Christ is with us, armed for our defense. Our place of safety is in the Savior. Perhaps we are being tempted right now in order to drive us nearer to Him. Blessed is any wind that blows us into the port of our Savior's love! Blessed are the wounds that make us seek the beloved Physician. You who are tempted, come to your tempted Savior. He can sympathize with your weaknesses. He will come to the aid of everyone who is tried and tempted.

If any man sin, we have an advocate with the Father,
Jesus Christ the righteous.
—1 John 2:1

f any man sin, we have an advocate." Yes, even though we may sin, we still have Him. John did not say, "If any man sins, he has forfeited his advocate" but, *"We have an advocate"*—sinners though we are. All the sins that a believer ever committed, or can commit, cannot destroy his right to have the Lord Jesus Christ as his Advocate. The name that our Lord is called in the text is significant. First, He is called *"Jesus."* He is just the Advocate we need, for *"Jesus"* is the name of the One whose business and delight it is to save. *"Thou shalt call his name JESUS: for he shall save his people from their sins"* (Matt. 1:21). His sweetest name implies His success. Second, He is *"Christ."* The word *"Christ"* in the Greek is *Christos,* meaning "anointed." This shows His authority to intercede on our behalf. The Christ has a right to intercede, for He is the Father's own appointed Advocate and elected Priest. If He were of our choosing, He might fail. However, if God has *"laid help upon one that is mighty"* (Ps. 89:19), we may safely lay our trouble where God has laid His help. He is Christ, and therefore He is authorized. He is Christ, and therefore He is qualified, for the anointing has fully equipped Him for His work. He can intercede in such as way that He moves the heart of God and prevails. What words of tenderness, what sentences of persuasion, will the Anointed One use when He stands up to intercede for me! One more part of His name remains: *"the righteous."* This title reflects not only His character, but also His plea. *"Righteous"* is His character, and if the Righteous One is my Advocate, then my cause is good, or He would not have espoused it. It is also His plea, for He meets the charge of unrighteousness against me by the plea that He is righteous. He declares Himself as my substitute, and puts His obedience to my account. You have a Friend who is well suited to be your Advocate. He cannot do anything but succeed. Therefore, leave yourself entirely in His hands.

He that believeth and is baptized shall be saved.
—Mark 16:16

Mr. MacDonald asked the inhabitants of the island of St. Kilda, Scotland, how a person must be saved. An old man replied, "We will be saved if we repent, forsake our sins, and turn to God." "Yes," said a middle-aged woman, "and with a true heart, too." "Aye," rejoined a third, "and with prayer." A fourth added, "It must be the prayer of the heart." "And we must be diligent, too," said a fifth, "in keeping the commandments." Each having contributed his thoughts, and feeling that a very decent creed had been put together, they all looked to the preacher and waited for his approval—but they had aroused his deepest pity. The carnal mind always maps out for itself a way in which self can work and become great. However, the Lord's way is quite the reverse. Believing and being baptized are not matters of merit to be gloried in. They are so simple that boasting is excluded. It is God's free grace that has won the victory. It may be that you are unsaved. If so, what is the reason? Do you think that the way of salvation prescribed in the text is doubtful? How can that be, when God has pledged His own Word for its certainty? Do you think it is too easy? Then why do you not obey it? Its ease leaves those who neglect it without excuse. To believe is simply to trust, to depend, to rely on Christ Jesus. To be baptized is to submit to the ordinance that our Lord fulfilled at the Jordan River (see Matthew 3:13–17), that the converted ones submitted to at Pentecost (see Acts 2:1–42), and that the jailer yielded obedience to on the very night of his conversion (see Acts 16:23–33). Baptism is an outward sign of inward faith. It does not save, but it demonstrates to us our death, burial, and resurrection with Jesus. Like the Lord's Supper, it is not to be neglected. Do you believe in Jesus? Then, dear friend, dismiss your fears, for you will be saved. Are you still an unbeliever? Then remember that there is only one Door. (See John 10:7–9.) If you will not enter by it, you will perish in your sins.

He had married an Ethiopian woman.
—Numbers 12:1

his was a strange choice for Moses. Yet how much stranger is the choice of Him who is a prophet *"like unto Moses"* (Deut. 34:10), but who is greater than he! (See Hebrews 3:1–3.) Our Lord, who is as fair as the lily, has entered into marriage with one who confesses herself to be *"black, because the sun hath looked upon me"* (Song 1:6). It is the marvel of angels that the love of Jesus is given to poor, lost, guilty men. Each believer, when filled with a sense of Jesus' love, must also be overwhelmed with astonishment that such love should be lavished on an object so utterly unworthy of it. Knowing, as we do, our secret guiltiness, unfaithfulness, and black-heartedness, we are overcome with grateful admiration for the incomparable freeness and sovereignty of grace. Jesus must have found the cause of His love in His own heart. He could not have found it in us, for it is not there. Even after our conversion, we have been *"black"* (Song 1:5), though grace has made us *"comely"* (v. 5). Rutherford said of himself what we must each subscribe to: "His relation to me is that I am sick, and He is the Physician of whom I stand in need. Alas! How often I play fast and loose with Christ! He binds, and I loose; He builds, and I cast down. I quarrel with Christ, and He agrees with me twenty times a day!" Most tender and faithful Husband of our souls, pursue Your gracious work of conforming us to Your image, until You can present us to Yourself without *"spot, or wrinkle, or any such thing"* (Eph. 5:27). Moses met with opposition because of his marriage. Both he and his spouse were the subjects of criticism and gossip. Do we wonder, then, if this vain world opposes Jesus and His spouse, especially when great sinners are converted? The Pharisee's ground of objection is always, *"This man receiveth sinners"* (Luke 15:2).

Now on whom dost thou trust?
—Isaiah 36:5

Reader, this is an important question. Listen to the Christian's answer, and see if it is yours. *"On whom dost thou trust?"* "I trust," says the Christian, "in a tri-une God. I trust the Father, believing that He has chosen me from *'before the foundation of the world'* (Eph. 1:4). I trust Him to provide for me in providence, to teach me, to guide me, to correct me, if need be, and to bring me home to His own house, where there are *'many mansions'* (John 14:2). I trust the Son. He is 'very God of very God,' the Man Christ Jesus. I trust in Him to take away all my sins by His own sacrifice, and to adorn me with His perfect righteousness. I trust Him to be my Intercessor, to present my prayers and desires before His Father's throne. I trust Him to be my Advocate at the Last Great Day, to plead my cause, and to justify me. I trust Him for who He is, what He has done, and what He has promised to do. I trust the Holy Spirit. He has begun to deliver me from my innate sins, and I trust Him to drive them all out. I trust Him to curb my temper, to subdue my will, to enlighten my understanding, to check my passions, to comfort my despondency, to help my weaknesses, and to illuminate my darkness. I trust Him to dwell in me as my life; to reign in me as my King; to sanctify me wholly, spirit, soul, and body; and to take me to dwell with the *'saints in light'* (Col. 1:12) forever." Oh, blessed trust! It is blessed to trust Him whose power will never be exhausted, whose love will never wane, whose kindness will never change, whose faithfulness will never fail, whose wisdom will never be baffled, and whose perfect goodness can never be diminished! Blessed are you, reader, if you have this trust! With it, you will enjoy sweet peace now, and glory in the next life. The foundation of your trust will never be removed.

Praying in the Holy Ghost.
—Jude 20

This is the great characteristic of true prayer: *"in the Holy Ghost."* The seed of acceptable devotion must come from heaven's storehouse. Only the prayer that comes from God can go to God. We must shoot the Lord's arrows back to Him. The desire that He writes on our hearts will move His heart and bring down a blessing; but the desires of the flesh have no power with Him. *"Praying in the Holy Ghost"* means praying with fervency. Cold prayers ask the Lord not to hear them. Those who do not intercede with fervency do not intercede at all. One may as well speak of lukewarm fire as of lukewarm prayer. It is essential that prayer be red-hot. Second, it means praying with perseverance. The true suppliant gathers force as he proceeds, and grows more fervent when God delays to answer. The longer the door of the gate is closed, the more vehemently he knocks. The longer the angel lingers, the more resolved he is that he will not let the angel go without receiving the blessing. (See Genesis 32:24–30.) Tearful, agonizing, unconquerable persistence is beautiful in God's sight. Third, it means praying humbly, for the Holy Spirit never puffs us up with pride. His role is to convict us of sin, and thus to cause us to bow down in contrition and brokenness of spirit. We will never sing *"Gloria in excelsis"* unless we also pray to God *de profundis.* That is, we will never see "glory in the highest" unless we cry to God "out of the depths." Fourth, it means praying with love. Prayer should be perfumed with love, saturated with love—love for our fellow saints and love for Christ. Last, it means offering prayers that are full of faith. A man prevails only as he believes. The Holy Spirit is the author of faith. He also strengthens faith, so that we may pray believing God's promise. May this blessed combination of excellent graces, as priceless and sweet as the spices of the merchant, be fragrant within us, because the Holy Spirit is in our hearts! Most blessed Comforter, help our weaknesses in prayer by exerting Your mighty power within us.

But he answered her not a word.
—Matthew 15:23

hose who are genuinely seeking salvation in Christ, but who have not yet obtained the blessing, may take comfort from the story from which our text is taken. The Savior did not immediately give the woman the blessing she sought, even though she had great faith in Him. He intended to give it, but He waited a while. *"He answered her not a word."* Were her prayers not good? Never in the world were there better prayers than hers. Was her case not needy? It was sorrowfully needy. Did she not feel her need sufficiently? She felt it overwhelmingly. Was she not earnest enough? She was intensely so. Did she have no faith? She had such a high degree of it that even Jesus marveled, and said, *"O woman, great is thy faith"* (Matt. 15:28). We may see, then, that although it is true that faith brings peace, it does not always bring it instantaneously. There may be certain reasons that call for the trial of faith, rather than the reward of faith. Genuine faith may be in the soul like a hidden seed, not yet having budded and blossomed into joy and peace. A painful silence from the Savior is the grievous trial of many seeking souls, but heavier still is the affliction of a harsh, cutting reply such as this: *"It is not meet to take the children's bread, and cast it to dogs"* (v. 26). Many people find immediate delight in waiting on the Lord, but this is not the case with all. Some, like the jailer, are turned from darkness to light in a moment (see Acts 16:23–33), but others are plants of slower growth. A deeper sense of sin may be given to you instead of a sense of pardon. In such a case, you will need patience to bear the heavy blow. Poor heart, even though, in a spiritual sense, Christ may beat and bruise you, or even slay you, trust Him. (See Job 13:15.) Though He may give you an angry word, believe in the love of His heart. Do not, I beg you, give up seeking or trusting my Master because you have not yet obtained the conscious joy that you long for. Cast yourself on Him, and perseveringly depend on Him, even when you cannot joyfully hope.

And I will deliver thee out of the hand of the wicked,
and I will redeem thee out of the hand of the terrible.
—Jeremiah 15:21

ote the glorious personality of this promise: *"I will...I will."* The Lord Jehovah Himself intervenes to deliver and redeem His people. He pledges Himself personally to rescue them. His own arm will do it, that He may have the glory. Not a word is said of any effort of our own that may be needed to assist the Lord. Neither our strength nor our weaknesses are taken into account. The lone *"I,"* like the sun in the heavens, shines out, resplendent in all-sufficiency. Why, then, do we calculate our forces and consult with flesh and blood—to our grievous wounding? Jehovah has power enough without borrowing from our puny strength. *"Peace, be still"* (Mark 4:39), you unbelieving thoughts, and know that the Lord reigns. There is no hint in the text about secondary means and causes. The Lord says nothing of friends and helpers. He undertakes the work alone, and feels no need of human strength to aid Him. All our looking around for the help of companions and relatives is useless. They will be to us as broken reeds if we lean on them. (See Isaiah 36:6.) They are often unwilling to help when they are able, and unable when they are willing. Since the promise comes from God alone, we would do well to wait only on Him. When we do so, our expectation never fails us. Who are the wicked that we should fear them? The Lord will utterly consume them; they are to be pitied rather than feared. As for terrible oppressors, they are only terrors to those who have no God to run to. For when the Lord is on our side, whom will we fear? If we run back into sin in order to please the wicked, we have reason to be alarmed. However, if we hold fast to our integrity, the rage of tyrants will be overruled for our good. When the fish swallowed Jonah, he encountered a morsel that he could not digest. Similarly, when the world devours the church, it is glad to be rid of it again. In all times of fiery trial, let us secure our souls through patient endurance.

Whom he did predestinate, them he also called.
—Romans 8:30

n 2 Timothy 1:9, we read, *"Who hath saved us, and called us with an holy calling."* In this verse, we find the first standard by which we may test our calling. It is *"an holy calling, not according to our works, but according to his own purpose and grace"* (v. 9). This calling forbids all trust in our own works, and directs us to Christ alone for salvation. Then, after we are saved, it purges us from *"dead works to serve the living God"* (Heb. 9:14). *"As he which hath called you is holy, so be ye holy"* (1 Pet. 1:15). If you are living in sin, you are not called. If you are truly Christ's, you will say, "Nothing pains me as much as sin; I desire to be rid of it. Lord, help me to be holy." Is this the longing of your heart? Is this the tenor of your life toward God and His divine will? Second, in Philippians 3:14, we are told of *"the high calling of God in Christ Jesus."* Is your calling a *"high calling"*? Has it ennobled your heart and set it on heavenly things? Has it elevated your hopes, your tastes, your desires? Has it raised the general tendency of your life, so that you spend it with God and for God? We find a third test in Hebrews 3:1: *"Partakers of the heavenly calling."* A *"heavenly calling"* means that the call must be from heaven. If man alone calls you, you are not called. Is your calling of God? Is it a call to heaven as well as from heaven? Unless you are a stranger on this earth, and heaven is your true home, you have not been called with a *"heavenly calling."* Those who have been called declare that they look for a *"city which hath foundations, whose builder and maker is God"* (Heb. 11:10), and that they themselves are *"strangers and pilgrims on the earth"* (v. 13). Is your calling *"holy," "high,"* and *"heavenly"*? Then, beloved, you have been called by God, for such is the calling by which God calls His people.

The Comforter, which is the Holy Ghost.
—John 14:26

We live in an age that is distinctively the dispensation of the Holy Spirit. Jesus comforts us, not by His physical presence, as He will do in the future, but by the indwelling and constant abiding of the Holy Spirit, who is the Comforter of the church. The Holy Spirit's role is to console the hearts of God's people. He convicts us of sin, and He illuminates and instructs us. However, the main part of His work lies in bringing joy to the hearts of the renewed, in strengthening the weak, and in lifting up all those who are bowed down. He does this by revealing Jesus to them. The Holy Spirit consoles, but Christ is the Consolation. If I may use this metaphor, the Holy Spirit is the Physician, but Jesus is the Medicine. The Holy Spirit heals the wound, but He does so by applying the holy ointment of Christ's name and grace. He does not draw from what is His, but from the things of Christ. So if we give to the Holy Spirit the name Paraclete (from the Greek word *parakletos*, meaning "comforter"), as we sometimes do, then our hearts may confer on our blessed Lord Jesus the title of Paraclesis. If the Holy Spirit is the Comforter, Jesus is the Comfort. Now, when the Christian has such rich provision for his needs, why should he be sad and despondent? The Holy Spirit has graciously pledged to be your Comforter. Do you imagine, O weak and trembling believer, that He will be negligent of His sacred trust? Do you suppose that He has undertaken what He cannot or will not perform? If it is His special work to strengthen and comfort you, do you suppose that He has forgotten His business or that He will fail in the loving duty that He performs on your behalf? Do not think so harshly of the tender and blessed Spirit, whose name is *"Comforter."* He delights to give *"the oil of joy for mourning, the garment of praise for the spirit of heaviness"* (Isa. 61:3). Trust in Him, and He will surely comfort you until the *"house of mourning"* (Eccl. 7:2) is closed forever, and the Marriage Feast (Rev. 19:9) has begun.

Love is strong as death.
—Song of Solomon 8:6

Whose love can this be that is as mighty as the destroyer of the human race, the conqueror of monarchs? Would it not sound like satire if it were applied to my poor, weak, and scarcely living love for Jesus my Lord? I do love Him, and perhaps, by His grace, I could even die for Him. However, as for my love, in itself, it can scarcely endure a scoff or a jeer, much less a cruel death. Surely, it is my Beloved's love that is spoken of in the text—the love of Jesus, the matchless Lover of souls. His love was indeed stronger than the most terrible death, for it endured the trial of the cross triumphantly. It was a lingering death, but love survived the torment. It was a shameful death, but love despised the shame. It was a punitive death, but love bore our iniquities. It was a forsaken, lonely death, from which the eternal Father hid His face, but love endured the curse and gloried over all. There has never been such love, or such a death. It was a desperate duel, but love won the victory. What then, my heart? Are no emotions stirred within you at the contemplation of such heavenly affection? Yes, my Lord, I long, I yearn, to feel Your love flaming like a furnace within me. Come and ignite the fervor of my spirit.

> For every drop of crimson blood
> Thus shed to make me live,
> O wherefore, wherefore have not I
> A thousand lives to give?

Why should I despair of loving Jesus with a love as *"strong as death"*? He deserves it, and I desire it. The martyrs felt such love, and they were only flesh and blood. Why not I? They mourned their weaknesses, yet *"out of weakness were made strong"* (Heb. 11:34). Grace gave them their unflinching constancy. The same grace is available for me. Jesus, Lover of my soul, pour out Your love, *"love…strong as death,"* into my heart this evening.

And be not conformed to this world.
—Romans 12:2

If a Christian can possibly be saved while he conforms to this world, it will only be by fire. Such a bare salvation is almost as much to be dreaded as desired. Reader, would you wish to leave this world in the darkness of despondency, and enter heaven as a shipwrecked sailor climbs the cliffs of his native country in order to reach home? Then be worldly. Be mixed up with those who love money but not God. (See Matthew 6:24.) Refuse to go outside the camp bearing Christ's reproach. (See Hebrews 13:11–13.) Or do you want to have a heaven below as well as a heaven above? Do you want to *"comprehend with all saints what is the…depth, and height; and to know the love of Christ, which passeth knowledge"* (Eph. 3:18–19)? Do you want to receive an abundant entrance into the joy of your Lord? Then *"come out from among them, and be ye separate, saith the Lord, and touch not the unclean thing"* (2 Cor. 6:17). Do you want to attain the *"full assurance of faith"* (Heb. 10:22)? You cannot attain it while you commune with sinners. Do you want to flame with fervent love for God? Your love will be dampened by the drenchings of godless society. You may be a babe in grace, but you cannot become a great Christian, you cannot be a *"perfect man"* (Eph. 4:13) in Christ Jesus, while you yield to the principles and business practices of worldly people. It is harmful for an heir of heaven to be a great friend of the heirs of hell. It looks bad when a courtier is too friendly with his king's enemies. Even small inconsistencies are dangerous. Little thorns make great blisters, little moths destroy fine garments, and a little frivolousness and disobedience will rob faith of a thousand joys. If you are a believer, but are compromising your faith, you do not know what you lose by your conformity to the world. It cuts the tendons of your strength, and makes you creep when you should be running. Therefore, for your own comfort's sake, and for the sake of your growth in grace, if you are a Christian, be a Christian, and be a marked and distinct one.

*But the firstling of an ass thou shalt redeem with a lamb: and if thou
redeem him not, then shalt thou break his neck.*
—Exodus 34:20

Every firstborn animal belonged to the Lord. However, since the donkey was unclean, it could not be presented in sacrifice. Then what was to be done with it? Could it be freed from the universal law? By no means. God allowed no exceptions. The donkey was His due, but He would not accept it. He would not nullify the claim, yet He could not be pleased with the victim. No way of escape remained but redemption—the animal could be saved only by the substitution of a lamb in its place. If it was not redeemed, it had to die. This Old Testament law provides us with an important lesson. That unclean animal is yourself. You are justly the property of the Lord who made you and preserves you. Yet you are so sinful that God will not, cannot, accept you. Therefore, it has come to this: the Lamb of God must take your place, or you must die eternally. Let all the world know of your gratitude to that spotless Lamb who has already bled for you, and thus redeemed you from the fatal curse of the law. The Israelite must sometimes have questioned which should die, the donkey or the lamb. Would not a good man pause to evaluate and compare? Assuredly, there is no comparison between the value of the soul of man and the life of the Lord Jesus. However, the Lamb died, and man the donkey was spared. Admire the boundless love of God to you and others of the human race. Imagine—worms are bought with the blood of the Son of the Highest; dust and ashes are redeemed with a price far above silver and gold! What a doom would have been ours if abundant redemption had not been provided! The breaking of the neck of the donkey was only a momentary penalty. Yet who can measure the *"wrath to come"* (Matt. 3:7), for which no limit can be imagined? Immeasurably precious is the glorious Lamb, who has redeemed us from such a fate.

With thee is the fountain of life.
—Psalm 36:9

here are times in our spiritual experience when human counsel or sympathy, or Christian ordinances, fail to comfort or help us. Why does our gracious God permit this? Perhaps it is because we have been living too much without Him. Therefore, He has taken away everything upon which we have been in the habit of depending, so that He may drive us to Himself. It is a blessed thing to live at the fountainhead. While our water bottles are full, we are content, like Hagar and Ishmael, to go into the wilderness. (See Genesis 21:14.) However, when they are dry, nothing will satisfy us but the knowledge that *"thou God seest me"* (Gen. 16:13). We are like the Prodigal Son. We love pig troughs but forget our Father's house. Remember, we can make pig troughs and husks even out of religious practices. Such practices are blessed things, but when we substitute them for God, they are of no value. Anything becomes an idol when it keeps us away from God. Even the bronze serpent is to be despised as *"Nehushtan"* (2 Kings 18:4) if we worship it instead of God. The Prodigal was never safer than when he was driven to the arms of his father, because he could find sustenance nowhere else. The Lord may allow a famine in the land in order to prompt us to seek Him all the more. The best position for a Christian to be in is to live wholly and directly on God's grace—remaining where he stood when he first came to Christ: *"Having nothing, and yet possessing all things"* (2 Cor. 6:10). Let us never for a moment think that our standing is in our sanctification, our self-denial, our graces, or our feelings. Let us recognize that we are saved because Christ offered a full atonement, for we are *"complete in him"* (Col. 2:10). Having nothing of our own to trust in, we rest on the merits of Jesus. His sacrifice and holy life furnish us with our only sure ground of confidence. Beloved, when we are brought into a thirsty condition, we are sure to turn to the *"fountain of life"* with eagerness.

He shall gather the lambs with his arm.
—Isaiah 40:11

ur Good Shepherd has a variety of sheep in His flock. Some are strong in the Lord, while others are weak in faith. However, He cares for all His sheep impartially. The weakest lamb is as dear to Him as the most advanced of the flock. Lambs tend to lag behind, wander, and grow weary. Yet the Shepherd protects them from the dangers of these tendencies with His arm of power. He finds newborn souls, like young lambs, ready to perish, and He nourishes them until they are strong. He finds weak minds ready to faint and die, and He comforts them and renews their strength. He gathers all the little ones, for it is not the will of our heavenly Father that any of them should perish. What a quick eye He must have to see them all, what a tender heart to care for them all, what a far-reaching and powerful arm to gather them all! During His lifetime on earth, He was a great gatherer of the weak. Now that He dwells in heaven, His loving heart yearns toward the meek and contrite, the timid and feeble, and the fearful and fainting here below. How gently He gathered me—to Himself, to His truth, to His blood, to His love, to His church! With great grace, He compelled me to come to Himself. Since my conversion, He has frequently restored me from my wanderings, and again embraced me within the circle of His everlasting arms. Best of all, He does all this Himself, personally. He does not delegate the task of love, but graciously takes it upon Himself to rescue and preserve even the most unworthy servant. How will I love Him enough or serve Him worthily? I would gladly make His name *"great unto the ends of the earth"* (Mic. 5:4). Yet what can my feebleness do for Him? Great Shepherd, add to Your mercies one other: a heart to love You more truly, as I should.

Behold, to obey is better than sacrifice.
—1 Samuel 15:22

aul had been commanded to slay all the Amalekites and their cattle. Instead of doing so, he preserved the king and allowed the Israelites to take the best of the oxen and sheep. When called to account for this, he declared that he had done it with the idea of offering sacrifices to God. However, Samuel immediately countered him with this certain truth: sacrifices are no excuse for an act of direct rebellion. The text for this evening is worthy to be printed in letters of gold, and to be hung up before the eyes of the present idolatrous generation. They are very fond of the fineries of worshipping their own wills, yet they utterly neglect the laws of God. Always remember that to keep strictly in the path of your Savior's commands is better than any outward form of religion. Listening to His precepts with an attentive ear is better than bringing the *"fat of rams"* (1 Sam. 15:22), or any other precious thing, to place on His altar. If you are failing to keep the least of Christ's commands to His disciples, I urge you not to be disobedient any longer. All the pretensions you make of attachment to your Master, and all the devout actions that you may perform, are no recompense for disobedience. *"To obey,"* even in the slightest thing, *"is better than sacrifice"*—no matter how elaborate it is. We are not to rely on Gregorian chant, sumptuous robes, incense, or banners in our desire to please God. The first thing that God requires of His child is obedience. Even though you might give your body to be burned, and all your goods to feed the poor, if you do not listen to the Lord's precepts, all your formalities will be of no profit to you. It is a blessed thing to be as teachable as a little child. However, it is a much more blessed thing, when one has been taught the lesson, to carry it out to the letter. How many people decorate their churches and adorn their clergymen, but refuse to obey the Word of the Lord! Do not be like one of them.

God my maker, who giveth songs in the night.
—Job 35:10

nyone can sing in the day. When the cup is full, man draws inspiration from it. When wealth flows around him in abundance, anyone can praise the God who gives a plenteous harvest or sends home a ship loaded with goods. It is easy enough for an aeolian harp to whisper music when the wind is blowing. The difficulty is in getting the music to swell when no wind is stirring. It is easy to sing when we can read the notes by daylight. Yet the one who can sing when there is not a ray of light to read by—who sings from his heart—is skillful. No one can compose a song in the night by his own ability. He may attempt it, but he will find that it must be divinely inspired. If everything is going well, I can weave songs wherever I go, forming them out of the flowers that grow on my path. However, put me in a desert, where nothing green grows, and then how will I create a hymn of praise to God? How can a mortal man make a crown for the Lord where there are no jewels? If my voice is clear, and my body is full of health, I can sing God's praises. Yet silence my tongue, and put me on a sickbed, and then how will I sing God's high praises, unless He Himself gives me the song? No, it is not in man's power to sing when everything is going badly, unless a coal from the altar touches his lips. (See Isaiah 6:5–7.) Habakkuk sang a divine song when he said, in the night, *"Although the fig tree shall not blossom, neither shall fruit be in the vines; the labour of the olive shall fail, and the fields shall yield no meat; the flock shall be cut off from the fold, and there shall be no herd in the stalls: yet I will rejoice in the LORD, I will joy in the God of my salvation"* (Hab. 3:17–18). Therefore, since our Maker gives *"songs in the night,"* let us wait on Him for the music. O Chief Musician, let us not remain songless when affliction is upon us. Tune our lips to the melody of thanksgiving.

Keep not back.
—Isaiah 43:6

lthough this message was given to the *"south"* (Isa. 43:6), referring to the children of Israel, we may benefit by considering it an exhortation to us, also. We are naturally unlearned in all good things, and it is a lesson of grace to learn to go forward in the ways of God. Reader, if you are unconverted, do you desire to trust in the Lord Jesus? Then *"keep not back."* Love invites you, the promises secure your success, and the precious blood of Jesus prepares the way. Do not let sins or fears hinder you, but come to Jesus just as you are. Do you long to pray? Do you want to pour out your heart before the Lord? *"Keep not back."* The mercy seat is prepared for those who need mercy. A sinner's cries will prevail with God. You are invited—not only so, you are commanded—to pray. Therefore, come with boldness to the throne of grace. Dear friend, are you already saved? Then *"keep not back"* from fellowshipping with the Lord's people. Do not neglect the ordinances of baptism and the Lord's Supper. You may have a timid disposition. However, you must strive against it, so that it will not lead you into disobedience. A sweet promise is given to those who confess Christ. By no means miss it, lest you come under the condemnation of those who deny Him. If you have talents, *"keep not back"* from using them. Do not hoard your wealth. Do not waste your time. Do not let your abilities rust or your influence go unused. Jesus did not hold back. Imitate Him by being foremost in self-denial and self-sacrifice. *"Keep not back"* from close communion with God, from boldly taking hold of covenant blessings, from advancing in the Christian life, from looking into the precious mysteries of the love of Christ. Beloved friend, do not be guilty of keeping others back by your coldness, harshness, or suspicions. For Jesus' sake, go forward yourself, and encourage others to do the same. Hell and the joint forces of superstition and unfaithfulness are on the frontlines of the fight. O soldiers of the Cross, *"keep not back."*

Why are ye troubled? and why do thoughts arise in your hearts?
—Luke 24:38

hy sayest thou, O Jacob, and speakest, O Israel, My way is hid from the LORD, and my judgment is passed over from my God?" (Isa. 40:27). The Lord cares for all things, and the humblest creatures share in His universal providence; but His particular providence is over His saints. *"The angel of the LORD encampeth round about them that fear him"* (Ps. 34:7). *"Precious shall their blood be in his sight"* (Ps. 72:14). *"Precious in the sight of the LORD is the death of his saints"* (Ps. 116:15). *"We know that all things work together for good to them that love God, to them that are the called according to his purpose"* (Rom. 8:28). Let this fact encourage and comfort you: while He is the *"Saviour of all men"* (1 Tim. 4:10), He is the Savior *"specially of those that believe"* (v. 10). You are His special care, His regal treasure that He guards as the *"apple of his eye"* (Deut. 32:10), His vineyard over which He watches day and night. *"The very hairs of your head are all numbered"* (Matt. 10:30). Let the thought of His special love for you be a spiritual painkiller, a dear soother of your troubles. *"I will never leave thee, nor forsake thee"* (Heb. 13:5). God speaks that promise to you as much as He did to any saint of old. *"Fear not,...I am thy shield, and thy exceeding great reward"* (Gen. 15:1). We lose much comfort by our habit of reading His promises as if they were only for the church as a whole, instead of applying them directly to ourselves. Believer, grasp the divine Word with a personal, appropriating faith. Hear Jesus say to you, *"I have prayed for thee, that thy faith fail not"* (Luke 22:32). See Him walking on the waters of your trouble, for He is there, and He is saying, *"Be of good cheer; it is I; be not afraid"* (Matt. 14:27). Oh, those sweet words of Christ! May the Holy Spirit enable you to think of them as words spoken to you. Forget others for a while, and accept the voice of Jesus as addressed to you. Say, "Jesus whispers comfort. I cannot refuse it. I will sit *'under his shadow with great delight'* (Song 2:3)."

He shall take of mine, and shall show it unto you.
—John 16:15

here are times when all the promises and doctrines of the Bible are of no benefit, unless a gracious hand applies them to us. We are thirsty, but we are too faint to crawl to the brook to drink. When a soldier is wounded in battle, it is of little use for him to know that there are those at the hospital who can bind up his wounds, and that there are medicines that can ease all the pain he is suffering. What he needs is to be carried to the hospital, and to have the remedies applied to his wounds. It is the same way with our souls. To meet this need, there is One, *"even the Spirit of truth"* (John 14:17), who takes of the things of Jesus and applies them to us. Do not think that Christ has placed His joys on heavenly shelves, and that we have to climb up to them ourselves. No, He draws near and pours His peace into our hearts. O Christian, if you are laboring under deep distresses tonight, your Father does not give you promises and then leave you to draw them up from the Word like buckets from a well. The promises He has written in the Word, He will write anew on your heart. He will manifest His love to you and, by His blessed Spirit, dispel your cares and troubles. O mourner, know that it is God's prerogative to wipe every tear from the eyes of His people. The Good Samaritan did not say to the wounded man, "Here are the oil and wine." He actually poured the oil and wine into the man's wounds. In the same way, Jesus does not only give you the sweet wine of the promise, but He also holds the golden chalice to your lips and pours the lifeblood into your mouth. The poor, sick, weary pilgrim is not merely strengthened to walk, but he is also carried on eagles' wings. What a glorious Gospel we have, which provides everything for the helpless, which draws near to us when we cannot reach for it, which brings us grace even before we seek it! There is as much glory in the way the gift is given as in the gift itself. Happy are those who have the Holy Spirit to bring Jesus to them.

Why sleep ye? rise and pray, lest ye enter into temptation.
—Luke 22:46

When is the Christian most liable to sleep? Is it not when his temporal circumstances are prosperous? Have you not found this to be the case? When you had daily troubles to take to the throne of grace, were you not more wakeful than you are now? Easy roads make sleepy travelers. Another dangerous time is when all is going well in spiritual matters. In Bunyan's *The Pilgrim's Progress*, Christian did not go to sleep when lions were in the way, when he was wading through the river, or when he was fighting with Apollyon. However, when he climbed halfway up the hill Difficulty and came to a delightful arbor, he sat down and immediately fell asleep, to his great sorrow and loss. The Enchanted Ground is a place of warm breezes, laden with fragrant scents and soft influences, all tending to lull pilgrims to sleep. Remember Bunyan's description: "Then they came at an arbor, warm, and promising much refreshing to the pilgrims; for it was finely wrought above-head, beautified with greens, furnished with benches and settles. It also had in it a soft couch, whereon the weary might lean....This arbor was called The Slothful's Friend, and was made on purpose to allure, if it might be, some of the pilgrims there to take up their rest when weary." Depend upon this truth: it is in easy places that men shut their eyes and wander into the dreamy land of forgetfulness. Erskine wisely remarked, "I like a roaring devil better than a sleeping devil." There is no temptation half as dangerous as not being tempted. The distressed soul does not sleep. It is after we enter into peaceful confidence and full assurance that we are in danger of slumbering. The disciples fell asleep after they had seen Jesus transfigured on the mountaintop. Take note, joyous Christian, that good circumstances are near neighbors to temptations. Be as happy as you wish, but also be watchful.

He…began to wash the disciples' feet.
—John 13:5

The Lord Jesus loves His people so much that, every day, He is still doing for them much that is analogous to washing their soiled feet. He accepts their poorest actions, feels their deepest sorrows, hears their slenderest wishes, and forgives all their transgressions. He is still their Servant, as well as their Friend and Master. He not only performs majestic deeds for them as their High Priest, such as wearing the turban on His head and the precious jewels glittering on His breastplate, and standing up to plead for them, but He also humbly and patiently goes among His people with basin and towel. He does this when, day by day, He removes our constant weaknesses and sins from us. Last night, when you prayed, you mournfully confessed that much of your conduct was not worthy of your profession of faith. Even tonight, you must mourn afresh that you have fallen again into the same folly and sin from which special grace delivered you long ago. Yet Jesus will have great patience with you. He will hear your confession of sin, and will say, *"I will; be thou clean"* (Matt. 8:3). He will again apply the *"blood of sprinkling"* (Heb. 12:24), speak peace to your conscience, and remove every spot. It is a great act of eternal love when Christ once for all absolves the sinner and puts him into the family of God. However, what gracious patience the Savior has when, with much longsuffering, He bears the often-recurring sins of His wayward disciple, day by day and hour by hour washing away the multiplied transgressions of His erring yet beloved child! To dry up a flood of rebellion is a marvelous thing. Yet to endure the constant dripping of repeated offenses—to bear with a perpetual trying of His patience—this is divine indeed! While we find comfort and peace in our Lord's daily cleansing, its real influence on us will be to increase our watchfulness and activate our desire for holiness. Is this the case with you?

*She…gleaned in the field after the reapers: and her hap was to
light on a part of the field belonging unto Boaz,
who was of the kindred of Elimelech.*
—Ruth 2:3

"*Her hap was.*" The situation seemed to come about from nothing but chance, yet it was the direct result of divine guidance. Ruth had gone out to the field to do humble but honorable work with her mother-in-law's blessing, and under the care of her mother-in-law's God, and the providence of God was guiding her every step. Little did she know that among the sheaves she would find a husband, that he would make her the joint owner of all those broad acres, and that she, a poor foreigner, would become one of the ancestors of the great Messiah. God is very good to those who trust in Him, and He often surprises them with unlooked-for blessings. Little do we know what may happen to us tomorrow, but this sweet fact may encourage us: no good thing will be withheld from us. (See Psalm 84:11.) Chance is banished from the faith of Christians, for they see the hand of God in everything. The trivial events of today or tomorrow may involve consequences of the highest importance. O Lord, deal as graciously with Your servants as You did with Ruth. What a blessing it would be if, while wandering in the field of meditation tonight, we happened to come upon the place where our next Kinsman (see Ruth 2:20) will reveal Himself to us! O Spirit of God, guide us to Him. We would rather glean in His field than carry away the whole harvest from any other. Oh, for the footsteps of His flock, which may conduct us to the green pastures where He dwells! This is a weary world when Jesus is away. We could better do without sun and moon than without Him. Yet how divinely beautiful all things become in the glory of His presence! Our souls know the virtue that dwells in Jesus, and can never be content without Him. We will wait in prayer tonight until we happen to come upon a part of the field belonging to Jesus, in which He will manifest Himself to us.

All the rivers run into the sea; yet the sea is not full; unto the place from whence the rivers come, thither they return again.
—Ecclesiastes 1:7

verything that is of this earth is on the move. Time knows nothing of rest. The solid earth is a rolling ball, and the great sun itself is a star obediently fulfilling its course around a greater luminary. Tides move the sea, winds stir the airy ocean, and erosion wears away the rock. Change and death rule everywhere. The sea is not a miser's storehouse for a wealth of waters, for as by one force the waters flow into it, by another they are lifted from it. Men are born, only to die. Everything is hurry, worry, and *"vexation of spirit"* (Eccl. 1:14). Friend of the unchanging Jesus, what a joy it is to reflect on your changeless heritage. Your sea of bliss will be full forever, since God Himself will pour eternal rivers of pleasure into it. We seek an abiding city beyond the skies, and we will not be disappointed. The text for this evening may well teach us gratitude. Father Ocean is a great receiver, but he is a generous distributor. What the rivers bring him, he returns to the earth in the form of clouds and rain. The person who takes everything but returns nothing is out of harmony with the universe. To give to others is to sow seed for ourselves. He who is a good steward, willing to use his substance for the Lord, will be entrusted with more. Friend of Jesus, are you giving back to Him according to the benefit you have received? Much has been given to you. What is your fruit? Have you done everything you can? Can you do more? To be selfish is to be wicked. Suppose the ocean gave up none of its watery treasure. It would bring ruin upon the human race. God forbid that any of us would follow the ungenerous and destructive policy of living for ourselves. Jesus did not please Himself. All fullness dwells in Him, but *"of his fulness have all we received"* (John 1:16). May we have Jesus' nature, so that, from this time forward, we may not live for ourselves!

We are all as an unclean thing.
—Isaiah 64:6

he believer is a new creation. He belongs to a holy generation, a special people. The Spirit of God is in him, and, in all respects, he is far removed from the natural man. Yet, for all that, the Christian is still a sinner. He is a sinner because of the imperfection of his nature, and will continue to be so to the end of his earthly life. The blackened fingers of sin leave smudges on our whitest robes. Sin mars our repentance before the great Potter has finished it on the wheel. Selfishness defiles our tears, and unbelief tampers with our faith. The best thing we ever did independent of the merit of Jesus only swelled the number of our sins. For even when we have been purest in our own sight, we, like the heavens, have not been pure in God's sight. (See Job 15:15.) Since He charged His angels with folly, how much more must He charge us with it, even in our most angelic frames of mind. The song that ascends to heaven and seeks to emulate angelic tunes has human discords in it. The prayer that moves the arm of God is still a bruised and battered prayer, and only moves His arm because the sinless One, the great Mediator, has stepped in to take away the sin of our supplication. The most golden faith or the purest degree of sanctification that a Christian ever attained on earth still has so much alloy in it that it is only worthy of the flames, considered in itself. Every night that we look in the mirror, we see a sinner, and we need to confess, *"We are all as an unclean thing, and all our righteousnesses are as filthy rags"* (Isa. 64:6). Oh, how precious the blood of Christ is to hearts such as ours! How priceless a gift His perfect righteousness is! How bright our hope of perfect holiness in the next world is! Although sin dwells in us, even now, its power is broken; it has no dominion. It is like a broken-backed snake. We are in bitter conflict with it, but we are dealing with a vanquished enemy. In a little while, we will enter victoriously into the city where nothing defiles. (See Revelation 21:27.)

His head is as the most fine gold, his locks are bushy,
and black as a raven.
—Song of Solomon 5:11

Comparisons fail to describe the Lord Jesus, but the spouse used the best analogies she could. The *"head"* of Jesus signifies His deity, for *"the head of Christ is God"* (1 Cor. 11:3). *"Most fine [pure] gold"* is the best conceivable metaphor. However, it is all too poor to describe One so precious, so pure, so dear, so glorious. Jesus is not a grain of gold, but a vast globe of it, a priceless mass of treasure that earth and heaven cannot excel. Created beings are mere iron and clay. They will all perish like *"wood, hay, [and] stubble"* (1 Cor. 3:12). Yet the ever living Head of the creation of God will shine on forever and ever. There is no mixture in Him, or even the smallest taint of alloy. He is forever infinitely holy and altogether divine. The "bushy locks" depict His manly vigor. There is nothing effeminate in our Beloved. He is the manliest of men—bold as a lion, industrious as an ox, swift as an eagle. Every conceivable and inconceivable beauty may be found in Him, though once He was *"despised and rejected of men"* (Isa. 53:3).

> His head the finest gold;
> With secret sweet perfume,
> His curled locks hang all as black
> As any raven's plume.

The glory of His head is not cut off—He is eternally crowned with peerless majesty. The *"black"* hair indicates youthful freshness, for Jesus has the dew of His youth upon Him. Others grow weak with age, but He is forever a Priest, as was Melchizedek. Others come and go, but He abides as God upon His throne, *"world without end"* (Eph. 3:21). Let us behold Him tonight and adore Him. Angels are gazing upon Him. His redeemed must not turn their eyes away from Him. Where else is there such a Beloved? Oh, for an hour's fellowship with Him! Away, you intruding cares! Jesus draws me, and I run after Him.

But their eyes were holden that they should not know him.
—Luke 24:16

The disciples ought to have known Jesus. They had heard His voice so often, and gazed upon His marred face so frequently, that it is amazing they did not perceive Him. Yet is this not the case with you, also? You have not seen Jesus lately. You have been to His Table, but you have not met Him there. You may be in the midst of dark trouble this evening, and though He plainly says, *"It is I; be not afraid"* (Matt. 14:27), you still cannot discern Him. Our eyes are *"holden."* We know His voice; we have looked into His face; we have leaned our heads upon His chest. However, although Christ is very near to us, we say, "If only I knew where I might find Him!" We should know Jesus, for the Scriptures reflect His image. Yet how possible it is for us to open that precious Book and to have no glimpse of the Well Beloved! Dear child of God, is this your situation? Jesus *"feedeth among the lilies"* (Song 2:16) of the Word, and you walk among those lilies, yet you do not see Him. He is accustomed to walking through the glades of Scripture, and communing with His people, as the Father did with Adam in the cool of the day. Yet you are in the garden of Scripture, and you cannot see Him, though He is always there. Why do we not see Him? In our case, as in the disciples' case, this lack of vision must be ascribed to unbelief. They evidently did not expect to see Jesus, and therefore they did not recognize Him. To a great extent, in spiritual things, we get what we expect from the Lord. Faith alone can bring us to see Jesus. Make this your prayer: "Lord, open my eyes, that I may see my Savior present with me." It is a blessed thing to want to see Him, but it is far better to gaze on Him! To those who seek Him, He is kind. However, to those who find Him, He is precious beyond expression!

Thou that dwellest in the gardens, the companions hearken
to thy voice: cause me to hear it.
—Song of Solomon 8:13

My sweet Lord Jesus remembers well the Garden of Gethsemane. Although He has left that Garden, He now dwells in the garden of His church. There He reveals Himself to those who keep His blessed company. The voice of love with which He speaks to His beloved is more musical than the harps of heaven. There is a depth of melodious love within it that leaves all human music far behind. Tens of thousands on earth, and millions above, are favored with its harmonious tones. Some whom I well know, and whom I greatly envy, are at this moment listening to the beloved voice. If only I were a partaker of their joys! It is true that some of them are poor, others are bedridden, and still others are near the gates of death. Yet, O my Lord, I would cheerfully starve with them, languish with them, or die with them, if I might only hear Your voice. Once I did hear it often, but I have grieved Your Spirit. Return to me in compassion, and once again say to me, *"I am thy salvation"* (Ps. 35:3). No other voice can satisfy me. I know Your voice, and cannot be deceived by another. I beg You, let me hear it. O my Beloved, I do not know what You will say, and I do not ask with any conditions. Only let me hear You speak. If it is a rebuke, I will bless You for it. Cleansing my dull ears may require an operation that is very grievous to the flesh. Yet whatever the cost, I do not turn from my one consuming desire: cause me to hear Your voice. Pierce my ears anew; pierce my ears with Your harshest notes. Only do not permit me to continue deaf to Your calls. Tonight, Lord, grant Your unworthy one his desire, for I am Yours, and You have bought me with Your blood. You have opened my eyes to see You, and the sight has saved me. Now, Lord, open my ears. I have read Your heart. Now let me hear Your voice.

I did know thee in the wilderness, in the land of great drought.
—Hosea 13:5

Yes, Lord, You did indeed know me in my fallen state, and even then, You chose me for Yourself. When I was loathsome, and abhorred myself, You received me as Your child and met my urgent needs. May Your name be blessed forever for this free, rich, abounding mercy. Since then, my inward experience has often been a wilderness. Yet You have still acknowledged me as Your beloved, and have poured streams of love and grace into me, to bring me joy and to make me fruitful. Yes, when my outward circumstances have been at their worst, and I have wandered in a land of drought, Your sweet presence has comforted me. Men have abandoned me when I have faced scorn, but You have known my soul in adversity, for no affliction dims the luster of Your love. Most gracious Lord, I magnify You for all Your faithfulness to me in trying circumstances. I deplore that I have at any time forgotten You and been prideful—since I have owed everything to Your gentleness and love. Have mercy on Your servant in this thing! My soul, since Jesus acknowledged you in your low estate, be sure that you acknowledge both Himself and His cause now that you are prosperous. Do not be not lifted up by your worldly successes, so that you are ashamed of the truth or of the poor church with which you have been associated. Follow Jesus into the wilderness. Bear the cross with Him when the heat of persecution grows hot. He acknowledged you, O my soul, in your poverty and shame. Never be so treacherous as to be ashamed of Him. Oh, for more shame at the thought of being ashamed of my Best Beloved! Jesus, my soul clings to You.

> I'll turn to You in days of light,
> As well as nights of care,
> You brightest amid all that's bright!
> You fairest of the fair!

*And knew not until the flood came, and took them all away; so shall
also the coming of the Son of man be.*
—Matthew 24:39

he doom was universal. Neither rich nor poor escaped. The learned and the illiterate, the admired and the hated, the religious and the profane, the old and the young, all sank in one common ruin. Some had undoubtedly ridiculed the patriarch Noah. Where are their lighthearted jests now? Others had threatened him for his zeal, which they had considered madness. Where are their boasting and harsh words now? The critic who judged the old man's work was drowned in the same sea that covered his sneering companions. Those who spoke patronizingly of the good man's faithfulness to his convictions, but did not share in them, sank to rise no more. All the workers who had helped to build the wondrous ark for pay were also lost. The flood swept them all away; it did not make a single exception. Similarly, for those who are outside of Christ, final destruction is sure. No rank, possession, or character will suffice to save a single soul who has not believed in the Lord Jesus. My soul, take note of this widespread judgment, and tremble at it. The general apathy of the people was astonishing! They were all *"eating and drinking, marrying and giving in marriage"* (Matt. 24:38), until the terrible morning dawned. There was not one wise man on earth outside the ark. Folly duped the whole race, folly in regard to self-preservation—the most foolish of all follies; folly in doubting the true God—the most malignant of foolishness. It is strange, is it not? All men are negligent of their souls until grace gives them reason. Then they leave their madness and act like rational beings—but not until then. May God be blessed, for all who were in the ark were safe. No ruin entered there. From the huge elephant down to the tiny mouse, all were safe. The timid hare was equally as secure as the courageous lion; the helpless coney was as safe as the industrious ox. Everyone who is in Jesus is safe. Are you in Him this evening?

Horror hath taken hold upon me because of the wicked
that forsake thy law.
—Psalm 119:53

o you experience a holy shuddering at the sins of others? If not, you lack inward holiness. David's cheeks were wet with rivers of water because of the prevailing unholiness. Jeremiah desired eyes like fountains, so that he might mourn the iniquities of Israel. Lot was oppressed by the conversation of the men of Sodom. In Ezekiel's vision, those upon whom the mark was put were those who sighed and cried for the abominations of Jerusalem. It cannot but grieve the godly to see what pains men take to go to hell. They know the evil of sin experientially, and they are alarmed to see others flying like moths into its blaze. Sin makes the righteous shudder because it violates holy law, which is in every person's highest interest to keep. It pulls down the pillars of the commonwealth. Sin in others horrifies the believer, because it reminds him of the baseness of his own heart. When he sees a transgressor, he cries, along with the saint mentioned by Bernard, "He fell today, and I may fall tomorrow." To the believer, sin is horrible because it crucified the Savior. He sees the nails and the spear in every iniquity. How can a saved soul not look with abhorrence on cursed sin, which killed Christ? My heart, is this how you feel about sin? It is an awful thing to insult God to His face. The good God deserves better treatment, the great God claims it, and the just God will have it, or repay His adversary to his face. An awakened heart trembles at the audacity of sin, and stands alarmed at the contemplation of its punishment. What a monstrous thing rebellion is! What dreadful doom is prepared for the ungodly! My soul, never laugh at sin's foolishness, lest you come to smile at sin itself. Sin is your enemy, and your Lord's enemy. Regard it with abhorrence, for only thus can you evidence the possession of *"holiness, without which no man shall see the Lord"* (Heb. 12:14).

Their prayer came up to his holy dwelling place, even unto heaven.
—2 Chronicles 30:27

rayer is the never-failing resource of the Christian, for any situation, in every plight. When you cannot use your sword, you may take up the weapon of all-prayer. Your gunpowder may be damp, your bowstring may be relaxed, but the weapon of all-prayer is never out of order. Leviathan laughs at the javelin, but he trembles at prayer. Sword and spear need furbishing, but prayer never rusts, and when we think it is the bluntest, it cuts the best. Prayer is an open door that no one can shut. Devils may surround you on all sides, but the way upward is always open. As long as that road is unobstructed, you will not fall into the enemy's hands. We can never be taken by blockade, escalade, mine, or storm, as long as heavenly help can come down to us by Jacob's ladder, to relieve us in our times of need. Prayer is never out of season: in summer and in winter, its merchandize is precious. Prayer gains an audience with heaven in the dead of night, in the midst of business, in the heat of noonday, and in the shades of evening. In every condition, whether poverty, sickness, obscurity, slander, or doubt, your covenant God will welcome your prayer and answer it from His holy place. Prayer is never futile. True prayer is always true power. You may not always receive what you ask for, but you will always have your real needs supplied. When God does not answer His children according to the letter, He does so according to the spirit. If you ask for coarse meal, will you become angry when He gives you the finest flour? If you seek bodily health, should you complain if, instead of physical healing, He causes your sickness to work for the healing of your spiritual maladies? Is it not better to have the cross sanctified than removed? This evening, do not forget to offer your petition and request, for the Lord is ready to grant your desires.

In thy light shall we see light.
—Psalm 36:9

No words can explain the love of Christ to the heart until Jesus Himself speaks within. All descriptions are empty and fall flat unless the Holy Spirit fills them with life and power. Until Immanuel reveals Himself within, the soul does not see Him. If you wanted to see the sun, would you gather together various lamps and candles, and then go out and try to view it using their light? No, the wise person knows that the sun must reveal itself, and that only by its own blaze can that mighty lamp be seen. It is the same way with Christ. *"Blessed art thou, Simon Barjona,"* He said to Peter, *"for flesh and blood hath not revealed it unto thee"* (Matt. 16:17). You may refine flesh and blood by any educational process you select; you may elevate mental faculties to the highest degree of intellectual power; yet neither of these methods can reveal Christ. The Spirit of God must come with power, overshadowing a person with His wings. Then, in that mysterious "Holy of Holies," the Lord Jesus will display Himself to the sanctified eye—as He will not do for the shortsighted sons of men. Christ must be His own mirror. The great mass of this bleary-eyed world can see nothing of the transcendent glories of Immanuel. He stands before them without *"form nor comeliness"* (Isa. 53:2), *"a root out of a dry ground"* (v. 2), rejected by the vain, and despised by the proud. Jesus is understood only where the Spirit has touched the eyes with balm, quickened the heart with divine life, and educated the soul to a heavenly taste. *"Unto you therefore which believe he is precious"* (1 Pet. 2:7). To you, He is the *"chief corner stone"* (Eph. 2:20), the Rock of your salvation, your all in all. Yet to others, He is *"a stone of stumbling, and a rock of offence"* (1 Pet. 2:8). Happy are those to whom our Lord manifests Himself, for His promise to them is that He will make His home with them. O Lord Jesus, our hearts are open. Come in, never to leave. Show Yourself to us now! Favor us with a glimpse of Your all-conquering charms.

Be thankful unto him, and bless his name.
—Psalm 100:4

Our Lord wants all His people to be rich in high and happy thoughts concerning His blessed person. Jesus is not content to have His brethren think poorly of Him. It is His pleasure that His espoused ones be delighted with His beauty. We are not to regard Him as a bare necessary, like bread and water, but as a luxurious delicacy, as a rare and exquisite delight. To this end, He has revealed Himself as the *"pearl of great price"* (Matt. 13:46) in its peerless beauty, as the *"bundle of myrrh"* (Song 1:13) in its refreshing fragrance, as the *"rose of Sharon"* (Song 2:1) in its lasting perfume, and as the *"lily"* (v. 1) in its spotless purity. To help yourself think high thoughts of Christ, remember the estimation that Christ is held in beyond the skies, where things are measured by the right standards. Think how God esteems the Only Begotten, His *"unspeakable gift"* (2 Cor. 9:15) to us. Consider what the angels think of Him, as they consider it their highest honor to veil their faces as they worship Him. Consider what the blood-washed saints think of Him, as day without night they sing His well-deserved praises. High thoughts of Christ will enable us to act consistently in our relationship with Him. The more exaltedly we see Christ enthroned, and the more humble we are when bowing before the foot of the throne, the more truly we will be prepared to act properly toward Him. Our Lord Jesus desires us to think well of Him, so that we may submit cheerfully to His authority. High thoughts of Him increase our love. Love and esteem go together. Therefore, believer, think much of your Master's excellencies. Study Him in His original glory, before He took your nature upon Himself. Think of the mighty love that drew Him from His throne to die on the cross! Admire Him as He conquers all the powers of hell! See Him risen, crowned, glorified! Bow before Him as *"Wonderful, Counsellor, The mighty God"* (Isa. 9:6), for only thus will your love for Him be what it should be.

This is the blood of the testament which God
hath enjoined unto you.
—Hebrews 9:20

There is a strange power about the word *blood*, and the sight of it is always affecting. A kind heart cannot bear to see a sparrow bleed, and unless it has become accustomed to it, it turns away with horror at the slaughter of an animal. As for the blood of men, it is a consecrated thing. It is murder to shed it in wrath, and it is a terrible crime to squander it in war. Is the reason for this solemnity the fact that *"the blood is the life"* (Deut. 12:23), and that the pouring out of blood is a sign of death? I think so. When we contemplate the blood of the Son of God, our awe is increased even more, and we shudder when we think of the guilt of sin and the terrible penalty that the Sin-bearer endured. Blood, always precious, is priceless when it streams from Immanuel's side. The blood of Jesus seals the covenant of grace and makes it forever sure. Covenants of old were made by sacrifice, and the everlasting covenant was ratified in the same manner. Oh, the delight of being saved on the sure foundation of divine pledges that cannot be dishonored! Salvation by the works of the law is a frail and broken vessel whose shipwreck is sure. However, the covenant vessel fears no storms, for the blood insures that it will stay intact. The blood of Jesus made His testament valid. Wills have no power unless the testators die. In this light, the soldier's spear that pierced the Savior's side is a blessed aid to faith, since it proved that our Lord was really dead. There can be no doubt about that matter; therefore, we may boldly take hold of the legacies He has left for His people. Happy are those who see their title to heavenly blessings assured them by a dying Savior. But does this blood have nothing to say to us? Does it not call us to sanctify ourselves to Him by whom we have been redeemed? Does it not call us to *"newness of life"* (Rom. 6:4) and stir us to entire consecration to the Lord? Oh, that the power of the blood might be known and felt in us this night!

And ye shall be witnesses unto me.
—Acts 1:8

In order to learn how to discharge your duty as a witness for Christ, look at His example. He was always witnessing: by the well of Samaria, in the temple at Jerusalem, by the Sea of Galilee, or at the top of a mountain. He witnessed night and day. His mighty prayers were as vocal to God as His daily services. He witnessed under all circumstances. Scribes and Pharisees could not silence Him. Even before Pilate, He *"witnessed a good confession"* (1 Tim. 6:13). He witnessed so clearly and distinctly that there was no mistake in Him. Christian, make your life a clear testimony. Be like a brook of which you can see every stone at the bottom—not like a muddy creek, of which you can see only the surface. Be clear and transparent, so that your heart's love for God and man may be visible to all. You do not need to say, "I am true." Instead, *be* true. Do not boast of integrity. Rather, *be* upright. Then your testimony will be such that people cannot help seeing it. Never suppress your witness out of a fear of man, who is weak. Your lips have been warmed with a coal from the altar. (See Isaiah 6:6–7.) Let them speak as heaven-touched lips should. *"In the morning sow thy seed, and in the evening withhold not thine hand"* (Eccl. 11:6). Do not watch the clouds or consult the wind. In season and out of season, witness for the Savior. If it happens that, for Christ's sake and the Gospel's sake, you must endure suffering in any form, do not shrink from it, but rejoice in the honor thus conferred on you, that you are counted worthy to suffer with your Lord. Rejoice also in this: your suffering, losses, and persecution will be a platform from which you can witness for Christ Jesus even more vigorously, and with greater power. Study your great Exemplar, and be filled with His Spirit. Remember that you need much teaching, much upholding, much grace, and much humility, if your witnessing is to be to your Master's glory.

*The Master saith, Where is the guestchamber, where I shall eat the
passover with my disciples?*
—Mark 14:14

Jerusalem at the time of the Passover was one great inn.
Each householder had invited his own friends, but no
one had invited the Savior, and He had no dwelling of
His own. It was by His own supernatural power that He
found an upper room in which to keep the Feast. This is the
case even to this day. Jesus is not received among the sons of
men, except where, by His supernatural power and grace, He
makes the heart anew. All doors are wide open to the prince
of darkness, but Jesus must clear a way for Himself, or else
lodge in the streets. It was through the mysterious power
exerted by our Lord that the householder raised no objec-
tions, but immediately, cheerfully, and joyfully opened his
guest room. Who he was, and what he was, we do not know.
However, he readily accepted the honor that the Redeemer
proposed to confer on him. Today, we discover who are the
Lord's chosen, and who are not, in much the same way. For
when the Gospel comes to some, they fight against it and
will not have it. Yet when people receive it, welcoming it,
this is a sure indication that there is a secret work going on
in their souls, and that God has chosen them for eternal life.
Are you willing, dear reader, to receive Christ? Then there is
no difficulty blocking the way. Christ will be your guest. His
own power is working in you, making you willing. What an
honor it is to entertain the Son of God! The heaven of heavens cannot contain Him, yet He graciously finds a home
within our hearts! We are not worthy for Him to come under
our roof, but what an unutterable privilege it is when He
graciously enters! For then He makes a banquet and causes
us to feast with Him on royal delicacies. We sit at a banquet
where the food is immortal and gives immortality to those
who feed on it. Blessed among the sons of Adam is he who
entertains the angels' Lord.

His place of defence shall be the munitions of rocks: bread shall be given him; his waters shall be sure.
—Isaiah 33:16

Christian, do you doubt whether God will fulfill His promise? Can the *"munitions of rocks"* be taken by storm? Can the storehouses of heaven fail? Do you think that your heavenly Father will forget you, even though He knows that you need food and clothing? When not one sparrow falls to the ground without your Father's knowledge, and the *"very hairs of your head are all numbered"* (Matt. 10:30), will you mistrust and doubt Him? Perhaps your affliction will continue until you dare to trust your God, and then it will end. There are a great many believers who have undergone trials and been very distressed, until at last they have been driven in sheer desperation to exercise faith in God—and the moment of their faith has been the instant of their deliverance. They have seen whether or not God would keep His promise. Oh, I urge you, do not doubt Him any longer! Do not please Satan, and do not distress yourself, by indulging in unbelieving thoughts about God any longer. Do not think it is a light matter to doubt Jehovah. Remember, it is a sin, and not a little sin, either; it is criminal in the highest degree. The angels never doubted Him, and neither did the demons. We alone, out of all the beings that God has made, dishonor Him by unbelief, and tarnish His honor by mistrust. Shame on us for this! Our God is not deserving of such low-minded suspicion. In the past, we have proven Him to be true and faithful to His Word. With the many examples of His love and kindness that we have received, and are daily receiving, from His hands, it is disgraceful and inexcusable for us to allow a doubt to stay within our hearts. From this time on, may we wage constant war against doubts about our God, which are enemies to our peace, and to His honor. With an unwavering faith, may we believe that what He has promised, He will also perform. *"Lord, I believe; help thou mine unbelief"* (Mark 9:24).

It is enough for the disciple that he be as his master.
—Matthew 10:25

No one can dispute this statement, for it would be improper for the servant to be exalted above his Master. When our Lord was on earth, what was the treatment He received? Were His claims acknowledged, His instructions followed, and His perfections worshipped by those whom He came to bless? No, He was *"despised and rejected of men"* (Isa. 53:3). His place was outside the camp. (See Hebrews 13:11–13.) Crossbearing was His occupation. Did the world give Him comfort and rest? *"Foxes have holes, and the birds of the air have nests; but the Son of man hath not where to lay his head"* (Matt. 8:20). That inhospitable country afforded Him no shelter: it cast Him out and crucified Him. If you are a follower of Jesus, and maintain a consistent, Christlike walk and conversation, you must expect to be treated in the same way in regard to the part of your spiritual life that, in its outward development, comes under the observation of men. They will treat it as they treated the Savior—they will despise it. Do not imagine that worldly people will admire you, or that the holier and more Christlike you are, the more peaceably people will act toward you. They did not prize the polished gem, so why should they value the jewel in the rough? *"If they have called the master of the house Beelzebub, how much more shall they call them of his household?"* (Matt. 10:25). If we were more like Christ, we would be more hated by His enemies. It would be a sad dishonor for a child of God to be the world's favorite. It is a very bad sign to hear a wicked world clap its hands and shout "Well done!" to the Christian. The believer may begin to examine his character, and wonder whether he has not been doing something wrong, when the unrighteous give him their approval. Let us be true to our Master and have no friendship with a blind and base world that scorns and rejects Him. Far be it from us to seek a crown of honor where our Lord found a crown of thorns.

He shall choose our inheritance for us.
—Psalm 47:4

Believer, if your earthly inheritance is a modest one, you should be satisfied with your portion, for you may rest assured that it is the best one for you. Unerring wisdom ordained your circumstances and selected for you the safest and best conditions. Suppose a ship of large tonnage were to be sailed up a river that had a sandbank in one part of it. If someone were to ask, "Why does the captain steer through the deep part of the channel and deviate so much from sailing in a straight line?" the captain's answer would be, "Because I would not get my ship into the harbor at all if I did not keep to the deep channel." Likewise, it may be that you would run aground and suffer shipwreck if your Divine Captain did not steer you into the depths of affliction, where waves of trouble follow each other in quick succession. Some plants die if they have too much sunshine. It may be that you are planted where you receive only a little. You are put there by the loving Farmer, because only in this situation will you bring forth *"fruit to perfection"* (Luke 8:14). Remember this: if any other condition had been better for you than the one you are in, divine love would have put you there. You have been placed by God in the most suitable circumstances. If you could choose your own situation, you would soon cry out, "Lord, choose my inheritance for me, for by my self-will I am *'pierced...through with many sorrows'* (1 Tim. 6:10)." Be content with what you have, since the Lord has ordered all things for your good. Take up your own daily cross. It is the burden best suited for your shoulder, and will prove most effective in making you perfect *"in every good word and work"* (2 Thess. 2:17), to the glory of God. Down, meddlesome self and proud impatience! It is not for you, but only for the Lord of Love, to choose!

> Trials must and will befall—
> But with humble faith to see
> Love inscribed upon them all;
> This is happiness to me.

And it came to pass in those days, that he went out into a mountain to pray, and continued all night in prayer to God.
—Luke 6:12

I f anyone might have lived without prayer, it was our spotless, perfect Lord. Yet no one ever prayed as much as He! Such was His love for His Father, that He cherished being in frequent communion with Him. Such was His love for His people, that He desired to intercede for them often. The prominent prayerfulness of Jesus is a lesson for us. He has given us an example, so that we may follow in His steps. The time of prayer that He chose—night—was admirable. It was the hour of silence, when the crowd would not disturb Him; the time of inaction, when all but He had stopped working; the season when sleep made people forget their troubles and cease coming to Him for help. While others found rest in sleep, He refreshed Himself with prayer. The place of prayer was also well selected. He was alone where no one would intrude, where no one could observe Him. Thus He was free from the pretentiousness of the Pharisees and the interruptions of the public. Those dark and silent hills were a fitting place of prayer for the Son of God. Heaven and earth in midnight stillness heard the groans and sighs of the mysterious Being in whom both worlds were blended. The duration of His supplication is remarkable. The long watches were not too long for Him. The cold wind did not chill His devotions. The grim darkness did not darken His faith, nor the loneliness inhibit His persistence. We are not able to watch with Him for one hour, but He watched for us during entire nights. The occasion of Jesus' night of prayer is notable. It was after His enemies had been enraged, and therefore prayer was His refuge and solace. It was also before He chose the twelve apostles, and so prayer was the entranceway to His ministry, the herald of His new work. Should we not learn from Jesus to resort to special prayer when we are under particular trial or when we contemplate fresh endeavors for the Master's glory? Lord Jesus, *"teach us to pray"* (Luke 11:1).

Men ought always to pray.
—Luke 18:1

I f *"men"* should always pray, and not lose heart (Luke 18:1), how much more should Christian men pray! Jesus has sent His church into the world on the same mission on which He Himself came, and this mission includes intercession. He has made us *"priests unto God"* (Rev. 1:6), and we are to intercede for the world. Creation is mute, but the church is to find a voice for it. It is the church's high privilege to pray with God's acceptance. The door of grace is always open for her petitions, and they never return empty-handed. The veil was torn for her, the blood was sprinkled on the altar for her, and God constantly invites her to ask what she desires. Will she refuse a privilege that even angels might envy? Is she not the bride of Christ? May she not go in to her King at every hour? Will she allow the precious privilege to go unused? The church is always in need of prayer. There are always some in her midst who are declining, or falling into open sin. There are lambs to be prayed for, that they may be carried in Christ's arms; there are the strong to be prayed for, lest they grow presumptuous, and the weak, lest they become despairing. If we maintained prayer meetings twenty-four hours a day, every day of the year, we might never be without a special subject for supplication. Are we ever without the sick and the poor, the afflicted and the wavering? Are we ever without those who seek the conversion of relatives, the reclaiming of backsliders, or the salvation of the wicked? No, with congregations constantly gathering, with ministers always preaching, with millions of sinners lying *"dead in trespasses and sins"* (Eph. 2:1), in a country over which the darkness of false religion is certainly descending, in a world full of idols, cruelty, and wickedness, if the church does not pray, how will she excuse her disgraceful neglect of the commission of her loving Lord? Let the church be constant in supplication, and let every individual believer cast his mite of prayer into the treasury.

And Laban said, It must not be so done in our country,
to give the younger before the firstborn.
—Genesis 29:26

e do not excuse Laban for his dishonesty, but we do not hesitate to learn from the custom that he quoted as his excuse. There are some things that must be taken in order, and if we want to gain the second, we must secure the first. The second may be more lovely in our eyes, but the rule of the heavenly country must stand, and the elder must be married first. For instance, many believers desire the *"beautiful and well favoured"* (Gen. 29:17) Rachel of *"joy and peace in believing"* (Rom. 15:13), but they must first be wedded to the *"tender eyed"* (Gen. 29:17) Leah of repentance. Everyone falls in love with happiness, and many would cheerfully serve twice seven years to enjoy it. However, according to the rule of the Lord's kingdom, the Leah of real holiness must be beloved to our souls before the Rachel of true happiness can be attained. Heaven does not come first but second, and only by persevering to the end can we gain a share in it. The cross must be carried before the crown can be worn. We must follow our Lord in His humiliation, or we will never rest with Him in glory. My soul, are you so vain as to hope to break through the heavenly rule? Do you hope for reward without labor, or honor without toil? Dismiss that idle expectation, and be content to take the difficult things for the sake of the sweet love of Jesus, which will compensate you for everything. In such a spirit, laboring and suffering, you will find that bitter things grow sweet, and hard things easy. Like Jacob, your years of service will seem to you but a few days, because of the love you have for Jesus. Then, when the dear hour of the Wedding Feast has come, all your toils will be as though they had never been. An hour with Jesus will make up for ages of pain and labor.

> Jesus, to win Yourself so fair,
> Your cross I will with gladness bear:
> Since so the rules of heaven ordain,
> The first I'll wed the next to gain.

Strengthen, O God, that which thou hast wrought for us.
—Psalm 68:28

It is our wisdom, as well as our necessity, to petition God continually to strengthen what He has worked in us. Many Christians have neglected to do this, and thus they may blame themselves when they experience trials and afflictions of spirit that arise from unbelief. It is true that Satan seeks to flood the fair garden of the heart and to make it a scene of desolation. However, it is also true that many Christians leave open the floodgates themselves, and let in the dreadful deluge through carelessness and lack of prayer to their strong Helper. We often forget that the Author of our faith must also be the Preserver of it. The lamp that was burning in the temple was never allowed to go out. It had to be replenished daily with fresh oil. Likewise, our faith can only live by being sustained with the oil of grace, and we can only obtain this grace from God Himself. We will prove to be foolish virgins if we do not secure the needed sustenance for our lamps. (See Matthew 25:1–13.) He who built the world also upholds it, or it would fall in one tremendous crash. He who made us Christians must maintain us by His Spirit, or our ruin will be speedy and final. Let us, then, evening by evening, go to our Lord for the grace and strength we need. We have a strong argument to plead, for it is His own work of grace that we ask Him to strengthen—*"That which thou hast wrought for us."* Do you think that He will fail to protect and sustain that work? Only let your faith take hold of His strength, and all the powers of darkness, led on by the master fiend of hell, cannot cast a cloud or shadow over your joy and peace. Why faint when you may be strong? Why suffer defeat when you may conquer? Oh, take your wavering faith and drooping graces to Him who can revive and replenish them! Earnestly pray, *"Strengthen, O God, that which thou hast wrought for us."*

Thine eyes shall see the king in his beauty.
—Isaiah 33:17

The more you know about Christ, the less you will be satisfied with superficial views of Him. The more deeply you study His transactions in the eternal covenant, His guarantees on your behalf as the eternal Surety, and the fullness of His grace, which shines in all His offices, the more you will truly *"see the king in his beauty."* Give yourself to such contemplation. Long more and more to see Jesus. Meditation and contemplation are often like windows of agate and gates of carbuncle, through which we see the Redeemer. Meditation puts the telescope to the eye and enables us to see Jesus better than we could have seen Him if we had lived in the days when He was on earth. If only our conduct were more heavenly, and that we were more taken up with the person, work, and beauty of our incarnate Lord! If we meditated more on Jesus, the beauty of the King would gleam upon us with more resplendence. Beloved, when it is time for us to die, it is very probable that we will have a sight of our glorious King such as we have never had before. Many saints, in dying, have looked up from amid the stormy waters and seen Jesus walking on the waves of the sea. They have heard Him say, *"It is I; be not afraid"* (Matt. 14:27). Ah, yes, when the house begins to shake, and the clay falls away, we see Christ through the openings; and between the rafters, the sunlight of heaven comes streaming in. Yet if we want to see the *"king in his beauty"* face-to-face, we must go to heaven for the sight, or the King must come here in person. Oh, that He would come on the *"wings of the wind"* (2 Sam. 22:11)! He is our Husband, and we are widowed by His absence. He is our dear and fair Brother, and we are lonely without Him. Thick veils and clouds hang between our souls and their true life. When will the *"day break, and the shadows flee away"* (Song 2:17)? Oh, long-expected day, begin!

He that cleaveth wood shall be endangered thereby.
—Ecclesiastes 10:9

Oppressors may have their way with the poor and needy as easily as they can split logs of wood. However, they had better beware, for they are involved in a dangerous business—a splinter from a tree has often killed a woodsman. Jesus is persecuted in every injured saint, and He is mighty to avenge His beloved ones. Success in treading down the poor and needy is a thing to be feared, for if there is no danger to persecutors on earth, there will be great danger in the next world. Splitting wood is a common, everyday task, yet it has its dangers. Similarly, reader, there are dangers connected with your calling and daily life, which it would benefit you to be aware of. I do not refer to hazards relating to floods, wars, disease, and sudden death, but to spiritual perils. Your occupation may be as humble as log splitting, yet the devil can tempt you in it. You may be a household servant, a farm laborer, or a mechanic, and you may be greatly screened from temptations to the more obvious vices, yet some secret sin may do you harm. Those who stay at home and do not associate with the rough world may still be endangered by their very seclusion. The person who thinks he is safe is not safe anywhere. Pride may enter a poor man's heart; greed may reign in a laborer's soul; uncleanness may venture into the quietest home; and anger, envy, and malice may insinuate themselves into the most rural dwelling. We may sin even in speaking a few words to a servant. A little purchase at a shop may be the first link in a chain of temptations. Merely looking out a window may be the beginning of evil. O Lord, how vulnerable we are! How will we be protected? Guarding ourselves is too hard a job for us. Only You are able to preserve us in such a world of evils. Spread Your wings over us, and we, like little chicks, will crouch down beneath You and feel safe!

Thou art from everlasting.
—Psalm 93:2

Christ is *"everlasting."* Of Him we may sing, with David, *"Thy throne, O God, is for ever and ever"* (Ps. 45:6). Rejoice, believer, in *"Jesus Christ the same yesterday, and to day, and for ever"* (Heb. 13:8). Jesus always was. The Babe born in Bethlehem was united to the Word, who was *"in the beginning"* (John 1:2), and by whom *"all things were made"* (v. 3). The title by which Christ revealed Himself to John in Patmos was, *"Him which is, and which was, and which is to come"* (Rev. 1:4). If He were not God *"from everlasting,"* we could not love Him so devoutly. We could not feel that He had any share in the eternal love that is the fountain of all covenant blessings. Yet since He was from all eternity with the Father, we trace the stream of divine love to Himself equally with His Father and the blessed Spirit. As our Lord always *was,* He also *is* eternally. Jesus is not dead: *"He ever liveth to make intercession for [us]"* (Heb. 7:25). Go to Him in all your times of need, for He is waiting to bless you still. Moreover, Jesus our Lord always *will be.* If God spares your life so that you have a full life span of *"threescore years and ten"* (Ps. 90:10), you will find that His cleansing fountain is still open, and that His precious blood has not lost its power. You will find that the Priest who filled the healing fountain with His own blood, lives to purge you from all iniquity. When only your last battle remains to be fought, you will find that the hand of your conquering Captain has not grown weak. The living Savior will encourage the dying saint. When you enter heaven, you will find Him there bearing the dew of His youth. Through eternity, the Lord Jesus will still remain the perennial spring of joy, life, and glory to His people. May you draw living waters from this sacred well! Jesus always was, always is, and always will be. He is eternal in all His attributes, in all His offices, in all His might, and in His willingness to bless, comfort, guard, and crown His chosen people.

Oh that I knew where I might find him!
—Job 23:3

In Job's extreme need, he cried out to the Lord. The greatest desire of an afflicted child of God is to see his Father's face once more. His first prayer is not, "Oh, that I might be healed of the disease that now festers in every part of my body!" or even, "Oh, that I might see my children restored from the jaws of the grave, and my property returned from the hand of the spoiler!" Instead, his first and foremost cry is, "*Oh that I knew where I might find him*' who is my God, that I might come even to His throne!" God's children run home when the storm comes on. It is the heaven-born instinct of the godly to seek shelter from all trouble beneath the wings of Jehovah. "He who has made God his refuge" might serve as the title of a true believer. A hypocrite, when afflicted by God, resents the infliction and, like a slave, wants to run from the Master who has scourged him. This is not the case with the true heir of heaven. He kisses the hand that struck him, and seeks shelter from the rod in the arms of the God who frowned on him. Job's desire to commune with God was intensified by the failure of all other sources of comfort. The patriarch turned away from his sorry friends and looked up to the heavenly throne, just as a traveler turns from his empty water bottle and hurries to the well. He bids farewell to earthborn hopes, and cries, "If only I knew where I might find my God!" Nothing teaches us the preciousness of the Creator as much as when we discover the emptiness of everything else. Turning away with bitter scorn from earth's hives, where we find no honey but many sharp stings, we rejoice in Him whose faithful Word is sweeter than honey or the honeycomb. In every trouble, we should first seek to realize God's presence with us. If we can only enjoy His smile, we can bear our daily cross with a willing heart, for His dear sake.

*The conies are but a feeble folk, yet make they
their houses in the rocks.*
—Proverbs 30:26

onscious of their own natural defenselessness, the coneys resort to burrows in the rocks, and are secure from their enemies. My heart, be willing to glean a lesson from these *"feeble folk."* You are as weak and as exposed to peril as the timid coney. Therefore, be as wise to seek a shelter. My best security is within the fortifications of an unchangeable Jehovah, where His unalterable promises stand like giant walls of rock. It will be well with you if you can always hide in the bulwarks of His glorious attributes, all of which are guarantees of safety for those who put their trust in Him. May the name of the Lord be blessed, for I have done so, and have found myself like David in Adullam (see 1 Samuel 22:1)—safe from the cruelty of my enemy. I do not now have to discover the blessedness of the man who puts his trust in the Lord. For, long ago, when Satan and my sins pursued me, I fled to the cleft of the Rock Christ Jesus, and in His torn side I found a delightful resting place. My heart, run to Him anew tonight, no matter what your present grief may be. Jesus feels for you; Jesus comforts you; Jesus will help you. No monarch in his impenetrable fortress is more secure than the coney in his rocky burrow. The captain of ten thousand chariots is not one bit better protected than the little dweller in the cleft of the mountain. In Jesus, the weak are strong, and the defenseless are safe. They could not be stronger if they were giants, or safer if they were in heaven. Faith gives to men on earth the protection of the God of heaven. They could not wish for anything more. The coneys cannot build a castle, but they avail themselves of what is already there. Similarly, I cannot make myself a refuge, but Jesus has provided it, His Father has given it, and His Spirit has revealed it. I enter it again tonight and am safe from every foe.

Lazarus was one of them that sat at the table with him.
—John 12:2

Lazarus is to be envied. It would have been good to have been Martha, and to have served Jesus. However, it would have been even better to have been Lazarus, and to have communed with Him. There are times for each purpose, and each is fitting in its season. Yet none of the trees of the garden yield clusters like the vine of fellowship. To sit with Jesus, to hear His words, to take note of His actions, and to receive His smiles, is such a blessing that it must have made Lazarus as happy as the angels. When it has been our happy circumstance to feast with our Beloved in His banquet hall, we would not have given half a sigh for all the kingdoms of the world, if such a breath could have bought them. Lazarus is also to be imitated. It would have been a strange thing if Lazarus had not been at the table where Jesus was, for he had been dead, and Jesus had raised him. For the one who had been raised to have been absent when the Lord who gave him life was at his house, would have been ungrateful, indeed. We, too, were once dead and, like Lazarus, were stinking in the grave of sin. Yet Jesus raised us, and by His life we live. Can we be content to live at a distance from Him? Do we neglect to remember Him at His table, where He graciously feasts with His brethren? Oh, this is cruel! We must repent and do as He has commanded us. His least wish should be law to us. To have lived without constant communion with the One of whom the Jews said, *"Behold how he loved him!"* (John 11:36), would have been disgraceful for Lazarus. Is it excusable in us, whom Jesus has loved *"with an everlasting love"* (Jer. 31:3)? To have been cold to Him who wept over his lifeless corpse would have demonstrated a great callousness in Lazarus. What does it show about us, over whom the Savior has not only wept, but also bled? Come, beloved, let us return to our heavenly Bridegroom and ask for His Spirit, so that we may have more intimate fellowship with Him. From this time forward, let us sit at the table with Him.

The power of his resurrection.
—Philippians 3:10

The doctrine of a risen Savior is exceedingly precious. The Resurrection is the cornerstone of the entire building of Christianity. It is the keystone of the arch of our salvation. It would take a volume to describe all the streams of living water that flow from this one sacred source, the resurrection of our dear Lord and Savior Jesus Christ. However, both to know that He has risen, and to have fellowship with Him in His resurrection—communing with the risen Savior by possessing a risen life, seeing Him leave the tomb by leaving the tomb of worldliness ourselves—is even more precious. The doctrine is the basis of the experience; but as the flower is lovelier than the root, so is the experience of fellowship with the risen Savior lovelier than the doctrine itself. I want you to believe that Christ rose from the dead in such a way that you can sing of His resurrection, and derive all the consolation that it is possible for you to extract from this well-ascertained and well-witnessed fact. However, I urge you not to be content with facts alone. Though you cannot, as the disciples did, see Him visibly, I urge you to aspire to see Christ Jesus by the eyes of faith. Though, like Mary Magdalene, you may not *"touch"* (John 20:17) Him, may you be privileged to converse with Him, and to know that He is risen—you yourselves being risen in Him to *"newness of life"* (Rom. 6:4). To know a crucified Savior as having crucified all my sins, is a high degree of knowledge. Yet to know a risen Savior as having justified me, and to realize that He has bestowed on me new life, since He has granted it to me to be a new creation through His own newness of life—this is a noble experience. Short of it, no one ought to rest satisfied. May you *"know him, and the power of his resurrection"* (Phil. 3:10). Why should those who are made alive with Jesus wear the grave clothes of worldliness and unbelief? Rise, for the Lord is risen.

Get thee up into the high mountain.
—Isaiah 40:9

ach believer should be thirsting *"for God, for the living God"* (Ps. 42:2), and longing to climb the hill of the Lord, to see Him face-to-face. We should not rest content in the mists of the valley when the summit of Mount Tabor awaits us. My soul thirsts to drink deeply of the cup that is reserved for those who reach the summit of the mountain, whose heads are wet with the dew of heaven. How pure is the dew of the hills, how fresh is the mountain air, how rich is the fare of those who dwell on high, whose windows look into the New Jerusalem! Many believers are content to live like men in the coal mines, who do not see the sun. They eat dust like the serpent, when they could taste the heavenly food of angels. They are content to wear miners' clothes, when they could put on royal robes. Tears mar their faces, when they could anoint them with heavenly oil. I am convinced that many believers languish in the dungeon when they could walk on the palace roof and view the *"goodly mountain, and Lebanon"* (Deut. 3:25). Rouse yourself, O believer, from your low condition! Cast away your sloth, your lethargy, your coldness, or whatever interferes with your spotless and pure love for Christ, your soul's Husband. Make Him the source, the center, and the circumference of your soul's entire range of delight. What beguiles you into such folly that you remain in a pit when you may sit on a throne? Do not live in the lowlands of bondage now that mountain liberty has been conferred on you. Do not be satisfied any longer with your dwarfish attainments, but press forward to more sublime and heavenly things. Aspire to a higher, nobler, and fuller life. Upward to heaven! Nearer to God!

> When will You come to me, Lord?
> Oh, come, my Lord most dear!
> Come near, come nearer, nearer still,
> I'm blessed when You are near.

Yet a little sleep, a little slumber, a little folding of the hands to sleep:
so shall thy poverty come as one that travelleth;
and thy want as an armed man.
—Proverbs 24:33–34

he worst of sluggards only ask for a *"little slumber."* They would be indignant if they were accused of thorough idleness. *"A little folding of the hands to sleep"* is all they crave, and they have a crowd of reasons to show that this indulgence is a very proper one. Yet by these "littles," the day goes by. The time for labor is all gone, and the field is grown over with thorns. It is by little procrastinations that people ruin their souls. They have no intention of delaying for years. They think a few months will bring a more convenient season. Tomorrow they will attend to serious things; but the present hour is so busy, and so altogether unsuitable, that they beg to be excused. Like sands from an hourglass, time slips by. Life is wasted one drop at a time, and seasons of grace are lost by "little slumbers." Oh, to be wise, to catch the hurrying hour, to use the moments that are flying by! May the Lord teach us this sacred wisdom. Otherwise, a poverty of the worst sort awaits us— eternal poverty—in which we will desire just one drop of water, though we will beg for it in vain. Like a traveler steadily pursuing his journey, poverty overtakes the lazy, and ruin overthrows the undecided. Each hour brings the dreaded pursuer nearer. He does not pause along the way, for he is on his master's business and must not delay. As an armed man enters with authority and power, poverty will come to the idle, and death to the unrepentant, and there will be no escape. Oh, if only men would be wise in good season, and would seek the Lord Jesus diligently before the solemn Day dawns. Then it will be too late to plow and sow, too late to repent and believe. In harvest, it is useless to mourn that seedtime was neglected. Faith and holy decision are sill timely. May we obtain them this night.

For he saith to Moses, I will have mercy on whom I will have mercy,
and I will have compassion on whom I will have compassion.
—Romans 9:15

With these words, the Lord clearly claims the right to give or withhold His mercy, according to His own sovereign will. As the prerogative of life and death is vested in the monarch, so the Judge of all the earth has a right to spare or condemn the guilty, as seems best in His sight. By their sins, men have forfeited all their claims on God. They deserve to perish for their sins, and if they all do so, they have no grounds for complaint. If the Lord steps in to save any, He may do so if the purposes of justice are not thwarted. However, if He judges that it is best to allow the condemned to suffer the righteous sentence, they may not arraign Him at their own court of opinion. Foolish and impudent are the discourses that say that all men have a right to be placed on the same footing. Ignorant, if not worse, are the contentions against discriminating grace, which are only the rebellion of proud human nature against the crown and scepter of Jehovah. When we understand our own utter ruin, that we are deserving of punishment, and the justice of the divine verdict against sin, we no longer quibble at the truth that the Lord is not obligated to save us. We do not complain if He chooses to save others, as though He were doing us an injury. Instead, we feel that if He graciously looks upon us, it will be His own free act of goodness, undeserved on our part, for which we will forever bless His name. How will those who are the subjects of divine election sufficiently adore the grace of God? They have no room for boasting, for sovereignty most effectively excludes it. The Lord's will alone is glorified, and the very notion of human merit is cast out to everlasting contempt. There is no more humbling doctrine in Scripture than that of election, none that promotes more gratitude, and, consequently, none more sanctifying. Believers should not be afraid of it, but rejoice in it with adoration.

They shall rejoice, and shall see the plummet in the hand of Zerubbabel.
—Zechariah 4:10

mall things" (Zech. 4:10) marked the beginning of the work in the *"hand of Zerubbabel,"* the work of rebuilding the temple in Jerusalem. Yet no one could despise these *"small things,"* for the Lord had raised up one who would persevere until the capstone could be brought forth with shouts (v. 7). The *"plummet"* or plumb line was in good hands. Spiritually, this is a comfort to every believer in the Lord Jesus. Even if the work of grace is very small in its beginnings, the plumb line is in good hands, for a Master Builder greater than Solomon has undertaken the building of the heavenly temple. He *"shall not fail nor be discouraged"* (Isa. 42:4) until the topmost pinnacle is raised. If the plumb line were in the hand of a mere human being, we might worry about the building. However, *"the pleasure of the LORD shall prosper"* (Isa. 53:10) in Jesus' hand. The work of rebuilding the temple did not proceed irregularly, and without care, for the overseer's hand carried a good instrument. If the walls had been constructed hurriedly, without due supervision, they might not have been built completely upright. Yet the plumb line was used by the chosen overseer. Similarly, Jesus is continuously watching over the construction of His spiritual temple, so that it may be built securely and well. We are for haste, but Jesus is for judgment. He will use the plumb line, and what is out of line must come down, every stone of it. This is why many promising works have failed and many glittering professions of faith have fallen by the wayside. It is not for us to judge the Lord's church, since Jesus has a steady hand and a true eye, and can use the plumb line well. Do we not rejoice that judgment is left to Him? The *"plummet"* was in active use—it was in the builder's hand, a sure indication that he meant to push forward with the work to completion. O Lord Jesus, how we would indeed be glad if we could see You at Your great work. O Zion the beautiful, your walls are still in ruins! Rise, glorious Builder, and make her ruins rejoice at Your coming.

The forgiveness of sins, according to the riches of his grace.
—Ephesians 1:7

an there be a sweeter word in any language than the word *"forgiveness,"* when it spoken in a guilty sinner's ear? It is like the silver notes of jubilee to the captive Israelite. May the dear star of pardon, which shines into the cells of the condemned, and gives the perishing a gleam of hope amid the midnight of despair, be forever blessed! Is it possible that sin, sin such as mine, can be forgiven—forgiven altogether and forever? Hell is my portion as a sinner. There is no possibility of my escaping from it while sin remains upon me. Can the load of guilt be lifted, the crimson stain removed? Can the impenetrable stones of my prison ever be loosed from their mortises, or the doors be lifted from their hinges? Jesus tells me that I can be blameless. Forever blessed is the revelation of atoning love, which tells me not only that pardon is possible, but also that it is secured to all who rest in Jesus. I have believed in the appointed propitiation, even Jesus, who was crucified. Therefore my sins are, at this moment and forever, forgiven by virtue of His substitutionary pains and death. What joy this forgiveness brings! How blissful it is to be a perfectly pardoned soul! I dedicate all that I am to Him who, out of His own love—unearned by me—became my Surety and worked redemption for me through His blood. What riches of grace free forgiveness exhibits! To forgive at all, to forgive fully, to forgive freely, to forgive forever—there is a constellation of wonders in this forgiveness. When I think about how great my sins were, how dear the precious drops of blood were that cleansed me from them, and how gracious the method was by which pardon was sealed for me, I am overcome with marveling, worshipping affection. I bow before the throne that absolves me, and I clasp the cross that delivers me. For the rest of my life, I will serve the Incarnate God, through whom I am a pardoned soul tonight.

Seeking the wealth of his people.
—Esther 10:3

Mordecai was a true patriot. Therefore, when he was exalted to the highest position under King Ahasuerus, he used his position to promote the prosperity of Israel. In this, he was a type of Jesus, who, upon His throne of glory, does not seek His own interests, but expends His power for His people. It would be a good thing if every Christian were a Mordecai to the church, striving, according to his ability, for its prosperity. Some believers have been placed in positions of affluence and influence. Let them honor their Lord in the high places of the earth, and testify for Jesus before great men. Others have what is far better, namely, close fellowship with the King of Kings. Let them be sure to plead daily for the weak among the Lord's people—the doubting, the tempted, and the comfortless. It will be to their honor if they intercede much for those who are in darkness and who do not dare to draw near to the mercy seat. Believers who are knowledgeable in the things of God may serve their Master greatly if they use their talents for the general good, and impart their wealth of heavenly learning to others by teaching them the things of God. Even the least person in the body of Christ may *seek* the welfare of his people. His desire, if he can give no more, will be acceptable. The most Christlike, as well as the happiest, way for a believer to live is to cease from living for himself. He who blesses others cannot fail to be blessed himself. On the other hand, seeking our own personal greatness is a wicked and unhappy way of life. Its way will be grievous, and its end will be fatal. Now is the time to ask you, my friend, whether you are, to the best of your ability, seeking the wealth of the church in your neighborhood. I trust you are not doing it harm by bitterness ar scandal, or weakening it by neglect. Friend, unite with t Lord's poor, bear their cross, do them all the good you c and you will not miss your reward.

Spices for anointing oil.
—Exodus 35:8

uch use was made of anointing oil under the law, and what it represents is of primary importance under the Gospel. The Holy Spirit, who anoints us for all holy service, is indispensable to us if we want to serve the Lord acceptably. Without His aid, our religious service is just an empty offering, and our inward experience is dead. Whenever the ministry of the church lacks anointing, it becomes a miserable thing—and when individual Christians lack anointing, their prayers, praises, meditations, and efforts aren't any better. A holy anointing is the life and soul of piety. Its absence is the most grievous of all calamities. Going before the Lord without anointing is the equivalent of a common Levite in Old Testament times thrusting himself into the office of priest. In such a situation, his ministering would have been sin rather than service. May we never undertake holy service without sacred anointing. Sacred anointing comes upon us from our glorious Head. From His anointing, we who are as the *"skirts of his garments"* (Ps. 133:2) partake of a plentiful anointing. Choice spices were skillfully mixed to form the anointing oil, to show us how rich all the influences of the Holy Spirit are. All good things are found in the divine Comforter. Matchless comfort, infallible instruction, immortal quickening, spiritual energy, and divine sanctification all lie compounded with other excellencies in that sacred ointment, the heavenly anointing oil of the Holy Spirit. It imparts delightful fragrance to the character and person of one on whom it is poured. Nothing like it can be found in the treasuries of the rich or the secrets of the wise. It cannot be imitated. It comes from God alone, and is freely given through Jesus Christ to every waiting soul. Let us seek, for we may have it—we may have it this very evening. O Lord, anoint Your servants.

*Michael and his angels fought against the dragon;
and the dragon fought and his angels.*
—Revelation 12:7

War will always rage between the two great kingdoms until one or the other is crushed. Peace between good and evil is an impossibility. In fact, the very pretense of it would mean the triumph of the powers of darkness. The archangel Michael will always fight. His holy soul is distressed with sin, and will not endure it. Jesus will always be the dragon's foe—not in a quiet sense, but actively, vigorously, and with full determination to exterminate evil. All His servants, whether angels in heaven or messengers on earth, will and must fight. Believers are born to be warriors. At the cross, they enter into covenant never to make a truce with evil. They are warlike—firm in defense and fierce in attack. The duty of every soldier in the army of the Lord is to fight against the dragon daily, with all his heart, soul, and strength. The dragon and his angels will not decline to fight. They are incessant in their onslaughts, sparing no weapon, fair or foul. We are foolish to expect to serve God without opposition from the enemy. The more zealous we are, the surer we are to be assailed by the followers of hell. The church may become lazy, but this is not the case with her great antagonist. His restless spirit never allows the war to pause. He hates the woman's seed (see Genesis 3:15) and would gladly devour the church if he could. The servants of Satan have much of the old dragon's energy and are usually active. War rages everywhere, and to dream of peace is dangerous and futile. Glory be to God, we know the outcome of the war! The great dragon will be cast out and destroyed forever, while Jesus and those who are with Him will receive the crown. Tonight, let us sharpen our sword and ask the Holy Spirit to strengthen our arms for the conflict. Never was there a more important battle; never was there a more glorious crown. Every soldier to his post, warriors of the Cross, and may the Lord *"bruise Satan under feet shortly"* (Rom. 16:20)!

*Oh that men would praise the LORD for his goodness, and for his
wonderful works to the children of men!*
—Psalm 107:8

f we complained less and praised more, we would be
happier, and God would be more glorified. Let us daily
praise God for common mercies—common as we frequently call them, yet so priceless that, when deprived of
them, we are ready to perish. Let us bless God for the eyes
with which we behold the sun, for the health and strength
to walk around, for the bread we eat, for the clothing we
wear. Let us praise Him that we are not cast out among the
hopeless or confined among the guilty. Let us thank Him
for liberty, for friends, for family, and for comforts. Let us
praise Him, in fact, for everything that we receive from His
bounteous hand; for we deserve little, yet we are abundantly endowed. But, beloved, the sweetest and the loudest
note in our songs of praise should be of redeeming love.
God's redeeming acts toward His chosen are forever the
favorite themes of their praise. If we know what redemption
means, let us not withhold our sonnets of thanksgiving. We
have been redeemed from the power of our corruptions, uplifted from the depth of sin in which we were naturally
plunged. We have been led to the cross of Christ. Our
hackles of guilt have been broken; we are no longer slaves,
it children of the living God. We can anticipate the time
en we will be presented before the throne without *"spot,
rinkle, or any such thing"* (Eph. 5:27). Even now by faith
ave the palm branch and wrap ourselves about with
r linen that is to be our everlasting array. Will we
easingly give thanks to the Lord our Redeemer?
God, can you be silent? Awake, awake, inheritors
nd lead your *"captivity captive"* (Ps. 68:18), as you
avid, *"Bless the LORD, O my soul: and all that is
ss his holy name"* (Ps. 103:1). Let the new month
w songs.

Behold, all is vanity.
—Ecclesiastes 1:14

Nothing can satisfy the entire man but the Lord's love and the Lord's own self. Saints have tried to anchor in other harbors, but they have been driven out of such deadly refuges. Solomon, the wisest of men, was permitted to make experiments for us all, and to do for us what we must not dare to do for ourselves. Here is his testimony in his own words: *"So I was great, and increased more than all that were before me in Jerusalem: also my wisdom remained with me. And whatsoever mine eyes desired I kept not from them, I withheld not my heart from any joy; for my heart rejoiced in all my labour: and this was my portion of all my labour. Then I looked on all the works that my hands had wrought, and on the labour that I had laboured to do: and, behold, all was vanity and vexation of spirit, and there was no profit under the sun"* (Eccl. 2:9–11). *"Vanity of vanities; all is vanity"* (Eccl. 1:2). What! The whole of it is vanity? O favored monarch, is there nothing in all your wealth? Nothing in that wide dominion reaching from the river even to the sea? Nothing in your glorious palaces? Nothing in the house of the forest of Lebanon? Is there nothing in all your music and dancing, and wine and luxury? "Nothing," he answers, "but weariness of spirit." This was his verdict when he had traveled the whole globe of pleasure. To embrace our Lord Jesus, to dwell in His love, and to be fully assured of union with Him—this is all in all. Dear reader, you do not need to try other forms of life in order to see whether they are better than the Christian's. If you roam the world over, you will see no sights like the sight of the Savior's face. If you could have all the comforts of life, but you lost your Savior, you would be wretched. But if you win Christ, then even if you rotted away in a dungeon, you would find it a paradise you lived in obscurity or died from starvation, you would still be satisfied with favor and be full of the goodness the Lord.

The LORD mighty in battle.
—Psalm 24:8

God is glorious in the eyes of His people, seeing that He has worked such wonders for them, in them, and by them. For them, the Lord Jesus on Calvary dispelled every foe, breaking all the weapons of the enemy in pieces by His finished work of satisfactory obedience. By His triumphant resurrection and ascension, He completely overturned the hopes of hell, leading *"captivity captive"* (Ps. 68:18), making an open show of our enemies, triumphing over them by His Cross. Every arrow of guilt that Satan might have shot at us is broken, for *"who shall lay any thing to the charge of God's elect"* (Rom. 8:33)? Vain are the sharp swords of infernal malice and the perpetual battles of the serpent's seed, for in the midst of the church, the lame take the prey, and the feeblest warriors are crowned. The saved may well adore their Lord for His conquests in them, since the arrows of their natural hatred are snapped, and the weapons of their rebellion are broken. What victories grace has won in our evil hearts! How glorious Jesus is when the will is subdued and sin is dethroned! As for our remaining corruptions, they will sustain an equally sure defeat; every temptation, doubt, and fear will be utterly destroyed. In the ʃalem of our peaceful hearts, the name of Jesus is great beyond comparison. He has won our love, and He will wear it. ʃre in His love, we may expect to be victorious. *"We are than conquerors through him that loved us"* (v. 37). By our zeal, and holiness, we will cast down the powers of s that are in the world. We will win sinners to Je- will overturn false systems, and we will convert or God is with us, and none will stand before us. ng let the Christian warrior chant the war song for tomorrow's fight. *"Greater is he that is in that is in the world"* (1 John 4:4).

*Even we ourselves groan within ourselves, waiting
for the adoption, to wit, the redemption of our body.*
—Romans 8:23

his groaning is universal among the saints; we all feel it to a greater or lesser extent. It is not the groan of murmuring or complaint; it is the note of desire rather than of distress. Having received a down payment, we desire the whole of our portion. We are yearning for the day when our entire personhood—in its trinity of spirit, soul, and body—may be set free from the last vestige of the Fall. We long to put off corruption, weakness, and dishonor and to wrap ourselves in incorruption, in immortality, in glory, in the spiritual body that the Lord Jesus will bestow upon His people. We long for the manifestation of our adoption as the children of God. We groan, but it is *"within ourselves."* It is not the hypocrite's groan, by which he would make men believe that he is a saint because he is wretched. Our sighs are sacred things, too hallowed for us to express. We keep our longings to our Lord alone. Then the apostle said that we are *"waiting,"* by which we learn that we are not to be petulant, like Jonah or Elijah, when they said, "Let me die." Neither are we to whimper and sigh for the end of life because we are tired of work. Nor should we wish to escape from our present sufferings until the will of the Lord is done. We are to groan for glorification, but we are to wait patiently for it, knowing that what the Lord appoints is best. Waiting implies being ready. We are to stand at the door, expecting the Beloved to open it and take us away to Himself. This *"groaning"* is a test. You may judge a man by what he groans after. Some men groan after wealth—the worship money. Some groan continually under the trouble of life; they are merely impatient. But the man who sig after God, who is uneasy until he is made like Christ, tha the blessed man. May God help us to groan for the con of the Lord and the resurrection that He will bring to u

And the LORD showed me four carpenters.
—Zechariah 1:20

In the vision described in this chapter, the prophet saw four terrible horns. They were pushing this way and that way, dashing down the strongest and the mightiest. The prophet asked, *"What be these?"* (Zech. 1:19). The answer was, *"These are the horns which have scattered Judah, Israel, and Jerusalem"* (v. 19). He saw before him a representation of those powers that had oppressed the church of God. There were four horns, for the church is attacked from all quarters. Well might the prophet have felt dismayed, but suddenly there appeared before him four carpenters. He asked, *"What come these to do?"* (v. 21). These are the men whom God has found to break those horns in pieces. God will always find men for His work, and He will find them at the right time. The prophet did not see the carpenters first, when there was nothing to do; he first saw the horns, then the carpenters. Moreover, the Lord finds enough men. He did not find three carpenters, but four; there were four horns, so there needed to be four workmen. God finds the right men—not four men with pens to write, not four architects to draw plans, but four carpenters to do rough work. Rest assured, you who tremble for the ark of God, that when the *"horns"* grow troublesome, the *"carpenters"* will be found. You do not need to fret concerning the weakness of the church of God at any moment; there may be growing up in obscurity the valiant reformer who will shake the nations. Church fathers like John Chrysostom or Augustine may come forth from our lowliest schools or from the thickest darkness of London's poverty. The Lord knows where to find His servants. He has in ambush a multitude of mighty men. At His word they will move to the battle, for *the battle is the Lord's"* (1 Sam. 17:47), and He will get to Himself the victory. Let us remain faithful to Him, and He, in the right time, will raise up for us a deliverer, be it in the day of our personal need or in the hour of His church.

Girt about the paps with a golden girdle.
—Revelation 1:13

*O*ne like unto the Son of man" (Rev. 1:13) appeared to John on Patmos, and the beloved disciple noted that He wore a *"girdle"* of gold—a girdle, for Jesus never was unprepared while on earth. He always stood ready for service. Now before the eternal throne, He continues His holy ministry; but as a priest, He is girded with *"the curious girdle of the ephod"* (Exod. 28:8). We are blessed that He has not ceased to fulfill His offices of love for us, since this is one of our choicest safeguards that He *"ever liveth to make intercession for [us]"* (Heb. 7:25). Jesus is never an idler; His garments are never loose, as though His ministry were over. He diligently carries on the cause of His people. A *"golden girdle"* manifests the superiority of His service, the royalty of His person, the dignity of His state, and the glory of His reward. No longer does He cry out of the dust, but He intercedes with authority. He is a King as well as a Priest. Our cause is safe enough in the hands of our enthroned Melchizedek. Our Lord presents all His people with an example. We must never unbind our girdles. This is not the time for lying down at ease; it is the season of service and warfare. We need to bind the girdle of truth more and more tightly around our loins. It is a *"golden girdle,"* so it will be our richest ornament. We greatly need it, for a heart that is not well braced up with the truth as it is in Jesus, and with the fidelity that is worked by the Spirit, will be easily entangled with the things of this life and tripped up by the snares of temptation. It is in vain that we possess the Scriptures unless we bind them around us like a girdle, surrounding our entire nature, keeping each part of our character in order, and giving substance to our whole man. If in heaven Jesus does not unbind His girdle, much less may we who are still on the earth. *"Stand therefore, having your loins girt about with truth"* (Eph. 6:14).

I am made all things to all men, that I might by all means save some.
—1 Corinthians 9:22

aul's great objective was not merely to instruct and to improve, but to save. Anything short of this goal would have disappointed him. He desired that people would be renewed in heart, forgiven, saved, and sanctified. Have our Christian labors been aimed at anything below this great point? Then let us amend our ways, for of what avail will it be at the Last Great Day to have taught and moralized men if they appear before God unsaved? Our skirts will be bloodred if through life we have sought inferior purposes and forgotten that people need to be saved. Paul knew the ruin of man's natural state. He did not try to educate men, but to save them. He saw men sinking to hell, and he did not talk about refining them, but of their being saved from the *"wrath to come"* (Matt. 3:7). To bring about their salvation, he gave himself up with untiring zeal to preaching the Gospel, to warning and beseeching men to be reconciled to God. His prayers were importunate, and his labors were incessant. To save souls was his consuming passion, his ambition, his calling. He became a servant to all men, toiling for his race, feeling a sorrow within him if he did not preach the Gospel. He laid aside his preferences to prevent prejudice; he submitted his will in things indifferent, and if men would but receive the Gospel, he raised no questions about forms or ceremonies. The Gospel was the one all-important business with him. If he might save some, he would be content. This was the crown for which he strove, the sole and sufficient reward of all his labors and self-denials. Dear reader, have you and I lived to win souls at this noble rate? Are we possessed with the same all-absorbing desire? If not, why not? Jesus died for sinners; can we not live for them? Where is our tenderness? Where is our love for Christ, if we do not seek His honor in the salvation of men? Oh, that the Lord would saturate us through and through with an undying zeal for the souls of men.

Thou, O God, hast prepared of thy goodness for the poor.
—Psalm 68:10

All God's gifts are prepared gifts laid up in store for needs that are foreseen. God anticipates our needs. Out of the fullness that He has treasured up in Christ Jesus, He provides of His goodness for the poor. You may trust Him for all the necessities that can occur, for He has infallibly foreknown every one of them. He can say of us in all conditions, "I knew that you would be in this situation." A man makes a journey across the desert, and when he has gone a day's distance and stops to rest, he discovers that he needs many comforts and necessaries that he has not brought in his luggage. "Ah!" says he, "I did not foresee this: if I had to take this journey again, I would bring things with me that are necessary for my comfort." But God has noticed with His all-seeing eyes all the requirements of His poor, wandering children; and when those needs occur, He has supplies ready. It is goodness that He has prepared for the poor in heart, goodness and goodness only. *"My grace is sufficient for thee"* (2 Cor. 12:9). *"As thy days, so shall thy strength be"* (Deut. 33:25). Reader, is your heart heavy this evening? God knew it would be. The comfort that your heart needs is treasured in the sweet assurance of the text. You are poor and needy, but He has thought about you. He has in store for you the exact blessing that you require. Plead the promise, believe it, and obtain its fulfillment. Do you feel that you never were so consciously vile as you are now? Behold, the crimson fountain is open still, with all its former effectiveness to wash your sin away. You will never come into such a position that Christ cannot help you. No trouble will ever arrive in your spiritual affairs in which Jesus Christ will not be equal to the emergency, for your history has all been foreknown and provided for in Jesus.

My people shall dwell in...quiet resting places.
—Isaiah 32:18

Peace and rest do not belong to the unregenerate. They are the special possession of the Lord's people, and for them alone. The God of Peace gives perfect peace to those whose hearts are fixed on Him. Before man fell, God gave him the flowery bowers of Eden as his quiet resting place; sadly, sin soon blighted the fair abode of innocence. In the day of universal wrath, when the flood swept away a guilty race, the chosen family were quietly secured in the resting place of the ark, which floated them from the old condemned world into the new earth of the rainbow and the covenant, herein typifying Jesus, the Ark of our salvation. Israel rested safely beneath the blood-sprinkled habitations of Egypt when the destroying angel smote the firstborn; in the wilderness, the shadow of the pillar of cloud and the flowing rock gave the weary pilgrims sweet repose. At this hour we rest in the promises of our faithful God, knowing that His words are full of truth and power. We rest in the doctrines of His Word, which are consolation itself. We rest in the covenant of His grace, which is a haven of delight. We are more highly favored than David in Adullam (see 1 Samuel 22:1) or Jonah beneath his gourd, for none can invade or destroy our shelter. The person of Jesus is the quiet resting place of His people. When we draw near to Him in the breaking of the bread, the hearing of the Word, the searching of the Scriptures, prayer, or praise, we find any form of approach to Him to be the return of peace to our spirits.

I hear the words of love, I gaze upon the blood,
I see the mighty sacrifice, and I have peace with God.
'Tis everlasting peace, sure as Jehovah's name,
'Tis stable as His steadfast throne, for evermore the same.
The clouds may go and come,
And storms may sweep my sky,
This blood-sealed friendship changes not,
The cross is ever nigh.

Whose heart the Lord opened.
—Acts 16:14

here are many points of interest in Lydia's conversion. It was brought about by providential circumstances. She was a *"seller of purple"* (Acts 16:4) in the city of Thyatira; however, just at the right time for hearing Paul, we find her at Philippi. Providence, the handmaiden of grace, led her to the right spot. Again, grace was preparing her soul for the blessing—grace preparing for grace. She did not know the Savior, but as a Jewish woman, she knew many truths that were excellent stepping-stones to a knowledge of Jesus. Her conversion took place as she used the means of grace. On the Sabbath she went when prayer was customarily made, and there prayer was heard. Never neglect the means of grace. God may bless us when we are not in His house, but we have greater reason to hope that He will when we are in communion with His saints. Observe the words, *"Whose heart the Lord opened."* She did not open her own heart. Her prayers did not do it; Paul did not do it. In order for us to receive the things that bring about our peace with God, the Lord Himself must open our hearts. He alone can put the key into the hole of the door, open it, and gain admittance for Himself. He is the heart's Master as He is the heart's Maker. The first outward evidence of the opened heart was obedience. As soon as Lydia had believed in Jesus, she was baptized. It is a sweet sign of a humble and broken heart when a child of God is willing to obey a command that is not essential to his salvation, that he does not feel forced to comply with out of a selfish fear of condemnation, but that is a simple act of obedience and communion with his Master. The next evidence was love, manifesting itself in acts of grateful kindness to the apostles. Love for the saints has always been a mark of the true convert. Those who do nothing for Christ or His church give but sorry evidence of an "opened" heart. Lord, give me an opened heart forever.

Ye serve the Lord Christ.
—Colossians 3:24

To what choice group of officials was this word spoken? To kings who proudly boast a divine right? No, too often they serve themselves or Satan and forget the God whose mercy permits them to wear their mock majesty for their little hour. Did the apostle, then, speak to those so-called "right reverend fathers in God," the bishops or the venerable archdeacons? No, indeed. Paul knew nothing of these mere inventions of man. Not even to pastors and teachers or to the wealthy and esteemed among believers was this word spoken, but to servants, yes, and to slaves. Among the toiling multitudes—the journeymen, the day laborers, the domestic servants, the drudges of the kitchen—the apostle found, as we find still, some of the Lord's chosen. To them he said, *"Whatsoever ye do, do it heartily, as to the Lord, and not unto men; knowing that of the Lord ye shall receive the reward of the inheritance: for ye serve the Lord Christ"* (Col. 3:23–24). This saying ennobles the weary routine of earthly employment and shines a halo around the most humble occupations. To wash feet may be servile, but to wash His feet is royal work. To untie shoelaces is a poor job, but to untie the great Master's shoe is a princely privilege. The shop, the barn, and the kitchen become temples when men and women do all to the glory of God! Divine service is not a thing of a few hours and a few places, but all life becomes holiness unto the Lord. Every place and thing may be as consecrated as the tabernacle and its golden candlestick.

Teach me, my God and King, in all things Thee to see;
And what I do in anything to do it as to Thee.
All may of Thee partake, nothing can be so mean,
Which with this tincture, for Thy sake,
Will not grow bright and clean.
A servant with this clause makes drudgery divine;
Who sweeps a room, as for Thy laws,
Makes that and the action fine.

They have dealt treacherously against the LORD.
—Hosea 5:7

Believer, here is a sorrowful truth: you are the beloved of the Lord, redeemed by blood, called by grace, preserved in Christ Jesus, *"accepted in the beloved"* (Eph. 1:6), and on your way to heaven, yet you *"have dealt treacherously"* with God, your best Friend; treacherously with Jesus, whose you are; and treacherously with the Holy Spirit, by whom you have been quickened unto life eternal! How treacherous you have been in the matter of vows and promises! Do you remember your first love, that happy time—the springtime of your spiritual life? Oh, how closely you clung to your Master then! You said, "He will never charge me with indifference. My feet will never grow slow in the way of His service. I will not permit my heart to wander after other loves. In Him is every store of inexpressible sweetness. I give all up for my Lord Jesus' sake." Has it been so? Sadly, if conscience speaks, it will say, "He who promised so well has performed most poorly. Prayer has often been neglected. It has been short, but not sweet; brief, but not fervent. Communion with Christ has been forgotten. Instead of a heavenly mind, there have been carnal cares, worldly vanities, and evil thoughts. Instead of service, there has been disobedience; instead of fervency, lukewarmness; instead of patience, petulance; instead of faith, confidence in an *"arm of flesh"* (2 Chron. 32:8). As a soldier of the Cross, there has been cowardice, disobedience, and desertion to a very shameful degree. You *"have dealt treacherously."* Treachery to Jesus! What words will be used in denouncing it? Words avail little. Let our penitent thoughts denounce the sin that is so surely in us. We have been treacherous to Your wounds, O Jesus! Forgive us, and let us not sin again. How shameful to be treacherous to Him who never forgets us, but who this day stands with our names engraved on His breastplate before the eternal throne.

I will make thy windows of agates.
—Isaiah 54:12

The church is most instructively symbolized by a building erected by heavenly power and designed by divine skill. Such a spiritual house must not be dark, for the Israelites had light in their dwellings; therefore, there must be windows to let the light in and to allow the inhabitants to gaze outside. These windows are precious as agates. The ways in which the church beholds her Lord and heaven, and spiritual truth in general, are to be held in the highest esteem. Agates are not the most transparent of gems. They are but semi-transparent at best. "Our knowledge of that life is small; our eye of faith is dim." Faith is one of these precious agate windows, but it is often so misty and cloudy that we see but dimly, and we mistake much that we do see. Yet if we cannot gaze through windows of diamonds and know even as we are known (see 1 Corinthians 13:12), it is a glorious thing to behold the One who is *"altogether lovely"* (Song 5:16), even though the glass is as hazy as the agate. Experience is another of these dim but precious windows, yielding to us a subdued religious light, in which we see the sufferings of the Man of Sorrows through our own afflictions. Our weak eyes could not endure windows of transparent glass to let in the Master's glory, but when they are dimmed with weeping, the beams of the Sun of Righteousness are tempered. Then they shine through the windows of agate with a soft radiance that is inexpressibly soothing to tempted souls. Sanctification, as it conforms us to our Lord, is another agate window. Only as we become heavenly can we comprehend heavenly things. The pure in heart see a pure God. Those who are like Jesus see Him as He is. Because we are so little like Him, the window is but agate; because we are somewhat like Him, it is agate. We thank God for what we have, and we long for more. When will we see God and Jesus, and heaven and truth, face-to-face?

I am crucified with Christ.
—Galatians 2:20

In what He did, the Lord Jesus Christ acted as a great public representative, and His dying on the cross was the virtual dying of all His people. Through Him, all His saints rendered unto justice what was due and made an atonement to divine vengeance for all their sins. Paul, the apostle to the Gentiles, delighted to think that as one of Christ's chosen people, he died upon the cross in Christ. He did more than believe this doctrinally. He accepted it confidently, resting his hope upon it. He believed that by virtue of Christ's death, he had satisfied divine justice and had found reconciliation with God. Beloved, what a blessed thing it is when the soul can, as it were, stretch itself upon the cross of Christ and feel, "I am dead. The law has slain me; therefore, I am free from its power. In my Surety I have borne the curse, and in my Substitute the whole that the law could do, by way of condemnation, has been executed upon me, for I am crucified with Christ!" But Paul meant even more than this. He not only believed in Christ's death and trusted in it, but also actually felt its power in himself in causing the crucifixion of his old corrupt nature. When he saw the pleasures of sin, he said, "I cannot enjoy these. I am dead to them." Such is the experience of every true Christian. Having received Christ, he is to this world as one who is utterly dead. Yet, while conscious of death to the world, he can, at the same time, exclaim with the apostle, "Nevertheless I live." He is fully alive to God. The Christian's life is a matchless riddle. No earthly-minded person can comprehend it; even the believer himself cannot understand it. Dead, yet alive! Crucified with Christ, yet at the same time risen with Christ in newness of life! Union with the suffering, bleeding Savior and death to the world and sin are soul-cheering things. Oh, for more enjoyment of them!

And lay thy foundations with sapphires.
—Isaiah 54:11

Not only that which is seen of the church of God, but also that which is unseen, is fair and precious. Foundations are out of sight. As long as they are firm, it is not expected that they should be valuable. But in Jehovah's work, everything is from Him; nothing is worthless or defective. The deep foundations of the work of grace are as precious sapphires; no human mind is able to measure their glory. We build on the covenant of grace, which is firmer than diamonds and as enduring as jewels on which age spends itself in vain. Sapphire foundations are eternal, and the covenant lasts throughout the lifetime of the Almighty. Another foundation is the person of the Lord Jesus, which is as clear, spotless, everlasting, and beautiful as the sapphire. It blends the deep blue of earth's ever-rolling ocean and the azure of its all-embracing sky. Once, as our Lord stood covered with His own blood, He might have been compared to the ruby; but now we see Him radiant with the soft blue of love, an abundant, everlasting, and deep love. Our eternal hopes are built on the justice and the faithfulness of God, which are as clear and cloudless as the sapphire. We are not saved by a compromise, by mercy defeating justice or law suspending its operations; no, we defy the eagle's eye to detect a flaw in the groundwork of our confidence—our foundation is of sapphire, and it will endure the fire. The Lord Himself has laid the foundation of His people's hopes. It is a matter for grave inquiry whether our hopes are built on such a basis. Good works and ceremonies are not a foundation of sapphires, but of *"wood, hay,* [and] *stubble"* (1 Cor. 3:12); neither are they laid by God, but by our own conceit. Foundations will all be tried before long. Woe unto him whose lofty tower comes down with a crash, because it is based on quicksand. He who is built on sapphires may await storm or fire with calmness, for he will withstand the test.

Yea, thou heardest not; yea, thou knewest not; yea, from that time that thine ear was not opened.
—Isaiah 48:8

It is painful to remember that, to a certain degree, this accusation may be laid at the door of believers, who too often are in a measure spiritually insensitive. We may well bewail ourselves that we do not hear the voice of God as we ought. *"Yea, thou heardest not."* There are gentle motions of the Holy Spirit in the soul that are unheeded by us. There are whisperings of divine command and of heavenly love that are alike unobserved by our leaden intellects. Alas! We have been carelessly ignorant—*"Yea, thou knewest not."* There are matters within that we should have seen, corruptions that have made headway into our lives unnoticed; sweet affections that are being blighted like flowers in the frost, untended by us; glimpses of the divine face that might be perceived if we did not wall up the windows of our soul. But we *"have not known"* (Isa. 44:18). As we think of it, we are humbled in the deepest self-abasement. How we must adore the grace of God as we learn from the context that all this folly and ignorance, on our part, was foreknown by God, and, notwithstanding that foreknowledge, He yet has been pleased to deal with us in a merciful way! Admire the marvelous sovereign grace that could have chosen us in the sight of all this! Wonder at the price that was paid for us when Christ knew what we would be! He who hung on the cross foresaw us as unbelieving, backsliding, coldhearted, indifferent, careless, lax in prayer, yet He said, *"I am the* LORD *thy God, the Holy One of Israel, thy Saviour....Since thou wast precious in my sight, thou hast been honourable, and I have loved thee: therefore will I give men for thee, and people for thy life"* (Isa. 43:3–4)! O redemption, how wondrously resplendent you shine when we think how black we are! O Holy Spirit, from this point on, give us a hearing ear and an understanding heart!

I am the door: by me if any man enter in, he shall be saved, and shall go in and out, and find pasture.
—John 10:9

esus, the great I AM, is the entrance into the true church, and the way of access to God Himself. He gives four choice privileges to the man who comes to God by Him. First, he will be saved. The fugitive man-slayer went through the gate of the city of refuge and was safe. Noah entered the door of the ark and was secure. None can be lost who take Jesus to their souls as the door of faith. Entrance through Jesus into peace is the guarantee of entrance by the same door into heaven. Jesus is the only door, an open door, a wide door, a safe door. Blessed is he who rests all his hope of admission to glory on the crucified Redeemer. Second, he will go in. He will be privileged to go in among the divine family, sharing the children's bread and participating in all their honors and enjoyments. He will go into the rooms of communion, to the banquets of love, to the treasures of the covenant, to the storehouses of the promises. He will go in to the King of Kings in the power of the Holy Spirit, and the secret of the Lord will be with him. Next, he will go out. This blessing is much forgotten. We go out into the world to labor and suffer, but what a mercy to go in the name and power of Jesus! We are called to bear witness to the truth, to cheer the disconsolate, to warn the careless, to win souls, and to glorify God. The angel said to Gideon, *"Go in this thy might"* (Judg. 6:14); likewise, the Lord wants us to proceed as His messengers in His name and strength. Fourth, he will find pasture. He who knows Jesus will never want. Going in and out will both be helpful to him: in fellowship with God he will grow, and in watering others he will be watered. Having made Jesus his all, he will find all in Jesus. His soul will *be like a watered garden, and like a spring of water, whose waters fail not* (Isa. 58:11).

Be thou diligent to know the state of thy flocks,
and look well to thy herds.
—Proverbs 27:23

very wise businessman will periodically take stock of his company. He will update his accounts, examine his inventory, and evaluate whether his trade is prospering or declining. Every man who is wise in the kingdom of heaven will cry, *"Search me, O God, and know my heart: try me"* (Ps. 139:23). He will frequently set apart special seasons for self-examination, to discover whether things are right between God and his soul. The God whom we worship is a great heart-searcher. In times past, His servants knew Him as the Lord who searches the heart and examines the minds of His children. (See Jeremiah 17:10.) Let me encourage you in His name to diligently search and solemnly investigate your spiritual condition, lest you come short of the promised rest. That which every wise man does, that which God Himself does with us all, I exhort you to do with yourself this evening. Let the oldest saint look well to the fundamentals of his faith, for gray heads may cover black hearts. Do not let the young believer despise the word of warning, for the greenness of youth may be joined to the rottenness of hypocrisy. Every now and then a cedar falls into our midst. The enemy still continues to sow tares among the wheat. It is not my aim to introduce doubts and fears into your mind; instead, I hope that the rough wind of self-examination may help to drive them away. It is not security, but carnal security, that we want to kill; not confidence, but fleshly confidence, that we want to overthrow; not peace, but false peace, that we want to destroy. By the precious blood of Christ, which was not shed to make you a hypocrite, but so that sincere souls might show forth His praise, I beg you, search and look, lest in the end it will be said of you, *"MENE, MENE...TEKEL; thou art weighed in the balances, and art found wanting"* (Dan. 5:25, 27).

And there was no more sea.
—Revelation 21:1

Scarcely could we rejoice at the thought of losing the glorious old ocean: the new heavens and the new earth are none the fairer to our imagination, if, indeed, literally there is to be no great and wide sea, with its gleaming waves and shelly shores. Is not the text to be read as a metaphor, tinged with the prejudice with which the Oriental mind universally regarded the sea in the olden times? A real, physical world without a sea is mournful to imagine. It would be an iron ring without the sapphire which made it precious. There must be a spiritual meaning here. In the new dispensation there will be no division—the sea separates nations and divides peoples from each other. To John in Patmos the deep waters were like prison walls, shutting him out from his brothers and his work. There will be no such barriers in the world to come. Leagues of rolling billows lie between us and many relatives whom tonight we prayerfully remember, but in the bright world to which we go, there will be unbroken fellowship for all the redeemed family. In this sense there will be no more sea. The sea is the emblem of change; with its ebbs and flows—its glassy smoothness and its mountainous billows, its gentle murmurs and its tumultuous roarings—it is never the same for long. Slave of the fickle winds and the changeful moon, its instability is proverbial. In this mortal state we have too much of this. Earth is constant only in her inconstancy. But in the heavenly state, all mournful change will be unknown, and with it all fear of storm to wreck our hopes and drown our joys. The sea of glass glows with a glory unbroken by a wave. No tempest howls along the peaceful shores of paradise. Soon we will reach that happy land where partings, changes, and storms will be ended! Jesus will carry us there. Are we in Him or not? This is the grand question.

Call the labourers, and give them their hire.
—Matthew 20:8

God is a good employer. He pays His servants while they work as well as when they have finished working. One of His payments is an easy conscience. If you have spoken faithfully of Jesus to one person, when you go to bed at night you feel happy in thinking, "Today, I have discharged my conscience of that man's blood." There is a great comfort in doing something for Jesus. Oh, what happiness it brings to place jewels in His crown and to allow Him to see the results of His saving work! There is also great reward in watching the first budding of conviction in a soul. To say of a girl in your class, "She is tenderhearted. I hope that her sensitivity reflects the Lord's work within"; to go home and pray over the boy who said something that made you think he must know more of divine truth than you had feared—oh, the joy of hope! As for the joy of success, it is unspeakable! This joy, overwhelming as it is, is a hungry thing—you long for more of it. To be a soulwinner is the happiest thing in the world. With every soul you bring to Christ, you get a new heaven on earth. Who can conceive the bliss that awaits us above? Oh, how sweet is that sentence, *"Enter thou into the joy of thy lord"* (Matt. 25:21)! Do you know what the joy of Christ is over a saved sinner? This is the very joy that we are to possess in heaven. Yes, when He mounts the throne, you will mount with Him. When the heavens ring with, "Well done, well done," you will partake in the reward. You have toiled with Him, and you have suffered with Him; now, you will reign with Him. You have sown with Him, and you will reap with Him. Your face was covered with sweat like His, and your soul was grieved as His soul was for the sins of men. Now your face will be bright with heaven's splendor as is His countenance, and your soul will be filled with blissful joy even as His soul is.

I clothed thee also with broidered work, and shod thee
with badgers' skin, and I girded thee about with fine linen,
and I covered thee with silk.
—Ezekiel 16:10

ee the matchless generosity with which the Lord provides for His people. They are clothed such that divine skill is seen producing an unrivalled embroidered work, in which every attribute takes its part and every divine beauty is revealed. There is no art like the art displayed in our salvation and no cunning workmanship like that beheld in the righteousness of the saints. Justification has engaged learned writers in all ages of the church, and it will be the theme of admiration in eternity. God has indeed "curiously wrought it." With all this elaboration, there is mingled utility and durability, comparable to our being shod with badgers' skins. The animal mentioned here is unknown, but its skin covered the tabernacle and formed one of the finest and strongest leathers known. The righteousness that is of God by faith endures forever, and he who is shod with this divine preparation will tread the desert safely. He may even set his foot *"upon the lion and adder"* (Ps. 91:12). Purity and dignity of our holy vesture are brought out in the fine linen. When the Lord sanctifies His people, they are clad as priests in pure white. The snow itself does not excel them. In the eyes of men and angels, they are fair to look upon; even in the Lord's eyes, they are without spot. Meanwhile the royal apparel is delicate and rich as silk. No expense is spared, no beauty is withheld, and no daintiness is denied. What then? Is there no inference from this? Surely there is gratitude to be felt and joy to be expressed. Come, my heart. Do not refuse your evening hallelujah! Tune your pipes! Touch your chords!

> Strangely, my soul, art thou arrayed
> By the Great Sacred Three!
> In sweetest harmony of praise
> Let all thy powers agree.

The spot of his children.
—Deuteronomy 32:5

hat is the secret *"spot"* that infallibly denotes the child of God? It would be vain presumption to decide this based on our own judgment, but God's Word reveals it to us. We may walk confidently where we have divine revelation as our guide. Now, we are told concerning our Lord, *"As many as received him, to them gave he power to become the sons of God, even to them that believe on his name"* (John 1:12). Then, if I have received Christ Jesus into my heart, I am a child of God. That reception is described in the same verse as believing on the name of Jesus Christ. If, then, I believe on Jesus Christ's name—that is, simply from my heart, I trust myself with the crucified, but now exalted, Redeemer—I am a member of the family of the Most High. Whatever else I may not have, if I have this, I have the privilege to become a child of God. Our Lord Jesus puts it another way: *"My sheep hear my voice, and I know them, and they follow me"* (John 10:27). Here is the matter in a nutshell. Christ appears as a Shepherd to His own sheep, not to others. As soon as He appears, His own sheep recognize Him. They trust Him and are prepared to follow Him. He knows them, and they know Him. There is a mutual knowledge, and there is a constant connection between them. Thus the one mark, the sure mark, the infallible mark of regeneration and adoption, is a hearty faith in the appointed Redeemer. Reader, are you in doubt? Are you uncertain whether you bear the secret mark of God's children? Then do not let an hour go by until you have said, *"Search me, O God, and know my heart"* (Ps. 139:23). Do not handle this matter lightly, I beg you! If you must trifle anywhere, let it be about some secondary matter: your health, if you will, or the deeds of your estate. But about your soul, your never-dying soul and its eternal destiny, I beseech you to be in earnest. Be certain about where you will spend eternity!

The night also is thine.
—Psalm 74:16

Lord, You do not abdicate Your throne when the sun goes down, nor do You leave the world all through these long wintry nights to be the prey of evil. Your eyes watch us as the stars, and Your arms surround us as the zodiac encircles the sky. The dews of benevolent sleep and all the influences of the moon are in Your hand. The alarms and solemnities of night are the same with You. This is very sweet to me when watching through the midnight hours or when tossing to and fro in anguish. There are precious fruits put forth by the moon as well as by the sun. May my Lord make me to be a favored partaker in them. The night of affliction is as much under the arrangement and control of the Lord of Love as the bright summer days when all is bliss. Jesus is in the tempest. His love wraps the night about itself as a mantle, but to the eye of faith, the sable robe is hardly a disguise. From the first watch of the night to the break of day, the eternal Watcher observes His saints. He overrules the shades and dews of midnight for His people's highest good. We believe in no rival deities of good and evil contending for mastery, but we hear the voice of Jehovah saying, "I create light, and I create darkness. I, the Lord, do all these things." Gloomy seasons of religious indifference and social sin are not exempted from the divine purpose. When the altars of truth are defiled, and the ways of God forsaken, the Lord's servants weep with bitter sorrow. But they do not need to despair, for the darkest times are governed by the Lord, and they will come to their end at His command. What may seem defeat to us may be victory to Him.

> Though enwrapt in gloomy night,
> We perceive no ray of light;
> Since the Lord Himself is here,
> 'Tis not meet that we should fear.

The glory of the LORD shall be revealed,
and all flesh shall see it together.
—Isaiah 40:5

We anticipate the happy day when the whole world will be converted to Christ; when the gods of the heathen will be cast *"to the moles and to the bats"* (Isa. 2:20); when the crescent of Mohammed will wane, never again to cast its baleful rays upon the nations; when kings will bow down before the Prince of Peace, and all nations will call their Redeemer blessed. Some despair of this. They look at the world as a vessel breaking up and going to pieces, never to float again. We know that the world and all that is in it will one day be burned up; afterward, we look for new heavens and a new earth. We cannot read our Bibles without the conviction that "Jesus shall reign where'er the sun / Does his successive journeys run." We are not discouraged by the length of His delays; we are not disheartened by the long period that He allots to the church in which to struggle with little success and much defeat. We believe that God will never permit this world, which has once seen Christ's blood shed upon it, to always be the devil's stronghold. Christ came here to deliver this world from the detested sway of the powers of darkness. What a shout that will be when men and angels unite to cry, *"Alleluia: for the Lord God omnipotent reigneth"* (Rev. 19:6)! What satisfaction it will be in that day to have had a share in the fight, to have helped to break the arrows of the bow, and to have aided in winning the victory for our Lord! Happy are they who trust themselves with this conquering Lord and who fight side by side with Him, doing their little in His name and by His strength! How unhappy are those on the side of evil! It is a losing side, and it is a matter wherein to lose is to lose and to be lost forever. On whose side are you?

And it was so, when the days of their feasting were gone about, that Job sent and sanctified them, and rose up early in the morning, and offered burnt offerings according to the number of them all: for Job said, It may be that my sons have sinned, and cursed God in their hearts. Thus did Job continually.
—Job 1:5

What the patriarch Job did early in the morning, after the family festivities, would be good for the believer to do for himself before he rests tonight. Amid the cheerfulness of family gatherings, it is easy to slide into sinful frivolities and to forget our avowed character as Christians. It should not be so, but it is. Our days of celebrating are very seldom days of sanctified enjoyment; too frequently, they degenerate into unholy levity. There is a joy that is as pure and sanctifying as though one bathed in the rivers of Eden. Holy gratitude should be as purifying an element as grief. Unfortunately, for our poor hearts, the fact is that the *"house of mourning"* (Eccl. 7:2) is better than the *"house of feasting"* (v. 2). Come, believer, in what have you sinned today? Have you been forgetful of your high calling? Have you been as those who speak idle words and have loose tongues? Then confess the sin, and fly to the Sacrifice. The Sacrifice sanctifies. The precious blood of the slain Lamb removes the guilt and purges away the defilement of our sins of ignorance and carelessness. The best ending for a Christmas Day would be to wash anew in the cleansing fountain. Believer, come to this sacrifice continually; if it is good to do so tonight, it is good every night. To live at the altar is the privilege of the royal priesthood. As great as it is, sin is nevertheless no cause for despair, since believers may yet again draw near to the sin-atoning Sacrifice, and have their consciences purged from dead works.

> Gladly I close this festive day,
> Grasping the altar's hallow'd horn;
> My slips and faults are washed away,
> The Lamb has all my trespass borne.

Lo, I am with you alway.
—Matthew 28:20

he Lord Jesus is in the midst of His church. He walks among the golden candlesticks. His promise is, *"Lo, I am with you alway."* He is as surely with us now as He was with the disciples at the lake, when they saw coals of fire, and fish laid thereon and bread. Not in the flesh, but still in real truth, Jesus is with us. And a blessed truth it is, for where Jesus is, love becomes inflamed. Of all the things in the world that can set the heart burning, there is nothing like the presence of Jesus! A glimpse of Him so overcomes us that we are ready to say, "Turn Your eyes away from me, for they have overcome me." Even the smell of the aloes, the myrrh, and the cassia, which comes from His perfumed garments, causes the sick and the faint to grow strong. Let there be but a moment's leaning of the head on that gracious breast, and a reception of His divine love into our poor cold hearts, and we are no longer cold. Instead, we glow like angels, equal to every labor and capable of every suffering. If we know that Jesus is with us, every power will be developed, and every grace will be strengthened. We will cast ourselves into the Lord's service with heart, soul, and strength; therefore, the presence of Christ is to be desired above all things. His presence will be most realized by those who are most like Him. If you desire to see Christ, you must grow in conformity to Him. Bring yourself, by the power of the Spirit, into union with Christ's desires, motives, and plans of action, and you are likely to be favored with His company. Remember that His presence may be felt. His promise is as true as ever. He delights to be with us. If He does not come, it is because we hinder Him by our indifference. He will reveal Himself to our earnest prayers. He graciously permits Himself to be detained by our entreaties and by our tears, for these are the golden chains that bind Jesus to His people.

And the LORD shall guide thee continually.
—Isaiah 58:11

he LORD *shall guide thee."* Not an angel, but Jehovah will guide you. He said He would not go through the wilderness before His people, that an angel would go before them to lead them in the way; but Moses said, *"If thy presence go not with me, carry us not up hence"* (Exod. 33:15). Christian, God has not left you in your earthly pilgrimage to an angel's guidance: He Himself leads the way. You may not see the cloudy, fiery pillar, but Jehovah will never forsake you. Notice the word *"shall"*—*"The LORD shall guide thee."* How certain this makes it! How sure it is that God will not forsake us! His precious *shall*s and *will*s are better than men's promises. *"I will never leave thee, nor forsake thee"* (Heb. 13:5). Then notice the adverb *"continually."* We are not merely to be guided sometimes, but we are to have a perpetual monitor. We are not occasionally to be left to our own understanding, and so to wander; but we are continually to hear the guiding voice of the Great Shepherd. If we follow close at His heels, we will not err. We will be led by a right way to a city to dwell in. If you have to change your position in life; if you have to move to distant shores; if it happens that you are cast into poverty or uplifted suddenly into a more responsible position than the one you now occupy; if you are thrown among strangers or cast among foes, do not fear, for *"the LORD shall guide thee continually."* If you live close to God and your heart is kept warm by His holy love, there are no dilemmas out of which you will not be delivered. You cannot go wrong when you follow in the company of God. Like Enoch, walk with God, and you cannot mistake your road. You have infallible wisdom to direct you, immutable love to comfort you, and eternal power to defend you. *Jehovah*—pay attention to that word—Jehovah will guide you continually.

I came not to send peace, but a sword.
—Matthew 10:34

he Christian is sure to make enemies. It will be one of his goals to make none; but if, in doing right and believing the truth, he loses every earthly friend, he will count it but a small loss, since his great Friend in heaven will be friendlier and will reveal Himself to him more graciously than anyone else ever could. You who have taken up His cross, do you not know what your Master said? *"I am come to set a man at variance against his father, and the daughter against her mother,…and a man's foes shall be they of his own household"* (Matt. 10:35–36). Christ is the great Peacemaker; but before peace, He brings war. Where the light comes, the darkness must retire. Where truth is, lies must flee; or, if falsehoods remain, there must be a stern conflict, for the truth cannot and will not lower its standard, and lies must be trodden underfoot. If you follow Christ, you will have all the dogs of the world yelping at your heels. If you wish to live so as to stand the test of the Last Judgment, depend on this: the world will not speak well of you. He who has the friendship of the world is an enemy to God; but if you are true and faithful to the Most High, men will resent your unflinching fidelity, since it is a testimony against their iniquities. Fearless of all consequences, you must do right. You will need the courage of a lion unhesitatingly to pursue a course that will turn your best friend into your fiercest foe; but, for the love of Jesus, you must be courageous. To risk reputation and affection for the truth's sake is such a deed that to do it constantly you will need a degree of moral principle that only the Spirit of God can work in you. Do not turn your back like a coward, but act like a man. Boldly follow in your Master's steps, for He has walked this rough way before you. Better a brief warfare and eternal rest than false peace and everlasting torment.

What think ye of Christ?
—Matthew 22:42

he great test of your soul's health is, What do you think of Christ? Is He to you *"fairer than the children of men"* (Ps. 45:2), *"chiefest among ten thousand"* (Song 5:10), the *"altogether lovely"* (v. 16)? Wherever Christ is thus esteemed, all the faculties of the spiritual man exercise themselves with energy. I will judge your faith by this barometer: does Christ stand high or low with you? If you have thought little of Christ, if you have been content to live without His presence, if you have cared little for His honor, if you have been neglectful of His laws, then I know that your soul is sick. May God grant that it will not be sick unto death! But if the first thought of your spirit has been, How can I honor Jesus? and if the daily desire of your soul has been, *"Oh that I knew where I might find him!"* (Job 23:3), I tell you that you may have a thousand infirmities and even scarcely know whether you are a child of God at all, yet I am persuaded, beyond a doubt, that you are safe, since Jesus is great in your esteem. I do not care about your rags; what do you think of His royal apparel? I do not care about your wounds, though they bleed in torrents; what do you think of His wounds? Are they like glittering rubies in your estimation? I think no less of you, though you lie like Lazarus on the dunghill, and dogs lick your sores. I do not judge you by your poverty; what do you think of the King in His beauty? Has He a glorious high throne in your heart? Would you set Him higher if you could? Would you be willing to die if you could but add another trumpet to the melody that proclaims His praise? Then it is well with you. Whatever you may think of yourself, if Christ is greater to you, you will be with Him before long.

> Though all the world my choice deride,
> Yet Jesus shall my portion be;
> For I am pleased with none beside,
> The fairest of the fair is He.

Knowest thou not that it will be bitterness in the latter end?
—2 Samuel 2:26

If you are merely a professor of faith but not a possessor of faith in Christ Jesus, the following lines are a true depiction of your end. You are a respectable attendant at a place of worship; you go because others go, not because your heart is right with God. This is your beginning. I will suppose that for the next twenty or thirty years, you will be spared to go on as you do now, professing religion by an outward attendance on the means of grace, but having no heart in the matter. Tread softly, for I must show you the deathbed of such a one as yourself. Let us gaze upon him gently. A clammy sweat is on his brow, and he wakes up crying, "O God, it is hard to die. Did you send for my minister?" "Yes, he is coming." The minister comes. "Sir, I fear that I am dying!" "Have you any hope?" "I cannot say that I have. I fear to stand before my God; oh, pray for me!" The prayer is offered for him with sincere earnestness, and the way of salvation is for the ten-thousandth time put before him, but before he has grasped the rope, I see him sink. I may put my finger on those cold eyelids, for they will never see anything here again. But where is the man, and where are the man's true eyes? It is written, *"In hell he lift up his eyes, being in torments"* (Luke 16:23). Oh, why did he not lift up his eyes before? Because he was so accustomed to hearing the Gospel that his soul slept under it. Alas! If you lift up your eyes there, how bitter will be your wailing. Let the Savior's own words reveal the woe: *"Father Abraham, have mercy on me, and send Lazarus, that he may dip the tip of his finger in water, and cool my tongue; for I am tormented in this flame"* (v. 24). There is a frightful meaning in those words. May you never have to understand its truth by the red light of Jehovah's wrath!

The harvest is past, the summer is ended, and we are not saved.
—Jeremiah 8:20

ot saved"! Dear reader, is this your mournful plight? You have been warned of the judgment to come, encouraged to escape for your life, yet at this moment, you are not saved! You know the way of salvation. You read it in the Bible, you hear it from the pulpit, and it is explained to you by friends; yet you neglect it and, therefore, are not saved. You will be without excuse when the Lord will *"judge the quick and the dead"* (2 Tim. 4:1). The Holy Spirit has given more or less of a blessing upon the Word that has been preached in your hearing. Times of refreshing have come from the divine presence, yet you are without Christ. All these hopeful seasons have come and gone—your summer and your harvest have passed—yet you are not saved. Years have followed one another into eternity, and your last year will soon be here. Youth has gone, and adulthood is going, yet you are not saved. Let me ask you: will you ever be saved? Is there any likelihood of it? Already the most propitious seasons have left you unsaved. Will other occasions alter your condition? Means—the best of means, used perseveringly and with the utmost affection—have failed with you. What more can be done for you? Affliction and prosperity have both failed to impress you. Tears and prayers and sermons have been wasted on your barren heart. Are not the probabilities dead against your ever being saved? Is it not more than likely that you will abide as you are until death forever bars the door of hope? Do you recoil from the supposition? Yet it is a most reasonable one. He who is not washed in the cleansing waters will, in all probability, go to his end filthy. The convenient time has not come yet. Why should it ever come? It is logical to fear that it never will arrive, and that like Felix (see Acts 24:24–25), you will find no convenient season to be saved—until you are in hell! Oh, think about what hell is and of the frightening probability that you will soon be cast into it! Reader, suppose you would die unsaved. No words can describe your doom. Write out your terrible state in tears and blood; talk of it with groans and gnashing of teeth. You will be punished with everlasting destruction from the glory of the Lord and from the glory of His power. A brother's voice would gladly startle you into earnestness. Be wise. Be wise in time, and before another year begins. Believe in Jesus, who is able to save *"to the uttermost"* (Heb. 7:25). Consecrate these last hours of this year to solitary thought, and if deep repentance is bred in you, it will be well; if it leads to a humble faith in Jesus, it will be best of all. See to it that this year does not pass away with your still having an unforgiven spirit. Do not let the New Year's midnight peals sound upon a joyless spirit! Believe *now* and live. *"Escape for thy life; look not behind thee, neither stay thou in all the plain; escape to the mountain, lest thou be consumed"* (Gen. 19:17).

About the Author

harles Haddon Spurgeon was born on June 19, 1834, at Kelvedon, Essex, England, the firstborn of eight surviving children. His parents were committed Christians, and his father was a preacher. Spurgeon was converted in 1850 at the age of fifteen. He began to help the poor and to hand out tracts, and he was known as "The Boy Preacher."

His next six years were eventful. He preached his first sermon at the age of sixteen. At age eighteen, he became the pastor of Waterbeach Baptist Chapel, preaching in a barn. Spurgeon preached over six hundred times before he reached the age of twenty. By 1854 he was well-known and was asked to become the pastor of New Park Street Chapel in London. In 1856, Spurgeon married Susannah Thompson; they had twin sons, both of whom later entered the ministry.

Spurgeon's compelling sermons and lively preaching style drew multitudes of people, and many came to Christ. Soon, the crowds had grown so large that they blocked the narrow streets near the church. Services eventually had to be held in rented halls, and Spurgeon often preached to congregations of more than ten thousand. The Metropolitan Tabernacle was built in 1861 to accommodate the large numbers of people.

Spurgeon published over thirty-five hundred sermons, which were so popular that they sold by the ton. At one point his sermons sold twenty-five thousand copies every week. An 1870 edition of the English magazine *Vanity Fair* called him an "original and powerful preacher...honest, resolute, sincere; lively, entertaining." The prime minister of England, members of the royal family, and Florence Nightingale, among others, went to hear him preach. Spurgeon preached to an estimated ten million people throughout his life. Not surprisingly, he is called the "Prince of Preachers."

About the Author

In addition to his powerful preaching, Spurgeon founded and supported charitable outreaches, including educational institutions. His pastors' college, which is still in existence today, taught nearly nine hundred students in Spurgeon's time. He also founded the famous Stockwell Orphanage.

Charles Spurgeon died in 1892, and his death was mourned by many.